Your All-in-One Resource

On the CD that accompanies this book, you'll find additional resources to extend your learning.

The reference library includes the following fully searchable titles:

- *Microsoft Computer Dictionary*, 5th ed.
- *First Look 2007 Microsoft Office System* by Katherine Murray
- Windows Vista Product Guide

Also provided are a sample chapter and poster from *Look Both Ways: Help Protect Your Family on the Internet* by Linda Criddle

The CD interface has a new look. You can use the tabs for an assortment of tasks:

- Check for book updates (if you have Internet access)
- Install the book's practice file
- Go online for product support or CD support
- Send us feedback

The following screen shot gives you a glimpse of the new interface.

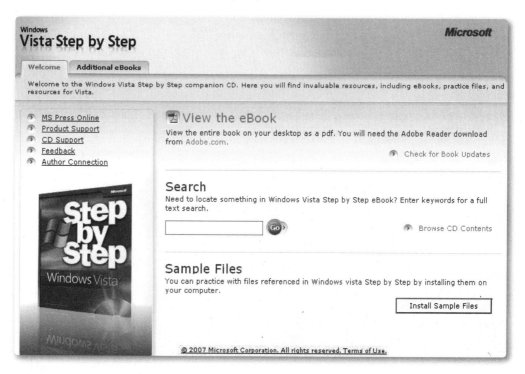

Microsoft® Office
Project 2007
Step by Step

Carl Chatfield
Timothy Johnson

PUBLISHED BY
Microsoft Press
A Division of Microsoft Corporation
One Microsoft Way
Redmond, Washington 98052-6399

Library of Congress Control Number: 2006937716

Printed and bound in the United States of America.

2 3 4 5 6 7 8 9   QWT   2 1 0 9 8 7

Distributed in Canada by H.B. Fenn and Company Ltd.

A CIP catalogue record for this book is available from the British Library.

Microsoft Press books are available through booksellers and distributors worldwide. For further information about international editions, contact your local Microsoft Corporation office or contact Microsoft Press International directly at fax (425) 936-7329. Visit our Web site at www.microsoft.com/mspress. Send comments to mspinput@microsoft.com.

Acquisitions Editor: Juliana Aldous Atkinson
Developmental Editor: Sandra Haynes
Project Editor: Rosemary Caperton
Editorial Production Services: Custom Editorial Productions, Inc.
Technical Reviewer: Brian Kennemer

Body Part No. X12-65182

Contents

What do you think of this book? We want to hear from you!

Microsoft is interested in hearing your feedback so we can continually improve our books and learning resources for you. To participate in a brief online survey, please visit:

www.microsoft.com/learning/booksurvey/

What do you think of this book? We want to hear from you!

Microsoft is interested in hearing your feedback so we can continually improve our books and learning resources for you. To participate in a brief online survey, please visit:

www.microsoft.com/learning/booksurvey/

Information for Readers Running Windows XP

The graphics and the operating system–related instructions in this book reflect the Windows Vista user interface. However, Windows Vista is not required; you can also use a computer running Microsoft Windows XP.

Most of the differences you will encounter when working through the exercises in this book on a computer running Windows XP center around appearance rather than functionality. For example, the Windows Vista Start button is round rather than rectangular and is not labeled with the word Start; window frames and window-management buttons look different; and if your system supports Windows Aero, the window frames might be transparent.

In this section, we provide steps for navigating to or through menus and dialog boxes in Windows XP that differ from those provided in the exercises in this book. For the most part, these differences are small enough that you will have no difficulty in completing the exercises.

Managing the Practice Files

The instructions given in the "Using the Book's CD" section are specific to Windows Vista. The only differences when installing, using, uninstalling, and removing the practice files supplied on the companion CD are the default installation location and the uninstall process.

On a computer running Windows Vista, the default installation location of the practice files is *Documents\Microsoft Press\Project 2007 SBS*. On a computer running Windows XP, the default installation location is *My Documents\Microsoft Press\Project 2007 SBS*. If your computer is running Windows XP, whenever an exercise tells you to navigate to your *Documents* folder, you should instead go to your *My Documents* folder.

To uninstall the practice files from a computer running Windows XP:

1. On the Windows taskbar, click the **Start** button, and then click **Control Panel**.
2. In **Control Panel**, click (or in Classic view, double-click) **Add or Remove Programs**.

3. In the **Add or Remove Programs** window, click **Microsoft Office Project 2007 Step by Step**, and then click **Remove**.

4. In the **Add or Remove Programs** message box asking you to confirm the deletion, click **Yes**.

> **Important** If you need help installing or uninstalling the practice files, please see the "Getting Help" section later in this book. Microsoft Product Support Services does not provide support for this book or its companion CD.

Using the Start Menu

To start Microsoft Office Project 2007 on a computer running Windows XP:

● Click the **Start** button, point to **All Programs**, click **Microsoft Office**, and then click **Microsoft Office Project 2007**.

Folders on the Windows Vista Start menu expand vertically. Folders on the Windows XP Start menu expand horizontally. You will notice this variation between the images shown in this book and your Start menu.

Navigating Dialog Boxes

On a computer running Windows XP, some of the dialog boxes you will work with in the exercises not only look different from the graphics shown in this book but also work differently. These dialog boxes are primarily those that act as an interface between Project and the operating system, including any dialog box in which you navigate to a specific location. For example, here are the Open dialog boxes from Project 2007 running on Windows Vista and Windows XP and some examples of ways to navigate in them.

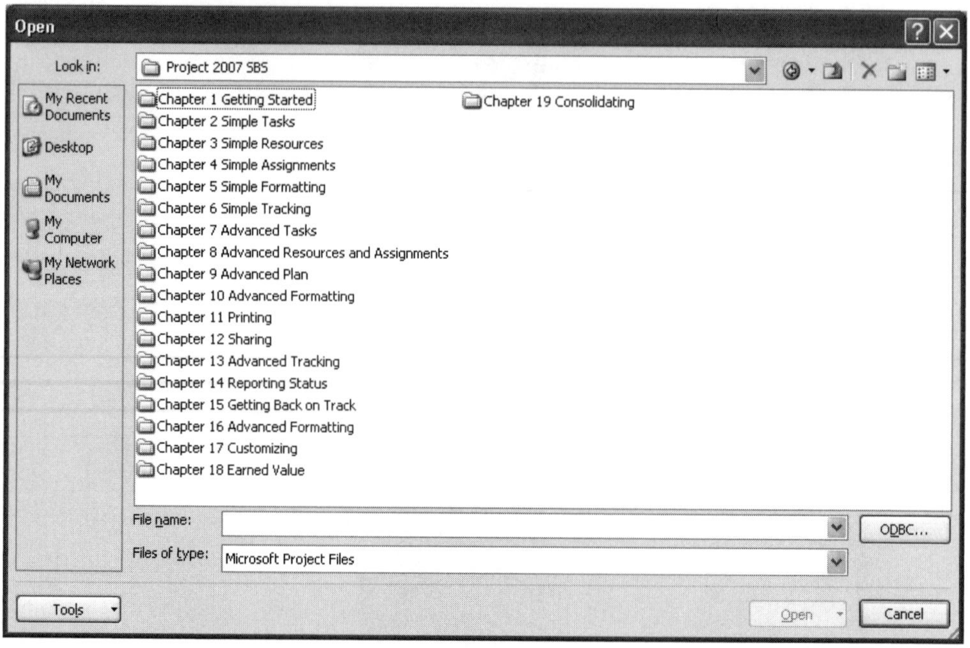
Open
Look in:
Project 2007 SBS
My Recent Documents
Desktop
My Documents
My Computer
My Network Places
Chapter 1 Getting Started
Chapter 2 Simple Tasks
Chapter 3 Simple Resources
Chapter 4 Simple Assignments
Chapter 5 Simple Formatting
Chapter 6 Simple Tracking
Chapter 7 Advanced Tasks
Chapter 8 Advanced Resources and Assignments
Chapter 9 Advanced Plan
Chapter 10 Advanced Formatting
Chapter 11 Printing
Chapter 12 Sharing
Chapter 13 Advanced Tracking
Chapter 14 Reporting Status
Chapter 15 Getting Back on Track
Chapter 16 Advanced Formatting
Chapter 17 Customizing
Chapter 18 Earned Value
Chapter 19 Consolidating
File name:
Files of type:
Microsoft Project Files
ODBC...
Tools
Open
Cancel

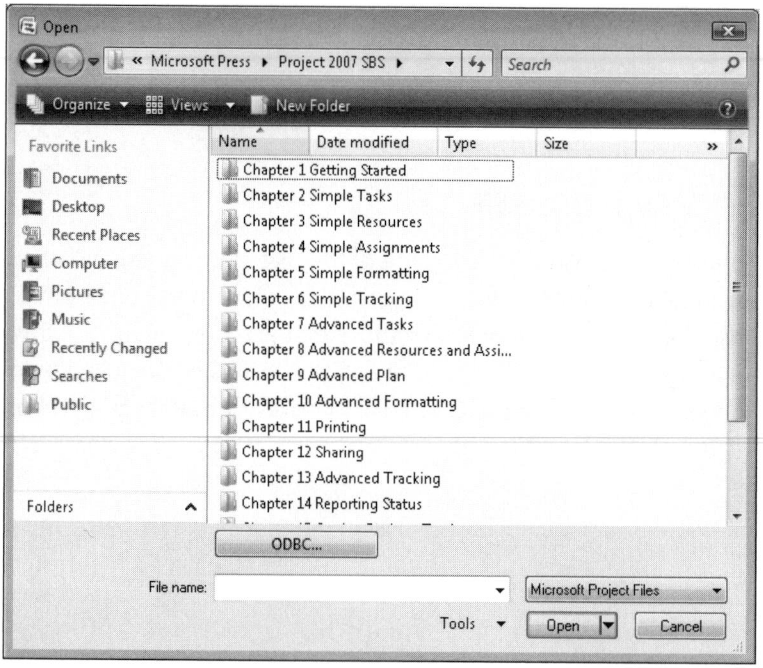
Open
« Microsoft Press ▸ Project 2007 SBS ▸
Search
Organize
Views
New Folder
Favorite Links
Documents
Desktop
Recent Places
Computer
Pictures
Music
Recently Changed
Searches
Public
Folders
Name
Date modified
Type
Size
Chapter 1 Getting Started
Chapter 2 Simple Tasks
Chapter 3 Simple Resources
Chapter 4 Simple Assignments
Chapter 5 Simple Formatting
Chapter 6 Simple Tracking
Chapter 7 Advanced Tasks
Chapter 8 Advanced Resources and Assi...
Chapter 9 Advanced Plan
Chapter 10 Advanced Formatting
Chapter 11 Printing
Chapter 12 Sharing
Chapter 13 Advanced Tracking
Chapter 14 Reporting Status
ODBC...
File name:
Microsoft Project Files
Tools
Open
Cancel

To navigate to the **Chapter 2 Simple Tasks** folder in Windows Vista:

● In the **Favorite Links** pane, click **Documents**. Then in the folder content pane, double-click **Microsoft Press**, **Project 2007 SBS**, and double-click **Chapter 2 Simple Tasks**.

To move back to the **Project 2007 SBS** folder in Windows Vista:

● In the upper-left corner of the dialog box, click the **Back** button.

To navigate to the **Chapter 2 Simple Tasks** folder in Windows XP:

● On the **Places** bar, click **My Documents**. Then in the folder content pane, double-click **Microsoft Press**, **Project 2007 SBS**, and double-click **Chapter 2 Simple Tasks**.

To move back to the **Project 2007 SBS** folder in Windows XP:

● On the toolbar, click the **Up One Level** button.

Features and Conventions of This Book

This book has been designed to lead you step-by-step through all the tasks you are most likely to want to perform in Microsoft Office Project 2007. If you start at the beginning and work your way through all the exercises, you will gain enough proficiency to be able to create and work with Project files. However, each topic is self contained. If you have worked with a previous version of Project, or if you completed all the exercises and later need help remembering how to perform a procedure, the following features of this book will help you look up specific tasks in Project 2007:

- Detailed table of contents. Get an overview of which topics are discussed in which chapters.
- Chapter thumb tabs. Easily open the book at the beginning of the chapter you want.
- Topic-specific running heads. Within a chapter, quickly locate the topic you want by looking at the running head of odd-numbered pages.
- Quick Reference. Refresh your memory about a task while working with your own documents.
- Detailed index. Look up specific tasks and features in the index, which has been carefully crafted with the reader in mind.
- Companion CD. Use to install the practice files needed for the step-by-step exercises, but also as a source of other useful information, including an online, searchable version of this book.

In addition, we provide a glossary of terms for those times when you need to look up the meaning of a word or the definition of a concept.

You can save time when you use this book by understanding how the Step by Step series shows special instructions, keys to press, buttons to click, and so on.

Convention	Meaning
	This icon indicates a reference to the book's companion CD.

BE SURE TO	This paragraph preceding or following a step-by-step exercise indicates any prerequisite requirements that you should attend to before beginning the exercise, or actions you should take to restore your system after completing the exercise.
OPEN	This paragraph preceding a step-by-step exercise indicates files that you should open before beginning the exercise.
CLOSE	This paragraph following a step-by-step exercise provides instructions for closing open files or programs before moving on to another topic.
1 2	Blue numbered steps guide you through step-by-step exercises and procedures in the "Quick Reference."
1 **2**	Black numbered steps guide you through procedures in sidebars and topic introductions.
●	A single solid blue circle indicates an exercise that has only one step.
See Also	These paragraphs direct you to more information about a given topic in this book or elsewhere.
Troubleshooting	These paragraphs explain how to fix a common problem that might prevent you from continuing with an exercise.
Tip	These paragraphs provide a helpful hint or shortcut that makes working through a task easier, or information about other available options.
Important	These paragraphs point out information that you need to know to complete a procedure.
[Save icon] Save	The first time you are told to click a button in an exercise, a picture of the button appears in the left margin. If the name of the button does not appear on the button itself, the name appears under the picture.
Enter	In step-by-step exercises, keys you must press appear in key-shaped boxes.
Ctrl + Home	A plus sign (+) between two key names means that you must hold down the first key while you press the second key. For example, "press Ctrl + Home" means "hold down the Ctrl key while you press the Home key."
Program interface elements	In steps, the names of program elements, such as buttons, commands, and dialog boxes, are shown in black bold characters.
User input	Anything you are supposed to type appears in blue bold characters.
Glossary terms	Terms that are explained in the glossary at the end of the book are shown in blue italic characters.

Getting Help

Every effort has been made to ensure the accuracy of this book and the contents of its companion CD. If you do run into problems, please contact the sources listed below for assistance.

Getting Help with This Book and Its Companion CD

If your question or issue concerns the content of this book or its companion CD, please first search the online Microsoft Press Knowledge Base, which provides support information for known errors in or corrections to this book, at the following Web site:

www.microsoft.com/mspress/support/search.asp

If you do not find your answer at the online Knowledge Base, send your comments or questions to Microsoft Press Technical Support at:

mspinput@microsoft.com

Getting Help with Project 2007

If your question is about Microsoft Office Project 2007, and not about the content of this Microsoft Press book, your first recourse is the Project Help system. This system is a combination of tools and files stored on your computer when you installed Project 2007 and, if your computer is connected to the Internet, information available from Microsoft Office Online. There are several ways to find general or specific Help information:

- To find out about an item on the screen, you can display a *ScreenTip*. For example, to display a ScreenTip for a button, point to the button without clicking it. The ScreenTip gives the button's name and the associated keyboard shortcut if there is one.

- In the Project program window, you can also type a question into the Search box in the upper right corner of the Project window. The Search box initially contains the text *Type a question for help*. You can also click the Microsoft Office Project Help command on the Help menu.

- After opening a dialog box, you can click the Help button to display the Project Help window with topics related to the functions of that dialog box already identified.

More Information

If your question is about Microsoft Office Project 2007 or another Microsoft software product and you cannot find the answer in the product's Help, please search the appropriate product solution center or the Microsoft Knowledge Base at:

support.microsoft.com

In the United States, Microsoft software product support issues not covered by the Microsoft Knowledge Base are addressed by Microsoft Product Support Services. Location-specific software support options are available from:

support.microsoft.com/gp/selfoverview/

Using the Book's CD

The companion CD included with this book contains the practice files you'll use as you work through the book's exercises, as well as other electronic resources that will help you learn how to use Microsoft Office Project 2007.

What's on the CD?

The following table lists the practice files supplied on the book's CD.

Chapter	Files
Chapter 1: Getting Started with Project	(no practice file)
Chapter 2: Creating a Task List	Wingtip Toys Commercial 2a
Chapter 3: Setting Up Resources	Wingtip Toys Commercial 3a
Chapter 4: Assigning Resources to Tasks	Wingtip Toys Commercial 4a
Chapter 5: Formatting and Printing Your Plan	Wingtip Toys Commercial 5a, Logo.gif
Chapter 6: Tracking Progress on Tasks	Wingtip Toys Commercial 6a
Chapter 7: Fine-Tuning Task Details	Short Film Project 7a
Chapter 8: Fine-Tuning Resource and Assignment Details	Short Film Project 8a
Chapter 9: Fine-Tuning the Project Plan	Short Film Project 9a
Chapter 10: Organizing and Formatting Project Details	Short Film Project 10a
Chapter 11: Printing Project Information	Short Film Project 11a
Chapter 12: Sharing Project Information with Other Programs	Short Film Project 12a, Letter to Client.rtf, Sample Task Lists.xls

Chapter 13: Tracking Progress on Tasks and Assignments	Short Film Project 13a, Short Film Project 13b, Short Film Project 13c, Short Film Project 13d
Chapter 14: Viewing and Reporting Project Status	Short Film Project 14a
Chapter 15: Getting Your Project Back on Track	Short Film Project 15a
Chapter 16: Applying Advanced Formatting	Parnell Film 16a
Chapter 17: Customizing Project	Parnell Aerospace Promo 17a, Wingtip Toys Commercial 17b
Chapter 18: Measuring Performance with Earned Value Analysis	Short Film Project 18a
Chapter 19: Consolidating Projects and Resources	Wingtip Toys Commercial 19a, Parnell Aerospace Promo 19b
Chapter 20: Planning Work with Project Server	(no practice files)
Chapter 21: Tracking Work with Project Server	(no practice files)
Chapter 22: Managing Risks, Issues, and Documents with Project Server	(no practice files)

In addition to the practice files, the CD contains some exciting resources that will really enhance your ability to get the most out of using this book and Project 2007, including the following:

- *Microsoft Office Project 2007 Step by Step* in eBook format
- *Microsoft Computer Dictionary*, Fifth Edition eBook
- *First Look 2007 Microsoft Office System* (Katherine Murray, 2006)
- Sample chapter and poster from *Look Both Ways: Help Protect Your Family on the Internet* (Linda Criddle, 2007)

> **Important** The companion CD for this book does not contain the Project 2007 software. You should purchase and install that program before using this book.

Minimum System Requirements

2007 Microsoft Office System

The 2007 Microsoft Office system includes the following programs:

- Microsoft Office Access 2007
- Microsoft Office Communicator 2007
- Microsoft Office Excel 2007
- Microsoft Office Groove 2007
- Microsoft Office InfoPath 2007
- Microsoft Office OneNote 2007
- Microsoft Office Outlook 2007
- Microsoft Office Outlook 2007 with Business Contact Manager
- Microsoft Office PowerPoint 2007
- Microsoft Office Publisher 2007
- Microsoft Office Word 2007

No single edition of the 2007 Office system installs all of the above programs. Specialty programs available separately include Microsoft Office Project 2007, Microsoft Office SharePoint Designer 2007, and Microsoft Office Visio 2007.

To run Project Standard or Professional, your computer needs to meet the following minimum requirements:

- 700 megahertz (MHz) processor or higher
- 512 megabytes (MB) RAM or higher
- CD or DVD drive
- 1.5 gigabyte (GB) hard disk space necessary for install; a portion of this disk space will be freed if you select the option to delete the installation files

> **Tip** Hard disk requirements will vary depending on configuration; custom installation choices may require more or less hard disk space.

- Monitor with minimum 800x600 screen resolution; 1024x768 or higher recommended

- Keyboard and mouse or compatible pointing device

- Internet connection, 128 kilobits per second (Kbps) or greater, for download and activation of products, accessing Microsoft Office Online and online Help topics, and any other Internet-dependent processes

- Windows Vista or later, Microsoft Windows XP with Service Pack (SP) 2 or later, or Microsoft Windows Server 2003 or later

- Windows Internet Explorer 6.0 or later for Internet functionality

Installing the Practice Files

You need to install the practice files in the correct location on your hard disk before you can use them in the exercises. Follow these steps:

1. Remove the companion CD from the envelope at the back of the book, and insert it into the CD drive of your computer.

   The Step By Step Companion CD License Terms appear. Follow the on-screen directions. To use the practice files, you must accept the terms of the license agreement. After you accept the license agreement, a menu screen appears.

   > **Important** If the menu screen does not appear, click the Start button and then click Computer. Display the Folders list in the Navigation Pane, click the icon for your CD drive, and then in the right pane, double-click the StartCD executable file.

2. Click **Install Practice Files**.

3. Click **Next** on the first screen, and then click **Next** to accept the terms of the license agreement on the next screen.

4. If you want to install the practice files to a location other than the default folder (*Documents\Microsoft Press\Project 2007 SBS*), click the **Change** button, select the new drive and path, and then click **OK**.

   > **Important** If you install the practice files to a location other than the default, you will need to substitute that path within the exercises.

5. Click **Next** on the **Choose Destination Location** screen, and then click **Install** on the **Ready to Install the Program** screen to install the selected practice files.

6. After the practice files have been installed, click **Finish**.

7. Close the **Step by Step Companion CD** window, remove the companion CD from the CD drive, and return it to the envelope at the back of the book.

Using the Practice Files

When you install the practice files from the companion CD that accompanies this book, the files are stored on your hard disk in chapter-specific subfolders under *Documents\ Microsoft Press\Project 2007 SBS*. Each chapter includes a paragraph that lists the files needed for that exercise and explains any preparations needed before you start working through the exercise. Here is an example:

> **OPEN** Short Film Project 9a from the *\Documents\Microsoft Press\Project 2007 SBS\ Chapter 9 Advanced Plan* folder.

You can browse to the practice files in Windows Explorer by following these steps:

1. On the Windows taskbar, click the **Start** button, and then click **All Programs**.

2. Next, click **Microsoft Press**, click **Project 2007 Step By Step**, and then select a specific chapter folder.

Removing and Uninstalling the Practice Files

You can free up hard disk space by uninstalling the practice files that were installed from the companion CD. The uninstall process deletes any files that you created in the chapter-specific folders while working through the exercises. Follow these steps:

1. On the Windows taskbar, click the **Start** button, and then click **Control Panel**.

2. In **Control Panel**, under **Programs**, click the **Uninstall a program** task.

3. In the **Programs and Features** window, click **Microsoft Office Project 2007 Step by Step**, and then on the toolbar at the top of the window, click the **Uninstall** button.

4. If the **Programs and Features** message box asking you to confirm the deletion appears, click **Yes**.

> **Important** Microsoft Product Support Services does not provide support for this book or its companion CD.

Quick Reference

1   Getting Started with Project

To Start Project Standard, page 6

1   On the Windows taskbar, click the **Start** button.
2   On the **Start** menu, point to **All Programs**, click **Microsoft Office**, and then click **Microsoft Office Project 2007**.

To start Project Professional and work offline, page 12

1   On the Windows taskbar, click the **Start** button.
2   On the **Start** menu, point to **All Programs**, click **Microsoft Office**, and then click **Microsoft Office Project 2007**.
3   If the Project Server Security Login dialog box appears, click **Cancel**.
4   In the Login dialog box, in the **Profile** box, select **Computer**, and then click **Work Offline**.

To create a project plan from a template, page 15

1   On the **File** menu, click **New**.
2   In the **New Project** task pane, under **Template**, click **On computer**.
3   In the Templates dialog box, click the **Project Templates** tab.
4   Click the template you want, and then click **OK**.

To switch to a different view, page 17

1   On the **View** menu, click the name of the view you want.
2   If the view is not listed, click **More Views**. In the More Views dialog box, click the name of the view you want, and click **Apply**.

To view a report in the Print Preview window, page 23

1   On the **Report** menu, click **Reports**.
2   Click a report category, or to see all reports, click **Custom**, and then click **Select**.
3   Select the report you want, and then click **Select** or **Preview**.

To create a visual report, page 25

1   On the **Report** menu, click **Visual Reports**.
2   Click a visual report tab, and then click the visual report you want.

3   Click **View**.

To create a new project plan and set its start date, page 28

1   On the **File** menu, click **New**.
2   In the **New Project** task pane, click **Blank Project**.
3   On the **Project** menu, click **Project Information**.
4   In the **Start Date** box, type or select the project start date you want.
5   Click **OK**.

To set nonworking time, page 30

1   On the **Tools** menu, click **Change Working Time**.
2   In the **For Calendar** box, select the base calendar you want to edit (normally **Standard**).
3   In the **Name** field on the **Exceptions** tab, enter a descriptive name for the nonworking time, such as Holiday.
4   In the **Start** and **Finish** fields, type or select the start and finish dates for the nonworking timespan.
5   Click **OK**.

To enter properties about a Project plan, page 32

1   On the **File** menu, click **Properties**.
2   In the Properties dialog box, click the **Summary** tab, and then enter the information you want.

2   Creating a Task List

To enter task names, page 38

1   In a task view, such as the Gantt Chart view, click a cell in the **Task Name** column.
2   Enter a task name and then press Enter.

To enter task durations, page 42

1   In a task view, such as the Gantt Chart view, click a cell in the **Duration** column.
2   Type the task duration, and then press Enter.

To enter a milestone, page 44

1   On the **Entry** table, enter a name for the milestone.
2   In the **Duration** field, type 0d, and then press Enter.

To organize tasks into phases, page 46

1   Select the names of tasks that you would like to become subtasks of a summary task.
2   On the **Project** menu, point to **Outline**, and then click **Indent**.

To link adjacent tasks, page 49

1   Select the adjacent tasks.
2   On the **Edit** menu, click **Link tasks**.

To link nonadjacent tasks, page 51

1   Select the first task, which will be the predecessor task.
2   While holding down the Ctrl key, select the second task. This will be the successor task.
3   On the **Edit** menu, click **Link tasks**.

To enter a task note, page 53

1   Select the name of a task.
2   On the **Project** menu, click **Task Notes**.
3   In the **Notes** box, type the note you want, and then click **OK**.

To enter a task hyperlink, page 54

1   Select the name of a task.
2   On the **Insert** menu, click **Hyperlink**.
3   In the **Text to display** box, type the text you want to appear when you hover over the hyperlink.
4   In the **Address** box, type the destination hyperlink you want, and then click **OK**.

To check a project plan's duration and other statistics, page 55

1   On the **Project** menu, click **Project Information**.
2   In the Project Information dialog box, click **Statistics**.

To display the project's entire duration in the Gantt Chart view, page 56

1   On the **View** menu, click **Zoom**.
2   Click **Entire Project**, and then click **OK**.

3   Setting Up Resources

To set up work (people and equipment) resources, page 61

1   On the **View** menu, click **Resource Sheet** (or another resource view).
2   In the **Resource Name** field, enter the resource's name.

3   In the **Type** field, click **Work**.

4   In the **Max. Units** field, type or click the maximum capacity of this resource to accomplish any task.

5   Enter whatever other resource information would be useful to your project.

6   Repeat steps 2 through 5 for each resource.

To set up material resources, page 66

1   On the **View** menu, click **Resource Sheet**.

2   In the **Resource Name** field, enter the material resource's name.

3   In the **Type** field, click **Material**.

4   In the **Material Label** field, enter the unit of measure you want to use for this resource. For example, you might measure cement in pounds or tons.

5   In the **Std. Rate** field, enter the cost per unit of measure for this material resource.

6   Enter whatever other resource information would be useful for our project.

7   Repeat steps 2 through 6 for each material resource.

To set up cost resources, page 67

1   On the **View** menu, click **Resource Sheet**.

2   In the **Resource Name** field, enter the cost resource's name.

3   In the **Type** field, click **Cost**.

To enter work (people and equipment) resource pay rates, page 68

1   On the **View** menu, click **Resource Sheet**.

2   In the **Std. Rate** field, enter the resource's pay rate per standard pay period (such as hourly, weekly, or monthly).

3   If the resource should accrue overtime pay, enter his or her overtime pay rate in the **Ovt. Rate** field.

4   If the resource accrues a per-use cost, enter that amount in the **Cost/Use** field.

5   In the **Accrue At** field, click the method by which the resource accrues cost.

6   Repeat steps 2 through 5 for each resource.

To make a one-time adjustment to an individual resource's working time, page 70

1   On the **Tools** menu, click **Change Working Time**.

2   In the **For calendar** box, click the name of the resource whose working time you want to change.

3   In the **Name** field on the **Exceptions** tab, enter a descriptive name for the nonworking time, such as Vacation.

4   In the **Start** and **Finish** fields, type or select the start and finish dates for the nonworking timespan.

5   Click **OK**.

To edit the regular work week for an individual resource, page 72

1   On the **Tools** menu, click **Change Working Time**.

2   In the **For calendar** box, click the name of the resource whose working time you want to change.

3   Click the **Work Weeks** tab in the Change Working Time dialog box.

4   Click **[Default]** or enter a new name and period, and then click **Details**.

5   Select the working time options you want for the work week, and then click **OK**.

To document resources with resource notes, page 74

1   Switch to a resource view, such as the Resource Sheet view.

2   Click the name of the resource for which you want to create a note.

3   On the **Project** menu, click **Resource Notes**.

4   In the Resource Information dialog box, type the note you want associated with this resource and then click **OK**.

4   Assigning Resources to Tasks

To assign resources to tasks, page 79

1   In a task view, such as the Gantt Chart view, on the **Tools** menu, click **Assign Resources**.

2   Click the name of the task to which you want to assign a resource.

3   In the **Resource Name** column of the Assign Resources dialog box, click a resource, and then click **Assign**.

To control how Project schedules the work on a task after assigning an additional resource, page 86

1   Assign an additional resource to a task.

2   Click the **Smart Tag Actions** button, and choose the action you want.

To assign material resources to tasks, page 90

1   On the **Standard** toolbar, click **Assign Resources**.

2   In the Gantt Chart view, click the name of the task to which you want to assign a material resource.

3   In the **Resource Name** column of the Assign Resources dialog box, click a resource, and in the **Units** column, enter the unit value you want.

4   Press ⎆Enter or click **Assign**.

To assign cost resources to tasks, page 92

1   On the **Standard** toolbar, click **Assign Resources**.

2   In the Gantt Chart view, click the name of the task to which you want to assign a cost resource.

3   In the **Resource Name** column of the Assign Resources dialog box, click a resource, and in the **Cost** column, enter the cost value you want.

4   Press ⎆Enter or click **Assign**.

5   Formatting and Printing Your Plan

To display the project summary task, page 99

1   On the **Tools** menu, click **Options**.

2   In the Options dialog box, click the **View** tab.

3   Under the **Outline options for** label, select the **Show project summary task** check box, and then click **OK**.

To create a new view based on an existing view, page 100

1   On the **View** menu, click **More Views**.

2   In the More Views dialog box, click the view's name, and then click **Copy**.

3   In the View Definition dialog box, enter a name for the new view.

4   Click **OK**.

To format Gantt bars with the Gantt Chart Wizard, page 101

1   On the **Format** menu, click **Gantt Chart Wizard**.

2   Follow the instructions that appear on your screen.

To draw a text box on a Gantt chart, page 106

1   On the **View** menu, point to **Toolbars**, and then click **Drawing**.

2   On the **Drawing** toolbar, click the **Text Box** button, and then drag a small box anywhere on the chart portion of a Gantt Chart view.

3   In the box you just drew, type the text you want.

To format a category of text in a view, page 109

1   On the **Format** menu, click **Text Styles**.

2   In the **Item to Change** list, click the type of text you want to format.

3   Select the font and other formatting options you want.

To format selected text in a view, page 111

1   Click the cell that contains the text you want to format.

2   On the **Format** menu, click **Font**.

3   Select the font and other formatting options you want.

To edit a report's header or footer, page 112

1   On the **Report** menu, click **Reports**.

2   Click a report category, or to see all reports, click **Custom**, and then click **Select**.

3   Select the report you want, and then click **Select** or **Preview**.

4   On the **Print Preview** toolbar, click **Page Setup**.

5   In the Page Setup dialog box, click the **Header** or **Footer** tab, and select the options you want.

6   Tracking Progress on Tasks

To set current values in a schedule as a baseline, page 124

1   On the **Tools** menu, point to **Tracking**, and then click **Set Baseline**.

2   Click **OK**.

To display the Variance table in the Task Sheet view, page 124

1   On the **View** menu, click **More Views** to display the More Views dialog box.

2   In the **Views** box, **click Task Sheet**, and click **Apply**.

3   On the **View** menu, point to **Table: Entry**, and click **Variance**.

To record project progress as scheduled, page 126

1   On the **Tools** menu, point to **Tracking**, and click **Update Project**.

2   In the Update Project dialog box, make sure the **Update work as complete through** option is selected. In the adjacent date list, type or click the date you want, and click **OK**.

To record a task's completion percentage, page 127

1   On the **View** menu, point to **Toolbars**, and then click **Tracking**.

2   Select the name of the task for which you want to record a percent complete.

3   Do one of the following:

- To record a predefined percentage complete, click the **0%**, **25%**, **50%**, **75%**, or **100% Complete** button.
- To record some other percentage complete, click the **Update Tasks** button, and enter the value you want in the **Percent Complete** field.

To enter actual work values for tasks, page 129

1   In a task view, such as the Task Sheet view, on the **View** menu, point to **Table: Entry**, and click **Work**.

2   In the **Actual** field, enter the actual hours of work you want, and then press `Enter`.

To enter actual start and duration values for tasks, page 130

1   Click the task for which you want to enter actual values.

2   On the **Tools** menu, point to **Tracking**, and then click **Update Tasks**.

3   In the **Start** field in the Actual box on the left side of the Update Tasks dialog box, type or click the start date you want.

4   In the **Actual dur** field, type or click the duration value you want, and then click **OK**.

7   Fine-Tuning Task Details

To display what affects the scheduling of a task in the Task Drivers pane, page 140

1   On the **Project** menu, click **Task Drivers**.

2   Click the task for which you want to display Task Drivers details.

To enter lead and lag time between predecessor and successor tasks, page 141

1   Click the successor task whose lead or lag time with a predecessor you want to change.

2   On the **Project** menu, click **Task Information**.

3   In the Task Information dialog box, click the **Predecessors** tab.

4   In the **Lag** field for a predecessor task, enter the value you want (enter a positive value for lag time or a negative value for lead time).

To change task relationships, page 141

1   Click the successor task whose predecessor relationship you want to change.

2   On the **Project** menu, click **Task Information**.

3   In the Task Information dialog box, click the **Predecessors** tab.

4   Click in the **Type** column for a predecessor task, and click the type of task relationship you want.

To apply a constraint to a task, page 145

1   Click the task to which you want to apply a constraint.

2   On the **Project** menu, click **Task Information**.

3   In the **Constraint Type** box, select the constraint type you want.

4   If you selected date-driven constraint, in the **Constraint Date** box, type or select the constraint date you want, and then click **OK**.

To view a project's critical path, page 148

1   On the **View** menu, click **More Views**.

2   In the More Views dialog box, click **Detail Gantt**, and then click **Apply**.

To interrupt work on a task, page 150

1   On the **Standard** toolbar, click the **Split Task** button.

2   Move the mouse pointer over the task's Gantt bar where you want to start the split, click, and then drag to the right.

To create a new base calendar, page 153

1   On the **Tools** menu, click **Change Working Time**.

2   In the Change Working Time dialog box, click **Create New Calendar**.

3   In the **Name** box, type a name for the base calendar.

4   Click **Create new base calendar**, or click **Make a copy of** and then choose the base calendar on which you want to base the new calendar.

5   Click **OK**.

6   Select the **Exceptions** and **Work Weeks** details you want.

To apply a task calendar to a task, page 154

1   In the Gantt Chart view, click a task.

2   On the **Project** menu, click **Task Information**.

3   In the Task Information dialog box, click the **Advanced** tab.

4   In the **Calendar** box, choose the base calendar you want applied to this task.

5   If you want the task calendar to override resource calendar settings, click the **Scheduling ignores resource calendars** box.

To change a task type to fixed units, duration, or work, page 158

1   In a task view, such as the Gantt Chart view, click a task.

2   On the **Project** menu, click **Task Information**.

3   In the Task Information dialog box, click the **Advanced** tab.

4   In the **Task Type** box, click the task type you want.

To enter a deadline date on a task, page 161

1   In a task view, such as the Gantt Chart view, select the name of the task for which you want to enter a deadline.

2   On the **Project** menu, click **Task Information**.

3   Click the **Advanced** tab.

4   In the **Deadline** box, type or select the deadline date you want, and then click **OK**.

To enter a fixed cost, page 163

1   In a task view, such as the Gantt Chart view, on the **View** menu, point to **Table: Entry**, and then click **Cost**.

2   In the **Fixed Cost** field for the task you want, type or click an amount.

3   In the **Fixed Cost Accrual** field, choose a method, and then press Enter.

To create a recurring task, page 164

1   In a task view, such as the Gantt Chart view, click the task above which you want to insert a recurring task.

2   On the **Insert** menu, click **Recurring Task**.

3   In the Recurring Task Information dialog box, select the options you want.

8   Fine-Tuning Resource and Assignment Details

To create multiple pay rates for a resource, page 172

1   Switch to a resource view, such as the Resource Sheet view.

2   Click the name of the resource for whom you want to create an additional pay rate.

3   On the **Project** menu, click **Resource Information**.

4   In the Resource Information dialog box, click the **Costs** tab.

5   Under **Cost rate tables**, the resource's initial pay rate information appears on tab A. Click one of the other tabs, and then enter the rate information you want.

6   To apply a different cost rate table to a specific resource assignment, pick the one you want in the **Cost Rate Tables** field when you are in a usage view.

To create multiple pay rates that apply at different times, page 174

1   Switch to a resource view, such as the Resource Sheet view.

2   Click the name of the resource for whom you want to create an additional pay rate.

3   On the **Project** menu, click **Resource Information**.

4   In the Resource Information dialog box, click the **Costs** tab.

5   Click the tab of the rate you want to edit.

6   In the second or later row of the **Effective Date** column, enter the date on which the new pay rate is to take effect.

7   In the **Standard Rate** column (and, if applicable, the **Overtime Rate** or **Per Use Cost** columns), enter either a dollar amount or a positive or negative percentage of the existing pay rate. If you enter a percentage value, Project will calculate the new pay rate amount.

To customize a resource's availability over time, page 176

1   Switch to a resource view, such as the Resource Sheet view.

2   Click the name of the resource whose availability you want to change.

3   On the **Project** menu, click **Resource Information**.

4   In the Resource Information dialog box, click the **General** tab.

5   In the **Resource Availability** grid, enter the date ranges and unit values you want.

To delay the start of an assignment, page 178

1   On the **View** menu, click **Task Usage** or **Resource Usage**.

2   Click the assignment you want to delay.

3   On the **Project** menu, click **Assignment Information**.

4   In the Assignment Information dialog box, click the **General** tab.

5   In the **Start** box, type or click the date on which you want the selected resource to start work on the assignment, and then click **OK**.

To apply a work contour to an assignment, page 180

1   On the **View** menu, click **Task Usage** or **Resource Usage**.

2   Click the assignment for which you want to contour to an assignment.

3   On the **Standard** toolbar, click the **Assignment Information** button.

4   In the Assignment Information dialog box, click the **General** tab.

5   In the **Work Contour** box, click the contour you want, and then click **OK**.

To apply a different cost rate to an assignment, page 184

1   On the **View** menu, click **Task Usage** or **Resource Usage**.

2   Click the assignment for which you want to apply a different cost rate table.

3   On the **Standard** toolbar, click the **Assignment Information** button.

4   In the Assignment Information dialog box, click the **General** tab.

5   In the **Cost Rate Table** box, type or click the rate table you want to apply to this assignment, and then click **OK**.

9   Fine-Tuning the Project Plan

To view resource overallocations, page 193

●   On the **View** menu, click **More Views**, click **Resource Allocation**, and then click **Apply**.

To manually resolve resource overallocations by changing assignment units, page 199

1   On the **View** menu, click **More Views**, click **Resource Allocation**, and then click **Apply**.

2   In the **Resource Name** column, click the name of an assignment for the resource you want to work with.

3   On the **Standard** toolbar, click the **Assignment Information** button.

4   In the Assignment Information dialog box, click the **General** tab.

5   In the **Units** box, enter the unit value you want, and then click **OK**.

To level overallocated resources, page 205

1   On the **Tools** menu, click **Level Resources**, and then choose the leveling options you want.

2   Click **Level Now**.

To examine project costs, page 210

1   On the **View** menu, click **More Views**, click **Task Sheet**, and then click **Apply**.

2   On the **Tools** menu, click **Options**.

3   In the Options dialog box, click the **View** tab.

4   Under the **Outline options** for label, select the **Show project summary task** check box, and then click **OK**.

5   On the **View** menu, point to **Table: Entry**, and click **Cost**.

To check a project's finish date, page 212

1   On the **Project** menu, click **Project Information**.

2   In the Project Information dialog box, click **Statistics**.

10 Organizing and Formatting Project Details

To sort data in a view, page 219

1 Switch to the view or table you want to sort.
2 On the **Project** menu, point to **Sort**, and then click the field by which you want to sort the view. To specify a custom sort, click **Sort By**, and in the Sort dialog box, choose the options you want.

To group data in a view, page 223

1 Switch to the view or table you want to group.
2 On the **Project** menu, point to **Group By: No Group**, and then choose the criteria by which you want to group the view. To specify different grouping options, click **Customize Group By**, and then choose the options you want in the Customize Group By dialog box.

To turn AutoFilter on or off, page 228

● On the **Project** menu, point to **Filtered For: All Tasks**, and then click **AutoFilter**.

To filter data in a view, page 228

1 Switch to the view you want to filter.
2 On the **Project** menu, point to **Filtered For**, and click **More Filters**.
3 In the More Filters dialog box, choose the filter you want, and then click **Apply**.

To create a custom filter, page 229

1 On the **Project** menu, point to **Filtered For: All Tasks** (for task views) or **All Resources** (for resource views), and then click **More Filters**.
2 In the More Filters dialog box, click **New**.
3 In the Filter Definition dialog box, select the options you want.

To remove a filter, page 231

● On the **Project** menu, point to **Filtered For:<filter name>**, and then click **All Tasks** (for task views) or **All Resources** (for resource views).

To create a custom table, page 231

1 On the **View** menu, point to **Table: Entry**, and then click **More Tables**.
2 Do one of the following:
   ● To create a new table, click **New**.

- To create a new table based on an exisiting table, select the task or resource table you want to use as a basis for a new custom table, and then click **Copy**.

3 In the Table Definition dialog box, select the options you want, and then click **OK**.

To create a custom view, page 235

1 On the **View** menu, click **More Views**.
2 In the More Views dialog box, do one of the following:
   - To create a view, click **New**. Click **Single View** or **Combination View** in the Define New View dialog box, and then click **OK**.
   - To redefine a view, click the view's name, and then click **Edit**.
   - To create a new view based on another view, click the view's name, and then click **Copy**.
3 In the View Definition dialog box, choose the options you want, and then click **OK**.

11 Printing Project Information

To see the page setup options for views, page 245

1 Switch to a view you want.
2 On the **File** menu, click **Page Setup**.

To see the page setup options for reports, page 247

1 On the **View** menu, click **Reports**.
2 In the Reports dialog box, click **Custom**, and then click **Select**.
3 In the Custom Reports dialog box, click a report, and then click **Setup**.

To preview a view before printing, page 249

- On the **File** menu, click **Print Preview**.

To work in the Print Preview window, page 249

1 On the **File** menu, click **Print Preview**.
2 Do one of the following:
   - To navigate between pages of a multi-page print job, click a page navigation button.
   - To zoom out to see all pages of a print job, click **Multiple Pages**.
   - To change page setup options, such as header or legend text, click **Page Setup**, and choose the options you want.

- To display the Print dialog box and set other options or to print what you see in the Print Preview window, click **Print**.
- To exit the Print Preview window, click **Close**.

To print a predefined report, page 254

1   On the **View** menu, click **Reports**.
2   In the Reports dialog box, click the category of report you want, and then click **Select**.
3   In the dialog box that appears next, click the specific report you want to print, and click **Select**.
4   In the Print Preview window, click **Print**.

To edit a predefined report, page 256

1   On the **View** menu, click **Reports**.
2   In the Reports dialog box, click the category of report you want, and then click **Select** (or for custom reports, click **Preview**).
3   In the dialog box that appears next, click the specific report you want to edit, and then click **Edit**.
4   In the dialog box that appears next, choose the options you want.

12   Sharing Project Information with Other Programs

To copy text from a Project table to the Windows Clipboard, page 262

1   Set up the table to display only the data you want to copy—for example, apply a filter or insert or hide columns.
2   Select the range of data you want to copy.
3   On the **Edit** menu, click **Copy Cell**, **Copy Task**, or **Copy Resource**.

To copy a snapshot of a view to the Windows Clipboard, page 264

1   Set up the view with the specific details you want such as tables, filters, or groups.
2   On the **Report** menu, click **Copy Picture**.
3   In the Copy Picture dialog box, click either **For screen**, to optimize the snapshot for online viewing, or **For printer**, to optimize it for printing.
4   Select whatever other options you want, and then click **OK**.

To open a file in a different format in Project, page 267

1   On the **File** menu, click **Open**.
2   In the **Files of type** box, click the file format you want.
3   Locate and click the specific file you want to open, and then click **Open**.

4   If the file you selected is not in Project format, the Import Wizard appears. Follow the instructions that appear on your screen.

To save a Project file in a different format, page 273

1   On the **File** menu, click **Save As**.
2   In the Save As dialog box, click the location, and enter the file name you want.
3   In the **Save as type** box, click the format you want, and then click **Save**.
4   Follow the instructions that appear on your screen in the Export Wizard.

To create a new Project summary report for Word, PowerPoint, or Visio, page 275

1   On the **View** menu, point to **Toolbars**, and click **Analysis**.
2   On the **Analysis** toolbar, click the **Copy Picture to Office Wizard** button, and then follow the instructions that appear on your screen.

To create a visual report with Excel or Visio, page 280

1   On the **Report** menu, click **Visual Reports**.
2   Under **Show report templates created in**, select the application for which you want to generate a visual report.
3   Select the tab that corresponds to the type of data you want in the visual report.
4   Select the visual report you want, and then click **View**.
5   In Excel or Visio, adjust the PivotTable (if Excel) or PivotDiagram (Visio) as needed.

13   Tracking Progress on Tasks and Assignments

To update a baseline, page 289

1   On the **Tools** menu, point to **Tracking**, and then click **Set Baseline**.
2   In the Set Baseline dialog box, select the baseline you want to update.
3   Under **For**, click either **Entire project** or **Selected tasks**.

To enter task-level or assignment-level actual work values, page 291

1   On the **View** menu, click **Task Usage**.
2   On the **View** menu, point to **Table: Usage**, and then click **Work**.
3   Enter the actual work values you want for a task or assignment in the **Actual** column.

To enter daily (or other time period's) actual work values per task or assignment, page 298

1   On the **View** menu, click **Task Usage**.
2   Scroll the timescale to the time period for which you want to record actual work.
3   On the **Format** menu, point to **Details**, and click **Actual Work**.
4   In the timescale grid, enter the task or assignment value you want in the **Act. Work** field.

To reschedule uncompleted work, page 304

1   On the **Tools** menu, point to **Tracking**, and then click **Update Project**.
2   Click **Reschedule uncompleted work to start after**, and in the **Date** box, type or click the date you want.

14   Viewing and Reporting Project Status

To identify tasks that have slipped in a view, page 312

●   On the **View** menu, click **Tracking Gantt**.

To filter for tasks that have slipped, page 314

1   On the **Project** menu, point to **Filtered For: All Tasks**, and then click **More Filters**.
2   In the More Filters dialog box, click **Slipping Tasks**, and then click **Apply**.

To see schedule variance, page 315

1   On the **View** menu, click **More Views**.
2   In the More Views dialog box, click **Task Sheet**, and then click **Apply**.
3   On the **View** menu, point to **Table: Entry**, and then click **Variance**.

To see task costs in a view, page 319

1   On the **View** menu, click **More Views**.
2   In the More Views dialog box, click **Task Sheet**, and then click **Apply**.
3   On the **View** menu, point to **Table: Entry**, and click **Cost**.

To filter for tasks that are overbudget, page 320

1   On the **Project** menu, point to **Filtered For: All Tasks**, and then click **More Filters**.
2   In the More Filters dialog box, click **Cost Overbudget**, and then click **Apply**.

To see resource costs in a view, page 322

1 On the **View** menu, click **Resource Sheet**.
2 On the **View** menu, point to **Table: Entry**, and then click **Cost**.

To view and sort resources by cost, page 322

1 On the **View** menu, click **Resource Sheet**.
2 On the **View** menu, point to **Table: Entry**, and click **Cost**.
3 On the **Project** menu, point to **Sort**, and click **Sort By**.
4 In the Sort dialog box, in the **Sort By** box, click **Cost**.
5 Make sure the **Permanently renumber resources** check box is cleared, and then click **Sort**.

To view and sort resources by cost variance, page 323

1 On the **View** menu, click **Resource Sheet**.
2 On the **View** menu, point to **Table: Entry**, and click **Cost**.
3 On the **Project** menu, point to **Sort**, and click **Sort By**.
4 In the Sort dialog box, in the **Sort By** box, click **Cost Variance**.
5 Make sure the **Permanently renumber resources** check box is cleared, and then click **Sort**.

To customize fields for a custom view, page 325

1 On the **Tools** menu, point to **Customize**, and then click **Fields**.
2 In the Customize Fields dialog box, select the options you want.

15 Getting Your Project Back on Track

To edit resource assignments' work values, page 338

1 On the **View** menu, click **Resource Usage**.
2 In the **Work** column, edit the values you want.

To replace one resource with another, page 340

1 On the **View** menu, click **Task Usage**.
2 In the **Task Name** column, select the task for which you want to replace the resource.
3 On the **Standard** toolbar, click the **Assign Resources** button.
4 In the Assign Resources dialog box, in the **Resource Name** column, click the name of the resource you want to replace, and then click **Replace**.
5 In the Replace Resource dialog box, click the name of the replacement resource, and click **OK**.

To filter for critical tasks, page 343

● On the **Project** menu, point to **Filtered For: All Tasks**, and then click **Critical**.

To enter overtime work values in the Task Form, page 343

1 On the **View** menu, click **Gantt Chart**.
2 In the **Task Name** column, select the task you want.
3 On the **Window** menu, click **Split**.
4 Click anywhere in the Task Form. On the **Format** menu, point to **Details**, and then click **Resource Work**.
5 In the **Ovt. Work** column for the resource to which you want to assign overtime work, enter the number of hours of overtime work you want and then click **OK**.

16 Applying Advanced Formatting

To format bar styles in a Gantt Chart view, page 353

1 On the **Format** menu, click **Bar Styles**.
2 In the Bar Styles dialog box, select the options you want.

To display horizontal gridlines on the chart portion of a Gantt chart view, page 357

1 On the **Format** menu, click **Gridlines**.
2 In the **Line to change** box, make sure that **Gantt Rows** is selected, and then in the **Type** box, click the type of line you want.

To format box styles in the Network Diagram view, page 358

1 On the **View** menu, click **Network Diagram**.
2 On the **Format** menu, click **Box Styles**.
3 In the Box Styles dialog box, select the options you want.

To format bars in the Calendar view, page 362

1 On the **View** menu, click **Calendar**.
2 On the **Format** menu, click **Bar Styles**.
3 In the Bar Styles dialog box, select the options you want.

17   Customizing Project

To copy a custom element (such as a view or table) from one project plan to another through the Organizer, page 370

1   First open the project plan that contains the custom element (such as a custom table), and then open the project plan to which you want to copy the custom element.
2   On the **Tools** menu, click **Organizer**.
3   Click the tab name that corresponds to the type of custom element you want to copy.
4   In the **<Custom Elements> available in** drop-down list on the left side of the Organizer dialog box, click the name of the project plan that contains the custom element.
5   Click **Copy**.

To record a macro, page 374

1   On the **Tools** menu, point to **Macro**, and then click **Record New Macro**.
2   In the **Macro name** box, enter a name for the macro (no spaces allowed).
3   In the **Store macro in** box, click **This Project** to store the macro in the active project plan or **Global File** to store it in the global template.
4   Click **OK**.
5   Perform the actions you want recorded in the macro.
6   On the **Tools** menu, point to **Macro**, and then click **Stop Recorder**.

To run a macro, page 375

1   On the **Tools** menu, point to **Macro**, and then click **Macros**.
2   In the **Macro name** box, click the name of the macro you want to run, and then click **Run**.

To edit a macro in the Visual Basic Editor, page 377

1   On the **Tools** menu, point to **Macro**, and then click **Macros**.
2   In the **Macro name** box, click the name of the macro you want to edit, and then click **Edit**.
3   In the Visual Basic Editor, edit the macro.
4   On the **File** menu in the Visual Basic Editor, click **Close and Return to Microsoft Project**.

To create a custom toolbar, page 382

1   On the **Tools** menu, point to **Customize**, and then click **Toolbars**.
2   Click the **Toolbars** tab.

3   Click **New**.

4   In the **Toolbar Name** box, type the toolbar name you want, and then click **OK**.

To add a command to a custom toolbar, page 383

1   On the **Tools** menu, point to **Customize**, and then click **Toolbars**.

2   Click the **Commands** tab.

3   In the **Categories** list, click the category you want.

4   Drag the command you want from the **Commands** list to the custom toolbar.

To edit the graphic image and text that appears on a custom toolbar button, page 384

1   On the **Tools** menu, point to **Customize**, and then click **Toolbars**.

2   Click the **Commands** tab.

3   Click the custom button you want to modify on the custom toolbar.

4   Click **Modify Selection**, and then point to **Change Button Image**.

5   In the list of images that appears, click the image you want.

6   Click **Modify Selection**, and in the **Name** box, type the text you want for the custom button name.

18   Measuring Performance with Earned Value Analysis

To set the project status date, page 392

1   On the **Project** menu, click **Project Information**.

2   In the Project Information dialog box, in the **Status Date** box, type or click the status date you want, and click **OK**.

To view earned value schedule indicators, page 392

1   On the **View** menu, click **More Views**.

2   In the More Views dialog box, click **Task Sheet**, and then click **Apply**.

3   On the **View** menu, point to **Table: Entry**, and click **More Tables**.

4   In the More Tables dialog box, click **Earned Value Schedule Indicators**, and click **Apply**.

To view earned value cost indicators, page 394

1   On the **View** menu, click **More Views**.

2   In the More Views dialog box, click **Task Sheet**, and then click **Apply**.

3   On the **View** menu, point to **Table: Entry**, and click **More Tables**.

4   In the More Tables dialog box, click **Earned Value Cost Indicators**, and click **Apply**.

To create an Earned Value visual report, page 398

1   On the **Report** menu, click **Visual Reports**.
2   Click the **Assignment Usage** tab.
3   Click **Earned Value Over Time**.
4   In the **Select level of usage data to include in the report** box, select the time interval you want for reporting.
5   Click **View**.
6   In Excel, adjust the PivotTable and chart as needed.

19   Consolidating Projects and Resources

To create a resource pool, page 406

1   Create a new project plan.
2   Save the new project plan that will become a resource pool.
3   Open one of the project plans you want to make a sharer plan.
4   On the **Tools** menu, point to **Resource Sharing**, and click **Share Resources**.
5   Under **Resources for <Sharer Plan Name>**, click **Use resources**.
6   In the **From** list, click the name of your resource pool, and click **OK** to close the Share Resources dialog box.
7   If you have more than one sharer plan, open another sharer plan.
8   Repeat steps 3 through 7 for the other sharer plans.
9   Save changes to the sharer plans and the resource pool.

To view cross-project assignment details in the resource pool, page 410

1   On the **View** menu, click **Resource Usage**.
2   In the **Resource Name** column, click the name of a resource.
3   On the **Window** menu, click **Split** to display the Resource Form.

To update a resource's working time in the resource pool, page 413

1   Open the resource pool as read/write.
2   On the **Tools** menu, click **Change Working Time**.
3   In the **For Calendar** box, select the name of the resource whose working time you want to change.
4   In the **Name** field on the **Exceptions** tab, enter a descriptive name for the nonworking time, such as Vacation.

5   In the **Start** and **Finish** fields, type or select the start and finish dates for the nonworking timespan.

6   Click **OK** to close the Change Working Time dialog box.

To update working time for all sharer plans from the resource pool, page 417

1   Open the resource pool as read/write.

2   On the **Tools** menu, click **Change Working Time**.

3   In the Change Working Time dialog box, in the **For calendar** box, click the base calendar you want to change, such as Standard (Project Calendar).

4   In the **Name** field on the **Exceptions** tab, enter a descriptive name for the nonworking time, such as Holiday.

5   In the **Start** and **Finish** fields, type or select the start and finish dates for the nonworking timespan.

6   Click **OK** to close the Change Working Time dialog box.

To link new project files to the resource pool, page 420

1   Open the resource pool as read/write.

2   On the **Standard** toolbar, click the **New** button.

3   On the **Tools** menu, point to **Resource Sharing**, and click **Share Resources**.

4   In the Share Resources dialog box, under **Resources for <File Name>**, click **Use resources**.

5   In the **From** list, click the name of the resource pool, and click **OK** to close the Share Resources dialog box.

6   Save the sharer plan and resource pool.

To edit a sharer plan and update assignment details in the resource pool, page 422

1   Open a sharer plan.

2   When prompted, open the resource pool.

3   In the sharer plan, make changes to assignments.

4   On the **Tools** menu, point to **Resource Sharing**, and click **Update Resource Pool**.

To create a consolidated project plan, page 426

1   On the **Standard** toolbar, click the **New** button.

2   Save the new project plan.

3   On the **Insert** menu, click **Project**.

4   In the Insert Projects dialog box, locate and click the project plan you want to insert into the consolidated project plan. To select multiple plans, hold down the ⌷Ctrl⌷ key while you click the name of each plan.

5   Click **Insert**.

To create task dependencies between projects, page 429

1   Open the two project plans between which you want to create a task dependency.

2   Switch to the project plan that contains the task you want to make the successor task.

3   On the **View** menu, click **Gantt Chart**.

4   Click the name of the task you want to make the successor task.

5   On the **Standard** toolbar, click the **Task Information** button.

6   Click the **Predecessors** tab.

7   In the **ID** column, click the next empty cell below any other predecessor tasks, and enter the name of the predecessor task from the other project file in this format: File name\Task ID, such as Parnell Aerospace Promo 19\8.

8   Press ⌷Enter⌷, and click **OK** to close the Task Information dialog box.

Part 1

Managing a Simple Project

Chapter at a Glance

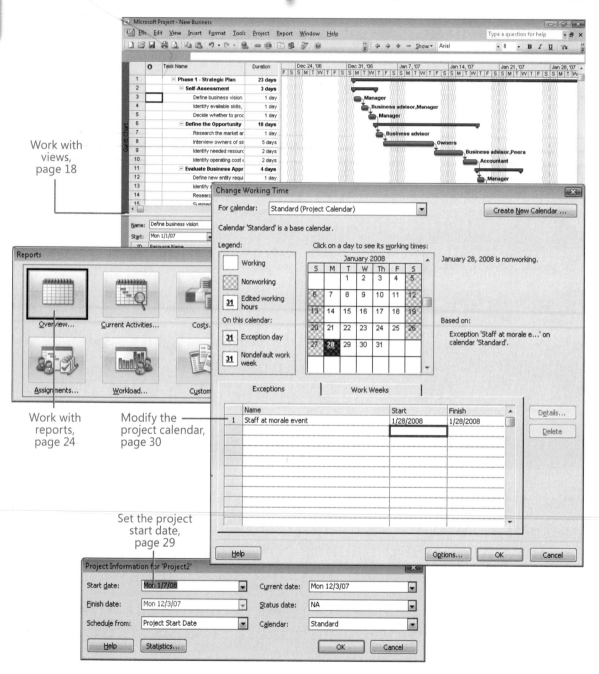

Work with views, page 18

Work with reports, page 24

Modify the project calendar, page 30

Set the project start date, page 29

1 Getting Started with Project

In this chapter, you will learn how to:

✔ Understand the family of Microsoft Office Project 2007 products.

✔ Understand what a good project management tool can help you accomplish.

✔ Start Project Standard or Project Professional, and identify the major parts of the Project window.

✔ Use views to work with project plan details in different ways.

✔ Use reports to print project plan details.

✔ Create a project plan and enter a project start date.

✔ Set the working and nonworking time for a project.

✔ Enter a project plan's properties.

> **Tip** Do you need only a quick refresher on the topics in this chapter? See the Quick Reference entries on pages xxv-xlviii.

Project management is a broadly practiced art and science. If you're reading this book, there's a good chance that either you're seriously involved in project management or you want to be.

At its heart, project management is a toolbox of skills and tools that help you predict and control the outcomes of endeavors undertaken by your organization. Your organization might be involved in other work apart from projects. *Projects* (such as a film project) are distinct from *ongoing operations* (such as payroll services) in that projects are temporary endeavors undertaken to create some unique deliverable or end result. With a good project management system in place, you should be able to answer such questions as

● What *tasks* must be performed, and in what order, to produce the *deliverable* of the project?

● When should each task be performed?

● Who will complete these tasks?

- How much will it cost?
- What if some tasks are not completed as scheduled?
- What's the best way to communicate project details to those who have an interest in the project?

Good project management does not guarantee the success of every project, but poor project management usually contributes to failure.

Microsoft Office Project 2007 should be one of the most frequently used tools in your project management toolbox. This book explains how to use Project to build project plans complete with tasks and resources, use the extensive formatting features in Project to organize and format the project plan details, track actual work against the plan, and take corrective action when things get off track.

If you are new to project management, stop right here and read Appendix A, "A Short Course in Project Management," before proceeding with this chapter. It won't take long, and it will help you to properly assess and organize your specific project-scheduling needs and build solid plans in Project.

Most of the exercises in this book revolve around a fictitious film production company, Southridge Video and Film Productions. Chances are you don't work for a film production company, but you probably have seen a TV commercial or film recently. Each commercial or film constitutes its own project; in fact, some are fairly complex projects involving hundreds of resources and aggressive *deadlines*. We think you'll be able to recognize many of the scheduling problems that Southridge Video encounters and apply the solutions to your own scheduling needs.

This chapter walks you through the Project interface and presents the steps necessary to create a new plan in Project.

There are no practice files in this chapter.

Managing Your Projects with Project

The best project management tool in the world can never replace your own good judgment. However, the tool can and should help you accomplish the following:

- Track all of the information you gather about the work, duration, costs, and resource requirements of your project.

- Visualize and present your project plan in standard, well-defined formats.

- Schedule tasks and resources consistently and effectively.

- Exchange project information with other Microsoft Office System applications.

- Communicate with resources and other stakeholders while you, the project manager, retain ultimate control of the project.

- Manage projects using a program that looks and feels like other desktop productivity applications.

The Microsoft Office Project 2007 family encompasses a broad range of products, including the following:

- **Microsoft Office Project Standard 2007** Windows-based desktop application for project management. The Standard edition is designed for the single project manager and does not interact with Project Server.

- **Microsoft Office Project Professional 2007** Windows-based desktop application that includes the complete feature set of the Standard edition, plus—when used with Project Server—additional project team planning and communications features. Project Professional plus Project Server represents Microsoft's *enterprise project management* (EPM) product offering.

- **Microsoft Office Project Server 2007** Intranet-based solution that enables enterprise-level project collaboration, timesheet reporting, and status reporting when used in conjunction with Project Professional.

- **Microsoft Office Project Web Access 2007** Internet Explorer–based interface for working with Project Server.

- **Microsoft Office Project Portfolio Server 2007** Portfolio management solution.

> **Tip** To learn more about the new features in Project 2007 as well as the differences between the Standard and Professional editions, check out the Project area of the Office Online Web site at microsoft.com Find it on the Web at www.office.microsoft.com, and then navigate to the Project page. For a list of the products that make up the Project Server–based enterprise project management, see "Understanding the Key Pieces of Enterprise Project Management" in Chapter 20.

Most of the chapters in this book focus on the feature set of Project Standard, the entry-level desktop project management tool. The chapters in Part 4 introduce you to the EPM features available with Project Professional and Project Server. All content in this book that applies to Project Standard also applies to Project Professional, so you can use either edition of Project to complete Parts 1 through 3 of this book. If you have Project Professional and access to Project Server, you can also explore the features introduced in Part 4. Otherwise, you can browse through Part 4 to help you decide whether you or your organization should be using Project Professional and Project Server.

What Can a Scheduling Engine Do for You?

Many projects are not managed with a real scheduling tool, such as Project, but they should be. It's common to see task and resource lists from spreadsheet programs, such as Microsoft Office Excel, or even nicely formatted Gantt charts from drawing programs, such as Visio. One big advantage that Project has over such applications is that it includes a scheduling engine—a computational brain that can handle issues such as ripple effects when task 1 in a 100-task sequence has a change in duration. This scheduling engine can also consider nonworking time, such as weekends, when calculating a task's start and finish dates. Applications such as Excel and Visio might have a place in your project management toolbox, but you'll need a scheduling engine such as Project to truly be successful.

Starting Project Standard

Important Follow the steps in this section if you have Microsoft Office Project Standard. If you have Microsoft Office Project Professional, skip this section and refer to the next section, "Starting Project Professional." If you are uncertain, here is an easy way to tell which edition of Project you have: After starting Project, look for a Collaborate menu between the Report and Window menus. If you see it, you have Project Professional; if not, you have Project Standard. You can also click About Microsoft Office Project on the Help menu any time after Project has been started. The dialog box that appears indicates which edition you have.

In this exercise, you'll start Project Standard, create a file based on a template (containing some initial data that you can use as a starting point for a new project plan), and view the major areas of the default Project interface.

1. On the Windows taskbar, click the **Start** button.

   The Start menu appears.

2. On the **Start** menu, point to **All Programs**, click **Microsoft Office**, and then click **Microsoft Office Project 2007**.

Project Standard appears. Your screen should look similar to the following illustration.

Toolbars

Menu bar   Project plan window   Search for Help box

Toolbar Options

> **Tip** Depending on the screen resolution that is set on your computer and the toolbar buttons you use most often, it's possible that not every button on every toolbar will appear on your Project toolbars. If a button mentioned in this book doesn't appear on a toolbar, click the Toolbar Options down arrow on that toolbar to display the rest of the available buttons.

If you've used other Office applications or if you're upgrading from a previous version of Project, you'll be familiar with many of the major interface elements in the Project window. Let's walk through them:

○ The main menu bar and shortcut menus allow you to give instructions to Project.

○ Toolbars provide quick access to the most common tasks; most toolbar buttons correspond to a menu bar command. Pop-up screen tips describe the toolbar buttons you point to. Project customizes its toolbars for you based on how frequently you use specific toolbar buttons. The most frequently used buttons will remain visible on the toolbars; those less frequently used will be temporarily hidden.

○ The project plan window contains a view of the active project plan. (We'll refer to the types of documents that Project works with as project plans, not documents or schedules.) The name of the active view appears on the left edge of the view—in this case, the Gantt Chart view is displayed.

○ The box labeled *Type a question for help* allows you to quickly search for instructions on performing common activities in Project. Simply type in a question and press Enter. Throughout this book, we'll suggest questions that you can enter into this box to learn more about specific features. If your computer is connected to the Internet, your search query will go to assistance content on Office Online (part of the Microsoft Web site), and the results displayed will reflect the most up-to-date content available from Microsoft. If your computer is not connected to the Internet, the search results will be limited to the Help installed with Project.

Next, you will view the templates included with Project and create a project plan based on one of them.

3. On the **File** menu, click **New**.

The New Project task pane appears.

4. In the **New Project** task pane, under **Templates**, click **On computer**.

The Templates dialog box appears.

5. Click the **Project Templates** tab.

Your screen should look similar to the following illustration.

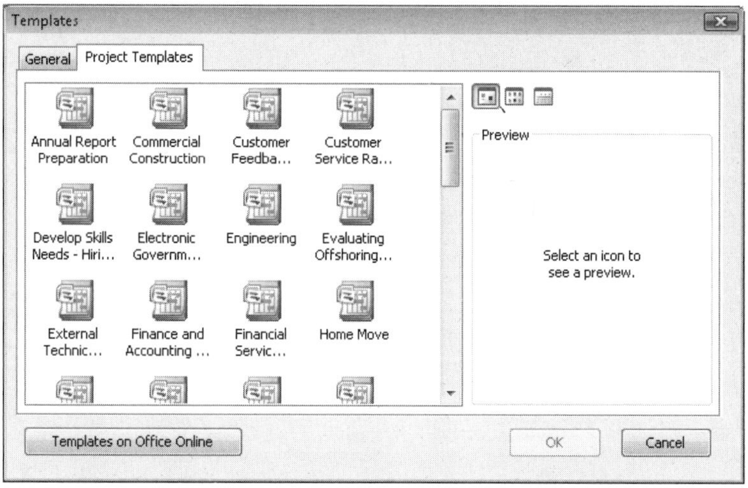

6. Click **New Business** (you may need to scroll down through the list of Project Templates to see it), and then click **OK**.

> **Tip** Depending on how Project was installed on your computer, the templates included with Project might not be installed at this point. This "install on first use" setting is one of the setup choices for optional components included with Project. If you have never seen the templates included with Project before, spend some time browsing through them. You might find one that matches an upcoming project for which you'd like to develop a full plan. Starting with a predefined template can save you a great deal of effort.

Project creates a project plan based on the New Business template and closes the New Project task pane. Your screen should look similar to the following illustration.

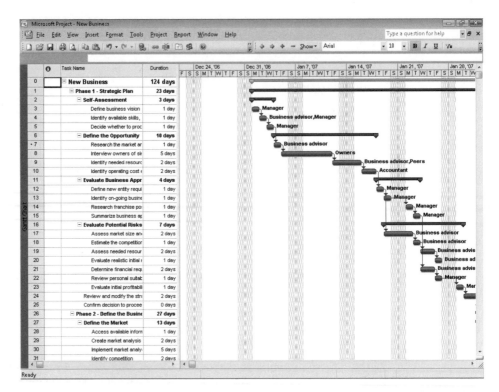

For the next few exercises in this chapter, you will use the sample data provided by the template to identify the major parts of the Project interface.

The Project Guide: Well Worth a Look

Project includes a wizard-like interface that you can use when creating or fine-tuning a project plan. This helper is called the Project Guide. You can use the Project Guide to perform many common activities relating to tasks, resources, and assignments.

In Project 2007, the Project Guide is turned off by default, but you can display the Project Guide by clicking Turn On Project Guide on the View menu or checking the Display Project Guide box on the Interface tab of the Options dialog box (Tools menu). Once you do this, the Project Guide appears in the left pane of the Project window.

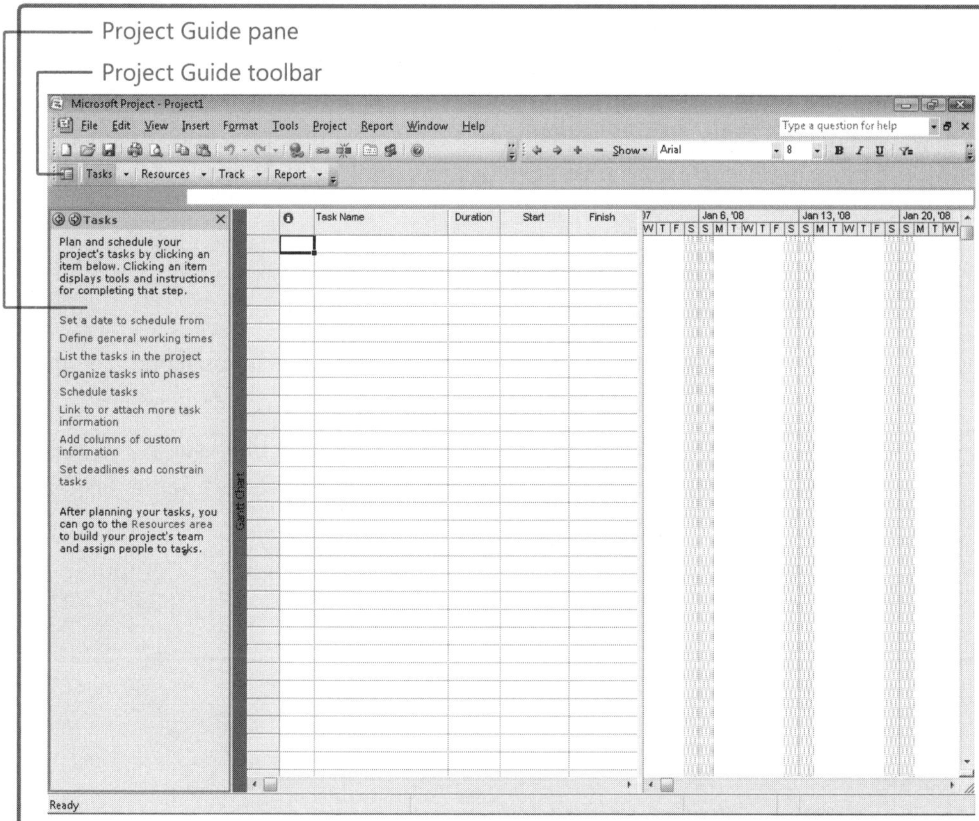

Project Guide pane

Project Guide toolbar

The Project Guide contains instructions, definitions, and commands that not only walk you through common activities, but can change views and other settings in Project to help you complete your chosen activity. You can view all activities in the Project Guide through the Project Guide toolbar. This toolbar is divided into the most common subject areas within Project (Tasks, Resources, Track, and Report).

Starting Project Professional

Important Follow the steps in this section if you have Microsoft Office Project Professional. If you have Microsoft Office Project Standard, skip this section and refer to the previous section, "Starting Project Standard." If you are uncertain, here is an easy way to tell which edition of Project you have: After starting Project, look for a Collaborate menu between the Report and Window menus. If you see it, you have Project Professional; if not, you have Project Standard. You can also click **About Microsoft Office Project** on the **Help** menu any time after Project has been started. The dialog box that appears indicates which edition you have.

In this exercise, you'll start Project Professional, create a file based on a template (containing some initial data that you can use as a starting point for a new project plan), and view the major areas of the default Project interface. If you use Project Professional connected to Project Server, you will also make a one-time adjustment to how Project Professional starts so that you can use this book's practice files without affecting Project Server.

1. On the Windows taskbar, click the **Start** button.

   The Start menu appears.

2. On the **Start** menu, point to **All Programs**, click **Microsoft Office**, and then click **Microsoft Office Project 2007.**

   Depending on how your enterprise options have been set in Project Professional, you might be prompted to log into or choose a Project Server account. If so, complete step 3. Otherwise, go to step 4.

3. If the Login dialog box appears, in the **Profile** box select **Computer**, and then click **OK**.

Login
Profile:	Computer
User Name:	Computer
Password:	
☐ Enter User Credentials
☑ Load Summary Resource Assignments
Work Offline	OK	Cancel

   Choosing this option sets Project Professional to work independently of your Project Server and helps ensure that none of the practice file data used for this chapter can accidentally be published to your Project Server.

   Project appears. Next, you'll review or adjust some enterprise options.

4. On the **Tools** menu, point to **Enterprise Options**, and then click **Microsoft Office Project Server Accounts**.

   The Project Server Accounts dialog box appears.

5. Note the Current account value:

   ○ If the Current account value is something other than Computer, click **Manually control connection state**, click **OK**, and then complete step 6.

   Or

   ○ If the Current account value is Computer, click **Cancel**, and then skip step 6.

   Choosing Manually Control Connection State will cause Project Professional to prompt you to choose an account to work with when you start Project Professional. This helps ensure that none of the practice file data used for this chapter can accidentally be published to your Project Server.

6. Close and restart Project Professional. If prompted to choose a profile, click **Computer**, and then click **OK**.

   Project Professional appears.

Toolbars

Menu bar

Project plan
window

The Collaborate menu
appears in Project
Professional only.

Search for Help box

Microsoft Project - Project1

File Edit View Insert Format Tools Project Report Collaborate Window Help

Type a question for help

Show ▾   Arial   ▾ 8   ▾ **B** *I* U

	❶	Task Name	Duration	Start	Finish	Dec 30, '07	Jan 6, '08	Jan 13, '08	Jan 20, '08	Jan 27, '08

Gantt Chart

Ready

Toolbar Options

Tip Depending on the screen resolution that is set on your computer and the toolbar buttons you use most often, it's possible that not every button on every toolbar will appear on your Project toolbars. If a button mentioned in this book doesn't appear on a toolbar, click the **Toolbar Options** down arrow on that toolbar to display the rest of the available buttons.

If you've used other Office applications or if you're upgrading from a previous version of Project, you'll be familiar with many of the major interface elements in the Project window. Let's walk through them:

○ The main menu bar and shortcut menus allow you to give instructions to Project.

○ Toolbars provide quick access to the most common tasks; most toolbar buttons correspond to a menu bar command. Project customizes its menus and toolbars for you based on how frequently you use specific commands or toolbar buttons. The most frequently used buttons will remain visible on the toolbars; those less frequently used will be temporarily hidden.

○ The project plan window contains a view of the active project plan. (We'll refer to the types of documents that Project works with as project plans, not documents or schedules.) The name of the active view appears on the left edge of the view—in this case, the Gantt Chart view is displayed.

○ The box labeled *Type a question for help* allows you to quickly search for instructions on performing common activities in Project. Simply type in a question and press Enter. Throughout this book, we'll suggest questions that you can enter into this box to learn more about specific features. If your computer is connected to the Internet, your search query will go to assistance content on Office Online (part of the Microsoft Web site), and the results displayed will reflect the most up-to-date content available from Microsoft. If your computer is not connected to the Internet, the search results will be limited to the Help installed with Project.

Next, you will view the templates included with Project and create a project plan based on one of them.

7. On the **File** menu, click **New**.

The New Project task pane appears.

8. In the **New Project** task pane, under **Templates**, click **On computer**.

The Templates dialog box appears.

9. Click the **Project Templates** tab.

When you are connected to Project Server an additional tab, Enterprise Templates, is displayed

10. Click **New Business** (you may need to scroll down through the list of Project Templates to see it), and then click **OK**.

> **Tip** Depending on how Project was installed on your computer, the templates included with Project might not be installed at this point. This "install on first use" setting is one of the setup choices for optional components included with Project. If you have never seen the templates included with Project before, spend some time browsing through them. You might find one that matches an upcoming project for which you'd like to develop a full plan. Starting with a predefined template can save you a great deal of effort.

Project creates a project plan based on the New Business template and closes the New Project task pane. Your screen should look similar to the following illustration.

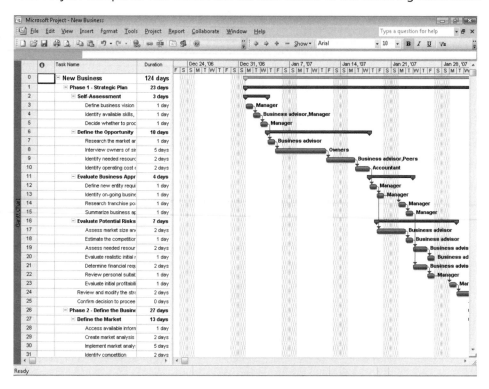

For the next few exercises in this chapter, you will use the sample data provided by the template to identify the major parts of the Project interface.

The Project Guide: Well Worth a Look

Project includes a wizard-like interface that you can use when creating or fine-tuning a project plan. This helper is called the Project Guide. You can use the Project Guide to perform many common activities relating to tasks, resources, and assignments.

In Project 2007, the Project Guide is turned off by default, but you can display the Project Guide by clicking Turn On Project Guide on the View menu or checking the Display Project Guide box on the Interface tab of the Options dialog box in the Tools menu. Once you do this, The Project Guide appears in the left pane of the Project window.

Project Guide pane

Project Guide toolbar

The Project Guide contains instructions, definitions, and commands that not only walk you through common activities, but can change views and other settings in Project to help you complete your chosen activity. You can view all activities in the Project Guide through the Project Guide toolbar. This toolbar is divided into the most common subject areas within Project (Tasks, Resources, Track, and Report).

Exploring Views

The working space in Project is called a *view*. Project contains dozens of views, but you normally work with just one view (sometimes two) at a time. You use views to enter, edit, analyze, and display your project information. The default view—the one you see when Project starts—is the *Gantt Chart view* shown here.

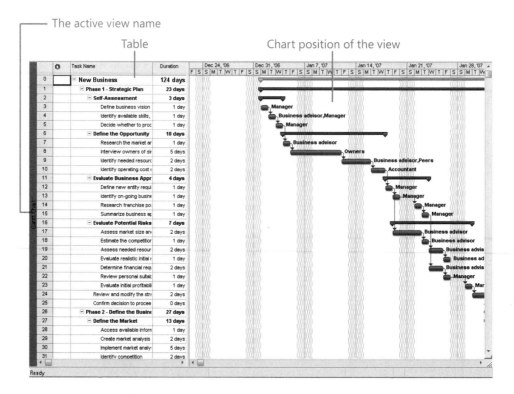

In general, views focus on either task or resource details. The Gantt Chart view, for example, lists task details in a table on the left side of the view and graphically represents each task as a bar in the chart on the right side of the view. The Gantt Chart view is a common way to represent a project plan, especially when presenting it to others. It is also useful for entering and fine-tuning task details and for analyzing your project.

In this exercise, you'll start at the Gantt Chart view and then switch to other views that highlight different aspects of a project plan. Finally, you'll explore combination views that let you focus on specific project details more easily.

1. On the **View** menu, click **Resource Sheet**.

   The Resource Sheet view replaces the Gantt Chart view.

The Resource Sheet view displays details about resources in a row-and-column format (called a *table*), with one resource per row. This view is called a sheet view. Another sheet view, called the Task Sheet view, lists the task details. Note that the Resource Sheet view doesn't tell you anything about the tasks to which resources might be assigned. To see that type of information, you'll switch to a different view.

2. On the **View** menu, click **Resource Usage**.

The Resource Usage view replaces the Resource Sheet view.

This usage view groups the tasks to which each resource is assigned. Another usage view, the Task Usage view, flips this around to display all of the resources assigned to each task. Usage views also show you the work assignments per resource on a timescale, such as daily or weekly.

Next, you'll switch to the Task Usage view.

3. On the **View** menu, click **Task Usage**.

The Task Usage view replaces the Resource Usage view.

4. In the table portion of the view on the left, click *Define business vision*, which is the name of task 3.

5. On the Standard toolbar, click the **Scroll To Task** button.

Scroll To Task

The timescale side of the view scrolls to show you the scheduled work values for this task.

Timescale

A usage view is a fairly sophisticated way of viewing project details. Next, you'll switch to a simpler view.

6. On the **View** menu, click **Calendar**.

The Calendar view appears.

This simple month- or week-at-a-glance view lacks the table structure, timescale, or chart elements you've seen in previous views. Task bars appear on the days they're scheduled to start; if a task's duration is longer than one day, its bar will span multiple days.

Another common view used in project management is the Network Diagram.

7. On the **View** menu, click **Network Diagram**.

The Network Diagram view appears. Use the scroll bars to view different parts of the Network Diagram view.

This view focuses on task relationships. Each box or node in the Network Diagram view displays details about a task, and lines between boxes indicate task relationships. Like the Calendar view, the Network Diagram view lacks a table structure; the entire view is a chart.

To conclude this exercise, you'll look at combination views. These split the project plan window into two panes, with each pane containing a different view. The views are synchronized; therefore, selecting a specific task or resource in one view causes the other view to display details about that task or resource.

8. On the **View** menu, click **More Views**.

The More Views dialog box appears. This dialog box lists all of the predefined views available in Project.

9. In the **Views** box, click **Task Entry**, and then click the **Apply** button.

The Task Entry view appears.

Drag divider bar to show more of either pane.

Gantt Chart view in the upper pane

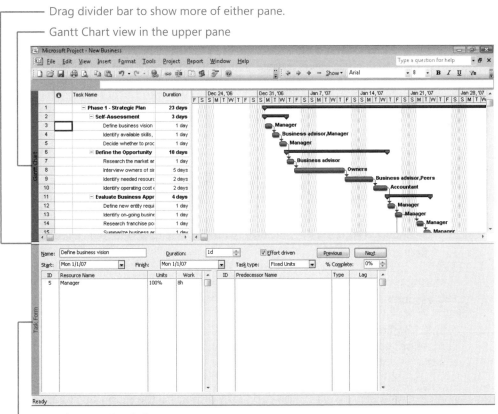

Task Form view in lower pane

This view is a predefined split-screen or combination view, with the Gantt Chart in the upper pane and the Task Form in the lower pane. A form is the final element of a view that you will see in this chapter. A form displays details about the selected task or resource, much like a dialog box. You can enter, change, or review these details in the form.

10. If the selection in the Gantt Chart portion of the view is not on task 3, *Define business vision,* click that task's name.

The details about task 3 appear in the Task Form portion of the view.

11. In the Gantt Chart portion of the view, click the name of task 4, *Identify available skills, information, and support.*

The details about task 4 appear in the Task Form.

> **Tip** Besides using the predefined combination views, you can display two views of your choice by clicking Split on the Window menu. After the Project window is split into two panes, click in the upper or lower pane and then choose the view you want to appear there. To return to a single view, on the Window menu, click Remove Split.

It is important to understand that, in all of these views as well as all of the other views in Project, you are looking at different aspects of the same set of details about a single project plan. Even a simple project plan can contain too much data to display at one time. You can use views to help you focus on the specific details you want.

In later exercises, you'll do more work with views to further focus on the most relevant project details.

Exploring Reports

Project contains two types of reports: tabular reports that are intended for printing, and visual reports that allow you to export Project data to Excel and Visio. Visual reports use Excel and Visio templates included with Project to produce nicely designed charts and diagrams.

You don't enter data directly into a report. Project includes several predefined task and resource reports that you can manipulate to obtain the information you want.

In this exercise, you view a report in the Print Preview window and then generate a visual report.

1. On the **Report** menu, click **Reports**.

    The Reports dialog box appears, displaying the six broad report categories available in Project.

2. Click **Custom**, and then click the **Select** button.

    The Custom Reports dialog box appears, listing all predefined reports in Project and any custom reports that have been added.

3. On the **Reports** list, click **Resource (work)**, and then click the **Preview** button.

    Project displays the Resource (work) report in the Print Preview window.

This report is a complete list of the resources available in this project plan, similar to what you'd see in the Resource Sheet view. If you want to zoom in closer, move the mouse pointer (shaped like a magnifying glass) to a specific portion of the report and click. Click again to toggle back to the full-page preview.

4. On the Print Preview toolbar, click the **Close** button.

The Print Preview window closes, and the Custom Reports dialog box reappears.

5. In the **Custom Reports** dialog box, click **Close**, and then click **Close** again to close the Reports dialog box.

Next, you will create a visual report to get a close look at overall resource work-load and availability through the life of the project. This exercise requires that you have Microsoft Office Excel 2003 or later installed on your computer. If you do not, skip ahead to step 11.

6. On the **Report** menu, click **Visual Reports**.

The Visual Reports dialog box appears, listing all predefined visual reports in Project.

For each available report, Project exports data to Excel or Visio and then generates charts, tables, or diagrams in one or the other of those applications.

7. For **Show Report Template Created In**, make sure that **Microsoft Office Excel** is selected and that the **All** tab is visible.

8. Click **Resource Remaining Work Report**, and then click **View**.

Excel starts and Project exports resource data to Excel (this may take a few moments).

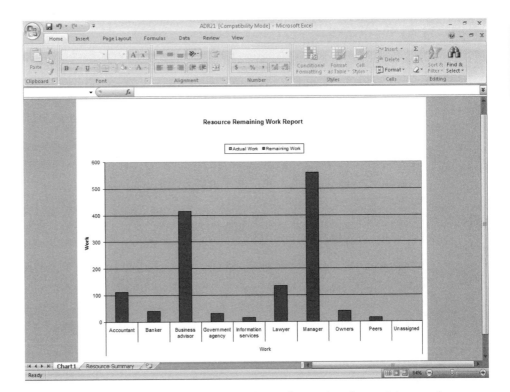

The Chart sheet contains a stacked bar chart of actual and remaining work per resource. You can also observe the data on which the chart is based on the Resource Summary sheet. Because the chart is based on an Excel PivotTable (visible on the Resource Summary sheet), you can substantially refine the data and corresponding chart.

9. Close Excel without saving the visual report.

> **Tip** Project users frequently go to a lot of trouble to customize views to include specific information in the format they want. Before you do that, check the predefined views (for online work or printing), reports (for printing), or visual reports (for charts and diagrams). There's a good chance that the Project designers have anticipated your needs and provided a predefined solution for you.

10. Click **Close** to close the Visual Reports dialog box.

To conclude this exercise, you'll close the file you've been using to explore views and reports.

11. On the **File** menu, click **Close** to close the New Business plan. When prompted to save changes, click the **No** button.

Creating a New Project Plan

A project plan is essentially a model you construct of some aspects of the real project you anticipate—what you think will happen or what you want to happen (it's usually best if these are not too different). This model focuses on some, but not all, aspects of the real project—tasks, resources, time frames, and possibly their associated costs.

As you might expect, Project focuses primarily on time. You might know the planned start date of a project, the planned finish date, or both. However, when working with Project, you specify only one date: the project start date or the project finish date. Why? Because after you enter the project start or finish date and the durations of the tasks, Project calculates the other date for you. Remember that Project is not merely a static repository of your schedule information; it is an active scheduling tool.

Most projects should be scheduled by using a start date, even if you know that the project must finish by a certain deadline date. Scheduling from a start date causes all tasks to start as soon as possible and gives you the greatest scheduling flexibility. In later chapters, you will witness this flexibility in action as we work with a project that is scheduled from a start date.

Project Management Focus: Project Is Part of a Larger Picture

Depending on your needs and the information to which you have access, the project plans you develop might not deal with other important aspects of real projects. For example, many large projects are undertaken in organizations that have a formal change management process. Before a major change to the scope of a project is allowed, it must first be evaluated and approved by the people managing and implementing the project. Even though this is an important project management activity, it is not something done directly within Project.

Now that you've had a brief look at the major parts of the Project interface, you are ready to create the project plan you will use in Part 1 of this book.

In this exercise, you create a new project plan.

1. On the **File** menu, click the **New** command. Then, in the **New Project** task pane, click **Blank Project**.

   Project creates a new, blank project plan. Next, you'll set the project's start date.

2. On the **Project** menu, click **Project Information**.

   The Project Information dialog box appears.

3. In the **Start date** box, type or select 1/7/08.

> **Tip** In most cases when you need to enter a date in Project, you can click the down arrow next to the Date field to show a small monthly calendar. There you can navigate to any month and then click the date you want, or click Today to quickly choose the current date.

Project Information for 'Project2'

Start date:	Mon 1/7/08	Current date:	Mon 12/3/07
Finish date:	Mon 12/3/07	Status date:	NA
Schedule from:	Project Start Date	Calendar:	Standard

Help   Statistics...   OK   Cancel

> **Important** If you are using Project Professional, the Project Information and some other dialog boxes you see will contain additional options. Throughout most of this book we show Project Standard screen illustrations, but point out some Project Server-related functionality that is supported in Project Professional and Project Server. In Part 4, "Introducing Project Server," we show Project Professional illustrations.

Save

4. Click **OK** to close the Project Information dialog box.

5. On the **Standard** toolbar, click the **Save** button.

   Because this project plan has not previously been saved, the Save As dialog box appears.

6. Locate the Chapter 1 Getting Started folder in the Project 2007 Step by Step folder on your hard disk. The default location for the Project 2007 Step by Step folder is \Documents\Microsoft Press.

7. In the **File name** box, type Wingtip Toys Commercial 1.

8. Click **Save** to close the Save As dialog box.

   Project saves the project plan as Wingtip Toys Commercial 1.

> **Tip** You can instruct Project to automatically save the active project plan at predefined intervals, such as every 10 minutes. On the **Tools** menu, click **Options**. In the **Options** dialog box, click the **Save** tab, select the **Save Every** check box, and then specify the time interval you want.

Setting Nonworking Days

This exercise introduces *calendars*—the primary means by which you control when each task and resource can be scheduled for work in Project. In later chapters, you will work with other types of calendars; in this chapter, you will work only with the project calendar.

The *project calendar* defines the general working and nonworking time for tasks. Think of the project calendar as your organization's normal working hours. For example, this might be Monday through Friday, 8 A.M. through 5 P.M., with a one-hour lunch break. Your organization or specific resources might have exceptions to this normal working time, such as holidays or vacation days. You'll address resource vacations in a later chapter, but here you'll address a holiday in the project calendar.

1. On the **Tools** menu, click **Change Working Time**.

   The Change Working Time dialog box appears.

2. In the **For calendar** box, click the down arrow.

The list that appears contains the three base calendars included with Project. These calendars are as follows:

- 24 Hours: Has no nonworking time.
- Night Shift: Covers a "graveyard" shift schedule of Monday night through Saturday morning, 11 P.M. to 8 A.M., with a one-hour break.
- Standard: The traditional working day, Monday through Friday from 8 A.M. to 5 P.M., with a one-hour lunch break.

Only one of the base calendars serves as the project calendar. For this project, you'll use the Standard base calendar as the project calendar, so leave it selected.

You know that the entire staff will be at a morale event on January 28; therefore, no work should be scheduled that day. You will record this as a calendar exception.

3. In the **Name** field on the **Exceptions** tab, type Staff at morale event, and then click in the **Start** field.

4. In the **Start** field, type 1/28/08, and then press Enter .

You could have also selected the date you want in the calendar above the Exceptions tab or from the drop-down calendar in the *Start* field.

This date is now scheduled as nonworking time for the project. In the dialog box, the date appears underlined and is formatted teal to indicate an exception day.

5. Click **OK** to close the Change Working Time dialog box.

To verify the change to the project calendar, scroll the chart portion of the Gantt Chart view (the portion on the right) to the right until Monday, January 28, is visible. Like the weekends, January 28 is formatted gray to indicate nonworking time.

Monday, January 28 is a nonworking day and
is formatted in gray (as are weekends) in the
Gantt chart

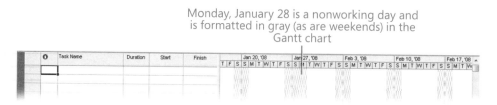

> **Tip** To learn more about calendars, type Overview of using calendars in Project into the box labeled *Type a question for help*.

Entering Project Properties

Like other Microsoft Office programs, Project keeps track of several file properties. Some of these properties are statistics, such as how many times the file has been revised. Other properties include information you might want to record about a project plan, such as the project manager's name or keywords to support a file search. Project also uses properties in page headers and footers when printing.

In this exercise, you enter some properties that you will use later when printing project information and for other purposes.

1. On the **File** menu, click **Properties**.

    The Properties dialog box appears.

2. Click the **Summary** tab if it is not already visible.

3. In the **Subject** box, type Video production schedule.

4. In the **Author** box, type your name.

5. In the **Manager** box, type your name, type your manager's name, or leave the box blank.

6. In the **Company** box, type Southridge Video.

7. Select the **Save preview picture** check box.

The next time this file appears in the Open dialog box with the Preview view option selected, a small image showing the first few tasks of the project will be displayed.

8. Click **OK** to close the dialog box.

CLOSE the Wingtip Toys Commercial 1 file.

"A Database That Knows About Time"

The project plans you create in Project have many things in common with databases, such as those you might work with in Access. If you were to peek inside a Microsoft Project Plan (MPP) file, you'd find it has much in common with a database file format. Data is stored in a set of tables, and relationships connect information in different tables. In fact, it's not uncommon for Project users in large organizations to save project plans in a database format, sometimes saving them to a central database on a network server.

However, what Project provides that a regular database application cannot provide is the active scheduling engine mentioned earlier. One Project expert we know describes it as "a database that knows about time."

Key Points

- The Project product family includes Project Standard, Project Professional, Project Server, and Project Web Access. Normally, you would use Project Standard on the desktop or the latter three in combination to form an EPM solution.

- One of the key distinguishing factors that separates Project from other list-keeping tools, such as Excel, is that Project has a scheduling engine that can work with time.

- Project includes several sophisticated templates that can provide you with a good start to a new project plan.

- The main working space in Project is a view. One or sometimes two views are typically displayed at a time. The Gantt Chart view is the default and probably best known view in Project.

- Project includes a large number of built-in reports that are intended for viewing (but not editing) Project data.

- You use calendars in Project to control when work can be scheduled to occur.

Chapter at a Glance

Create a task list, page 37

	❶	Task Name	Duration	Start	Finish
1		Pre-Production	1 day?	Mon 1/7/08	Mon 1/7/08
2		Develop script	5 days	Mon 1/7/08	Fri 1/11/08
3		Develop production boards	3 days	Mon 1/7/08	Wed 1/9/08
4		Pick locations	2 days	Mon 1/7/08	Tue 1/8/08
5		Hold auditions	2 days	Mon 1/7/08	Tue 1/8/08
6		Production	1 day?	Mon 1/7/08	Mon 1/7/08
7		Rehearse	2 days	Mon 1/7/08	Tue 1/8/08
8		Shoot video	2 days	Mon 1/7/08	Tue 1/8/08
9		Log footage	1 day	Mon 1/7/08	Mon 1/7/08

Create summary tasks, page 46

	❶	Task Name	Duration	Start	Finish
1		Pre-Production	5 days	Mon 1/7/08	Fri 1/11/08
2		Develop script	5 days	Mon 1/7/08	Fri 1/11/08
3		Develop production boa	3 days	Mon 1/7/08	Wed 1/9/08
4		Pick locations	2 days	Mon 1/7/08	Tue 1/8/08
5		Hold auditions	2 days	Mon 1/7/08	Tue 1/8/08
6		Pre-Production complet	0 days	Mon 1/7/08	Mon 1/7/08
7		Production	2 days	Mon 1/7/08	Tue 1/8/08
8		Rehearse	2 days	Mon 1/7/08	Tue 1/8/08
9		Shoot video	2 days	Mon 1/7/08	Tue 1/8/08
10		Log footage	1 day	Mon 1/7/08	Mon 1/7/08

Link tasks to create dependencies, page 49

	❶	Task Name	Duration	Start	Finish
1		Pre-Production	12 days	Mon 1/7/08	Tue 1/22/08
2		Develop script	5 days	Mon 1/7/08	Fri 1/11/08
3		Develop production boa	3 days	Mon 1/14/08	Wed 1/16/08
4		Pick locations	2 days	Thu 1/17/08	Fri 1/18/08
5		Hold auditions	2 days	Mon 1/21/08	Tue 1/22/08
6		Pre-Production complet	0 days	Tue 1/22/08	Tue 1/22/08
7		Production	2 days	Mon 1/7/08	Tue 1/8/08
8		Rehearse	2 days	Mon 1/7/08	Tue 1/8/08
9		Shoot video	2 days	Mon 1/7/08	Tue 1/8/08
10		Log footage	1 day	Mon 1/7/08	Mon 1/7/08

Add notes and hyperlinks to the Web, page 53

	❶	Task Name	Duration	Start	Finish
1		Pre-Production	12 days	Mon 1/7/08	Tue 1/22/08
2		Develop script	5 days	Mon 1/7/08	Fri 1/11/08
3		Develop production boa	3 days	Mon 1/14/08	Wed 1/16/08
4		Pick locations	2 days	Thu 1/17/08	Fri 1/18/08
5		Hold auditions	2 days	Mon 1/21/08	Tue 1/22/08
6		Check recent agent postings		Tue 1/22/08	Tue 1/22/08
7		Production	5 days	Wed 1/23/08	Tue 1/29/08
8		Rehearse	2 days	Wed 1/23/08	Thu 1/24/08
9		Shoot video	2 days	Fri 1/25/08	Mon 1/28/08
10		Log footage	1 day	Tue 1/29/08	Tue 1/29/08

2 Creating a Task List

In this chapter, you will learn how to:

✔ Enter task information.

✔ Estimate and enter how long each task should last.

✔ Create a milestone to track an important event.

✔ Organize tasks into phases.

✔ Create task relationships by linking tasks.

✔ Record task details in notes and insert a hyperlink to content on the Internet.

✔ Check a project plan's overall duration.

> **Tip** Do you need only a quick refresher on the topics in this chapter? See the Quick Reference entries on pages xxv-xlviii.

> **Important** Before you can use the practice files provided for this chapter, you need to install them from the book's companion CD to their default locations. See "Using the Book's CD" on page xix for more information.

Entering Tasks

Tasks are the most basic building blocks of any project—tasks represent the work to be done to accomplish the goals of the project. Tasks describe project work in terms of sequence, duration, and resource requirements. Later in this chapter, you will work with two special types of tasks: summary tasks (which summarize or "roll up" the durations, costs, and so on of subtasks) and milestones (which indicate significant events in the life of a project).

In this exercise, you enter the first tasks required in the video project.

> **BE SURE TO** start Microsoft Office Project 2007 if it's not already running.

> **Important** If you are running Project Professional, you may need to make a one-time adjustment to use the Computer account and to work offline. This ensures that the practice files you work with in this chapter do not affect your Project Server data. For more information, see "Starting Project Professional" on page 11.

> **OPEN** Wingtip Toys Commercial 2a from the *Documents**Microsoft Press**Project 2007 SBS**Chapter 2 Simple Tasks* folder. You can also access the practice files for this book by clicking Start, All Programs, Microsoft Press, Project 2007 Step by Step, and then selecting the chapter folder of the file you want to open.

1. On the **File** menu, click **Save As**.

   The Save As dialog box appears.

2. In the **File name** box, type Wingtip Toys Commercial 2, and then click **Save**.

3. In the first cell directly below the **Task Name** column heading, type Pre-Production, and then press Enter.

Default estimated duration   Bar representing task on Gantt chart

The task you entered is given an ID number. Each task has a unique ID number, but it does not necessarily represent the order in which tasks occur.

Project assigns a duration of one day to the new task, and the question mark indicates that this is an estimated duration. A corresponding task bar of one day's length appears in the Gantt chart. By default, the task start date is the same as the project start date.

4. Enter the following task names below the Pre-Production task name, pressing Enter after each task name.

Develop script

Develop production boards

Pick locations

Hold auditions

Production

Rehearse

Shoot video

Log footage

When you complete this step, you should have nine tasks entered.

		Task Name	Duration	Start	Finish	
1		Pre-Production	1 day?	Mon 1/7/08	Mon 1/7/08	
2		Develop script	1 day?	Mon 1/7/08	Mon 1/7/08	
3		Develop production boards	1 day?	Mon 1/7/08	Mon 1/7/08	
4		Pick locations	1 day?	Mon 1/7/08	Mon 1/7/08	
5		Hold auditions	1 day?	Mon 1/7/08	Mon 1/7/08	
6		Production	1 day?	Mon 1/7/08	Mon 1/7/08	
7		Rehearse	1 day?	Mon 1/7/08	Mon 1/7/08	
8		Shoot video	1 day?	Mon 1/7/08	Mon 1/7/08	
9		Log footage	1 day?	Mon 1/7/08	Mon 1/7/08	

Tip In addition to typing task information directly into Project, you can develop task lists in other applications and then import them into Project. For example, Project installs an Excel template named Microsoft Project Task List Import Template, which you or others can complete and then import into Project with the proper structure. In Excel, this template appears on the Spreadsheet Solutions tab of the Templates dialog box. You can also import your Outlook task list into a project plan. In Project, on the Tools menu, click Import Outlook Tasks.

> **Project Management Focus:**
> **Defining the Right Tasks for the Right Deliverable**
>
> Every project has an ultimate goal or intent: the reason that the project was started. This is called the project *deliverable*. This deliverable is usually a product, such as a TV commercial, or a service or event, such as a software training session. Defining the right tasks to create the right deliverable is an essential skill for a project manager. The task lists you create in Project should describe all of the work required, and only the work required, to complete the project successfully.
>
> In developing your task lists, you might find it helpful to distinguish product scope from project scope. *Product scope* describes the quality, features, and functions of the deliverable of the project. In the scenario used in Part 1 of this book, for example, the deliverable is a TV commercial, and the product scope might include its length, subject, and audience. *Project scope*, on the other hand, describes the work required to deliver such a product or service. In our scenario, the project scope includes detailed tasks relating to the creation of a TV commercial such as holding auditions, shooting the video, editing it, and so on.

Estimating Durations

A task's *duration* is the amount of time you expect it will take to complete the task. Project can work with task durations that range from minutes to months. Depending on the scope of your project, you'll probably want to work with task durations on the scale of hours, days, and weeks.

For example, a project might have a *project calendar* with working time defined as 8 A.M. through 5 P.M. with a one-hour lunch break Monday through Friday, leaving non-working time defined as evenings and weekends. If you estimate that a task will take 16 hours of working time, you could enter its duration as 2d to schedule work over two eight-hour workdays. By starting the task at 8 A.M. on a Friday, you should then expect that it wouldn't be completed until 5 P.M. on the following Monday. No work would be scheduled over the weekend because Saturday and Sunday have been defined as non-working time.

> **Tip** You determine the overall duration of a project by calculating the difference between the earliest start date and the latest finish date of the tasks that compose it. The project duration is also affected by other factors, such as task relationships, which are discussed in the "Linking Tasks" section of this chapter. Because Project distinguishes between working and nonworking time, a task's duration doesn't necessarily correlate to elapsed time.

When working in Project, you can use abbreviations for durations.

If you enter this abbreviation	It appears like this	And it means
m	min	minute
h	hr	hour
d	day	day
w	wk	week
mo	mon	month

> **Tip** You can schedule tasks to occur during working and nonworking time. To do this, assign an elapsed duration to a task. You enter elapsed duration by preceding the duration abbreviation with an e. For example, type 3ed to indicate three elapsed days. You might use an *elapsed duration* for a task that you don't directly control but that nonetheless is critical to your project. For instance, you might have the tasks *Pour foundation concrete* and *Remove foundation forms* in a construction project. If so, you might also want a task called *Wait for concrete to cure* because you don't want to remove the forms until the concrete has cured. The task *Wait for concrete to cure* should have an elapsed duration because the concrete will cure over a contiguous range of days, whether they are working or nonworking days. If the concrete takes 48 hours to cure, you can enter the duration for that task as 2ed, schedule the task to start on Friday at 9 A.M., and expect it to be complete by Sunday at 9 A.M. In most cases, however, you'll work with nonelapsed durations in Project.

Project uses standard values for minutes and hours for durations: one minute equals 60 seconds, and one hour equals 60 minutes. However, you can define nonstandard durations for days, weeks, and months for your project. To do this, on the Tools menu, click the Options command, and in the Options dialog box, click the Calendar tab, illustrated here.

With a setting of 8 hours per day, entering a two-day
task duration (2 days) is the same as entering 16 hours.

Options

Interface	Security		
Schedule	Calculation	Spelling	Save
View	General	Edit	Calendar

Calendar options for 'Wingtip Toys Commercial 2'

Week starts on: Sunday

Fiscal year starts in: January

☐ Use starting year for FY numbering

Default start time: 8:00 AM

Default end time: 5:00 PM

These times are assigned to tasks when you enter a start or finish date without specifying a time. If you change this setting, consider matching the project calendar using the Change Working Time command on the Tools menu.

Hours per day: 8.00

Hours per week: 40.00

Days per month: 20

Set as Default

Help   OK   Cancel

With a setting of 40 hours
per week, entering a three-
week task duration (3 wks)
is the same as entering 120
hours.

With a setting of 20 days
per month, entering a one-
month task duration (1 mon)
is the same as entering 160
hours (8 hours per day x 20
days per month).

The exercises in this chapter use default values: eight hours per day, 40 hours per week, and 20 days per month.

> **Tip**   Although it's beyond the scope of this book, Program Evaluation and Review Technique (PERT) analysis can be a useful tool for estimating task durations. For more information, type Use PERT analysis to estimate task durations into the Type a question for help search box in the upper right corner of the Project window.

In this exercise, you enter durations for the tasks you've created. When you created those tasks, Project entered an estimated duration of one day for each task. (The question mark in the Duration field indicates that the duration is an explicit estimate, although realistically you should consider all task durations to be estimates until the task is completed.) To enter durations:

1. Click the cell below the **Duration** column heading for task 2, Develop script.

   The *Duration* field for task 2 is selected.

2. Type 5d, and then press Enter .

The value 5 days appears in the *Duration* field.

3. Enter the following durations for the remaining tasks.

Task ID	Task Name	Duration
3	Develop production boards	3d
4	Pick locations	2d
5	Hold auditions	2d
6	Production	(Press Enter to skip this task for now)
7	Rehearse	2d
8	Shoot video	2d
9	Log footage	1d

As you complete this step, you see the length of the Gantt bars change.

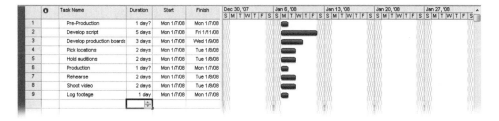

Project Management Focus:
How Do You Come Up with Accurate Task Durations?

You should consider two general rules when estimating task durations.

- Overall project duration often correlates to task duration; long projects tend to have tasks with longer durations than do tasks in short projects.

- If you track progress against your project plan (described in Chapter 6, "Tracking Progress on Tasks," and in Part 2, "Advanced Project Scheduling"), you must consider the level of detail you want to apply to your project's tasks. If you have a multi-year project, for example, it might not be practical or even possible to track tasks that are measured in minutes or hours. In general, you should measure task durations at the lowest level of detail or control that is important to you, but no lower.

The durations are supplied for you for the projects you work on in this book. For your real-world projects, you will often estimate task durations. Good sources of task duration estimates include:

- Historical information from previous, similar projects.
- Estimates from the people who will complete the tasks.
- Expert judgment of those who have managed similar projects.
- Standards of professional or industrial organizations that undertake projects similar to yours.

For complex projects, you probably would combine these and other sources to estimate task durations. Because inaccurate task duration estimates are a major source of risk in any project, making good estimates is well worth the effort expended.

One general rule of thumb to consider is called the *8/80 rule*. This rule suggests that task durations between eight hours (or one day) and 80 hours (10 working days, or two weeks) are generally sized to a manageable duration. Tasks shorter than one day might be too granular, and tasks longer than two weeks might be too long to manage properly. There are many legitimate reasons to break this rule, but its guidelines are worth considering for most tasks in your projects.

Entering a Milestone

In addition to tracking tasks to be completed, you might want to track an important event for your project, such as when the pre-production phase of the project will end. To do this, you will create a milestone.

Milestones are significant events that are either reached within the project (such as completion of a phase of work) or imposed upon the project (such as a deadline by which to apply for funding). Because the milestone itself doesn't normally include any work, milestones are represented as tasks with zero duration.

In this exercise, you create a milestone.

1. Click the name of task 6, *Production*.

2. On the **Insert** menu, click **New Task**.

   Project inserts a row for a new task and renumbers the subsequent tasks.

> **Tip** You can also press the ⌨Insert⌨ key to insert a new task above the selected task. To insert multiple new tasks, select multiple tasks first, and then press Insert. Project will insert the same number of new tasks.

3. Type Pre-Production complete! and then press the ⌨Tab⌨ key to move to the Duration field.

4. In the *Duration* field, type 0d and then press the ⌨Enter⌨ key.

   The milestone is added to your plan.

On the Gantt chart, the milestone appears as a black diamond.

	❶	Task Name	Duration	Start	Finish	Dec 30, '07	Jan 6, '08	Jan 13, '08	Jan 20, '08	Jan 27, '08
1		Pre-Production	1 day?	Mon 1/7/08	Mon 1/7/08					
2		Develop script	5 days	Mon 1/7/08	Fri 1/11/08					
3		Develop production boards	3 days	Mon 1/7/08	Wed 1/9/08					
4		Pick locations	2 days	Mon 1/7/08	Tue 1/8/08					
5		Hold auditions	2 days	Mon 1/7/08	Tue 1/8/08					
6		Pre-Production complete!	0 days	Mon 1/7/08	Mon 1/7/08	♦ 1/7				
7		Production	1 day?	Mon 1/7/08	Mon 1/7/08					
8		Rehearse	2 days	Mon 1/7/08	Tue 1/8/08					
9		Shoot video	2 days	Mon 1/7/08	Tue 1/8/08					
10		Log footage	1 day	Mon 1/7/08	Mon 1/7/08					

> **Tip** You can also mark a task of any duration as a milestone. Double-click the task name to display the Task Information dialog box, and then click the Advanced tab. Select the Mark task as milestone option.

Organizing Tasks into Phases

It is helpful to organize groups of closely related tasks that represent a major portion of the project's work into *phases*. When reviewing a project plan, observing phases of tasks helps you and others to think in terms of major work items and detailed work items. For example, it is common to divide a film or video project into major phases of work such as pre-production, production, and post-production. You create phases by indenting and outdenting tasks. You can also collapse a task list into phases, much as you can work with an outline in Word. In Project, phases are represented by summary tasks.

A *summary task* behaves differently from other tasks. You can't edit its duration, start date, or other calculated values directly because this information is derived or "rolled up" from the detail tasks, called *subtasks* (these appear indented under the summary tasks). Project calculates the duration of a summary task as the span of time from the earliest start date to the latest finish date of its subtasks.

Project Management Focus:
Top-Down and Bottom-Up Planning

The two most common approaches to developing tasks and phases are top-down and bottom-up planning.

- *Top-down planning.* Identifies major phases or products of the project before filling in the tasks required to complete those phases. Complex projects can have several layers of phases. This approach works from general to specific.

- *Bottom-up planning.* Identifies as many bottom-level detailed tasks as possible before organizing them into logical groups, called phases or summary tasks. This approach works from specific to general.

Creating accurate tasks and phases for most complex projects requires a combination of top-down and bottom-up planning. It is common for the project manager to begin with established, broad phases for a project (top-down) and for the resources who will execute the project to provide the detailed tasks that fill out each phase (bottom-up).

In this exercise, you create two summary tasks by indenting tasks.

1. Select the names of tasks 2 through 6.

2. On the **Project** menu, point to **Outline**, and then click **Indent**.

Indent Tasks

> **Tip** You can also click the Indent Tasks button on the Formatting toolbar.

Task 1 becomes a summary task. A summary task bar for it appears in the Gantt chart, and the summary task name is formatted in bold type.

Summary task   Summary task bar in the Gantt Chart

	❶	Task Name	Duration	Start	Finish
1		− **Pre-Production**	**5 days**	**Mon 1/7/08**	**Fri 1/11/08**
2		Develop script	5 days	Mon 1/7/08	Fri 1/11/08
3		Develop production bo	3 days	Mon 1/7/08	Wed 1/9/08
4		Pick locations	2 days	Mon 1/7/08	Tue 1/8/08
5		Hold auditions	2 days	Mon 1/7/08	Tue 1/8/08
6		Pre-Production complet	0 days	Mon 1/7/08	Mon 1/7/08
7		Production	1 day?	Mon 1/7/08	Mon 1/7/08
8		Rehearse	2 days	Mon 1/7/08	Tue 1/8/08
9		Shoot video	2 days	Mon 1/7/08	Tue 1/8/08
10		Log footage	1 day	Mon 1/7/08	Mon 1/7/08

Subtasks

3. Next, select the names of tasks 8 through 10.

4. On the **Project** menu, point to **Outline**, and then click **Indent**.

Task 7 becomes a summary task, and a summary task bar for it appears in the Gantt chart.

	❶	Task Name	Duration	Start	Finish
1		− **Pre-Production**	**5 days**	**Mon 1/7/08**	**Fri 1/11/08**
2		Develop script	5 days	Mon 1/7/08	Fri 1/11/08
3		Develop production bo	3 days	Mon 1/7/08	Wed 1/9/08
4		Pick locations	2 days	Mon 1/7/08	Tue 1/8/08
5		Hold auditions	2 days	Mon 1/7/08	Tue 1/8/08
6		Pre-Production complet	0 days	Mon 1/7/08	Mon 1/7/08
7		− **Production**	**2 days**	**Mon 1/7/08**	**Tue 1/8/08**
8		Rehearse	2 days	Mon 1/7/08	Tue 1/8/08
9		Shoot video	2 days	Mon 1/7/08	Tue 1/8/08
10		Log footage	1 day	Mon 1/7/08	Mon 1/7/08

> **Tip** If your organization uses a work breakdown structure (WBS) process in the project-planning phase, you may find it helpful to view WBS codes in Project. For information about using WBS codes with Project, type **Create WBS codes** into the *Type a question for help* search box.

Linking Tasks

Projects require tasks to be performed in a specific order. For example, the task of film-ing a scene must be completed before the task of editing the filmed scene can occur. These two tasks have a finish-to-start *relationship* (also called a link or dependency) that has two aspects:

- The second task must occur later than the first task; this is a *sequence*.
- The second task can occur only if the first task is completed; this is a *dependency*.

In Project, the first task ("film the scene") is called the *predecessor* because it precedes tasks that depend on it. The second task ("edit the filmed scene") is called the *successor* because it succeeds tasks on which it is dependent. Any task can be a predecessor for one or more successor tasks. Likewise, any task can be a successor to one or more prede-cessor tasks.

Although this might sound complicated, tasks can have one of only four types of task relationships.

This task relationship	Means	Looks like this in the Gantt chart	Example
Finish-to-start (FS)	The finish date of the predecessor task deter-mines the start date of the successor task.		A film scene must be shot before it can be edited.
Start-to-start (SS)	The start date of the predecessor task deter-mines the start date of the successor task.		Reviewing a script and developing the script breakdown and sched-ule are closely related, and they should occur simultaneously.
Finish-to-finish (FF)	The finish date of the predecessor task deter-mines the finish date of the successor task.		Tasks that require spe-cific equipment must end when the equip-ment rental ends.
Start-to-finish (SF)	The start date of the predecessor task deter-mines the finish date of the successor task.		The time when the edit-ing lab becomes avail-able determines when a pre-editing task must end. (This type of rela-tionship is rarely used.)

Representing task relationships and handling changes to scheduled start and finish dates is one area in which the use of a scheduling engine, such as Project, really pays off. For example, you can change task durations or add or remove tasks from a chain of linked tasks, and Project will reschedule tasks accordingly.

Task relationships appear in several ways in Project:

- In the Gantt Chart and Network Diagram views, task relationships appear as the lines connecting tasks.

- In tables, such as the Entry table, task ID numbers of predecessor tasks appear in the *Predecessor* fields of successor tasks.

You create task relationships by creating links between tasks. Currently, all of the tasks in the project plan are scheduled to start on the same day—the project start date. In this exercise, you use different methods to create links between several tasks, thereby creating finish-to-start relationships.

First you'll create a finish-to-start dependency between two tasks.

1. Select the names of tasks 2 and 3.

2. On the **Edit** menu, click **Link Tasks**.

> **Tip** To create a finish-to-start dependency, you can also click the Link Tasks button on the Standard toolbar.

Tasks 2 and 3 are linked with a finish-to-start relationship. Note that Project changed the start date of task 3 to the next working day following the completion of task 2 (skipping over the weekend), and the duration of the Pre-Production summary task grew correspondingly.

Link line   Nonworking time

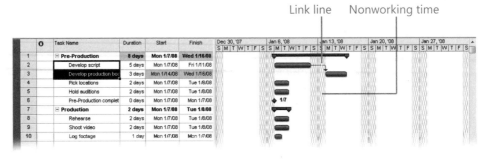

Unlink Tasks

> **Tip** To unlink tasks, select the tasks you want to unlink, and then click the Unlink Tasks button on the Standard toolbar. You can also click Unlink Tasks on the Edit menu. If you unlink a single task that is within a chain of linked tasks with finish-to-start relationships, Project reestablishes links between the remaining tasks.

Next, you will link several tasks at once.

3. Select the names of tasks 3 through 6.

4. On the **Edit** menu, click **Link Tasks**.

Tasks 3 through 6 are linked with a finish-to-start relationship.

Change Highlighting indicates the values that are affected after you make a change in a project plan.

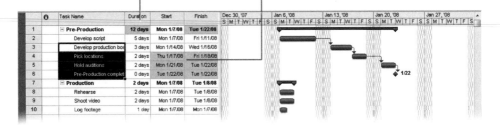

Have you noticed the blue highlighting of some of the *Duration*, *Start*, and *Finish* fields as you linked tasks? Project highlights the values that are affected after each change you make in a project plan. This feature is called Change Highlighting, and you can turn it off or on via the View menu.

Next, you will link two tasks in a different way by making task 8 the predecessor of task 9.

5. Select the name of task 9.

6. On the **Project** menu, click **Task Information**.

Task Information

> **Tip** You can also click the Task Information button on the Standard toolbar.

The Task Information dialog box appears.

7. Click the **Predecessors** tab.

8. Click the empty cell below the **Task Name** column heading, and then click the down arrow that appears.

9. On the **Task Name** list, click **Rehearse**, and press ⊞Enter.

ID	Task Name	Type	Lag
8	Rehearse	Finish-to-Start (FS)	0d

Task Information — Name: Shoot video   Duration: 2d   ☐ Estimated

10. Click **OK** to close the Task Information dialog box.

Tasks 8 and 9 are linked with a finish-to-start relationship.

To finalize this exercise, you'll link the remaining production tasks and then link the two summary tasks.

11. Select the names of tasks 9 and 10.

12. On the **Edit** menu, click **Link Tasks**.

13. Select the name of task 1 and, while holding down the ⌨Ctrl key, select the name of task 7. This is how you make a nonadjacent selection in a table in Project.

14. On the **Edit** menu, click **Link Tasks** to link the two summary tasks.

> **Tip** When working with summary tasks, you can either link summary tasks directly (as you did above) or link the latest task in the first phase with the earliest task in the second phase. The scheduling end result is the same in either situation, but it's preferable to link the summary tasks to better reflect the sequential nature of the two phases. Under no circumstances, however, can you link a summary task to one of its own subtasks. Doing so would create a circular scheduling problem, and therefore Project doesn't allow it.

15. If needed, scroll the chart portion of the Gantt Chart view to the right until the second phase of the project plan is visible.

	❶	Task Name	Duration	Start	Finish
1		− Pre-Production	12 days	Mon 1/7/08	Tue 1/22/08
2		Develop script	5 days	Mon 1/7/08	Fri 1/11/08
3		Develop production bo	3 days	Mon 1/14/08	Wed 1/16/08
4		Pick locations	2 days	Thu 1/17/08	Fri 1/18/08
5		Hold auditions	2 days	Mon 1/21/08	Tue 1/22/08
6		Pre-Production complet	0 days	Tue 1/22/08	Tue 1/22/08
7		− Production	5 days	Wed 1/23/08	Tue 1/29/08
8		Rehearse	2 days	Wed 1/23/08	Thu 1/24/08
9		Shoot video	2 days	Fri 1/25/08	Mon 1/28/08
10		Log footage	1 day	Tue 1/29/08	Tue 1/29/08

> **Tip** You can also create a finish-to-start relationship between tasks right in the Gantt chart. Point to the task bar of the predecessor task until the pointer changes to a four-pointed star. Then, drag the mouse pointer up or down to the task bar of the successor task. While you're dragging the mouse pointer to create a task relationship, the pointer image changes to a chain link.

Documenting Tasks

You can record additional information about a task in a *note*. For example, you might have detailed descriptions of a task and still want to keep the task's name succinct. You can add such details to a task note. In that way, the information resides in the Project file and can be easily viewed or printed.

There are three types of notes: task notes, resource notes, and assignment notes. You enter and review task notes on the Notes tab in the Task Information dialog box. (You can open the Notes tab by clicking the Task Notes command on the Project menu.) Notes in Project support a wide range of text formatting options; you can even link to or store graphic images and other types of files in notes.

Hyperlinks allow you to connect a specific task to additional information that resides outside of the project plan such as another file, a specific location in a file, a page on the Internet, or a page on an intranet.

In this exercise, you enter task notes and hyperlinks to document important information about some tasks.

1. Select the name of task 4, *Pick locations*.

2. On the **Project** menu, click **Task Notes**.

Task Notes

> **Tip** You can also click the Task Notes button on the Standard toolbar, or right-click the task name and click Task Notes in the shortcut menu that appears.

Project displays the Task Information dialog box with the Notes tab visible.

3. In the **Notes** box, type Includes exterior street scene and indoor studio scenes.

Task Information						

Tabs: General | Predecessors | Resources | Advanced | Notes | Custom Fields

Name: Pick locations   Duration: 2d   Estimated

Notes:

Includes exterior street scene and indoor studio scenes.

Help   OK   Cancel

4. Click **OK**.

A note icon appears in the Indicators column.

5. Point to the note icon.

	❶	Task Name	Duration	Start	Finish
1		− Pre-Production	12 days	Mon 1/7/08	Tue 1/22/08
2		Develop script	5 days	Mon 1/7/08	Fri 1/11/08
3		Develop production bo	3 days	Mon 1/14/08	Wed 1/16/08
4		Pick locations	2 days	Thu 1/17/08	Fri 1/18/08
5		Notes: 'Includes exterior street scene and indoor studio scenes.'		Mon 1/21/08	Tue 1/22/08
6				Tue 1/22/08	Tue 1/22/08
7		− Production	5 days	Wed 1/23/08	Tue 1/29/08
8		Rehearse	2 days	Wed 1/23/08	Thu 1/24/08
9		Shoot video	2 days	Fri 1/25/08	Mon 1/28/08
10		Log footage	1 day	Tue 1/29/08	Tue 1/29/08

The note appears in a *ScreenTip*. For notes that are too long to appear in a ScreenTip, you can double-click the note icon to display the full text of the note.

To conclude this exercise, you create a hyperlink.

6. Select the name of task 5, *Hold auditions*.

7. On the **Insert** menu, click **Hyperlink**.

Insert Hyperlink

> **Tip** You can also click the Insert hyperlink button on the Standard toolbar, or right-click the task name and then click Hyperlink on the shortcut menu.

The Insert Hyperlink dialog box appears.

8. In the **Text to display** box, type Check recent agent postings

9. In the **Address** box, type http://www.southridgevideo.com

10. Click **OK**.

A hyperlink icon appears in the Indicators column. Pointing to the icon displays the descriptive text you typed earlier.

Clicking the icon opens the Web page in your browser.

Checking the Plan's Duration

At this point, you might want to know how long the project is expected to take. You haven't directly entered a total project duration or finish date, but Project has calculated these values based on individual task durations and task relationships. An easy way to view the project's scheduled finish date is via the Project Information dialog box.

In this exercise, you see the current total duration and scheduled finish date of the project based on the task durations and relationships you've entered.

1. On the **Project** menu, click **Project Information**.

   The Project Information dialog box appears.

Project Information for "Wingtip Toys Commercial 2"			
Start date:	Mon 1/7/08	Current date:	Mon 12/3/07
Finish date:	Tue 1/29/08	Status date:	NA
Schedule from:	Project Start Date	Calendar:	Standard
Help	Statistics...	OK	Cancel

2. Note the finish date: 1/29/08.

> **Tip** This tip describes enterprise project management (EPM) functionality. If you are running Project Professional, you will see a slightly different dialog box. The Project Information dialog box in Project Professional includes an Enterprise Custom Fields section. Enterprise custom fields are used only with Project Server. For more information about Project Server, see Part 4, "Introducing Project Server."

You can't edit the finish date directly because this project is set to be scheduled from the start date. Project calculates the project's finish date based on the total number of working days required to complete the tasks, starting at the project's start date. As this project plan is now built, any change to the start date will cause Project to recalculate the finish date.

Next, let's look at the duration information in more detail.

3. Click the **Statistics** button.

   The Project Statistics dialog box appears.

Project Statistics for 'Wingtip Toys Commercial 2'			

	Start		Finish
Current		Mon 1/7/08	Tue 1/29/08
Baseline		NA	NA
Actual		NA	NA
Variance		0d	0d

	Duration	Work	Cost
Current	17d	0h	$0.00
Baseline	0d?	0h	$0.00
Actual	0d	0h	$0.00
Remaining	17d	0h	$0.00

Percent complete:

Duration: 0%   Work: 0%   Close

You don't need to pay attention to all of these numbers yet, but the current finish date and current duration are worth noting. The duration is the number of working days in the project calendar between the project's start date and finish date.

4. Click the **Close** button to close the Project Statistics dialog box.

Next, you will display the complete project by changing the timescale in the Gantt Chart view.

5. On the **View** menu, click **Zoom**.

The Zoom dialog box appears.

Zoom

Zoom to

○ 1 week
○ 2 weeks
◉ 1 month
○ 3 months
○ Selected task
○ Entire project
○ Custom: 34   Day(s) ▼

Reset   OK   Cancel

6. Click **Entire project**, and then click **OK**.

The entire project appears on the screen.

Zoom In

Zoom Out

Tip You can also click the Zoom In and Zoom Out buttons to change the timescale of the Gantt Chart view.

You can see the project's overall duration in the Gantt Chart view.

CLOSE the Wingtip Toys Commercial 2 file.

Key Points

- Essential aspects of tasks in a project plan include their duration and order of occurrence.

- Task links, or relationships, cause the start or end of one task to affect the start or end of another task. A common task relationship is a finish-to-start relationship in which the completion of one task controls the start of another task.

- In Project, phases of a schedule are represented as summary tasks.

- You can document additional details using task notes and create hyperlinks to the Internet.

- The Project Information dialog box (Project menu) is an excellent way to observe the key values of a project plan, such as its scheduled finish date and duration.

Chapter at a Glance

Create a list of resources, page 61

Change a resource's capacity to perform work, page 63

Enter resource cost rates, page 68

Change a resource's working time, page 70

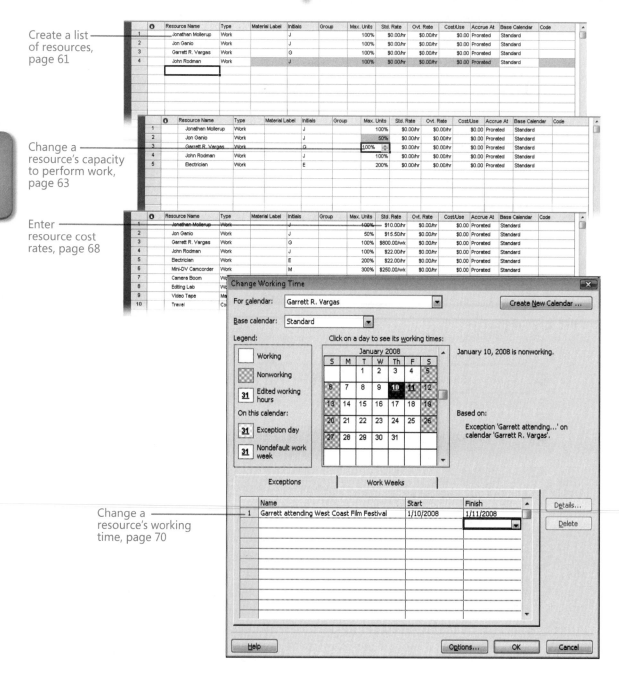

3 Setting Up Resources

In this chapter, you will learn how to:

✔ Set up basic resource information for the people who work on projects.

✔ Enter basic resource information for the equipment that will be used in projects.

✔ Enter resource information for the materials that will be consumed as the project progresses.

✔ Enter cost resource information for financial tracking.

✔ Set up cost information for work resources.

✔ Change a resource's availability for work.

✔ Record additional information about a resource in a note.

> **Tip** Do you need only a quick refresher on the topics in this chapter? See the Quick Reference entries on pages xxv-xlviii.

Resources include the people and equipment needed to complete the tasks in a project. Microsoft Office Project 2007 focuses on two aspects of resources: their availability and their costs. Availability determines when specific resources can work on tasks and how much work they can perform, and *costs* refer to how much money will be required to pay for those resources. In addition, Project supports two other types of special resources: material and cost.

In this chapter, you will set up the resources you need to complete the TV commercial project. Effective resource management is one of the most powerful advantages of using Project instead of task-focused planning tools, such as paper-based organizers. You do not need to set up resources and assign them to tasks in Project; however, without this information, you might be less effective in managing your schedule. Setting up resource information in Project takes a little effort, but the time is well spent if your project is primarily driven by time or cost *constraints* (and nearly all complex projects are driven by one, if not both, of these factors).

> **Important** Before you can use the practice files provided for this chapter, you need to install them from the book's companion CD to their default locations. See "Using the Book's CD" on page xix for more information.

Setting Up People Resources

Project works with three types of resources: work, material, and cost resources. *Work resources* are the people and equipment that do the work of the project. We will focus on work resources first and then turn to material and cost resources later in this chapter.

Some examples of work resources are listed below.

Work Resource	Example
Individual people identified by name	Jon Ganio; Jim Hance
Individual people identified by job title or function	Director; camera operator
Groups of people who have common skills (When assigning such interchangeable resources to a task, do not be concerned who the individual resource is as long as the resource has the right skills.)	Electricians; carpenters; extras
Equipment	Video camera; 600-watt light

Equipment resources don't need to be portable; a fixed location or piece of machinery, such as a video editing studio, can also be considered equipment.

All projects require some people resources, and some projects require only people resources. Project can help you make smarter decisions about managing work resources and monitoring financial costs.

> **Tip** This tip describes enterprise project management (EPM) functionality. The combination of Project Professional and Project Server provides substantial, enterprise-level resource management capabilities, such as skills-based resource assignments and a centralized enterprise resource pool. For more information, see Part 4, "Introducing Project Server."

In this exercise, you set up resource information for several people resources.

BE SURE TO start Microsoft Office Project 2007 if it's not already running.

Important If you are running Project Professional, you may need to make a one-time adjustment to use the Computer account and to work offline. This ensures that the practice files you work with in this chapter do not affect your Project Server data. For more information, see "Starting Project Professional" on page 11.

OPEN Wingtip Toys Commercial 3a from the \Documents\Microsoft Press\Project 2007 SBS\Chapter 3 Simple Resources folder. You can also access the practice files for this book by clicking Start, All Programs, Microsoft Press, Project 2007 Step by Step, and then selecting the chapter folder of the file you want to open.

1. On the **File** menu, click **Save As**.

   The Save As dialog box appears.

2. In the **File name** box, type Wingtip Toys Commercial 3, and then click **Save**.

3. On the **View** menu, click **Resource Sheet**.

   You will use the Resource Sheet view to help set up the initial list of resources for the Wingtip Toys TV commercial project.

4. In the Resource Sheet view, click the cell directly below the **Resource Name** column heading.

5. Type Jonathan Mollerup, and press [Enter].

   Project creates a new resource.

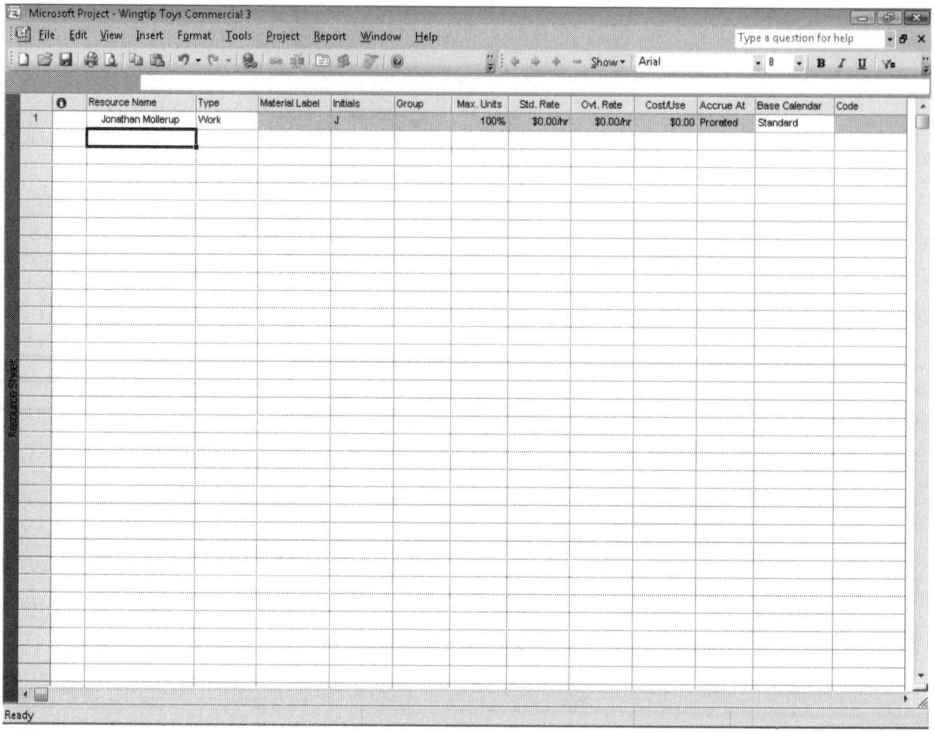

6. On the next empty rows in the **Resource Name** column, enter the following names:

   Jon Ganio

   Garrett R. Vargas

   John Rodman

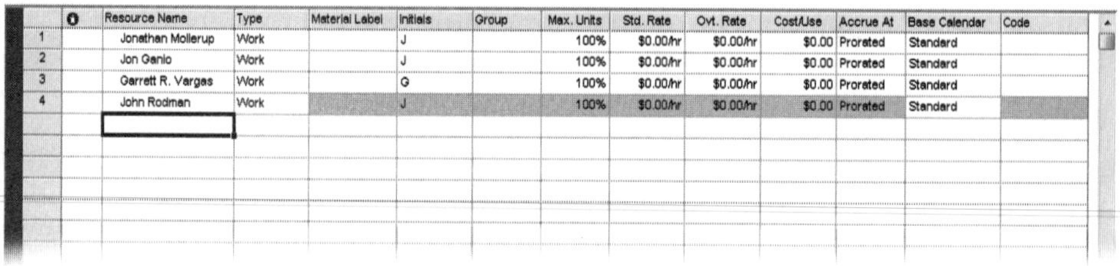

You can also have a resource that represents multiple people.

7. In the *Resource Name* field below the last resource, type Electrician, and then press [Tab].

8. In the **Type** field, make sure that **Work** is selected, and then press [Tab] several times to move to the *Max. Units* field.

The *Max. Units* field represents the maximum capacity of a resource to accomplish any task. Specifying that a resource, such as Jon Ganio, has 100% maximum units means that 100% of Jon's time is available to work on the tasks to which you assign him. Project will alert you if you assign Jon to more tasks than he can accomplish at 100% maximum units (in other words, if Jon becomes *overallocated*). As you can see, 100% is the default Max. Units value for new resources.

9. In the **Max. Units** field for the electrician, type or select 200%, and then press Enter.

> **Tip** When you click a numeric field, up and down arrows appear. You can click these to display the number you want, or simply type the number in the field.

The resource named *Electrician* does not represent a single person; instead, it represents a category of interchangeable people called electricians. Because the Electrician resource has a Max. Units setting of 200%, you can plan on two electricians being available to work full time every workday. At this point in the planning phase, it is alright that you do not know exactly who these electricians will be. You can still proceed with more general planning.

Now you'll update the Max. Units value for Jon Ganio to indicate that he works half time.

10. Click the *Max. Units* field for Jon Ganio, type or select 50%, and then press Enter.

When you create a new work resource, Project assigns it 100% Max. Units by default.

	❶	Resource Name	Type	Material Label	Initials	Group	Max. Units	Std. Rate	Ovt. Rate	Cost/Use	Accrue At	Base Calendar	Code	
1		Jonathan Mollerup	Work		J		100%	$0.00/hr	$0.00/hr	$0.00	Prorated	Standard		
2		Jon Ganio	Work		J		50%	$0.00/hr	$0.00/hr	$0.00	Prorated	Standard		
3		Garrett R. Vargas	Work		G		100%	$0.00/hr	$0.00/hr	$0.00	Prorated	Standard		
4		John Rodman	Work		J		100%	$0.00/hr	$0.00/hr	$0.00	Prorated	Standard		
5		Electrician	Work		E		200%	$0.00/hr	$0.00/hr	$0.00	Prorated	Standard		

> **Tip** If you prefer, you can enter maximum units as partial or whole numbers (.5, 1, 2) rather than as percentages (50%, 100%, 200%). To use this format, on the Tools menu, click Options, and then click the Schedule tab. In the Show assignment units as a box, click Decimal.

What Is the Best Way to Enter Resource Names?

In Project, work resource names can refer to specific people (Jon Ganio) or to specific job titles, such as Camera Operator or Actor. Use whatever method makes the most sense to you and to those who will see your project plan information. The important questions are *who* will see these resource names and *how* will they identify the resources. The resource names you choose will appear both in Project and in any information published from Project. For example, in the default Gantt Chart view, the name of the resource appears next to the bars of the tasks to which that resource is assigned.

A resource might refer to somebody who is already on staff or to a position to be filled later. If you have not yet filled all of the resource positions required, you might not have real people's names to enter. In that case, use placeholder names or job titles when setting up resources in Project.

Setting Up Equipment Resources

In Project, you set up people and equipment resources in exactly the same way because people and equipment are both examples of work resources. However, you should be aware of important differences in how you can schedule these two work resources. Most people resources have a working day of no more than 12 hours, but equipment resources might work around the clock. Moreover, people resources might be flexible in the tasks they can perform, but equipment resources tend to be more specialized. For example, a director of photography for a film or video project might also act as a camera operator in a pinch, but a video camera cannot replace an editing studio.

You do not need to track every piece of equipment that will be used in your project, but you might want to set up equipment resources when

- Multiple teams or people might need a piece of equipment to accomplish different tasks simultaneously, and the equipment might be overbooked.
- You want to plan and track costs associated with the equipment.

In this exercise, you enter information about equipment resources in the Resource Information dialog box.

1. In the Resource Sheet, click the next empty cell in the **Resource Name** column.

2. On the Standard toolbar, click the **Resource Information** button.

   The Resource Information dialog box appears.

Resource
Information

> **Tip** You can also double-click a resource name or an empty cell in the Resource Name column to display the Resource Information dialog box.

3. Click the **General** tab if it is not already displayed.

   In the upper portion of the General tab, you might recognize the fields you saw in the Resource Sheet view. As with many types of information in Project, you can usually work in at least two ways: a table or a dialog box.

4. In the **Resource name** field, type Mini-DV Camcorder

5. In the **Type** field, click **Work**.

The Resource Information dialog box contains many of the same fields you in the Resource Sheet view.

> **Tip** The Resource Information dialog box contains a button labeled Details. If you have an e-mail program that complies with the Messaging Application Programming Interface (MAPI) and the program is installed on the same computer as Project, you can click Details to see contact information about the selected resource. MAPI-compliant programs include Microsoft Office Outlook and Outlook Express.

6. Click **OK** to close the Resource Information dialog box and return to the Resource Sheet.

   The *Max. Units* field shows 100% for this resource; next, you will change this percentage.

> **Tip** You can also double-click on an empty cell in the Resource Name column to create a new resource using the Resource Information dialog box. Note that when creating a resource in this way, you cannot enter a Max. Units value. However, you can edit this value in the dialog box, as well as in the Resource Sheet, after you create the resource.

7. In the **Max. Units** field for the Mini-DV Camcorder, type or click the arrows until the value shown is 300% and press Enter.

    This means that you plan to have three camcorders available every workday.

8. Enter the following information about equipment resources directly in the Resource Sheet or in the **Resource Information** dialog box, whichever you prefer. In either case, make sure **Work** is selected in the **Type** field.

Resource name	Max. Units
Camera Boom	200%
Editing Lab	100%

	O	Resource Name	Type	Material Label	Initials	Group	Max. Units	Std. Rate	Ovt. Rate	Cost/Use	Accrue At	Base Calendar	Code	
1		Jonathan Mollerup	Work		J		100%	$0.00/hr	$0.00/hr	$0.00	Prorated	Standard		
2		Jon Ganio	Work		J		50%	$0.00/hr	$0.00/hr	$0.00	Prorated	Standard		
3		Garrett R. Vargas	Work		G		100%	$0.00/hr	$0.00/hr	$0.00	Prorated	Standard		
4		John Rodman	Work		J		100%	$0.00/hr	$0.00/hr	$0.00	Prorated	Standard		
5		Electrician	Work		E		200%	$0.00/hr	$0.00/hr	$0.00	Prorated	Standard		
6		Mini-DV Camcorder	Work		M		300%	$0.00/hr	$0.00/hr	$0.00	Prorated	Standard		
7		Camera Boom	Work		C		200%	$0.00/hr	$0.00/hr	$0.00	Prorated	Standard		
8		Editing Lab	Work		E		100%	$0.00/hr	$0.00/hr	$0.00	Prorated	Standard		

Setting Up Material Resources

Material resources are consumables that you use up as the project proceeds. On a construction project, material resources might include nails, lumber, and concrete. For the toy commercial project, video tape is the consumable resource that interests you most. You work with material resources in Project mainly to track the rate of consumption and the associated cost. Although Project is not a complete system for tracking inventory, it can help you stay better informed about how quickly you are consuming your material resources.

In this exercise, you enter information about a material resource.

1. In the Resource Sheet, click the next empty cell in the **Resource Name** column.

2. Type Video Tape and press Tab.

3. In the **Type** field, click the down arrow, select **Material**, and press Tab.

4. In the **Material Label** field, type 30-min. cassette and press Enter.

You will use 30-minute cassettes as the unit of measure to track video tape consumption during the project.

	🛈	Resource Name	Type	Material Label	Initials	Group	Max. Units	Std. Rate	Ovt. Rate	Cost/Use	Accrue At	Base Calendar	Code	
1		Jonathan Mollerup	Work		J		100%	$0.00/hr	$0.00/hr	$0.00	Prorated	Standard		
2		Jon Ganio	Work		J		50%	$0.00/hr	$0.00/hr	$0.00	Prorated	Standard		
3		Garrett R. Vargas	Work		G		100%	$0.00/hr	$0.00/hr	$0.00	Prorated	Standard		
4		John Rodman	Work		J		100%	$0.00/hr	$0.00/hr	$0.00	Prorated	Standard		
5		Electrician	Work		E		200%	$0.00/hr	$0.00/hr	$0.00	Prorated	Standard		
6		Mini-DV Camcorder	Work		M		300%	$0.00/hr	$0.00/hr	$0.00	Prorated	Standard		
7		Camera Boom	Work		C		200%	$0.00/hr	$0.00/hr	$0.00	Prorated	Standard		
8		Editing Lab	Work		E		100%	$0.00/hr	$0.00/hr	$0.00	Prorated	Standard		
9		Video Tape	Material	30-min. cassett	V			$0.00		$0.00	Prorated			

This Material Label field only
applies to material resources.

Note that you cannot enter a Max. Units value for a material resource. Since a material resource is a consumable item and not a person or piece of equipment that performs work, the Max. Units value doesn't apply.

Setting Up Cost Resources

The third and final type of resource that you can use in Project is the cost resource. You can use a *cost resource* to represent a financial cost associated with a task in a project. While work resources, such as people and equipment, can have associated costs (hourly rates and fixed costs per assignment), the sole purpose of a cost resource is to associate a particular type of cost with one or more tasks. Common types of cost resources might include categories of expenses you'd want to track on a project for accounting purposes such as travel, entertainment, or training. Like material resources, cost resources do no work and have no effect on the scheduling of a task. However, after you assign a cost resource to a task and specify the cost amount per task, you can then see the cumulative costs for that type of cost resource, such as total travel costs in a project.

1. In the Resource Sheet, click the next empty cell in the **Resource Name** column.

2. Type Travel and press Tab.

3. In the **Type** field, click the down arrow, select **Cost**, and press Enter.

	🛈	Resource Name	Type	Material Label	Initials	Group	Max. Units	Std. Rate	Ovt. Rate	Cost/Use	Accrue At	Base Calendar	Code	
1		Jonathan Mollerup	Work		J		100%	$0.00/hr	$0.00/hr	$0.00	Prorated	Standard		
2		Jon Ganio	Work		J		50%	$0.00/hr	$0.00/hr	$0.00	Prorated	Standard		
3		Garrett R. Vargas	Work		G		100%	$0.00/hr	$0.00/hr	$0.00	Prorated	Standard		
4		John Rodman	Work		J		100%	$0.00/hr	$0.00/hr	$0.00	Prorated	Standard		
5		Electrician	Work		E		200%	$0.00/hr	$0.00/hr	$0.00	Prorated	Standard		
6		Mini-DV Camcorder	Work		M		300%	$0.00/hr	$0.00/hr	$0.00	Prorated	Standard		
7		Camera Boom	Work		C		200%	$0.00/hr	$0.00/hr	$0.00	Prorated	Standard		
8		Editing Lab	Work		E		100%	$0.00/hr	$0.00/hr	$0.00	Prorated	Standard		
9		Video Tape	Material	30-min. cassett	V			$0.00		$0.00	Prorated			
10		Travel	Cost		T						Prorated			

Entering Resource Pay Rates

Almost all projects have some financial aspect, and cost limits drive the *scope* of many projects. Tracking and managing cost information allows the project manager to answer such important questions as

- What is the expected total cost of the project based on our task duration and re-source estimates?

- Are we using expensive resources to do work that less expensive resources could do?

- How much money will a specific type of resource or task cost over the life of the project?

- How have we allocated a particular type of expense, such as travel, in a project?

- Are we spending money at a rate that we can sustain for the planned duration of the project?

For the TV commercial project, you have been entrusted with pay rate information for all people resources used in the project. In the information below, note that the fees for the camcorders and editing lab are rental fees. Because the Southridge Video Company already owns the camera booms, you will not bill yourself for them.

> **Important** You deal with the per-task cost of a cost resource only when you assign the cost resource to the task. You will do this in Chapter 4, "Assigning Resources to Tasks."

In this exercise, you enter cost information for each work resource.

1. In the Resource Sheet, click the **Std. Rate** field for Jonathan Mollerup.

2. Type 10 and press Enter .

   Jonathan's standard hourly rate of $10 appears in the Std. Rate column. Note that the default standard rate is hourly, so you did not need to specify cost per hour.

3. In the **Std. Rate** field for Jon Ganio, type 15.50 and press Enter .

   Jon's standard hourly rate appears in the Std. Rate column.

	❶	Resource Name	Type	Material Label	Initials	Group	Max. Units	Std. Rate	Ovt. Rate	Cost/Use	Accrue At	Base Calendar	Code	
1		Jonathan Mollerup	Work		J		100%	$10.00/hr	$0.00/hr	$0.00	Prorated	Standard		
2		Jon Ganio	Work		J		50%	$15.50/hr	$0.00/hr	$0.00	Prorated	Standard		
3		Garrett R. Vargas	Work		G		100%	$0.00/hr	$0.00/hr	$0.00	Prorated	Standard		
4		John Rodman	Work		J		100%	$0.00/hr	$0.00/hr	$0.00	Prorated	Standard		
5		Electrician	Work		E		200%	$0.00/hr	$0.00/hr	$0.00	Prorated	Standard		
6		Mini-DV Camcorder	Work		M		300%	$0.00/hr	$0.00/hr	$0.00	Prorated	Standard		
7		Camera Boom	Work		C		200%	$0.00/hr	$0.00/hr	$0.00	Prorated	Standard		
8		Editing Lab	Work		E		100%	$0.00/hr	$0.00/hr	$0.00	Prorated	Standard		
9		Video Tape	Material	30-min. cassett	V			$0.00		$0.00	Prorated			
10		Travel	Cost		T						Prorated			

4. Enter the following standard pay rates for the given resources.

Resource Name	Standard Rate
Garrett R. Vargas	800/w
John Rodman	22
Electrician	22
Mini-DV camcorder	250/w
Camera boom	0
Editing lab	200/d
Video tape	5

	ⓘ	Resource Name	Type	Material Label	Initials	Group	Max. Units	Std. Rate	Ovt. Rate	Cost/Use	Accrue At	Base Calendar	Code	
1		Jonathan Mollerup	Work		J		100%	$10.00/hr	$0.00/hr	$0.00	Prorated	Standard		
2		Jon Ganio	Work		J		50%	$15.50/hr	$0.00/hr	$0.00	Prorated	Standard		
3		Garrett R. Vargas	Work		G		100%	$800.00/wk	$0.00/hr	$0.00	Prorated	Standard		
4		John Rodman	Work		J		100%	$22.00/hr	$0.00/hr	$0.00	Prorated	Standard		
5		Electrician	Work		E		200%	$22.00/hr	$0.00/hr	$0.00	Prorated	Standard		
6		Mini-DV Camcorder	Work		M		300%	$250.00/wk	$0.00/hr	$0.00	Prorated	Standard		
7		Camera Boom	Work		C		200%	$0.00/hr	$0.00/hr	$0.00	Prorated	Standard		
8		Editing Lab	Work		E		100%	$200.00/day	$0.00/hr	$0.00	Prorated	Standard		
9		Video Tape	Material	30-min. cassett	V			$5.00			$0.00	Prorated		
10		Travel	Cost		T						Prorated		

Cost resources do not have a pay rate. Instead, you specify a cost per each assignment.

Note that you enter a fixed amount rather than a rate (hourly, daily, or weekly) for the video tape's cost. For material resources, the standard rate value is per unit of consumption—in our case, 30-minute cassettes.

Note also that you cannot enter a standard pay rate for the Travel cost resource. You specify the cost when you assign the cost resource to a task.

Project Management Focus: Getting Resource Cost Information

Work resources can account for the majority of costs in many projects. To take full advantage of the extensive cost management features in Project, the project manager should know the costs associated with each work resource. For people resources, it might be difficult to obtain such information. In many organizations, only senior management and human resource specialists know the pay rates of all resources working on a project, and they might consider this information confidential. Depending on your organizational policies and project priorities, you might not be able to track resource pay rates. If you cannot track this information, your effectiveness as a project manager might be reduced, and the *sponsors* of your projects should understand this limitation.

Adjusting Working Time for Individual Resources

Project uses different types of calendars for different purposes. In this exercise, we will focus on the resource calendar. A *resource calendar* controls the working and nonworking times of a resource. Project uses resource calendars to determine when work for a specific resource can be scheduled. Resource calendars apply only to work resources (people and equipment) and not to material or cost resources.

When you initially create resources in a project plan, Project creates a resource calendar for each work resource. The initial working time settings for resource calendars exactly match those of the *Standard base calendar*, which is a calendar built into Project that accommodates a default work schedule from 8 A.M. to 5 P.M., Monday through Friday. If all of the working times of your resources match the working time of the Standard base calendar, you do not need to edit any resource calendars. However, chances are that some of your resources will need exceptions to the working time in the Standard base calendar—such as

- A flex-time work schedule
- Vacation time
- Other times when a resource is not available to work on the project, such as time spent training or attending a conference

Any changes that you make to the Standard base calendar are automatically reflected in all resource calendars based on the Standard base calendar. However, any specific changes you have made to the working time of a resource are not changed.

> **Tip** If you have a resource who is only available to work on your project part-time, you might be tempted to set the working time of the resource in your project to reflect a part-time schedule, such as 8 A.M. to 12 P.M. daily. However, a better approach would be to adjust the availability of the resource as recorded in the *Max. Units* field to 50%. Changing the unit availability of the resource keeps the focus on the capacity of the resource to work on the project rather than on the specific times of the day when that work might occur. You set the maximum units for a resource in the Resource Sheet view, which you display by clicking Resource Sheet on the View menu. For more information about resource units, see "Setting Up People Resources," on page 60.

In this exercise, you specify the working and nonworking times for individual work resources.

1. On the **Tools** menu, click **Change Working Time**.

    The Change Working Time dialog box appears.

2. In the **For calendar** box, click **Garrett R. Vargas**.

Garrett R. Vargas's resource calendar appears in the Change Working Time dialog box. Garrett has told you he will not be available to work on Thursday and Friday, January 10 and 11, because he plans to attend a film festival.

3. On the **Exceptions** tab in the **Change Working Time** dialog box, click in the first row directly below the **Name** column heading and type Garrett attending West Coast Film Festival

   The description for the calendar exception is a handy reminder for you and others who may view the project plan later.

4. Click in the **Start** field and type or select 1/10/2008.

5. Click in the **Finish** field, type or select 1/11/ 2008, and then press Enter.

Every resource calendar is based on the Standard base calendar unless you pick a different base calendar.

Project will not schedule work for Garrett on these dates.

Tip To set up a partial working time exception for a resource, such as a portion of a day when a resource cannot work, click Details. In the Details dialog box, you can also create recurring exceptions to the resource's availability.

To conclude this exercise, you will set up a "4 by 10" work schedule (that is, 4 days per week, 10 hours per day) for a resource.

6. In the **For** box, click **John Rodman**.

7. When prompted to save the resource calendar changes that you made for Garrett, click **Yes**.

8. Click the **Work Weeks** tab in the **Change Working Time** dialog box.

9. Click **[Default]**, and then click **Details**.

10. Under **Selected Day(s)**, select **Monday** through **Thursday**.

11. Click **Set day(s) to these specific working times**.

12. In the lower **To** box, click **5:00 PM** and replace it with 7:00 PM, and then press Enter .

13. Click **Friday**.

14. Click **Set days to nonworking time**.

Now Project can schedule work for John as late as 7 P.M. every Monday through Thursday, but it will not schedule work for him on Fridays.

15. Click **OK** to close the Details dialog box.

Now you can see that Fridays are marked as nonworking days for John Rodman.

15. Click **OK** to close the Change Working Time dialog box.

Because you have not yet assigned these resources to tasks, you don't see the scheduling effect of their nonworking time settings. You will observe this later in Chapter 4.

> **Tip** If you find that you must edit several resource calendars in a similar way (to handle a night shift, for example), it may be easier to assign a different base calendar to a resource or collection of resources. This is more efficient than editing individual calendars, and it allows you to make project-wide adjustments to a single base calendar if needed. For example, if your project includes a day shift and a night shift, you can apply the Night Shift base calendar to those resources who work the night shift. You change a base calendar in the Change Working Time dialog box on the Tools menu. For collections of resources, you can select a specific base calendar directly in the Base Calendar column on the Entry table in the Resource Sheet view.

Documenting Resources

You might recall from Chapter 2, "Creating a Task List," that you can record any additional information about a task, resource, or assignment in a *note*. For example, if a resource has flexible skills that can help the project, it is a good idea to record this in a note. In that way, the note resides in the project plan and can be easily viewed or printed.

In this exercise, you enter resource notes to document that a resource can assume multiple roles in the TV commercial project.

1. In the **Resource Name** column, click **Garrett R. Vargas**.

2. On the **Project** menu, click **Resource Notes**.

Resource Notes

> **Tip** You can also click the Resource Notes button on the Standard toolbar.

Project displays the Resource Information dialog box with the Notes tab visible.

3. In the **Notes** box, type Garrett is trained on camera and lights and then click **OK**.

A note icon appears in the Indicators column.

4. Point to the note icon.

	ⓘ	Resource Name	Type	Material Label	Initials	Group	Max. Units	Std. Rate	Ovt. Rate	Cost/Use	Accrue At	Base Calendar	Code	
1		Jonathan Mollerup	Work		J		100%	$10.00/hr	$0.00/hr	$0.00	Prorated	Standard		
2		Jon Ganio	Work		J		50%	$15.50/hr	$0.00/hr	$0.00	Prorated	Standard		
3		Garrett R. Vargas	Work		G		100%	$800.00/wk	$0.00/hr	$0.00	Prorated	Standard		
4		Notes: 'Garrett is trained on camera and lights'			J		100%	$22.00/hr	$0.00/hr	$0.00	Prorated	Standard		
5					E		200%	$22.00/hr	$0.00/hr	$0.00	Prorated	Standard		
6		Mini-DV Camcorder	Work		M		300%	$250.00/wk	$0.00/hr	$0.00	Prorated	Standard		
7		Camera Boom	Work		C		200%	$0.00/hr	$0.00/hr	$0.00	Prorated	Standard		
8		Editing Lab	Work		E		100%	$200.00/day	$0.00/hr	$0.00	Prorated	Standard		
9		Video Tape	Material	30-min. cassette	V			$5.00		$0.00	Prorated			
10		Travel	Cost		T						Prorated			

The note appears in a ScreenTip. For notes that are too long to appear in a ScreenTip, you can double-click the note icon to display the full text of the note.

CLOSE the Wingtip Toys Commercial 3 file.

Key Points

- Recording resource information in your project plans helps you better control who does what work when and at what cost.

- People and equipment resources perform the work in a project.

- Cost resources account for types of expenses across a project.

- Material resources are consumed during a project.

Chapter at a Glance

Assign work resource to tasks, page 79

Control how effort-driven scheduling affects task durations, page 84

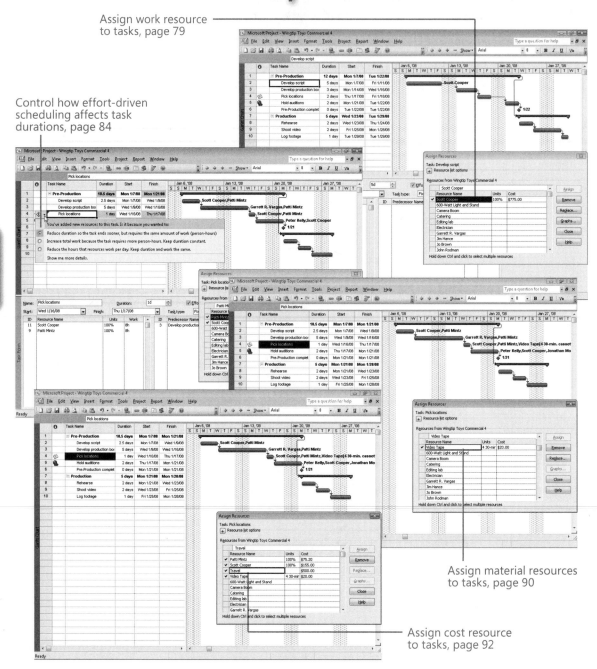

Assign material resources to tasks, page 90

Assign cost resource to tasks, page 92

4 Assigning Resources to Tasks

In this chapter, you will learn how to:

✔ Assign work resources to tasks.

✔ Control how Project schedules additional resource assignments.

✔ Assign material and cost resources to tasks.

> **Tip** Do you need only a quick refresher on the topics in this chapter? See the Quick Reference entries on pages xxv-xlviii.

If you completed Chapter 2, "Creating a Task List," and Chapter 3, "Setting Up Resources," you have already created tasks and resources. You are now ready to assign resources to tasks. An *assignment* is the matching of a resource to a task to do work. From the perspective of tasks, you might call the process of assigning a resource a task assignment; from the perspective of resources, you might call it a resource assignment. It is the same thing in either case: a task plus a resource equals an assignment.

> **Important** When we talk about resources throughout this chapter, we are talking about work resources (people and equipment) unless we specify material or cost resources. For a refresher on resource types, see Chapter 3.

You do not have to assign resources to tasks in Microsoft Office Project 2007; you could work with only tasks. Yet there are several good reasons for assigning resources in your project plan. If you assign resources to tasks, you can answer questions such as

● Who should be working on what tasks and when?

● Do you have the correct number of resources to accomplish the scope of work your project requires?

● Are you expecting a resource to work on a task at a time when that resource will not be available to work (for example, when the resource will be on vacation)?

- Have you assigned a resource to so many tasks that you have exceeded the capacity of the resource to work—in other words, have you *overallocated* the resource?

In this chapter, you assign resources to tasks. You assign work resources (people and equipment) as well as material and cost resources to tasks, and you observe where work resource assignments should affect task duration and where they should not.

> **Important** Before you can use the practice files provided for this chapter, you need to install them from the book's companion CD to their default locations. See "Using the Book's CD" on page xix for more information.

Assigning Work Resources to Tasks

Assigning a *work resource* to a task enables you to track the progress of the resource's work on the task. If you enter resource pay rates, Project also calculates resource and task costs for you.

You might recall from Chapter 3 that the capacity of a resource to work is measured in *units* (a level of effort measurement), and recorded in the *Max. Units* field. Unless you specify otherwise, Project assigns 100% of the units for the resource to the task—that is, Project assumes that all of the resource's work time can be allotted to the task. If the resource has less than 100% maximum units, Project assigns the resource's Max. Units value.

In this exercise, you make the initial resource assignments to tasks in the project plan.

> **BE SURE TO** start Microsoft Office Project 2007 if it's not already running.

> **Important** If you are running Project Professional, you may need to make a one-time adjustment to use the Computer account and to work offline. This ensures that the practice files you work with in this chapter do not affect your Project Server data. For more information, see "Starting Project Professional" on page 11.

> **OPEN** Wingtip Toys Commercial 4a from the *Documents**Microsoft Press**Project 2007 SBS**Chapter 4 Simple Assignments* folder. You can also access the practice files for this book by clicking Start, All Programs, Microsoft Press, Project 2007 Step by Step, and then selecting the chapter folder of the file you want to open.

1. On the **File** menu, click **Save As**.

   The Save As dialog box appears.

2. In the **File name** box, type Wingtip Toys Commercial 4, and then click **Save**.

3. On the **Tools** menu, click **Assign Resources**.

Assign Resources

> **Tip** You can also click the Assign Resources button on the Standard toolbar.

The Assign Resources dialog box appears, in which you see the resource names you entered in Chapter 3, plus additional resources. Except for assigned resources, which always appear at the top of the list, resources are sorted alphabetically in the Assign Resources dialog box.

> **Tip** If you are using Project Professional, you also see the R/D (request or demand) column in the Assign Resources dialog box. This relates to setting a priority for a resource assignment when using a Project Server feature called Resource Substitution. For more information about Project Server in general, see Part 4, "Introducing Project Server."

4. In the **Task Name** column, click task 2, **Develop script**.

5. In the **Resource Name** column in the **Assign Resources** dialog box, click **Scott Cooper**, and then click the **Assign** button.

A cost value and check mark appears next to Scott's name, indicating that you have assigned him to the task of developing the script. Because Scott has a cost standard rate recorded, Project calculates the cost of the assignment (Scott's standard pay rate times his scheduled amount of work on the task) and displays that value, $775, in the *Cost* field of the Assign Resources dialog box.

Next, you'll take a closer look at the scheduling values affecting task 2. You'll use a handy view called the Task Form.

6. On the **Window** menu, click **Split**.

Project splits the window into two panes. In the upper pane is the Gantt Chart view, and below it is the Task Form.

The resources assigned to the selected task have a check mark next to their names in the Assign Resources dialog.

The names of assigned resources appear next to the Gantt bars.

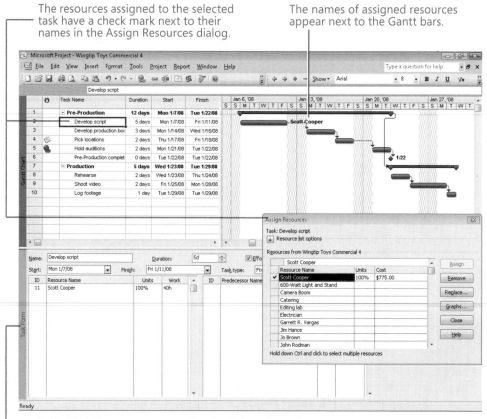

In the Task Form you can see details of the selected task's duration, assignment units, and work.

In the Task Form, you can see the essential scheduling values for this task: five days' duration, 40 hours of work, and 100% assignment units. Because the Task

Form is a handy way to see a task's duration, units, and work values, you'll leave it displayed for now.

Next, you assign two resources simultaneously to a task.

7. In the **Task Name** column, click task 3, **Develop production boards**.

8. In the **Assign Resources** dialog box, click **Garrett R. Vargas**, hold down the Ctrl key to make a nonadjacent selection, click **Patti Mintz**, and then click **Assign**.

Check marks appear next to Garrett's and Patti's names and their assignment costs are calculated, indicating that you have assigned both to task 3. You can also see the resulting assignment information (units and work per resource) and the task's duration in the Task Form.

The name of the selected task also appears here.

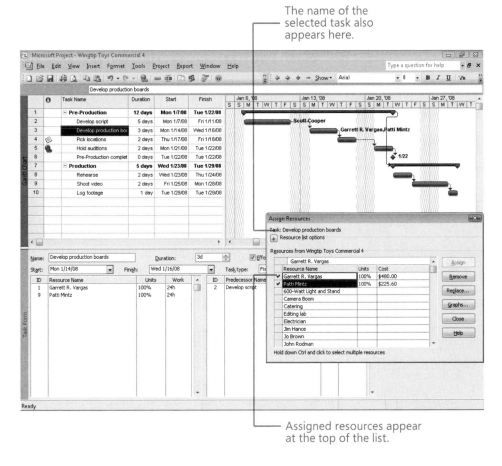

Assigned resources appear at the top of the list.

> **Troubleshooting** If you should accidentally assign only a single resource when you intended to assign multiple resources, you can undo the assignment. On the Edit menu, click Undo Assignment.

To conclude this exercise, you will make initial resource assignments for the remaining pre-production tasks.

9. In the **Task Name** column, click the name of task 4, *Pick locations*.

10. In the **Assign Resources** dialog box, click **Scott Cooper**, and then click **Assign**.

A check mark and cost value appear next to Scott's name, indicating that you have assigned him to task 4.

> **Tip** To remove or unassign a resource from a selected task, in the Assign Resources dialog box, click the resource name, and then click the Remove button.

11. In the **Task Name** column, click the name of task 5, *Hold auditions*.

12. In the **Assign Resources** dialog box, click **Peter Kelly**, hold down the `Ctrl` key, click **Scott Cooper**, and then click **Assign**.

Check marks and cost values appear next to Peter's and Scott's names, indicating that you have assigned both to task 5.

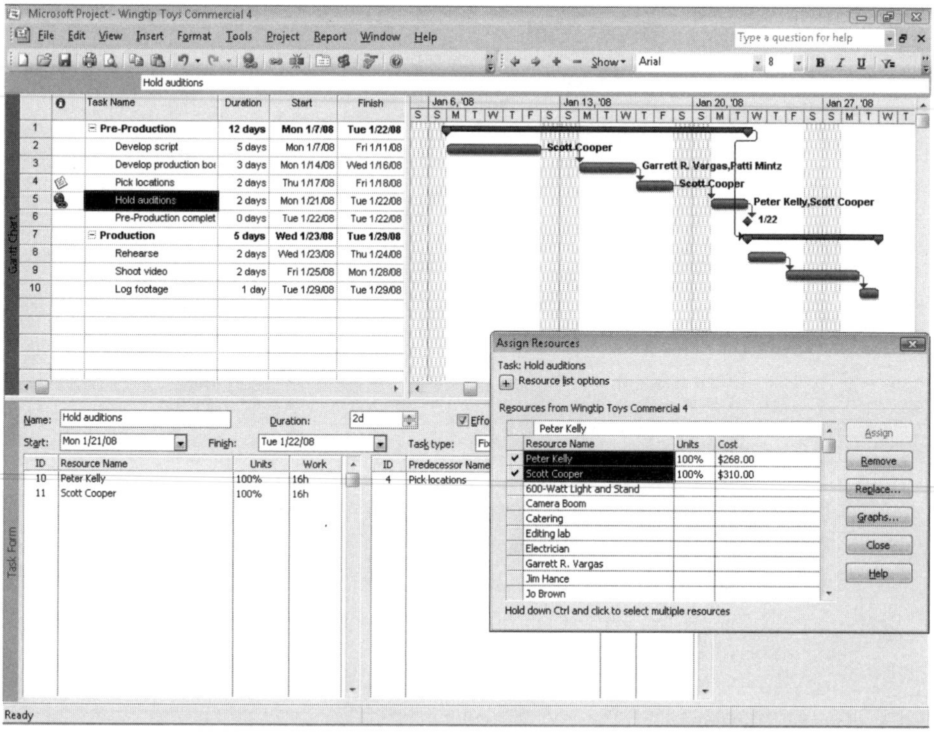

The Scheduling Formula: Duration, Units, and Work

After you create a task but before you assign a resource to it, the task has duration but no work associated with it. Why no work? *Work* represents the amount of effort a resource or resources will spend to complete a task. For example, if you have one person working full-time, the amount of time measured as work is the same as the amount of time measured as duration. In general, the amount of work will match the duration unless you assign more than one resource to a task or the one resource you assign is not working full-time.

Project calculates work using what is sometimes called the *scheduling formula*:

Duration × Units = Work

Let's look at a specific example. The duration of task 2 is five days. For our TV commercial project, five days equals 40 hours. When you assigned Scott Cooper to task 2, Project applied 100% of Scott's working time to this task. The scheduling formula for task 2 looks like this:

40 hours task duration × 100% assignment units = 40 hours work

In other words, with Scott assigned to task 2 at 100% units, the task should require 40 hours of work.

Here's a more complex example. You assigned two resources to task 5, each at 100% assignment units. The scheduling formula for task 5 looks like this:

16 hours task duration × 200% assignment units = 32 hours work

The 32 hours of work is the sum of Peter's 16 hours of work plus Scott's 16 hours of work. In other words, both resources will work on the task in parallel.

Assigning Additional Resources to a Task

Now you will assign additional resources to some of the pre-production tasks to observe the effect on the overall duration of the tasks. By default, Project uses a scheduling method called *effort-driven scheduling*. This means that the task's initial work value, or amount of effort, remains constant regardless of the number of resources you assign. The most visible effect of effort-driven scheduling is that, as you assign additional resources to a task, that task's duration decreases. Project applies effort-driven scheduling only when you assign resources to or remove resources from tasks.

As you saw previously, you define the amount of work that a task represents when you initially assign a resource or resources to it. If you later add resources to that task with effort-driven scheduling turned on, the amount of work for the task does not change, but the task's duration decreases. Or you might initially assign more than one resource to a task and later remove one of those resources. When effort-driven scheduling is used, the amount of work for the task stays constant; however, its duration, or time it takes the remaining resource to complete that task, increases.

> **Tip** By default, effort-driven scheduling is enabled for all tasks you create in Project. To change the default setting for all new tasks in a project plan, on the Tools menu, click Options, and in the Options dialog box, click the Schedule tab. Select or clear the New tasks are effort-driven check box. To control effort-driven scheduling for a specific task or tasks, first select the task or tasks. Then on the Project menu, click Task Information, and on the Advanced tab of the Task Information dialog box, select or clear the Effort driven check box.

In this exercise, you assign additional resources to tasks and observe how this affects task durations.

1. In the Gantt Chart view, click the name of task 2, **Develop script**.

   Currently, Scott Cooper is assigned to this task. A quick check of the scheduling formula looks like this:

   40 hours (the same as five days) task duration × 100% of Scott's assignment units = 40 hours work

   You can see these values in the Task Form.

   Next, you will assign a second resource to the task.

2. In the **Resource Name** column in the **Assign Resources** dialog box, click **Patti Mintz**, and click **Assign**.

   Patti Mintz is assigned to task 2.

The duration of this task decreases as additional resources are assigned to it. In addition, change highlighting indicates changes in the schedules of the successor tasks.

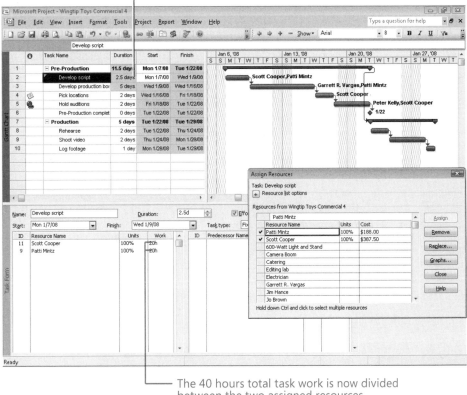

The 40 hours total task work is now divided between the two assigned resources.

As you can see, Project reduced the duration of task 2 from 5 days to 2.5 days. Why? The total work required is still 40 hours, as it was when only Scott was assigned to the task, but now the work is distributed evenly between Scott and Patti at 20 hours apiece. This demonstrates how effort-driven scheduling works. If you add resources to a task after an initial assignment, the total work remains constant but is distributed among the assigned resources. Furthermore, the task's duration decreases accordingly.

The scheduling formula now looks like this:

20 hours (the same as 2.5 days) task duration × 200% assignment units = 40 hours work

The 200% assignment units is the sum of Scott's 100% plus Patti's 100%, and the 40 work hours is the sum of Scott's 20 hours plus Patti's 20 hours.

The other important effect of reducing the duration of task 2 is that the start dates of all successor tasks have changed as well. The change highlighting that is now visible throughout the project illustrates the changes to successor tasks. In Chapter 2, you created task relationships, or links, for these tasks. In our current example, you see the benefit of creating task relationships rather than entering fixed start and finish dates. Project adjusts the start dates of successor tasks that do not have a constraint, such as a fixed start or finish date.

Next, you use a feature called a *Smart Tag* to control how Project schedules the work on a task when assigning multiple resources.

3. In the Gantt Chart view, click the name of task 4, *Pick locations*.

Currently, only Scott Cooper is assigned to this two-day task. You'd like to assign an additional resource and reduce the task's duration to one day.

4. In the **Resource Name** column of the **Assign Resources** dialog box, click **Patti Mintz**, and then click **Assign**.

Patti Mintz is also assigned to task 4.

Note the small triangle in the upper left corner of the name of task 4. This is a graphical indicator that a Smart Tag is now available. Until you perform another action, you can use the Smart Tag to choose how you want Project to handle the additional resource assignment.

Smart Tag
Actions

5. Click the name of task 4, and then click the **Smart Tag Actions** button that appears just to the left of the task name.

Look over the options on the list that appears.

Clicking the Smart Tag Actions button displays a list of
options and is available until you perform another action.

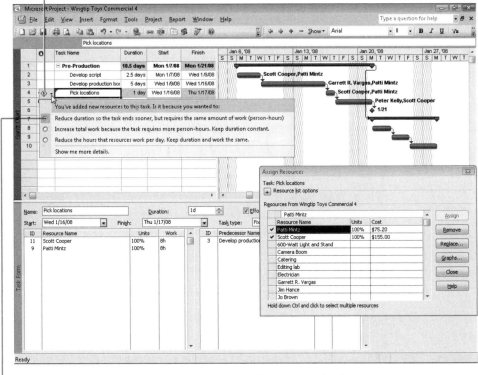

In the Actions list, the selected option describes the result of your most
recent action; if this is not the result you want, pick another option.

These options allow you to choose the scheduling result you want if it should differ from the effort-driven scheduling result. You can adjust the task's duration, the
resource's work, or the assignment units.

For this task, you want the additional resource assignment to reduce the task's duration. Because this is the default setting on the Smart Tag Actions list, you don't
need to make any changes.

6. Click the **Smart Tag Actions** button again to close the list.

Tip You will see other Smart Tag indicators while using Project. They generally appear
when you might otherwise ask yourself, "Hmm, why did Project just do that?" (such as when
a task's duration changes after you assign an additional resource). The Smart Tag Actions list
gives you the chance to change how Project responds to your actions.

To conclude this exercise, you will assign additional resources to a task and change
how Project schedules the work on the task.

7. In the Gantt Chart view, click the name of task 5, **Hold auditions**.

8. In the **Resource Name** column of the **Assign Resources** dialog box, click **Jonathan Mollerup**, hold down the ⎡Ctrl⎤ key, click **Patti Mintz**, and then click **Assign**.

   Project assigns Jonathan and Patti to the task. Because effort-driven scheduling is turned on for this task, Project reduces the duration of the task and adjusts the start dates of all successor tasks.

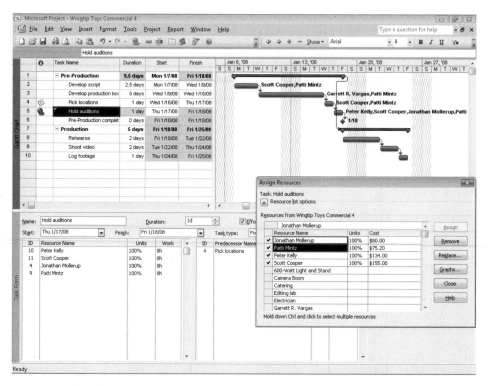

However, this time you do not want the additional resource assignments to change the task's duration. Jonathan and Patti will perform additional work on the task beyond the scope of the task's original work, which was assigned to Peter and Scott.

9. Click the name of task 5, and then click the **Smart Tag Actions** button when it appears.

10. On the **Smart Tag Actions** list, select the option **Increase total work because the task requires more person-hours. Keep duration constant.**

Project changes the task's duration back to two days and adjusts the start dates of all successor tasks. The additional resources receive the same work values (16 hours per resource) that the initially assigned resources had received, so total work on the task increases.

> **Tip** If you *initially assign two resources* to a task with a duration of three days (equal to 24 hours), Project schedules each resource to work 24 hours for a total of 48 hours of work on the task. However, you might *initially assign one resource* to a task with a duration of 24 hours and later *add a second resource*. In this case, effort-driven scheduling will cause Project to schedule each resource to work 12 hours in parallel for a total of 24 hours of work on the task. Remember that effort-driven scheduling adjusts task duration only if you add or delete resources from a task.

11. On the **Window** menu, click **Remove Split**.

Project hides the Task Form.

> **Project Management Focus:**
> **When Should Effort-Driven Scheduling Apply?**
>
> You should consider the extent to which effort-driven scheduling should apply to the tasks in your projects. For example, if one resource should take 10 hours to complete a task, could 10 resources complete the task in one hour? How about 20 resources in 30 minutes? Probably not; the resources would likely get in each other's way and require additional coordination to complete the task. If the task is very complicated, it might require significant ramp-up time before a resource could contribute fully. Overall productivity might even decrease if you assign more resources to the task.
>
> No single rule exists about when you should apply effort-driven scheduling and when you should not. As the project manager, you should analyze the nature of the work required for each task in your project and use your best judgment.

Assigning Material Resources to Tasks

In Chapter 3, you created the *material resource* named Video Tape. As you may recall from Chapter 3, material resources are used up or "consumed" as a project progresses. Common examples for a construction project include lumber and concrete. In our TV commercial project, we are interested in tracking the use of video cassettes and their cost. When assigning a material resource, you can handle consumptions and cost in one of two ways:

- Assign a fixed-unit quantity of the material resource to the task. Project will multiply the unit cost of this resource by the number of units assigned to determine the total cost. (You'll use this method in the following exercise.)

- Assign a variable-rate quantity of the material resource to the task. Project will adjust the quantity and cost of the resource as the task's duration changes. (You'll use this method in Chapter 9, "Fine-Tuning the Project Plan.")

In this exercise, you assign the material resource Video Tape to a task and enter a fixed-unit quantity of consumption.

1. In the **Task Name** column, click the name of task 4, **Pick locations**.

   You plan to use up to four tapes while picking locations.

2. In the **Assign Resources** dialog box, select the **Units** field for the Video Tape resource.

3. Type or select 4, and then press [Enter].

   Project assigns the video tape to the task and calculates the $20 cost of the assignment ($5 per video tape times four tapes).

When you assign a material resource to a task, its label value appears in the Units column...

...and next to the Gantt bar to which it is assigned.

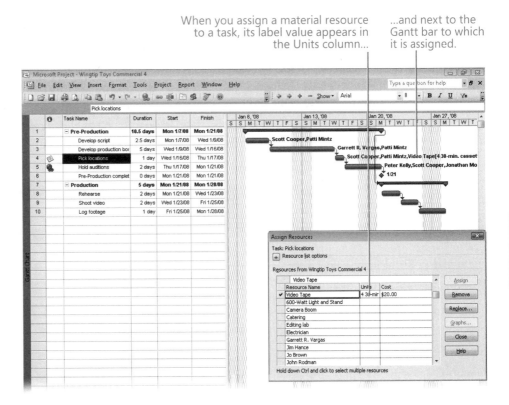

Because video tape is a material resource, it cannot do work. Therefore, assigning a material resource does not affect the duration of a task.

Assigning Cost Resources to Tasks

If you completed Chapter 3, recall that *cost resources* are used to represent a financial cost associated with a task in a project. Like material resources, cost resources do no work and have no effect on the scheduling of a task. Cost resources might include categories of expenses that you want to budget and track for accounting purposes that are separate from the costs associated with work or material resources. Broadly speaking, the costs that tasks can incur can include the following:

● Work resource costs, such as a person's standard pay rate times the amount of work they perform on the task.

● Material resource consumption costs, which are the material resource's per-unit cost times the number of units consumed by the task.

● Cost resource costs, which are a fixed dollar amount that you enter when assigning the cost resource to a task. The amount is not affected by changes in duration or any other schedule changes to the task, although you can edit the amount at any time.

For the TV commercial project, you'd like to enter planned travel and catering costs for certain tasks. Since work has not yet started on this project, at this time these costs represent budget or planned costs (indeed, you should consider all costs that Project has calculated so far in the schedule to be planned costs, such as those resulting from work resource assignments to tasks). Later, you can enter actual costs if you wish to compare them with the budget.

1. If task 4, **Pick locations**, is not already selected, click it the **Task Name** column.

2. In the **Assign Resources** dialog box, select the *Cost* field for the Travel cost resource.

3. Type 500, and then press [Enter].

   Project assigns the cost resource to the task. You can see in the Assign Resources dialog box all of the resources assigned to task 4 and their associated costs.

This task has all three resource types assigned to it: work, material, and cost.

Task 4 now includes costs resulting from all three types of resource assignments: work, material, and cost.

4. Click the name of task 5, **Hold auditions**.

5. In the **Assign Resources** dialog box, select the *Cost* field for the Catering cost resource.

6. Type 250, and then click **Assign**.

Project assigns the cost resource to the task.

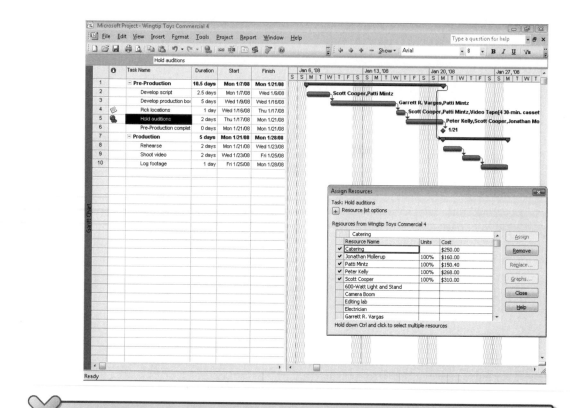

CLOSE the Wingtip Toys Commercial 4 file.

Key Points

- In Project, a task normally has work associated with it after a work resource (people or equipment) has been assigned to the task.

- When resources are assigned more work than they can complete in a specific period of time, they are said to be overallocated during that time period.

- You must assign resources to tasks before you can track their progress or cost.

- Project follows the scheduling formula: duration times units equals work.

- Effort-driven scheduling determines whether work remains constant when you assign additional resources to a task.

- The easiest way to understand effort-driven scheduling is to ask yourself, "If one person can do this task in 10 days, could two people do it in five days?" If so, then effort-driven scheduling should apply to the task.

- Smart Tags appear after you perform certain actions in Project. They allow you to quickly change the effect of your action to something other than the default effect.

- Assigning material resources to tasks allows you to track consumables.

- Assigning cost resources allows you to associate financial costs with a task other than those derived from work or material resources.

Chapter at a Glance

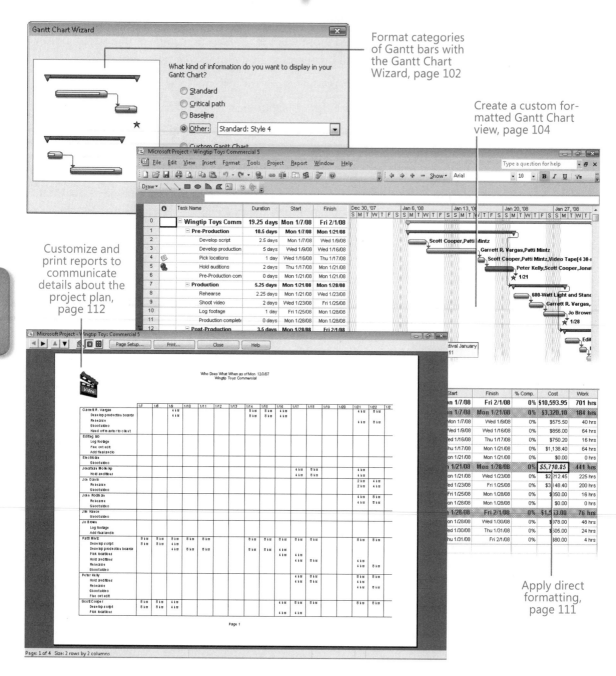

Format categories of Gantt bars with the Gantt Chart Wizard, page 102

Create a custom formatted Gantt Chart view, page 104

Customize and print reports to communicate details about the project plan, page 112

Apply direct formatting, page 111

5 Formatting and Printing Your Plan

In this chapter, you will learn how to:

✔ Customize a view and preview the way it will look when printed.

✔ Draw on the chart portion of a Gantt Chart view.

✔ Change the formatting of text in a project plan.

✔ Edit and print reports.

> **Tip** Do you need only a quick refresher on the topics in this chapter? See the Quick Reference entries on pages xxv–xlviii.

In this chapter, you use some of the formatting features in Microsoft Office Project 2007 to change the way your data appears and then preview the results in the Print Preview window. As you might recall from Chapter 1, "Getting Started with Project," a Project plan is really a database of information, not unlike a Microsoft Office Access database file. You don't normally see all of the data in a project plan at one time. Instead, you focus on the aspect of the plan that you're currently interested in viewing. *Views* and *reports* are the most common ways to observe or print a project plan's data. In both cases (especially with views), you can substantially format the data to meet your needs.

The primary way in which Project represents tasks graphically is as bars on the chart portion of a Gantt Chart view. These are called Gantt bars. On a Gantt chart, tasks, summary tasks, and milestones all appear as Gantt bars or symbols, and each type of bar has its own format. Whenever you work with Gantt bars, keep in mind that they represent tasks in a project plan.

> **Tip** This chapter introduces you to some of the simpler view and report formatting features in Project. You'll find quite a bit more material about formatting, printing, and publishing your project plans in Chapter 10, "Organizing and Formatting Project Details," Chapter 11, "Printing Project Information," and Chapter 12, "Sharing Project Information with Other Programs." Of particular note are the visual reports introduced with this release of Project. You work with visual reports in Part 2, "Advanced Project Scheduling."

> **Important** Before you can use the practice files provided for this chapter, you need to install them from the book's companion CD to their default locations. See "Using the Book's CD" on page xix for more information.

Creating a Custom Gantt Chart View

The Gantt chart became a standard way of visualizing project plans when, in the early twentieth century, American engineer Henry Gantt developed a bar chart showing the use of resources over time. For many people, a Gantt chart is synonymous with a project plan. In Project, the default view is the Gantt Chart view. You are likely to spend a lot of your time in this view when working in Project.

The Gantt Chart view consists of two parts: a *table* on the left and a bar chart on the right. The bar chart includes a *timescale* band across the top that denotes units of time. The bars on the chart graphically represent the tasks in the table in terms of start and finish dates, duration, and status (for example, whether work on the task has started or not). Other elements on the chart, such as link lines, represent *relationships* between tasks. The Gantt chart is a popular and widely understood representation of project information throughout the project management world.

> **Tip** By default, Project displays the Gantt Chart view when you start the program. However, you can change this setting to display any view you want at startup. On the Tools menu, click Options. In the Options dialog box, click the View tab. In the Default View box, click the view you want. The next time you start Project and create a new project plan, the view you have chosen will appear.

The default formatting applied to the Gantt Chart view works well for onscreen viewing, sharing with other programs, and printing. However, you can change the formatting of almost any element on the Gantt chart. In this exercise, we will focus on Gantt bars.

There are three distinct ways to format Gantt bars:

- Format whole categories of Gantt bars in the Bar Styles dialog box, which you can open by clicking the Bar Styles command on the Format menu. In this case, the formatting changes you make to a particular type of Gantt bar (a *summary task*, for example) apply to all such Gantt bars in the Gantt chart.

- Format whole categories of Gantt bars using the Gantt Chart Wizard, which you can start by clicking the Gantt Chart Wizard command on the Format menu. This wizard contains a series of pages in which you select formatting options for the most commonly used Gantt bars on the Gantt chart. Use the Gantt Chart Wizard to step you through some of the formatting actions that you can perform in the Bar Styles dialog box.

● Format individual Gantt bars directly. The formatting changes you make have no effect on other bars in the Gantt chart. You can double-click a Gantt bar on the Gantt chart to view its formatting options, or click Bar on the Format menu.

In this exercise, you create a custom Gantt chart and apply predefined formatting to it using the Gantt Chart Wizard. You then preview the results for printing.

> **BE SURE TO** start Microsoft Office Project 2007 if it's not already running.

> **Important** If you are running Project Professional, you may need to make a one-time adjustment to use the Computer account and to work offline. This ensures that the practice files you work with in this chapter do not affect your Project Server data. For more information, see "Starting Project Professional" on page 11.

> **OPEN** Wingtip Toys Commercial 5a from the *\Documents\Microsoft Press\Project 2007 SBS\Chapter 5 Simple Formatting* folder. You can also access the practice files for this book by clicking Start, All Programs, Microsoft Press, Project 2007 Step by Step, and then selecting the chapter folder of the file you want to open.

1. On the **File** menu, click **Save As**.

    The Save As dialog box appears.

2. In the **File name** box, type Wingtip Toys Commercial 5, and then click **Save**.

    Next, you will display the *project summary task* to see the top-level or rolled-up details of the project. Project automatically generates the project summary task but doesn't display it by default.

3. On the **Tools** menu, click **Options**.

4. In the **Options** dialog box, click the **View** tab.

5. Under the **Outline options for** label, select the **Show project summary task** check box, and then click **OK**.

    Project displays the project summary task at the top of the Gantt Chart view. You might see pound signs (##) or only part of the value in the project summary task's *Duration* field. If so, complete step 6.

6. Double-click the right edge of the **Duration** column in the column heading to expand the column so that you can see the entire value.

> **Tip** You can also double-click anywhere in a column heading and, in the Column Definition dialog box that appears, click the Best Fit button. To quickly move the vertical divider bar to the edge of the nearest column in the table, double-click the divider bar.

The Duration column widens to show the widest value in the column.

Double-click the right edge of a column heading to widen that column.

Drag the divider bar to show more of less of the table and chart portions of the Gantt Chart view.

Next, you will create a copy of the Gantt Chart view so that the formatting changes you make will not affect the original Gantt Chart view.

7. On the **View** menu, click **More Views**.

The More Views dialog box appears, with the current view (the Gantt Chart view) selected.

8. Click the **Copy** button.

The View Definition dialog box appears.

The Name field contains the proposed name of the new view as it will appear in the More Views dialog box and, if you specify, on the View menu. Note the ampersand (&) in the Name field. This is a code that indicates the keyboard shortcut character of the new view name, should you wish to include one.

9. In the **Name** field, type Custom Gantt Chart, and then click **OK**.

   The View Definition dialog box closes. The Custom Gantt Chart view appears and is selected in the More Views dialog box.

10. In the **More Views** dialog box, click the **Apply** button.

11. On the **Standard** toolbar, click **Scroll to Task**.

    At this point, the Custom Gantt Chart view is an exact copy of the original Gantt Chart view, so the two views look alike. Note, however, that the view title on the left edge of the view is updated.

    Next, you will use the Gantt Chart Wizard to format the Gantt bars and milestones in the chart portion of the Custom Gantt Chart view.

12. On the **Format** menu, click **Gantt Chart Wizard**.

    The welcome page of the Gantt Chart Wizard appears.

13. Click **Next**.

    The next screen of the Gantt Chart Wizard appears.

14. Click **Other**, and on the drop-down list next to the Other option, click **Standard: Style 4**.

The preview shows you the formatting options you choose on the right.

To see all of the elements the Gantt Chart Wizard can format, click here.

> **Tip** If you want to view the other built-in Gantt chart formats available in the wizard, click them in the Other box to see the preview on the left side of the wizard's window. When you are done, make sure that Standard: Style 4 is selected.

15. This is the only selection you'll make in the Gantt Chart Wizard for now, so click the **Finish** button.

    The final page of the Gantt Chart Wizard appears.

16. Click the **Format It** button, and then click the **Exit Wizard** button.

    The Gantt Chart Wizard applies the Standard: Style 4 formatting to the Custom Gantt Chart view and then closes.

The reformatted Gantt bars (summary, task, and milestone)
appear in the chart portion of the view.

Here you can see the effects of the Standard: Style 4 formatting applied to the project plan. Note that none of the data in the project plan has changed; only the way it is formatted has changed. These formatting changes affect only the Custom Gantt Chart view; all other views in Project are unaffected.

Next, you will format an individual Gantt bar. You'd like to give more visual attention to the Gantt bar for the *Hold auditions* task.

17. Click the name of task 5, *Hold auditions*.

18. On the **Format** menu, click **Bar**.

19. On the **Bar Shape** tab, under **Middle**, click the **Color** box.

20. Click **Blue**, and then click **OK**.

Project applies the blue color to the Task 5 Gantt bar.

After applying direct formatting,
only this bar is uniquely formatted.

To conclude this exercise, you will preview the Custom Gantt Chart view. What you see on the screen closely approximates what you'd see on the printed page, and you'll verify this now.

21. On the **File** menu, click **Print Preview**.

Project displays the Custom Gantt Chart view in the Print Preview window. You will do more work in the Print Preview window later in this chapter and in Chapter 11.

> **Important** If you have a plotter (a device used to draw charts, diagrams, and other line-based graphics) selected as your default printer or you have a different page size selected for your default printer, what you see in the Print Preview window might differ from what you see here.

22. On the Print Preview toolbar, click **Close**.

You can now print the project plan if desired, but previewing it is adequate for the purposes of this chapter. When printing in Project, you have additional options in the Print dialog box, which you can open by clicking the Print command on the File menu. For example, you can choose to print a specific date range of a timescaled view, such as the Gantt Chart view, or you can print a specific page range.

Drawing on a Gantt Chart

Project includes a Drawing toolbar with which you can draw objects directly on the chart portion of a Gantt chart. For example, if you would like to note a particular event or graphically call out a specific item, you can draw objects, such as text boxes, arrows, and other items, directly on a Gantt chart. You can also link a drawn object to either end of a Gantt bar or to a specific date on the timescale. Here's how to choose the type of link you need:

- Link objects to a Gantt bar when the object is specific to the task the Gantt bar represents. The object will move with the Gantt bar if the task is rescheduled.

- Link objects to a date when the information the object refers to is date sensitive. The object will remain in the same position relative to the timescale no matter which part of the timescale is displayed.

> **Tip** If the Drawing toolbar does not have the type of item you would like to add, you can add bitmap images or documents using the Object command on the Insert menu.

In this exercise, you display the Drawing toolbar and add a text box to the Custom Gantt Chart view.

1. On the **View** menu, point to **Toolbars**, and then click **Drawing**.

   The Drawing toolbar appears.

> **Tip** You can also click Drawing on the Insert menu to display the Drawing toolbar.

Text Box

2. On the Drawing toolbar, click the **Text Box** button, and then drag a small box anywhere on the chart portion of the Custom Gantt Chart view.

3. In the box that you just drew, type Film festival January 10 and 11

4. On the **Format** menu, point to **Drawing**, and then click **Properties**.

   The Format Drawing dialog box appears.

> **Tip** You can also double-click the border of the text box to view its properties.

5. Click the **Line & Fill** tab if it is not already selected.

6. In the **Color** box under the **Fill** label, click **Yellow**.

   Next, you'll attach the text box to a specific date on the timescale.

7. Click the **Size & Position** tab.

8. Make sure that **Attach To Timescale** is selected, and in the **Date** box, type or click 1/10/08.

9. In the **Vertical** box under **Attach To Timescale**, type 2.75 (this is the number of inches below the timescale where the top of the box will be positioned), and then click **OK** to close the Format Drawing dialog box.

   Project colors the text box yellow and positions it below the timescale near the date you specified.

10. Click in an empty area of the Gantt Chart view to unselect the text box.

Double-click the border of a drawn object to change its formatting or other properties.

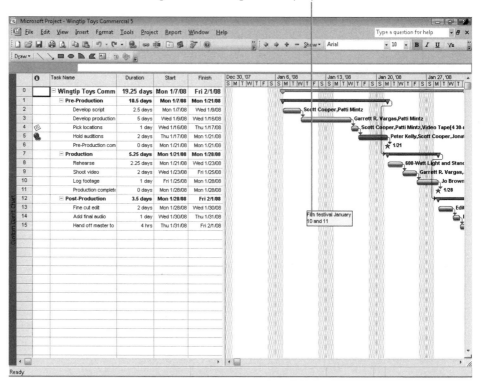

Because you attached the text box to a specific date on the timescale, it will always appear near this date even if you zoom the timescale in or out or scroll the chart left or right. Had you attached the text box to a Gantt bar, it would move with the Gantt bar if the task were rescheduled. To conclude this exercise, you will hide the Drawing toolbar.

11. On the **View** menu, point to **Toolbars**, and then click **Drawing**.

   The Drawing toolbar is hidden.

Formatting Text in a View

You can format text in tables, such as task names in a Gantt Chart view. There are two distinct ways to format text:

- Format whole categories of text in the Text Styles dialog box, which you can open by clicking the Text Styles command on the Format menu. The formatting changes you make to a category (such as milestones or summary tasks) apply to all cases of that category in the active view. You can view the categories for which you can change text formatting in the Item to Change box in the Text Styles dialog box.

- Format individual selections of text directly. The formatting changes you make have no effect on other text in the view.

> **Tip** You might notice some similarities between Project and Word in how you can format text. In Project, style-based formatting (available through the Text Styles command on the Format menu) is similar to applying paragraph styles in Word. Likewise, the direct formatting of text (available through the Font command on the Format menu) is similar to direct text formatting in Word.

As with all formatting options in Project, the formatting changes you make to any view or report affect only that view or report and only the active project plan. Later chapters will introduce methods of copying custom views or reports between project plans.

In this exercise, you switch to a different view and then use text styles and direct formatting to change the appearance of the text in that view.

1. On the **View** menu, click **More Views**.

   The More Views dialog box appears, with the current view (the Custom Gantt Chart view) selected.

2. In the **Views** box, click **Task Sheet**, and then click **Apply**.

   The Task Sheet view appears. Unlike Gantt Chart views, this view does not include a chart component; it consists of a single table.

   Next, you will change the table displayed in the Task Sheet view.

3. On the **View** menu, point to **Table: Entry**, and then click **Summary**.

Select All

> **Tip** You also can right-click the Select All button in the upper left corner of the active table to switch to a different table.

The Summary table appears in the Task Sheet view. Like the Entry table, this table focuses on task details, but it includes a different set of *fields*. The field of most interest to us now is the *Cost* field.

	Task Name	Duration	Start	Finish	% Comp.	Cost	Work
0	⊟ Wingtip Toys Comm	19.25 days	Mon 1/7/08	Fri 2/1/08	0%	$10,593.95	701 hrs
1	⊟ Pre-Production	10.5 days	Mon 1/7/08	Mon 1/21/08	0%	$3,320.10	184 hrs
2	Develop script	2.5 days	Mon 1/7/08	Wed 1/9/08	0%	$575.50	40 hrs
3	Develop production	5 days	Wed 1/9/08	Wed 1/16/08	0%	$856.00	64 hrs
4	Pick locations	1 day	Wed 1/16/08	Thu 1/17/08	0%	$750.20	16 hrs
5	Hold auditions	2 days	Thu 1/17/08	Mon 1/21/08	0%	$1,138.40	64 hrs
6	Pre-Production com	0 days	Mon 1/21/08	Mon 1/21/08	0%	$0.00	0 hrs
7	⊟ Production	5.25 days	Mon 1/21/08	Mon 1/28/08	0%	$5,710.85	441 hrs
8	Rehearse	2.25 days	Mon 1/21/08	Wed 1/23/08	0%	$2,212.45	225 hrs
9	Shoot video	2 days	Wed 1/23/08	Fri 1/25/08	0%	$3,148.40	200 hrs
10	Log footage	1 day	Fri 1/25/08	Mon 1/28/08	0%	$350.00	16 hrs
11	Production complete	0 days	Mon 1/28/08	Mon 1/28/08	0%	$0.00	0 hrs
12	⊟ Post-Production	3.5 days	Mon 1/28/08	Fri 2/1/08	0%	$1,563.00	76 hrs
13	Fine cut edit	2 days	Mon 1/28/08	Wed 1/30/08	0%	$978.00	48 hrs
14	Add final audio	1 day	Wed 1/30/08	Thu 1/31/08	0%	$505.00	24 hrs
15	Hand off master to	4 hrs	Thu 1/31/08	Fri 2/1/08	0%	$80.00	4 hrs

Next, you'll change the way in which Project formats an entire category of information—in this case, summary tasks.

4. On the **Format** menu, click **Text Styles**.

The Text Styles dialog box appears.

Tip The Item To Change list displays all of the types of information in a project plan that you can consistently format.

5. On the **Item to Change** list, click **Summary Tasks**.

The current format settings of summary tasks appear in the dialog box, and a preview appears in the Sample box.

Next, you will change the formatting so that the summary task text stands out.

6. In the **Size** box, click **10**.

7. In the **Color** box, click **Blue**.

8. In the **Background Color** box, click **Silver**.

9. In the **Background Pattern** box, click the dark dot pattern at the bottom of the drop-down list.

10. Click **OK**.

Project applies the new format settings to all summary task text in the project (except for the project summary task, which appears separately on the Item To Change list). Any new summary tasks added to the project plan will also appear with the new formatting.

After applying the text style formatting change, all summary tasks are reformatted.

Double-click the right hand edge of column headings for any columns that need to be widened.

	Task Name	Duration	Start	Finish	% Comp.	Cost	Work
0	Wingtip Toys Comm	19.25 days	Mon 1/7/08	Fri 2/1/08	0%	$10,593.95	701 hrs
1	Pre-Production	10.5 days	Mon 1/7/08	Mon 1/21/08	0%	$3,320.10	184 hrs
2	Develop script	2.5 days	Mon 1/7/08	Wed 1/9/08	0%	$575.50	40 hrs
3	Develop production	5 days	Wed 1/9/08	Wed 1/16/08	0%	$856.00	64 hrs
4	Pick locations	1 day	Wed 1/16/08	Thu 1/17/08	0%	$750.20	16 hrs
5	Hold auditions	2 days	Thu 1/17/08	Mon 1/21/08	0%	$1,138.40	64 hrs
6	Pre-Production com	0 days	Mon 1/21/08	Mon 1/21/08	0%	$0.00	0 hrs
7	Production	5.25 days	Mon 1/21/08	Mon 1/28/08	0%	$5,710.85	441 hrs
8	Rehearse	2.25 days	Mon 1/21/08	Wed 1/23/08	0%	$2,212.45	225 hrs
9	Shoot video	2 days	Wed 1/23/08	Fri 1/25/08	0%	$3,148.40	200 hrs
10	Log footage	1 day	Fri 1/25/08	Mon 1/28/08	0%	$350.00	16 hrs
11	Production complet	0 days	Mon 1/28/08	Mon 1/28/08	0%	$0.00	0 hrs
12	Post-Production	3.5 days	Mon 1/28/08	Fri 2/1/08	0%	$1,563.00	76 hrs
13	Fine cut edit	2 days	Mon 1/28/08	Wed 1/30/08	0%	$978.00	48 hrs
14	Add final audio	1 day	Wed 1/30/08	Thu 1/31/08	0%	$505.00	24 hrs
15	Hand off master to	4 hrs	Thu 1/31/08	Fri 2/1/08	0%	$80.00	4 hrs

The format changes you've made apply only to the active view (in this case, the Task Sheet view) and not to the table. If you displayed the Summary table in the Gantt Chart view, for example, these format changes would not appear there.

To conclude this exercise, you will apply direct formatting to a specific item in a view. As with styles in Word, you can use direct formatting in conjunction with text style formatting. In this project plan, you'll apply italic formatting to the production phase's cost.

11. In the **Summary** table, click the **Cost** field for task 7, the *Production* summary task.

12. On the **Format** menu, click **Font**.

The Font dialog box appears, which is similar to the Text Styles dialog box that you worked with earlier. However, the options you choose here apply only to the selected text.

> **Troubleshooting** The Font command on the Format menu applies only to selections of text; you cannot use this command to affect the formatting of empty rows in a table. To set the default formatting of rows, use the Text Styles command on the Format menu instead.

13. In the **Font Style** box, click **Bold Italic**.

14. In the **Background Color** box, click **Yellow**.

15. Click **OK**.

Project applies bold italic and background color formatting to the *Cost* field of task 7.

After applying direct formatting only this value is formatted.

> **Troubleshooting** You can remove direct formatting that's been applied to text and re-store that text to the formatting defined by the Text Styles dialog box (Format menu). First, select the cell containing the formatted text. Next, on the Edit menu, point to Clear, and click Formats.

In conclusion, use the Text Styles command on the Format menu to change the formatting of entire categories of information, such as all summary tasks. When you want to reformat a specific item (such as the cost value of one task) to draw attention to it, use the Font command on the Format menu. Note that the Font command is not available in some views, such as the Calendar view.

> **Tip** Some buttons such as Font and Bold on the Formatting toolbar correspond to the options available with the Font command on the Format menu. These options control direct formatting, not the style-based formatting you might apply by using the Text Styles dialog box.

Formatting and Printing Reports

Reports are intended for printing Project data. Unlike views, which you can either print or work with on the screen, tabular reports are designed only for printing or for viewing in the Print Preview window. You do not enter data directly into a report. Project includes several predefined task, resource, and assignment reports that you can edit to obtain the information you want.

In this exercise, you view a report in the Print Preview window and then edit its format to include additional information. You will work with *visual reports*, a new feature introduced with this release of Project, in Part 2.

1. On the **Report** menu, click **Reports**.

   The Reports dialog box appears, showing the categories of reports available.

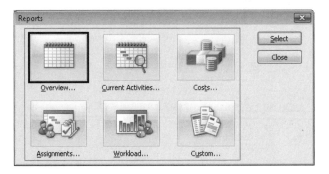

2. Click **Overview**, and then click the **Select** button.

The Overview Reports dialog box appears, listing the five predefined reports in Project that provide project-wide overview information.

3. In the **Overview Reports** dialog box, click **Project Summary**, and then click **Select**.

Project displays the Project Summary report in the Print Preview window. This is a handy summary of the project plan's tasks, resources, costs, and current status. You could use this report, for example, as a recurring status report that you share with the clients or other *stakeholders* of the project.

Depending on your screen resolution, the text in the report might not be readable when you view a full page.

> **Tip** Here's a quick way to see vital project statistics on the screen: Click the Project Information command on the Project menu, and then click Statistics.

4. In the Print Preview window, click the upper half of the page with the mouse pointer.

Project zooms in to show the page at a legible resolution.

The project title and company name come from the values entered in the Properties dialog box (File menu).

Click to zoom out.

At this point in the project life cycle, the most pertinent pieces of information in the report are the planned start and finish dates and the total cost. If any of these values did not fit within the expectations of the project *sponsor* or other stakeholders, now would be a good time to find out this information.

5. On the Print Preview toolbar, click **Close**.

   The Print Preview window closes, and the Reports dialog box reappears.

   Next, you will preview and edit a different report. For a small, simple project such as the TV commercial, a report is a simple way to communicate assignments to the resources involved. To do this, you will work with the Who Does What When report.

Tip This tip describes enterprise project management (EPM) functionality. For more detailed projects, communicating resource assignments (and subsequent changes) as well as other project details can be a significant responsibility for a project manager. Project Server offers an intranet-based solution for communicating such project details in conjunction with Project Professional. **For more information, see Part 4, "Introducing Project Server."**

---

6. Click **Assignments**, and then click **Select**.

   The Assignment Reports dialog box appears, listing four predefined reports in Project that provide resource assignment information.

7. In the **Assignment Reports** dialog box, click **Who Does What When**, and then click **Select**.

   Project displays the first page of the Who Does What When report in the Print Preview window.

Note that the status bar message informs you that this report spans four pages. To get a broader view of the output, you will switch to a multipage view.

8. On the Print Preview toolbar, click the **Multiple Pages** button.

Multiple Pages

The entire report appears in the Print Preview window.

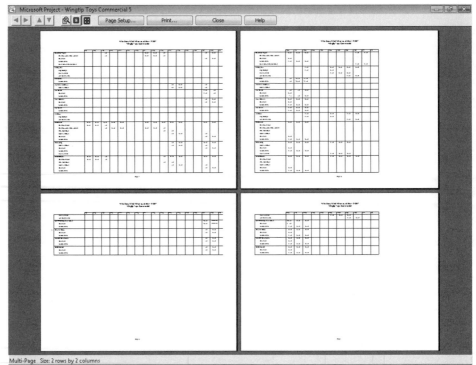

To conclude this exercise, you will customize the header that appears at the top of each printed page so that it includes a logo graphic.

9. On the Print Preview toolbar, click the **Page Setup** button.

   The Page Setup dialog box for the Who Does What When report appears.

10. Click the **Header** tab.

Page Setup - Who Does What When

| Page | Margins | Header | Footer | Legend | View |

Preview:

Who Does What Whenas of Mon 10/30/06
Wing ip Toys Commercial

Alignment: Left   Center   Right

&[Report] as of &[Date]
&[Project Title]
&[Manager]

General: Page Number   ▼   Add

Project fields: % Complete   ▼   Add

Print Preview...   Options...   Print...   OK   Cancel

As you can see in the Preview and Alignment boxes, codes such as &[Date] determine the specific text that appears in the header. You will add a logo to the left side of the header.

11. Next to Alignment, click the **Left** tab.

As with all regions of the header and footer, you can insert standard elements, such as page numbers, as well as any Project field. In this exercise, you'll insert a logo graphic that's supplied for you.

Insert Picture

12. Click the **Insert Picture** button.

13. Navigate to the Chapter 5 Simple Formatting folder and double-click the Logo file.

The logo image appears on the left side of the header in the Page Setup dialog box.

14. Click **OK** to close the Page Setup dialog box.

The updated header appears on each page in the Print Preview window.

One Page

15. For a closer look at the updated header, on the Print Preview toolbar, click the **One Page** button.

Project displays the first page of the report.

16. On the Print Preview toolbar, click **Close**.

17. Click **Close** again to close the Reports dialog box. The Task Sheet view reappears.

> **Tip** You can change the headers and footers of views in the same way you change them in reports. Keep in mind that changes made to the page setup of any view or report apply only to that view or report. However, the general method used to customize the page setup is the same for any report or view.

CLOSE the Wingtip Toys Commercial 5 file.

Key Points

- To format whole categories of Gantt bars, you can use either the Bar Styles dialog box or the Gantt Chart Wizard, both found on the Format menu. To format individual Gantt bars, use the Bar command on the Format menu.

- You can redefine the formatting of a built-in view, or copy a view first and then reformat it.

- You can draw or insert graphic objects on the chart portion of a Gantt chart view, but not on the table portion.

- Reports are intended for print-previewing or printing only; you cannot enter or edit data directly in a report.

Chapter at a Glance

Set a baseline to take a "snapshot" of the current schedule for future comparison, page 123.

Set progress on tasks through a specific date, page 125.

Enter percent complete on specific tasks, page 127.

Record a task's actual duration, page 129.

6 Tracking Progress on Tasks

In this chapter, you will learn how to:

✔ Save current values in a schedule as a baseline.

✔ Record progress on tasks through a specific date.

✔ Record a task's percentage of completion.

✔ Enter actual work and duration values for tasks.

> **Tip** Do you need only a quick refresher on the topics in this chapter? See the Quick Reference entries on pages xxv-xlviii.

Until now, you have focused on project *planning*—developing and communicating the details of a project before actual work begins. When work begins, so does the next phase of project management: tracking progress. *Tracking* means recording project details such as who did what work, when the work was done, and at what cost. These details are often called *actuals*.

Tracking actuals is essential to properly managing, as opposed to just planning, a project. The project manager must know how well the project team is performing and when to take corrective action. Properly tracking project performance and comparing it with the original plan allows you to answer such questions as these:

● Are tasks starting and finishing as planned? If not, what will be the impact on the project's finish date?

● Are resources spending more or less time than planned to complete tasks?

● Are higher-than-anticipated task costs driving up the overall cost of the project?

Microsoft Office Project 2007 supports several ways to track progress. Your choice of a tracking method should depend on the level of detail or control required by you, your project *sponsor*, and other *stakeholders*. Tracking the fine details of a project requires additional work from you and possibly from the resources working on the project.

Therefore, before you begin tracking progress, you should determine the level of detail you need. The different levels of tracking detail include the following:

- Record project work as scheduled. This level works best if everything in the project occurs exactly as planned. Hey, it could happen!

- Record each task's percentage of completion, either at precise values or at increments such as 25, 50, 75, or 100%.

- Record the actual start, actual finish, actual work, and actual and remaining duration for each task or assignment.

- Track assignment-level work by time period. This is the most detailed level of tracking. Here you record actual work values per day, week, or other interval.

Because different portions of a project might have different tracking needs, you might need to apply a combination of these approaches within a single project. For example, you might want to track high-risk tasks more closely than low-risk ones. In this chapter, you will perform the first three actions in the preceding list; the fourth (tracking assignment-level work by time period) is addressed in Part 2, "Advanced Project Scheduling." For users of Project Professional and Project Server, enterprise-level tracking is addressed in Part 4, "Introducing Project Server."

> **Important** Before you can use the practice files provided for this chapter, you need to install them from the book's companion CD to their default locations. See "Using the Book's CD" on page xix for more information.

Saving a Project Baseline

After developing a project plan, one of a project manager's most important activities is to record actuals and evaluate project performance. To judge project performance properly, you will need to compare it with your original plan. This original plan is called the baseline plan or just the baseline. A *baseline* is a collection of important values in a project plan such as the planned start dates, finish dates, and costs of the tasks, resources, and assignments. When you save a baseline, Project takes a "snapshot" of the existing values and saves it in your Project plan for future comparison.

The specific values saved in a baseline include the task, resource, and assignment fields, as well as the timephased fields, which are shown on the following list.

Task Fields	Resource Fields	Assignment Fields
Start	Work and timephased work	Start
Finish	Cost and timephased cost	Finish
Duration		Work and timephased work
Work and timephased work		Cost and timephased cost
Cost and timephased cost		

> **Tip** *Timephased fields* show task, resource, and assignment values distributed over time. For example, you can look at a task with five days of work planned at the weekly, daily, or hourly level and see the specific baseline work values per time increment. In Part 2, you will work with timephased values.

You should save the baseline when:

- You have developed the project plan as fully as possible. (However, this does not mean that you cannot add tasks, resources, or assignments to the project after work has started, for this is often unavoidable.)

- You have not yet started entering actual values, such as a task's percentage of completion.

The TV commercial project plan is now fully developed, and actual work on the project will soon begin. In this exercise, you save the baseline for the TV commercial project and then view the baseline task values.

> **BE SURE TO** start Microsoft Office Project 2007 if it's not already running.

> **Important** If you are running Project Professional, you may need to make a one-time adjustment to use the Computer account and to work offline. This ensures that the practice files you work with in this chapter do not affect your Project Server data. For more information, see "Starting Project Professional" on page 11.

> **OPEN** Wingtip Toys Commercial 6a from the \Documents\Microsoft Press\Project 2007 SBS\Chapter 6 Simple Tracking folder. You can also access the practice files for this book by clicking Start, All Programs, Microsoft Press, Project 2007 Step by Step, and then selecting the chapter folder of the file you want to open.

1. On the **File** menu, click **Save As**.

   The Save As dialog box appears.

2. In the **File name** box, type **Wingtip Toys Commercial 6**, and then click **Save**.

3. On the **Tools** menu. point to **Tracking**, and then click **Set Baseline**.

The Set Baseline dialog box appears.

You'll set the baseline for the entire project by using the default settings of the dialog box.

4. Click **OK**.

Project saves the baseline, even though there's no indication in the Gantt Chart view that anything has changed. You will now see some of the changes caused by saving the baseline.

> **Tip** You can set up to 11 baselines in a single plan. (The first one is called Baseline, and the rest are Baseline 1 through Baseline 10.) Saving multiple baselines can be useful for projects with exceptionally long planning phases in which you might want to compare different sets of baseline values. For example, you might want to save and compare the baseline plans every month as the planning details change. To clear a previously set baseline, click Clear Baseline on the Tools menu, Tracking submenu. To learn more about baselines in Project's online Help, type create baseline.

5. On the **View** menu, click **More Views**.

The More Views dialog box appears.

6. In the **Views** box, click **Task Sheet**, and then click the **Apply** button.

Because the Task Sheet view does not include the Gantt chart, more room is available to see the fields in the table. Now you'll switch to the Variance table in the Task Sheet view. The Variance table is one of several predefined tables that includes baseline values.

7. On the **View** menu, point to **Table: Entry**, and click **Variance**.

Select All

> **Tip** You also can right-click the Select All button in the upper left corner of the active table to switch to a different table.

The Variance table appears. This table includes both the scheduled and baseline start and finish columns, shown side by side for easy comparison.

	Task Name	Start	Finish	Baseline Start	Baseline Finish	Start Var.	Finish Var.
0	⊟ Wingtip Toys Co	Mon 1/7/08	Fri 2/1/08	Mon 1/7/08	Fri 2/1/08	0 days	0 days
1	⊟ Pre-Production	Mon 1/7/08	Mon 1/21/08	Mon 1/7/08	Mon 1/21/08	0 days	0 days
2	Develop script	Mon 1/7/08	Wed 1/9/08	Mon 1/7/08	Wed 1/9/08	0 days	0 days
3	Develop produ	Wed 1/9/08	Wed 1/16/08	Wed 1/9/08	Wed 1/16/08	0 days	0 days
4	Pick locations	Wed 1/16/08	Thu 1/17/08	Wed 1/16/08	Thu 1/17/08	0 days	0 days
5	Hold auditions	Thu 1/17/08	Mon 1/21/08	Thu 1/17/08	Mon 1/21/08	0 days	0 days
6	Pre-Production	Mon 1/21/08	Mon 1/21/08	Mon 1/21/08	Mon 1/21/08	0 days	0 days
7	⊟ Production	Mon 1/21/08	Mon 1/28/08	Mon 1/21/08	Mon 1/28/08	0 days	0 days
8	Rehearse	Mon 1/21/08	Wed 1/23/08	Mon 1/21/08	Wed 1/23/08	0 days	0 days
9	Shoot video	Wed 1/23/08	Fri 1/25/08	Wed 1/23/08	Fri 1/25/08	0 days	0 days
10	Log footage	Fri 1/25/08	Mon 1/28/08	Fri 1/25/08	Mon 1/28/08	0 days	0 days
11	Production cor	Mon 1/28/08	Mon 1/28/08	Mon 1/28/08	Mon 1/28/08	0 days	0 days
12	⊟ Post-Production	Mon 1/28/08	Fri 2/1/08	Mon 1/28/08	Fri 2/1/08	0 days	0 days
13	Fine cut edit	Mon 1/28/08	Wed 1/30/08	Mon 1/28/08	Wed 1/30/08	0 days	0 days
14	Add final audic	Wed 1/30/08	Thu 1/31/08	Wed 1/30/08	Thu 1/31/08	0 days	0 days
15	Hand off mast	Thu 1/31/08	Fri 2/1/08	Thu 1/31/08	Fri 2/1/08	0 days	0 days

Because no actual work has occurred yet and no changes to the scheduled work have been made, the values in the Start and Baseline Start fields are identical, as are the values in the Finish and Baseline Finish fields. After actual work is recorded or later schedule adjustments are made, the scheduled start and finish values might differ from the baseline values. You would then see the differences displayed in the variance columns.

Now that you've had a look at some baseline fields, it is time to enter some actuals!

Tracking a Project as Scheduled

The simplest approach to tracking progress is to report that the actual work is proceeding exactly as planned. For example, if the first month of a five-month project has elapsed and all of its tasks have started and finished as scheduled, you can quickly record this in the Update Project dialog box.

In the TV commercial project, suppose that some time has now passed since saving the baseline. Work has started, and so far, so good. In this exercise, you record project actuals by updating work to a specific date.

1. On the **View** menu, click **Gantt Chart**.

The Gantt Chart view appears.

2. On the **Tools** menu, point to **Tracking**, and click **Update Project**.

    The Update Project dialog box appears.

3. Make sure the **Update work as complete through** option is selected. In the adjacent date box, type or select 1/16/08.

> **Tip** You can also click the down arrow in the Update Work As Complete Through date box and, in the calendar that appears, select January 16, 2008. There are several date fields in the Project interface that use this pop-up calendar.

4. Click **OK**.

    Project records the completion percentage for the tasks that were scheduled to start before January 16. It then displays that progress by drawing *progress bars* in the Gantt bars for those tasks.

Check marks appear in the Indicators column for tasks that have been completed.

Progress bars indicate what portion of the task has been completed.

In the Gantt Chart view, the progress bar shows how much of each task has been completed. Because tasks 2 and 3 have been completed, a check mark appears in the Indicators column for those tasks, and the progress bars extend through the full length of those tasks' Gantt bars.

Entering a Task's Completion Percentage

After work has begun on a task, you can quickly record its progress as a percentage. When you enter a completion percentage other than 0, Project changes the task's actual start date to match its scheduled start date. It then calculates actual duration, remaining duration, actual costs, and other values based on the percentage you enter. For example, if you specify that a four-day task is 50% complete, Project calculates that it has had two days of actual duration and has two days of remaining duration.

Here are some ways of entering completion percentages:

- Use the Tracking toolbar (on the View menu, point to Toolbars, and then click Tracking). This toolbar contains buttons for quickly recording that a task is 0, 25, 50, 75, or 100% complete.

- Enter any percentage value you want in the Update Tasks dialog box (on the Tools menu, point to Tracking, and then click Update Tasks).

> **Tip** If you can collect the actual start date of a task, it is a good practice to record the actual start date (described in the next section), and then record a completion percentage.

In this exercise, you record completion percentages of tasks via the Tracking toolbar.

1. On the **View** menu, point to **Toolbars**, and then click **Tracking**.

   The Tracking toolbar appears.

You can use the Tracking toolbar to quickly set progress on tasks.

2. Click the name of task 4, *Pick Locations*.

3. On the Tracking toolbar, click the **100% Complete** button.

Project records the actual work for the task as scheduled and extends a progress bar through the length of the Gantt bar.

Next, you'll get a better look at the task's Gantt bar. You will enter a completion percentage value for a different task.

4. Click the name of task 5, *Hold auditions*.

5. On the Tracking toolbar, click the **50% Complete** button.

Project records the actual work for the task as scheduled and then draws a progress bar through part of the Gantt bar. Note that although 50% of task 5 is completed, the progress bar does not span 50% of the width of the Gantt bar. This is because Project measures duration in working time, but draws the Gantt bars to extend over nonworking time, such as weekends.

> **Tip** By default Project shows Gantt bars in front of nonworking time (such as weekends), like you see in this section. However Project can show nonworking time in front of task bars, visually indicating that no work on the task will occur during the nonworking time. If you prefer this type of presentation, click Timescale on the Format menu, and then click the Non-working time tab. Next to Draw, click In front of task bars.

6. In the chart portion (on the right) in the Gantt Chart view, hold the mouse pointer over the progress bar in task 5's Gantt bar. When the mouse pointer changes to a percent symbol and right arrow, a Progress screentip appears.

Depending on the type of bar or symbol you point to, in this case the progress bar, a ScreenTip will pop up providing information about that item.

The mouse pointer changes to a percent symbol and arrow when pointing to a progress bar.

	❶	Task Name	Duration	Start	Finish
0		⊟ Wingtip Toys Comm	19.25 days	Mon 1/7/08	Fri 2/1/08
1		⊟ Pre-Production	10.5 days	Mon 1/7/08	Mon 1/21/08
2	✓	Develop script	2.5 days	Mon 1/7/08	Wed 1/9/08
3	✓	Develop production	5 days	Wed 1/9/08	Wed 1/16/08
4	✓ 📝	Pick locations	1 day	Wed 1/16/08	Thu 1/17/08
5	🖐📝	Hold auditions	2 days	Thu 1/17/08	Mon 1/21/08
6		Pre-Production com	0 days	Mon 1/21/08	Mon 1/21/08
7		⊟ Production	5.25 days	Mon 1/21/08	Mon 1/28/08
8		Rehearse	2.25 days	Mon 1/21/08	Wed 1/23/08
9		Shoot video	2 days	Wed 1/23/08	Fri 1/25/08
10		Log footage	1 day	Fri 1/25/08	Mon 1/28/08
11		Production completi	0 days	Mon 1/28/08	Mon 1/28/08
12		⊟ Post-Production	3.5 days	Mon 1/28/08	Fri 2/1/08
13		Fine cut edit	2 days	Mon 1/28/08	Wed 1/30/08
14		Add final audio	1 day	Wed 1/30/08	Thu 1/31/08
15		Hand off master to	4 hrs	Thu 1/31/08	Fri 2/1/08

Scott Cooper,Patti Mintz

Garrett R. Vargas,Patti Mintz

Scott Cooper,Patti Mintz,Video Tape[4 30-i

Peter Kelly,Scott Cooper,Jona

Progress
Task: Hold auditions
Actual Start: Thu 1/17/08   Duration: 2d
Complete Through: Fri 1/18/08
% Complete: 50%

◆ 1/21

600-Watt Light and Stand

Garrett R. Vargas,

Jo Brown

◆ 1/28

Edit

The Progress ScreenTip informs you of the task's completion percentage and other tracking values.

So far, you have recorded actual work that started and finished on schedule. While this might prove true for some tasks, you often need to record actuals for tasks that lasted longer or shorter than planned, or occurred sooner or later than scheduled. This is the subject of the next topic.

Entering Actual Values for Tasks

A more detailed way to keep your schedule up to date is to record what actually happens for each task in your project. You can record each task's actual start, finish, work, and duration values. When you enter these values, Project updates the schedule and calculates the task's completion percentage. Project uses the following rules:

- When you enter a task's actual start date, Project moves the scheduled start date to match the actual start date.

- When you enter a task's actual finish date, Project moves the scheduled finish date to match the actual finish date and sets the task to 100% complete.

- When you enter a task's actual work value, Project recalculates the task's remaining work value, if any.

- When you enter a task's actual duration, if it is less than the scheduled duration, Project subtracts the actual duration from the scheduled duration to determine the remaining duration.

- When you enter a task's actual duration, if it is equal to the scheduled duration, Project sets the task to 100% complete.

- When you enter a task's actual duration, if it is longer than the scheduled duration, Project adjusts the scheduled duration to match the actual duration and sets the task to 100% complete.

Suppose that a few more days have passed and work on the TV commercial has progressed. In this exercise, you record actual work values for some tasks as well as start dates and durations for other tasks.

1. If it is not already selected, click the name of task 5, **Hold auditions**.

2. On the **View** menu, point to **Table: Entry**, and click **Work**.

    The Work table appears. This table includes both the scheduled work (labeled "Work") and actual work (labeled "Actual") columns. You'll refer to values in both columns as you update tasks.

	Task Name	Work	Baseline	Variance	Actual	
0	⊟ Wingtip Toys Comm	701 hrs	701 hrs	0 hrs	152 hrs	
1	⊟ Pre-Production	184 hrs	184 hrs	0 hrs	152 hrs	
2	Develop script	40 hrs	40 hrs	0 hrs	40 hrs	Scott Cooper,Patti Mintz
3	Develop production	64 hrs	64 hrs	0 hrs	64 hrs	Garrett R. Vargas,Patti Mintz
4	Pick locations	16 hrs	16 hrs	0 hrs	16 hrs	Scott Cooper,Patti Mintz,Video Tape[4 30
5	Hold auditions	64 hrs	64 hrs	0 hrs	32 hrs	Peter Kelly,Scott Cooper,Jon
6	Pre-Production com	0 hrs	0 hrs	0 hrs	0 hrs	1/21
7	⊟ Production	441 hrs	441 hrs	0 hrs	0 hrs	
8	Rehearse	225 hrs	225 hrs	0 hrs	0 hrs	600-Watt Light and Star
9	Shoot video	200 hrs	200 hrs	0 hrs	0 hrs	Garrett R. Vargas
10	Log footage	16 hrs	16 hrs	0 hrs	0 hrs	Jo Brow
11	Production complete	0 hrs	0 hrs	0 hrs	0 hrs	1/28
12	⊟ Post-Production	76 hrs	76 hrs	0 hrs	0 hrs	
13	Fine cut edit	48 hrs	48 hrs	0 hrs	0 hrs	Ed
14	Add final audio	24 hrs	24 hrs	0 hrs	0 hrs	
15	Hand off master to	4 hrs	4 hrs	0 hrs	0 hrs	

In the chart portion of the Gantt Chart view, you can see that task 5 is partially complete. In the Work table, you can see the actual work value of 32 hours. You want to record that the task is now complete but required more actual work than expected.

3. In the **Actual** field for task 5, type or select 80, and then press Enter .

Project records that 80 hours of work have been completed on task 5. It extends the Gantt bar of the task to indicate its longer duration and reschedules subsequent tasks.

Actual work is rolled up from
the subtasks to summary tasks.

	Task Name	Work	Baseline	Variance	Actual	
0	⊟ Wingtip Toys Comm	717 hrs	701 hrs	16 hrs	200 hrs	
1	⊟ Pre-Production	200 hrs	184 hrs	16 hrs	200 hrs	
2	Develop script	40 hrs	40 hrs	0 hrs	40 hrs	Scott Cooper,Patti Mintz
3	Develop production	64 hrs	64 hrs	0 hrs	64 hrs	Garrett R. Vargas,Patti Mintz
4	Pick locations	16 hrs	16 hrs	0 hrs	16 hrs	Scott Cooper,Patti Mintz,Video Tape[4 30
5	Hold auditions	80 hrs	64 hrs	16 hrs	80 hrs	Peter Kelly,Scott Cooper,Jo
6	Pre-Production com	0 hrs	0 hrs	0 hrs	0 hrs	1/21
7	⊟ Production	441 hrs	441 hrs	0 hrs	0 hrs	
8	Rehearse	225 hrs	225 hrs	0 hrs	0 hrs	600-Watt Light and St
9	Shoot video	200 hrs	200 hrs	0 hrs	0 hrs	Garrett R
10	Log footage	16 hrs	16 hrs	0 hrs	0 hrs	Jo Brc
11	Production complete	0 hrs	0 hrs	0 hrs	0 hrs	1/29
12	⊟ Post-Production	76 hrs	76 hrs	0 hrs	0 hrs	
13	Fine cut edit	48 hrs	48 hrs	0 hrs	0 hrs	
14	Add final audio	24 hrs	24 hrs	0 hrs	0 hrs	
15	Hand off master to	4 hrs	4 hrs	0 hrs	0 hrs	

Now suppose that more time has passed. To conclude this exercise, you will enter actual start dates and durations of tasks in the Production phase.

4. In the **Task Name** column, click task 8, **Rehearse**.

This task started one working day behind schedule (the Wednesday after its scheduled start date) and took a total of two days to complete. You will record this information in the Update Tasks dialog box.

5. On the **Tools** menu, point to **Tracking**, and then click **Update Tasks**.

Update Tasks

> **Tip** You can also click the Update Tasks button on the Tracking toolbar.

The Update Tasks dialog box appears. This dialog box shows both the actual and scheduled values for the task's duration, start, and finish, as well as its remaining duration. In this box, you can update the actual and remaining values.

6. In the **Start** field in the **Actual** box on the left side of the dialog box, type or select 1/23/08.

7. In the **Actual dur** field, type or select 3d.

Update Tasks	
Name: Rehearse	Duration: 2.25d
% Complete: 0% Actual dur: 3d Remaining dur: 2.25d	
Actual	**Current**
Start: Wed 1/23/08	Start: Tue 1/22/08
Finish: NA	Finish: Thu 1/24/08
Help Notes... OK Cancel	

8. Click **OK**.

Project records the actual start date, duration, and scheduled and actual work of the task. These values also roll up to the Production summary task (task 7) and the project summary task (task 0), as indicated by the change highlighting.

	Task Name	Work	Baseline	Variance	Actual
0	− Wingtip Toys Comm	792 hrs	701 hrs	91 hrs	500 hrs
1	− Pre-Production	200 hrs	184 hrs	16 hrs	200 hrs
2	Develop script	40 hrs	40 hrs	0 hrs	40 hrs
3	Develop production	64 hrs	64 hrs	0 hrs	64 hrs
4	Pick locations	16 hrs	16 hrs	0 hrs	16 hrs
5	Hold auditions	80 hrs	64 hrs	16 hrs	80 hrs
6	Pre-Production com	0 hrs	0 hrs	0 hrs	0 hrs
7	− Production	516 hrs	441 hrs	75 hrs	300 hrs
8	Rehearse	300 hrs	225 hrs	75 hrs	300 hrs
9	Shoot video	200 hrs	200 hrs	0 hrs	0 hrs
10	Log footage	16 hrs	16 hrs	0 hrs	0 hrs
11	Production completr	0 hrs	0 hrs	0 hrs	0 hrs
12	− Post-Production	76 hrs	76 hrs	0 hrs	0 hrs
13	Fine cut edit	48 hrs	48 hrs	0 hrs	0 hrs
14	Add final audio	24 hrs	24 hrs	0 hrs	0 hrs
15	Hand off master to	4 hrs	4 hrs	0 hrs	0 hrs

To conclude this exercise, you will record that task 9 started on time but took longer than planned to complete.

9. In the **Task Name** column, click task 9, **Shoot Video**.

10. On the **Tools** menu, point to **Tracking**, and then click **Update Tasks**.

The Update Tasks dialog box appears.

11. In the **Actual dur** field, type or select **3d**, and then click **OK**.

Project records the actual duration of the task.

Scroll to Task

12. On the Standard toolbar, click **Scroll To Task**.

	Task Name	Work	Baseline	Variance	Actual
0	⊟ Wingtip Toys Comm	892 hrs	701 hrs	191 hrs	800 hrs
1	⊟ Pre-Production	200 hrs	184 hrs	16 hrs	200 hrs
2	Develop script	40 hrs	40 hrs	0 hrs	40 hrs
3	Develop production	64 hrs	64 hrs	0 hrs	64 hrs
4	Pick locations	16 hrs	16 hrs	0 hrs	16 hrs
5	Hold auditions	80 hrs	64 hrs	16 hrs	80 hrs
6	Pre-Production com	0 hrs	0 hrs	0 hrs	0 hrs
7	⊟ Production	616 hrs	441 hrs	175 hrs	600 hrs
8	Rehearse	300 hrs	225 hrs	75 hrs	300 hrs
9	Shoot video	300 hrs	200 hrs	100 hrs	300 hrs
10	Log footage	16 hrs	16 hrs	0 hrs	0 hrs
11	Production complete	0 hrs	0 hrs	0 hrs	0 hrs
12	⊟ Post-Production	76 hrs	76 hrs	0 hrs	0 hrs
13	Fine cut edit	48 hrs	48 hrs	0 hrs	0 hrs
14	Add final audio	24 hrs	24 hrs	0 hrs	0 hrs
15	Hand off master to	4 hrs	4 hrs	0 hrs	0 hrs

Because you did not specify an actual start date, Project assumes that the task started as scheduled; yet, the actual duration you entered causes Project to calculate an actual finish date that is later than the originally scheduled finish date.

13. On the **View** menu, point to **Toolbars** and then click **Tracking**.

Project hides the Tracking toolbar.

Project Management Focus: Is the Project on Track?

Properly evaluating a project's status can be tricky. Consider the following issues:

- For many tasks, it is very difficult to evaluate a completion percentage. When is an engineer's design for a new motor assembly 50% complete? Or when is a programmer's code for a software module 50% complete? Reporting work in progress is in many cases a "best guess" effort and inherently risky.

- The elapsed portion of a task's duration is not always equal to the amount of work accomplished. For example, a task might require relatively little effort initially, but require more work as time passes. (This is referred to as a back-loaded task.) When 50% of its duration has elapsed, far less than 50% of its total work will have been completed.

- The resources assigned to a task might have different criteria for what constitutes the task's completion than the criteria determined by the project manager or the resources assigned to successor tasks.

Good project planning and communication can avoid or mitigate these and other problems that arise in project execution. For example, developing proper task durations and status-reporting periods should help you identify tasks that have varied substantially from the baseline early enough to make adjustments. Having well-documented and well-communicated task completion criteria should help prevent "downstream" surprises. Nevertheless, large, complex projects will almost always vary from the baseline.

CLOSE the Wingtip Toys Commercial 6 file.

Key Points

- Before tracking actual work in a project plan, you should set a baseline. This provides you with a "snapshot" of your initial project plan for later comparison against actual progress and is one way to tell whether your project is on track.

- The ability to track actual work in a project plan is a major advantage that a real project management tool, such as Project, has over a list-keeping tool, such as Excel. In Project, you can track actual work at a very broad or very granular level.

- To properly evaluate a project's status after you begin tracking requires a combination of recording accurate data in Project and using your good judgment when interpreting the results.

Part 2

Advanced Project Scheduling

Chapter at a Glance

Change how tasks are related to each other, page 140

Apply constraints to control when tasks can be scheduled, page 142

View the project's critical path and identify slack, page 148

Change a task's duration, work, or assignments units and control how Project handles the change, page 157

7 Fine-Tuning Task Details

In this chapter, you will learn how to:

✔ Adjust task links to have more control over how tasks are related.

✔ Apply a constraint to a task.

✔ Identify the tasks on the critical path.

✔ Split a task to record an interruption in work.

✔ Create a task calendar and apply it to tasks.

✔ Change a task type to control how Project schedules tasks.

✔ Record deadlines for tasks.

✔ Enter a fixed cost and specify how it should accrue.

✔ Set up a recurring task in the project schedule.

> **Tip** Do you need only a quick refresher on the topics in this chapter? See the Quick Reference entries on pages xxv-xlviii.

In this chapter, you examine and use a variety of advanced features in Microsoft Office Project 2007. These features focus on fine-tuning task details prior to saving a baseline as well as commencing work on the project with the goal of developing the most accurate schedule representation of the tasks you anticipate for the plan.

> **Important** Before you can use the practice files provided for this chapter, you need to install them from the book's companion CD to their default locations. See "Using the Book's CD" on page xix for more information.

Adjusting Task Relationships

You might recall from Chapter 2, "Creating a Task List," that there are four types of task dependencies, or relationships:

- Finish-to-start (FS): The finish date of the predecessor task determines the start date of the successor task.

- Start-to-start (SS): The start date of the predecessor task determines the start date of the successor task.

- Finish-to-finish (FF): The finish date of the predecessor task determines the finish date of the successor task.

- Start-to-finish (SF): The start date of the predecessor task determines the finish date of the successor task.

When you enter tasks in Project and link them by clicking the Link Tasks button on the Standard toolbar, the tasks are given a finish-to-start (FS) relationship. This should be fine for most tasks, but you will most likely change some task relationships as you fine-tune a project plan. The following are some examples of tasks that require relationships other than finish-to-start:

- You can start setting up the lighting for a film scene as soon as you start setting up the props (start-to-start relationship). This reduces the overall time required to complete the two tasks, as they are completed in parallel.

- Planning the filming sequence can begin before the script is complete, but it cannot be finished until the script is complete. You want the two tasks to finish at approximately the same time (finish-to-finish relationship).

Task relationships should reflect the sequence in which work should be performed. After you have established the correct task relationships, you can fine-tune your schedule by entering overlap (called *lead time*) or delay (called *lag time*) between the finish or start dates of predecessor and successor tasks.

Assuming that two tasks have a finish-to-start relationship:

- Lead time causes the successor task to begin before its predecessor task concludes.

- Lag time causes the successor task to begin some time after its predecessor task concludes.

The following is an illustration of how lead and lag time affect task relationships. Assume that you initially planned the following three tasks using finish-to-start relationships.

Initially the tasks are linked with finish-to-start relationships, so the
successor tasks begin as soon as the predecessor tasks finish.

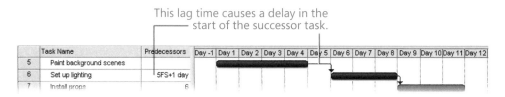

Before task 6 can begin, you need to allow an extra day for the paint applied in task 5 to
dry. You do not want to add a day to the duration of task 5 because no real work will occur on that day. Instead, you enter a one-day lag between tasks 5 and 6.

This lag time causes a delay in the
start of the successor task.

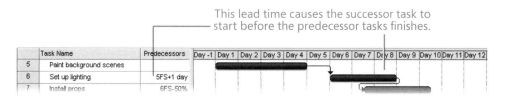

However, task 7 can start as soon as task 6 is halfway completed. To make this happen,
enter a 50% lead time between tasks 6 and 7.

This lead time causes the successor task to
start before the predecessor tasks finishes.

	Task Name	Predecessors													
5	Paint background scenes														
6	Set up lighting	5FS+1 day													
7	Install props	6FS-50%													

You can enter lead and lag time as units of time, such as two days, or as a percentage of
the duration of the predecessor task, such as 50%. Lag time is entered in positive units
and lead time in negative units (for example, *-2d* or *-50%*). You can apply lead or lag
time to any type of task relationship: finish-to-start, start-to-start, and so on.

> **Tip** Places in which you can enter lead or lag time include the Task Information dialog box
> (Project menu), the Predecessors column in the Entry table, and the Task Dependency dialog
> box (viewable by double-clicking a link line between Gantt bars).

In this exercise, you enter lead time and change task relationships between predecessor
and successor tasks.

BE SURE TO start Microsoft Office Project 2007 if it's not already running.

> **Important** If you are running Project Professional, you may need to make a one-time adjustment to use the Computer account and to work offline. This ensures that the practice files you work with in this chapter do not affect your Project Server data. For more information, see "Starting Project Professional" on page 11.

> **OPEN** Short Film Project 7a from the *\Documents\Microsoft Press\Project 2007 SBS\ Chapter 7 Advanced Tasks* folder. You can also access the practice files for this book by clicking Start, All Programs, Microsoft Press, Project 2007 Step by Step, and then selecting the chapter folder of the file you want to open.

1. On the **File** menu, click **Save As**.

    The Save As dialog box appears.

2. In the **File name** box, type Short Film Project 7, and then click **Save**.

3. On the **Project** menu, click **Task Drivers**.

Task Drivers

> **Tip** You can also click the **Task Drivers** button on the **Standard** toolbar.

The Task Drivers pane appears. This pane succinctly reveals all of the scheduling factors that affect the selected task, such as predecessor task relationships, resource calendars, and/or task calendars.

4. Select the name of task 9, **Reserve camera equipment**.

    In the Task Drivers pane, you can view the scheduling factors affecting this task.

For task 9, you can see that its predecessor is task 8, *Apply for filming permits*. You can see in the pane that the two tasks have a finish-to-start relationship with zero lag time. Next, you'll adjust the lag value on the task relationship. Because you cannot edit this value directly in the pane, you'll display the Task Information dialog box.

Task Information

5. On the Standard Toolbar, click the **Task Information** button.

6. Click the **Predecessors** tab.

7. In the **Lag** field for predecessor task 8, type –50%.

Entering lag time as a negative value produces lead time.

8. Click **OK** to close the Task Information dialog box.

Scroll To Task

9. To observe the effect of adjusting lag on the Gantt bars, on the **Standard** toolbar, click the **Scroll To Task** button.

Lead time causes the successor task to start before the predecessor task has finished, although the two tasks still have a finish-to-start relationship.

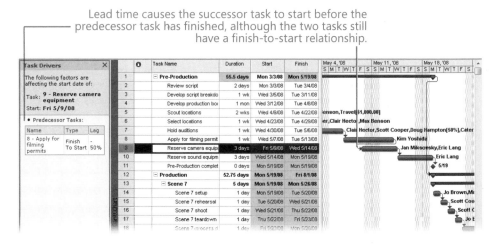

Task 9 is now scheduled to start at 50% of the duration of task 8. Should the duration of task 8 change, Project will reschedule the start of task 9 so that it maintains a 50% lead time.

Next, you will change the task relationship between two tasks.

10. Double-click the name of task 10, **Reserve sound equipment**.

The Task Information dialog box appears. The Predecessors tab should be visible. Note also that the Task Drivers pane in the background updates to display the scheduling details for task 10, the currently selected task.

11. On the **Predecessors** tab, click in the **Type** column for predecessor task 9. Select **Start-to-Start (SS)**, and click **OK**.

Project changes the task relationship between tasks 9 and 10 to start-to-start.

The start-to-start task relationship causes the successor task to start at the
same time as the predecessor task. If the start date of the predecessor task
changes, then the start date of the successor task will change as well.

> **Important** Assigning tasks' start-to-start relationships and entering lead times where
> appropriate are both excellent techniques to shorten overall project duration. However,
> Project cannot automatically make such schedule adjustments for you. As project manager,
> you must analyze the sequences and relationships of your tasks and make those adjust-
> ments where necessary.

Setting Task Constraints

Every task you enter into Project has some type of constraint applied to it. A *constraint*
controls the start or finish date of a task and the degree to which that task can be rescheduled. There are three categories of constraints:

- *Flexible constraints* Project can change the start and finish dates of a task. For
  example, the task *Select locations to film* can start as soon as possible. This type
  of flexible constraint is called As Soon As Possible, or ASAP for short, and is the
  default constraint type in Project. No constraint date is associated with flexible
  constraints.

- *Inflexible constraints* A task must begin or end on a certain date. For example, a
  task, such as *Set up lighting*, must end on June 14, 2008. Inflexible constraints are
  sometimes called hard constraints.

- *Semi-flexible constraints* A task has a start or finish date boundary. However,
  within that boundary, Project has the scheduling flexibility to change the start and
  finish dates of a task. For example, a task such as *Install props* must finish no later
  than June 13, 2008. However, the task could finish before this date. Semi-flexible
  constraints are sometimes called soft or moderate constraints.

In total, there are eight types of task constraints.

This constraint category	Includes these: constraint types	And means
Flexible	As Soon As Possible (ASAP)	Project will schedule a task to occur as soon as it can occur. This is the default constraint type applied to all new tasks when scheduling from the project start date. There is no constraint date for an ASAP constraint.
	As Late As Possible (ALAP)	Project will schedule a task to occur as late as it can occur. This is the default constraint type applied to all new tasks when scheduling from the project finish date. There is no constraint date for an ALAP constraint.
Semi-flexible	Start No Earlier Than (SNET)	Project will schedule a task to start on or after the constraint date you specify. Use this constraint type to ensure that a task will not start before a specific date.
	Start No Later Than (SNLT)	Project will schedule a task to start on or before the constraint date you specify. Use this constraint type to ensure that a task will not start after a specific date.
	Finish No Earlier Than (FNET)	Project will schedule a task to finish on or after the constraint date you specify. Use this constraint type to ensure that a task will not finish before a specific date.
	Finish No Later Than (FNLT)	Project will schedule a task to finish on or before the constraint date you specify. Use this constraint type to ensure that a task will not finish after a specific date.
Inflexible	Must Start On (MSO)	Project will schedule a task to start on the constraint date you specify. Use this constraint type to ensure that a task will start on an exact date.
	Must Finish On (MFO)	Project will schedule a task to finish on the constraint date you specify. Use this constraint type to ensure that a task will finish on an exact date.

> **Important** Beginning Project users are often tempted to enter start or finish dates for tasks. However, doing so applies semi-flexible constraints, such as Start No Earlier Than or Finish No Earlier Than. This essentially prevents users from taking full advantage of the Project scheduling engine. Although this is one of the most common scheduling problems that people create when using Project, it is usually avoidable.

These three constraint categories have very different effects on the scheduling of tasks:

- Flexible constraints, such as As Soon As Possible, allow tasks to be scheduled without any limitations other than their predecessor and successor relationships. No fixed start or end dates are imposed by these constraint types. Use these constraint types whenever possible.

- Semi-flexible constraints, such as Start No Earlier Than or Start No Later Than, limit the rescheduling of a task within the date boundary that you specify.

- Inflexible constraints, such as Must Start On, completely prevent the rescheduling of a task. Use these constraint types only when absolutely necessary.

The type of constraint that you apply to the tasks in your projects depends on what you need from Project. You should use inflexible constraints only if the start or finish date of a task is fixed by factors beyond the control of the project team. Examples of such tasks include handoffs to clients and the end of a funding period. For tasks without such limitations, you should use flexible constraints. Flexible constraints provide the most discretion in adjusting start and finish dates, and they allow Project to adjust dates if your project plan changes. For example, if you have used ASAP constraints and the duration of a predecessor task changes from four days to two days, Project adjusts or "pulls in" the start and finish dates of all successor tasks. However, if a successor task had an inflexible constraint applied, Project could not adjust its start or finish dates.

In this exercise, you apply a Start No Earlier Than constraint to a task.

1. Select the name of task 20, **Scene 3 setup**.

   This scene must be shot at a location that is not available to the film crew until May 26, 2008.

2. On the **Standard** toolbar, click **Task Information**.

3. In the **Task Information** dialog box, click the **Advanced** tab.

4. In the **Constraint Type** box, select **Start No Earlier Than**.

5. In the **Constraint Date** box, type or select 5/26/08.

The constraint date does not apply
if the constraint type is As Soon As
Possible or As Late As Possible.

Task Information	

| General | Predecessors | Resources | Advanced | Notes | Custom Fields |

Name: Scene 3 setup   Duration: 1d   ☐ Estimated

Constrain task

Deadline: NA

Constraint type: Start No Earlier Than   Constraint date: Mon 5/26/08

Task type: Fixed Units   ☑ Effort driven
Calendar: None   ☐ Scheduling ignores resource calendars
WBS code: 2.2.1
Earned value method: % Complete

☐ Mark task as milestone

Help   OK   Cancel

6. Click **OK**.

   Project applies a Start No Earlier Than (SNET) constraint to the task, and a constraint icon appears in the Indicators column. You can point to the icon to see the constraint details in a ScreenTip. You can also see the constraint details in the Task Drivers pane.

Position your mouse pointer over a
constraint indicator (or any icon in the
Indicators column) to see a ScreenTip.

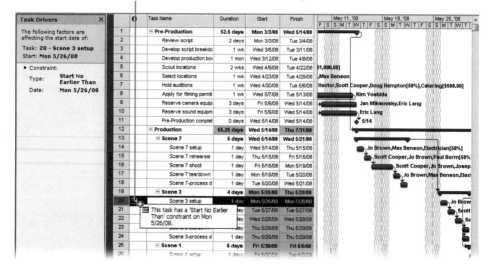

Task 20 is rescheduled to start on May 26 instead of May 21. All tasks that depend
on task 20 are also rescheduled. One way to view this rescheduling is by the light
blue change highlighting that Project applies to the Start and Finish dates of the
successor tasks of task 20. Because the duration of the Production phase was also
changed by applying the constraint to task 20, the *Duration* and *Finish* fields for
the *Production summary* task (task 12) are also highlighted. Change highlighting
remains visible until you perform another editing action or save the file, and it is
an effective visual way to see the broader consequences of your specific actions in
your schedule.

7. Click the **Close** button (the "X" button in the upper right corner) on the Task
   Drivers pane.

Here are a few other things to keep in mind when applying constraints to tasks:

- Entering a Finish date for a task (for example, in the Finish column) applies a Finish
  No Earlier Than (FNET) constraint to the task.

- Entering a Start date for a task (for example, in the Start column) or dragging a
  Gantt bar directly on the Gantt chart applies a Start No Earlier Than (SNET) constraint to the task.

- In many cases, entering a deadline date is a preferable alternative to entering a
  semi-flexible or inflexible constraint. You will work with deadline dates later in this
  chapter.

- Unless you specify a time, Project schedules a constraint date's start or finish time using the Default Start Time or Default End Time values on the Calendar tab (Tools menu, Options command). In this project, the default start time is 8 A.M. If you want a constrained task to be scheduled to start at a different time, enter that time along with the start date. For example, if you want to schedule a task to start at 10 A.M. on May 26, enter 5/26/08 10AM in the Start field.

- To remove a constraint, first select the task or tasks and, on the Project menu, click Task Information. In the Task Information dialog box, click the Advanced tab. In the Constraint Type box, select As Soon As Possible or (if scheduling from the project finish date) As Late As Possible.

- If you must apply semi-flexible or inflexible constraints to tasks in addition to task relationships, you might create what is called negative slack. For example, assume that you have a successor task that has a finish-to-start relationship with its predecessor task. If you entered a Must Start On constraint on the successor task earlier than the finish date of the predecessor task, this would result in negative slack and a scheduling conflict. By default, the constraint date applied to the successor task will override the relationship. However, if you prefer, you can set Project to honor relationships over constraints. On the Tools menu, click Options, and in the Options dialog box, click the Schedule tab. Clear the Tasks Will Always Honor Their Constraint Dates check box. This setting applies only to the current project file.

- If you must schedule a project from a finish date rather than a start date, some constraint behaviors change. For example, the As Late As Possible (ALAP) rather than the As Soon As Possible (ASAP) constraint type becomes the default for new tasks. You should pay close attention to constraints when scheduling from a finish date to make sure they create the effect you intend.

Viewing the Project's Critical Path

A *critical path* is the series of tasks that will push out the project's end date if the tasks are delayed. The word *critical* has nothing to do with how important these tasks are to the overall project. It refers only to how their scheduling will affect the project's finish date; however, the project finish date is of great importance in most projects. If you want to shorten the duration of a project to bring in the finish date, you must begin by shortening (also referred to as "crashing") the critical path.

Over the life of a project, the project's critical path is likely to change from time to time as tasks are completed ahead of or behind schedule. Schedule changes, such as assigning resources to tasks, can also alter the critical path. After a task on the critical path is completed, it is no longer critical because it cannot affect the project finish date. In

Chapter 15, "Getting Your Project Back on Track," you will work with a variety of techniques to shorten a project's overall duration.

A key to understanding the critical path is to understand slack, also known as float. There are two types of slack: free and total. *Free slack* is the amount of time a task can be delayed before it delays another task. *Total slack* is the amount of time a task can be delayed before it delays the completion of the project.

A task is on the critical path if its total slack is less than a certain amount—by default, if it is zero. In contrast, *noncritical tasks* have slack, meaning they can start or finish earlier or later within their slack time without affecting the completion date of a project.

In this exercise, you view the project's critical path. One way to see the critical path is to switch to the Detail Gantt view.

1. On the **View** menu, click **More Views**.

2. In the More Views dialog box, select **Detail Gantt**, and then click the **Apply** button.

   The project appears in the Detail Gantt view.

3. On the **Edit** menu, click **Go To**.

> **Tip** Ctrl+G is the keyboard shortcut for Go To.

4. In the **ID** box, type 12, and then click **OK**.

   Project displays task 12, the *Production* summary task.

Noncritical tasks have free slack, displayed here.

This task and its successor tasks are critical. If there is a change in the scheduling of these tasks, it will affect the project finish date.

The Scene 3 tasks and later tasks are critical tasks. In the Detail Gantt view, Project distinguishes between critical and noncritical tasks. Critical task bars are red, but noncritical task bars are blue. In this view, you can also see tasks with free slack.

Notice the Gantt bar of task 18, *Scene 7–process dailies*. The blue bar represents the duration of the task. The thin teal line and the number next to it represent free slack for this task. As you can see, this particular task has some slack and is therefore a noncritical task. (Remember that the term critical in this sense has nothing to do with the task's importance, but only with how much or little total slack is associated with the task—and, ultimately, what effect the task has on the project's finish date.) The slack on task 18 was caused by the Start No Earlier Than constraint applied to task 20. Without that constraint being applied, all tasks in the project would have been critical.

5. On the **View** menu, click **Gantt Chart**.

   Working with the critical path is the most important way to manage a project's overall duration. In later exercises, you will make adjustments that might extend the project's duration. Checking the project's critical path and, when necessary, shortening the overall project duration are important project management skills.

> **Tip** "Critical path" is a frequently misused phrase on many projects. Just listen for references to critical path work on your current projects to determine how frequently the phrase is used correctly. Remember that critical has nothing to do with the relative importance of a task, but only with its effect on the project finish date.

Here are a few other things to keep in mind when working with the critical path:

- By default, Project defines a task as critical if it has zero slack. However, you can change the amount of slack required for a task to be considered critical. You might do this, for example, if you wanted to more easily identify tasks that were within one or two days of affecting the project's finish date. On the Tools menu, click Options, and in the Options dialog box, click the Calculation tab. In the Tasks Are Critical If Slack Is Less Than Or Equal To box, enter the number of days you want.

- Project constantly recalculates the critical path even if you never display it.

- You see free slack represented in the chart portion of the Detail Gantt view, and you can also see the values of free and total slack in the Schedule table. You can apply the Schedule table to any Gantt Chart or Task Sheet view.

> **Tip** To learn more about managing a critical path, type critical path into the Search box in the upper right corner of the Project window. The Search box initially contains the text *Type a question for help.*

Interrupting Work on a Task

When initially planning project tasks, you might know that work on a certain task will be interrupted. You can split the task to indicate times when the work will be interrupted and when it can resume. The following are some reasons why you might want to split a task:

- You anticipate an interruption in a task. For example, a resource might be assigned to a week-long task, but needs to attend an event on Wednesday that is unrelated to the task.

- A task is unexpectedly interrupted. After a task is under way, a resource might have to stop work on the task because another task has taken priority. After the second task is completed, the resource can resume work on the first task.

In this exercise, you split a task to account for a planned interruption of work on that task.

1. On the **Edit** menu, click **Go To**.

2. In the **ID** box, type 4, and then click **OK**.

   Project displays task 4, *Develop production boards*.

   You know that work on this task will be interrupted for two days starting March 17.

The timescale is divided onto tiers. The time setting of the lowest tier determines how you can split tasks. In this example, you can split tasks into one-day increments.   Point at the timescale to see the date.

	O	Task Name	Duration	Start	Finish
1		☐ Pre-Production	52.5 days	Mon 3/3/08	Wed 5/14/08
2		Review script	2 days	Mon 3/3/08	Tue 3/4/08
3		Develop script breakdo	1 wk	Wed 3/5/08	Tue 3/11/08
4		Develop production bo	1 mon	Wed 3/12/08	Tue 4/8/08
5		Scout locations	2 wks	Wed 4/9/08	Tue 4/22/08
6		Select locations	1 wk	Wed 4/23/08	Tue 4/29/08

Split Task

3. On the Standard toolbar, click the **Split Task** button.

   Tip You can also click the Split Task command on the Edit menu.

Split Task
Mouse Pointer

A ScreenTip appears, and the mouse pointer changes.

4. Move the mouse pointer over the Gantt bar of task 4.

   This ScreenTip is essential for accurately splitting a task, because it contains the date at which you would start the second segment of the task if you dragged the mouse pointer from its current location on the Gantt bar. As you move the mouse pointer along the Gantt bar, you will see the start date in the ScreenTip change.

5. Move (but don't click) the mouse pointer over the Gantt bar of task 4 until the start date of Monday, 3/17/08, appears in the ScreenTip.

Use this ScreenTip to help you accurately split tasks. This information will change as you move the Split Task mouse pointer.

Split Task mouse pointer

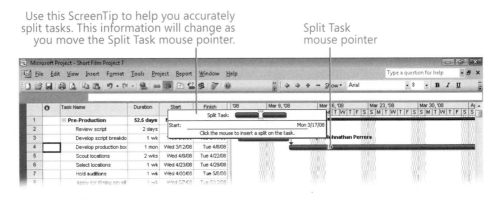

6. Click and drag the mouse pointer to the right until the start date of Wednesday, 3/19/08, appears in the ScreenTip, and then release the mouse button.

Project inserts a task split, represented in the Gantt chart as a dotted line, between the two segments of the task.

The split appears as a dotted line connecting the segments of the task. The split indicates an interruption of work on the task.

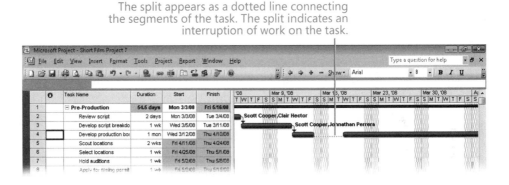

Four-headed Arrow Mouse Pointer

Tip Splitting tasks with the mouse might take a little practice. In step 6, if you didn't split task 4 so that the second segment starts on 3/19/08, just point to it again. When the mouse pointer changes to a four-headed arrow, drag the segment to the correct start date.

Here are a few other things to keep in mind when splitting tasks:

● Adjusting the bottom tier of the timescale is important for splitting tasks: the calibration of the bottom tier determines the smallest time increment into which you can split a task. With the bottom tier set at the Days level, you must split a task by at least one day. If you want to split a task at the Hourly level, you must adjust the bottom tier further (through the Timescale command on the Format menu).

- You can split a task into as many segments as you want.

- You can drag a segment of a split task either left or right to reschedule the split.

- The time of the task split, represented by the dotted line, is not counted in the duration of the task. No work occurs during the split.

- If the duration of a split task changes, the last segment of the task is increased or decreased.

- If a split task is rescheduled (for example, if its start date changes), the entire task is rescheduled, splits and all. The task keeps the same pattern of segments and splits.

- Resource leveling or manually contouring assignments over time can cause tasks to split. You will level resources in Chapter 8, "Fine-Tuning Resource and Assignment Details," and contour assignments in Chapter 9, "Fine-Tuning the Project Plan."

- To rejoin two segments of a split task, drag one segment of the task until it touches the other segment.

- If you do not want to display splits as a dotted line, you can remove them. On the Format menu, click Layout, and in the Layout dialog box, clear the Show Bar Splits check box.

Adjusting Working Time for Individual Tasks

You might want specific tasks to occur at times that are outside of the working time of the project calendar (or for assigned resources, the resource calendar). To accomplish this, you apply a *task calendar* to these tasks. As with the project calendar, you specify which base calendar to use as a task calendar. The following are some examples of when you might need a task calendar:

- You are using the Standard base calendar as your project calendar, and you have a task that must run overnight.

- You have a task that must occur on a specific weekday.

- You have a task that must occur over the weekend.

Unlike resources and resource calendars, Project does not create task calendars as you create tasks. When you need a custom task calendar, you assign one of the base calendars provided with Project (or, more likely, a new base calendar you have created) to the task. For example, if you assign the 24 Hours base calendar to a task, Project will schedule that task according to a 24-hour workday rather than the working time specified in the project calendar.

For tasks that have both a task calendar and resource assignments, Project schedules work during the working times that are common between the task calendar and re-source calendar(s). If there is no common working time, Project alerts you when you ap-ply the task calendar or assign a resource to the task.

> **Tip** When you assign a base calendar to a task, you can choose to ignore resource calen-dars for all resources assigned to the task. Doing so causes Project to schedule the resources to work on the task according to the task calendar and not their own resource calendars (for example, to work 24 hours per day). If this would result in resources working in what would otherwise be their nonworking time, you might want to first discuss this with the affected resources.

In the film project, one of the scenes must be filmed at night. However, the project calendar does not include working time late enough to cover the filming of this scene. Because this task is really an exception to the normal working time of the project, you do not want to change the project calendar. In this exercise, you create a new base calendar and apply it to the appropriate task.

1. On the **Tools** menu, click **Change Working Time**.

2. In the **Change Working Time** dialog box, click the **Create New Calendar** button.

   The Create New Base Calendar dialog box appears.

3. In the **Name** box, type Evening Shoot.

4. Make sure that the **Make a copy of** option is selected and that **Standard** is selected in the drop-down menu.

5. Click **OK**.

> **Tip** The benefit of basing the new calendar on the Standard calendar is that all of the working day exceptions from the Standard calendar, such as Independence Day, will also appear in the new calendar.

Note that *Evening Shoot* now appears in the For calendar box.

6. In the **Change Working Time** dialog box, click the **Work Weeks** tab.

   Next you'll enter the working time details for this new calendar.

7. Make sure that the Name value **[default]** in Row 1 is selected, and then click the **Details** button.

8. In the **Select Day(s)** box, select **Monday** through **Friday**.

   You want to set this calendar's working time to 5:00 PM and 11:00 PM, Monday through Friday.

9. Click **Set day(s) to these specific working times:**.

10. Select the number 2 row heading in the **Working Times** box, and press [Del].

11. In the **From** field for the first row, type 5:00 PM, and then press the [→] key.

12. Type 11:00 PM, and then press [Enter].

Details for '[Default]'

Set working time for this work week

Select day(s):

○ Use Project default times for these days.
○ Set days to nonworking time.
● Set day(s) to these specific working times:

| Sunday |
| Monday |
| Tuesday |
| Wednesday |
| Thursday |
| Friday |
| Saturday |

	From	To
1	5:00 PM	11:00 PM

Help   OK   Cancel

13. Click **OK** to close the Details dialog box, and then click **OK** again to close the Change Working Time dialog box.

    Now that you've created the Evening Shoot calendar, you're ready to apply it to a task that must be filmed in the evening.

Task Information

14. Select the name of task 34, **Scene 2 shoot**.

15. On the Standard toolbar, click **Task Information**.

    The Task Information dialog box appears.

16. Click the **Advanced** tab if it is not already selected.

17. In the **Calendar** box, select **Evening Shoot** from the list.

18. Click the **Scheduling ignores resource calendars** check box.

19. Click **OK** to close the dialog box.

Project applies the Evening Shoot calendar to task 34. A calendar icon appears in the Indicators column, reminding you that this task has a task calendar applied to it.

20. Point to the calendar icon.

This indicator appears when a task calendar has been applied to a task.

A screentip appears, showing the calendar details.

Because you chose to ignore resource calendars in the previous step, the resources assigned to these tasks will be scheduled at times that would otherwise be non-working times for them (specifically, 5:00 P.M. through 11:00 P.M.).

> **Tip** To remove a task calendar from a task, on the Advanced tab of the Task Information dialog box, click None in the Calendar box.

Changing Task Types

You might recall from Chapter 4, "Assigning Resources to Tasks," that Project uses the following formula, called the scheduling formula, to calculate a task's work value:

Work = Duration × Units

where Units refers to the resource assignment units, normally expressed as a percentage. Remember also that a task has work when it has at least one work (people or equipment) resource assigned to it. Each value in the scheduling formula corresponds to a task type. A *task type* determines which of the three scheduling formula values remains fixed if the other two values change.

The default task type is *fixed units*: when you change a task's duration, Project recalculates work. Likewise, if you change a task's work, Project recalculates the duration. In either case, the units value is unchanged. The two other task types are fixed duration and fixed work.

For a *fixed-duration* task, you can change the task's units or work value, and Project will recalculate the other value. For a *fixed-work* task, you can change the task's units or duration value, and Project will recalculate the other value. Note that you cannot turn off *effort-driven scheduling* for a fixed-work task.

Which is the right task type to apply to each of your tasks? It depends on how you want Project to schedule that task. The following table summarizes the effects of changing any value for any task type. You read it like a multiplication table.

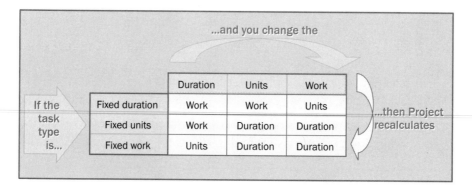

		...and you change the			
		Duration	Units	Work	
If the task type is...	Fixed duration	Work	Work	Units	...then Project recalculates
	Fixed units	Work	Duration	Duration	
	Fixed work	Units	Duration	Duration	

To view the task type of the selected task, on the Standard toolbar, click the Task Information button. Then in the Task Information dialog box, click the Advanced tab. You can also view the task type in the Task Form. (When in the Gantt Chart view, you can display the Task Form by clicking the Split command on the Window menu.) You can change a task type at any time. Note that characterizing a task type as fixed does not mean that its duration, units, or work values are unchangeable. You can change any value for any task type.

In this exercise, you change scheduling formula values (work, duration, and units) and task types.

1. On the **View** menu, click **Task Usage**.

   The Task Usage view appears.

2. On the **Edit** menu, click **Go To**.

3. In the **ID** box, type 2, and then click **OK**.

   Project displays task 2, *Review script*, and its assignments.

   The Task Usage view groups the assigned resources below each task and shows you, among other things, each task's and assignment's duration and work—two of the three variables of the scheduling formula.

4. Drag the vertical divider bar to the right so that the Start column is visible.

   Next, you'll add a column to the Task Usage view so you can see the assignment units—the third variable of the scheduling formula. You don't need to modify this view every time you want to use it, but for our purposes here, this is a good way to illustrate the effect of changing task types on the three variables of the scheduling formula.

5. Click the **Start** column heading, and then on the **Insert** menu, click **Column**.

   The Column Definition dialog box appears.

6. In the **Field Name** box, select **Assignment Units**, and then click **OK**.

   Project inserts the Assignment Units column to the left of the Start column.

	❶	Task Name	Work	Duration	Assignment Units	Details	Mar 2, '08								Mar 9, '08		
							S	S	M	T	W	T	F	S	S	M	
2		⊟ Review script	32 hrs	2 days		Work			16h	16h							
		Clair Hector	16 hrs		100%	Work			8h	8h							
		Scott Cooper	16 hrs		100%	Work			8h	8h							
3		⊟ Develop script breakdo	80 hrs	1 wk		Work					16h	16h	16h			16h	
		Johnathan Perret	40 hrs		100%	Work					8h	8h	8h			8h	
		Scott Cooper	40 hrs		100%	Work					8h	8h	8h			8h	
4		⊟ Develop production boo	480 hrs	1 mon		Work											
		Johnathan Perret	160 hrs		100%	Work											
		Kim Yoshida	160 hrs		100%	Work											

You can see that task 2 has a total work value of 32 hours (that is, 16 hours each for two resources), resource units of 100% each, and a duration of two days. Next, you will change the task's duration to observe the effects on the other values.

After a discussion among all of the resources who will review the script, all agree that the task's duration should double but that the work required to complete the task should remain the same.

7. In the **Duration** field for task 2, type or select **4d**, and press `Enter`.

   Project changes the duration of task 2 to four days and increases the work per re-source to 32 hours each. Note the change highlighting applied to the Work and Duration values. You wanted the duration to double (it did) but the work to remain the same (it didn't), so you will use the Smart Tag to adjust the results of the new task duration.

8. Point at the **Duration** field and then click the **Smart Tag Actions** button.

   Review the options on the list that appears.

	●	Task Name	Work	Duration	Assignment Units	Details		Mar 2, '08								Mar 9, '08	
							S	S	M	T	W	T	F	S	S	M
2		⊟ Review script		◇ 4 days ⊜		Work			16h	16h	16h	16h				
		Clair Hector								8h	8h				
		Scott Cooper		You just increased the duration of this task. Is it because the:					8h	8h				
3		⊟ Develop script breakdo		◉ Work required to do this task has increased, so it will take longer.				16h				16h
		Johnathan Perrer		○ Resources will work fewer hours per day, so the task will take longer.				8h				8h
		Scott Cooper		Show me more details.				8h				8h
4		⊟ Develop production bo				Work										
		Johnathan Perrer	160 hrs		100%	Work										
		Kim Yoshida	160 hrs		100%	Work										

Because task 2's task type is fixed units (the default task type), the Smart Tag's de-fault selection is to increase work as the duration increases. However, you'd like to keep the work value the same and decrease assignment units for the task's new duration.

9. On the **Smart Tag Actions** list, click **Resources will work fewer hours per day so that the task will take longer**.

   The assignment units value of each resource decreases to 50%, and the total work on the task remains unchanged at 32 hours (that is, 16 hours per each assigned resource).

	●	Task Name	Work	Duration	Assignment Units	Details		Mar 2, '08								Mar 9, '08	
							S	S	M	T	W	T	F	S	S	M
2		⊟ Review script	32 hrs	4 days ⊜		Work			8h	8h	8h	8h				
		Clair Hector	16 hrs		50%	Work			4h	4h	4h	4h				
		Scott Cooper	16 hrs		50%	Work			4h	4h	4h	4h				
3		⊟ Develop script breakdo	80 hrs	1 wk		Work							16h			16h
		Johnathan Perrer	40 hrs		100%	Work							8h			8h
		Scott Cooper	40 hrs		100%	Work							8h			8h
4		⊟ Develop production bo	480 hrs	1 mon		Work										
		Johnathan Perrer	160 hrs		100%	Work										
		Kim Yoshida	160 hrs		100%	Work										

Next, you will change a task type using the Task Information dialog box.

10. On the **Edit** menu, click **Go To**.

11. In the **ID** box, type **67**, and then click **OK**.

    Project displays task 67, *Hold formal approval showing*.

12. On the Standard toolbar, click **Task Information**.

The Task Information dialog box appears.

13. Click the **Advanced** tab if it is not already selected.

The selected task describes the formal screening of the film for the financial backers of the project. As you can see in the Task Type box, this task currently has a fixed-units task type.

The task is scheduled for a full day, although a few of the assigned resources will work for the equivalent of half a day. To reflect this (and properly manage resource costs for the task), you will make this a fixed-duration task and adjust the assignment unit values for some of the assigned resources.

14. In the **Task Type** box, select **Fixed Duration**.

15. Click the **Resources** tab.

16. In the **Units** column, set the units values for Mark Hassall and Scott Cooper to 50% each.

17. Click **OK** to close the Task Information dialog box.

The change highlighting shows you the updated work values of the two resources on the task in the Task Usage view. Note that the duration value remains unchanged.

18. On the **View** menu, click **Gantt Chart**.

> **Important** A summary task always has a fixed-duration task type, and you cannot change it. Because a summary task is based on the earliest start date and the latest finish date of its subtasks, its duration is calculated based on its subtasks and is not directly editable. If you want to confirm this, double-click Summary Task 1, Pre-Production (or a different summary task) and view the Advanced tab in the Task Information dialog box.

> ### Task Types and Effort-Driven Scheduling
>
> Many people misunderstand task types and effort-driven scheduling and conclude that these two issues are more closely related than they really are. Both settings can affect your schedule. Whereas the effect of a task type applies whenever you edit a task's work, duration, or unit values, effort-driven scheduling affects your schedule only when you're assigning or removing resources from tasks. For more information about effort-driven scheduling, see Chapter 4.

Entering Deadline Dates

One common mistake made by new Project users is to place semi-flexible or inflexible constraints on too many tasks in their projects. Such constraints severely limit your scheduling flexibility.

Yet, if you know that a specific task must be completed by a certain date, why not enter a Must Finish On constraint? This is the reason why not: Assume that you have a five-day task that you want to see completed by October 17, and today is October 6. If you enter a Must Finish On constraint on the task and set it to October 17, Project will move it out so that it will, indeed, end on October 17.

Pointing to the constraint indicator will give you the constraint details.

This task has a Must Finish On constraint, so Project schedules it to finish on the specified date, but no earlier.

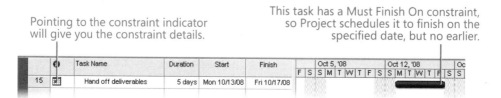

Even if the task could be completed earlier, Project will not reschedule it to start earlier. In fact, by applying that constraint, you have increased the risk for this task. If the task is delayed for even one day for any reason (a required resource is sick, for example), the task will miss its planned finish date.

A better approach to scheduling this task is to use the default As Soon As Possible (ASAP) constraint and enter a deadline of October 17. A *deadline* is a date value you enter for a task that indicates the latest date by which you want the task to be completed, but the deadline date itself does not constrain the task.

With an As Soon As Possible constraint applied, the task starts earlier and leaves slack between the finish date and the deadline date.

The deadline marker appears on the Gantt chart.

	ⓘ	Task Name	Duration	Start	Finish	Oct 5, '08	Oct 12, '08	Oc
15		Hand off deliverables	5 days	Mon 10/6/08	Fri 10/10/08			

Now the task has the greatest scheduling flexibility. It might be completed well before its deadline depending on resource availability, predecessor tasks, and whatever other scheduling issues apply.

Entering a deadline date causes Project to display a deadline indicator on the chart portion of the Gantt Chart view. If the task's finish date moves past its deadline, Project displays a missed deadline indicator in the *Indicator* field for that task.

In this exercise, you enter deadline dates for some tasks.

1. On the **Edit** menu, click **Go To**.

2. In the **ID** box, type 11 and click **OK**.

   Project displays task 11. This task is a milestone marking the scheduled finish date of the pre-production phase of the project. You want to make sure that the pre-production tasks conclude by May 22, 2008, so you will enter a deadline date for this milestone.

3. On the **Standard** Toolbar, click **Task Information**.

4. Click the **Advanced** tab.

5. In the **Deadline** box, type or select 5/22/08, and then click **OK**.

   Project inserts a deadline indicator in the chart portion of the Gantt Chart view.

Deadline marker

You can now see at a glance how close the pre-production phase has come to meeting or missing its deadline. If the scheduled completion of the pre-production phase moves past May 22, Project will display a missed deadline indicator in the Indicators column.

With one exception, entering a deadline date has no effect on the scheduling of a summary or subtask. However, a deadline date will cause Project to alert you if the scheduled completion of a task exceeds its deadline date.

The one situation in which the deadline date can affect the scheduling of a task involves slack. When a task is given a deadline date, its slack does not extend beyond the deadline date.

> **Tip** To remove a deadline from a task, clear the Deadline field on the Advanced tab of the Task Information dialog box (available by clicking Task Information on the Project menu).

Entering Fixed Costs

Projects that budget or track financial costs can deal with several different sources of costs. These include costs associated with resources, as well as costs associated directly with a specific task.

For many projects, financial costs are derived mainly from costs associated with work resources, such as people and equipment, or with material resources. To handle costs of similar types for which you want to track aggregate sums (travel and catering are two examples used in the short film project), Project 2007 has introduced cost resources (introduced in Chapter 3, "Setting Up Resources.").

However, you may occasionally want to associate a cost with a task that is not tied to resources or work and is not something you want to aggregate across the project. Project calls this a fixed cost, and it is applied per task. A *fixed cost* is a specific monetary amount budgeted for a task. It remains the same regardless of any resources assigned to the task. The following are common examples of fixed costs in projects:

- A setup fee, charged in addition to a per-day rental fee, for a piece of equipment.
- A permit to film in a public location.

If you assign resources with cost rates, assign cost resources, or add fixed costs to a task, Project adds it all together to determine the task's total cost. If you do not enter resource cost information into a project plan (perhaps because you do not know how much your work resources will be paid), you can still gain some control over the project's total cost by entering fixed costs per task.

As with resources, you can specify when fixed costs should accrue:

- **Start.** The entire fixed cost is scheduled for the start of the task. When you track progress, the entire fixed cost of the task is incurred as soon as the task starts.

- **End.** The entire fixed cost is scheduled for the end of the task. When you track progress, the entire fixed cost of the task is incurred only after the task is completed.

- **Prorated.** The fixed cost is distributed evenly over the duration of the task. When you track progress, the project incurs the cost of the task at the rate at which the task is completed. For example, if a task has a $100 fixed cost and is 75% complete, the project has incurred $75 against that task.

When you plan a project, the *accrual* method you choose for fixed costs determines how these costs are scheduled over time. This can be important in anticipating budget and cash-flow needs. By default, Project assigns the prorated accrual method for fixed costs, but you can change that to match your organization's cost accounting practices.

For the film project, you know from past experience that the filming permits will cost $500, payable when you apply for the permits. In this exercise, you assign a fixed cost to a task and specify its accrual method.

1. On the **View** menu, click **More Views**.

2. In the **More Views** dialog box, click **Task Sheet**, and then click **Apply**.

   The Task Sheet view appears.

3. On the **View** menu, point to **Table: Entry**, and click **Cost**.

   The Cost table appears, replacing the Entry table.

4. In the **Fixed Cost** field for task 8, **Apply for filming permits**, type 500, and press Tab.

5. In the **Fixed Cost Accrual** field, select **Start**, and press Tab.

A fixed cost value is either accrued at the start or finish of a task or prorated over the duration of the task, depending on the option you choose.

	Task Name	Fixed Cost	Fixed Cost Accrual	Total Cost	Baseline	Variance	Actual	Remaining
1	⊟ Pre-Production	**$0.00**	Prorated	**$27,402.00**	**$0.00**	**$27,402.00**	**$0.00**	**$27,402.00**
2	Review script	$0.00	Prorated	$712.00	$0.00	$712.00	$0.00	$712.00
3	Develop script breakdo	$0.00	Prorated	$1,880.00	$0.00	$1,880.00	$0.00	$1,880.00
4	Develop production bo	$0.00	Prorated	$10,144.00	$0.00	$10,144.00	$0.00	$10,144.00
5	Scout locations	$0.00	Prorated	$6,840.00	$0.00	$6,840.00	$0.00	$6,840.00
6	Select locations	$0.00	Prorated	$2,860.00	$0.00	$2,860.00	$0.00	$2,860.00
7	Hold auditions	$0.00	Prorated	$2,600.00	$0.00	$2,600.00	$0.00	$2,600.00
8	Apply for filming permit	$500.00	Start	$1,156.00	$0.00	$1,156.00	$0.00	$1,156.00
9	Reserve camera equipr	$0.00	Prorated	$966.00	$0.00	$966.00	$0.00	$966.00
10	Reserve sound equipm	$0.00	Prorated	$444.00	$0.00	$444.00	$0.00	$444.00
11	Pre-Production complet	$0.00	Prorated	$0.00	$0.00	$0.00	$0.00	$0.00

Project will now schedule a $500 cost against the task *Apply for filming permits* at the task's start date, and the project will incur this cost when the task starts. This cost is independent of the task's duration and of the costs of resources assigned to it. In fact, the task's total cost of $1,156 (visible in the Total Cost column) includes both the $500 fixed cost and the cost of the resources assigned to the task.

Setting Up a Recurring Task

Many projects require repetitive tasks, such as attending project status meetings, creating and publishing status reports, or running quality-control inspections. Although it is easy to overlook the scheduling of such events, you should account for them in your project plan. After all, status meetings and similar events that indirectly support the project require time from resources, and such events take time away from your resources' other assignments.

To help account for such events in your project plan, create a *recurring task*. As the name suggests, a recurring task is repeated at a specified frequency such as daily, weekly, monthly, or yearly. When you create a recurring task, Project creates a series of tasks with Start No Earlier Than constraints, no task relationships, and effort-driven scheduling turned off.

In this exercise, you create a recurring task that will represent a weekly meeting associated with this project.

1. On the **View** menu, click **Gantt Chart**.

   The Gantt Chart view appears.

2. Select the name of task 12, **Production**.

   You want the recurring tasks to be inserted into the project as the last items in the pre-production phase, directly above task 12, the *Production* task.

3. On the **Insert** menu, click **Recurring Task**.

   The Recurring Task Information dialog box appears.

4. In the **Task Name** box, type Staff planning meeting

5. In the **Duration** box, type 2h

6. Under **Recurrence pattern**, make sure **Weekly** is selected, and then select the **Monday** check box.

   Next, you will specify the date of its first occurrence. By default, it is the project start date. However, you want the weekly status meetings to begin one week later.

7. In the **Start** box, type or select 3/10/08.

Next, you will specify the number of recurrences. You do this by entering either an exact number of recurrences or a date by which the task should end.

8. Select **End after**, and type or select **10** occurrences.

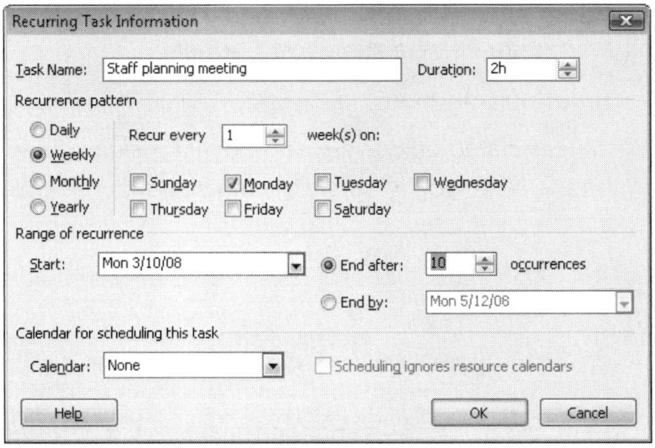

Recurring Task

9. Click **OK** to create the recurring task.

Project inserts the recurring tasks, nested within the pre-production phase. Initially, the recurring task is collapsed. A recurring task icon appears in the Indicators column.

Scroll To Task

10. To view the first occurrences of the recurring meeting's Gantt bars, on the Standard toolbar, click **Scroll To Task**.

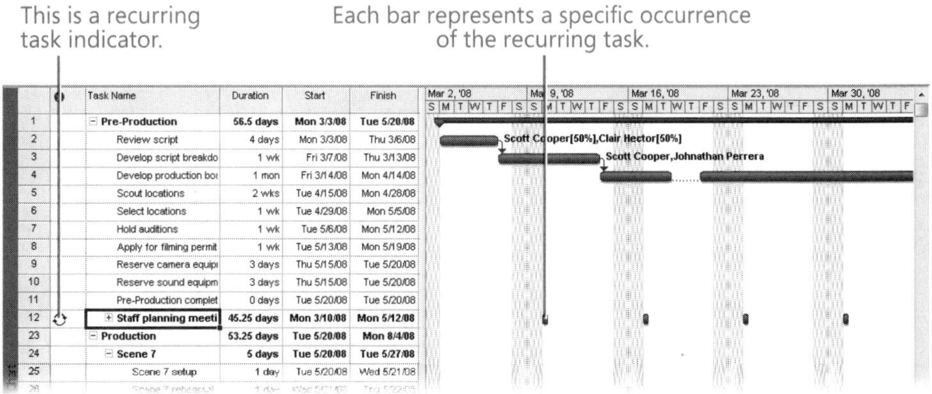

This is a recurring task indicator.

Each bar represents a specific occurrence of the recurring task.

Note that the Gantt bar for the recurring task does not look like the other Gantt bars in the Gantt chart. A Gantt bar for a recurring task shows only the occurrences or roll-ups of the individual occurrences of the task. For example, contrast the summary Gantt bar for the recurring task with that of task 1, Pre-Production.

Next, you will assign resources to the recurring task.

Assign Resources

11. Verify that task 12, *Staff planning meeting*, is selected, and then, on the **Standard** toolbar, click **Assign Resources**.

12. In the **Assign Resources** dialog box, click **Clair Hector**. Then hold down the Ctrl key while clicking **Johnathan Perrera** and **Scott Cooper**.

13. Click the **Assign** button, and then click **Close**.

The Assign Resources dialog box closes, and Project assigns the selected resources to the recurring task. Next, you will view the individual occurrences of the recurring task.

14. Click the plus sign next to the recurring task's title, *Staff planning meeting*.

The names of recurring tasks are automatically numbered sequentially. Pointing to a value that isn't fully visible in a cell will display the value in a ScreenTip.

		Task Name	Duration	Start	Finish
1		Pre-Production	56.5 days	Mon 3/3/08	Tue 5/20/08
2		Review script	4 days	Mon 3/3/08	Thu 3/6/08
3		Develop script breakdo	1 wk	Fri 3/7/08	Thu 3/13/08
4		Develop production bo	1 mon	Fri 3/14/08	Mon 4/14/08
5		Scout locations	2 wks	Tue 4/15/08	Mon 4/28/08
6		Select locations	1 wk	Tue 4/29/08	Mon 5/5/08
7		Hold auditions	1 wk	Tue 5/6/08	Mon 5/12/08
8		Apply for filming permit	1 wk	Tue 5/13/08	Mon 5/19/08
9		Reserve camera equip	3 days	Thu 5/15/08	Tue 5/20/08
10		Reserve sound equipm	3 days	Thu 5/15/08	Tue 5/20/08
11		Pre-Production complet	0 days	Tue 5/20/08	Tue 5/20/08
12	○	Staff planning meeti	45.25 days	Mon 3/10/08	Mon 5/12/08
13		Staff planning meeting 1	2 hrs	Mon 3/10/08	Mon 3/10/08
14		Staff planning meet	2 hrs	Mon 3/17/08	Mon 3/17/08
15		Staff planning meet	2 hrs	Mon 3/24/08	Mon 3/24/08
16		Staff planning meet	2 hrs	Mon 3/31/08	Mon 3/31/08
17		Staff planning meet	2 hrs	Mon 4/7/08	Mon 4/7/08
18		Staff planning meet	2 hrs	Mon 4/14/08	Mon 4/14/08
19		Staff planning meet	2 hrs	Mon 4/21/08	Mon 4/21/08
20		Staff planning meet	2 hrs	Mon 4/28/08	Mon 4/28/08
21		Staff planning meet	2 hrs	Mon 5/5/08	Mon 5/5/08
22		Staff planning meet	2 hrs	Mon 5/12/08	Mon 5/12/08
23		Production	53.25 days	Tue 5/20/08	Mon 8/4/08
24		Scene 7	5 days	Tue 5/20/08	Tue 5/27/08
25		Scene 7 setup	1 day	Tue 5/20/08	Wed 5/21/08
26		Scene 7 rehearsal	1 day	Wed 5/21/08	Thu 5/22/08

The individual occurrences of the recurring task bars are rolled up to the recurring task.

Each occurrence of the recurring task is sequentially numbered (if you wish to verify this, widen the Task Name column, or point to the task's name and note the content of the ScreenTip), and the resource assignments appear for the individual occurrences.

15. Click the minus sign next to the recurring task's title, *Staff planning meeting*, to hide the individual occurrences.

Here are a few other things to keep in mind when creating recurring tasks:

- By default, Project schedules a recurring task to start at the Default Start Time value entered on the Calendar tab (on the Tools menu, click Options); in this project, that value is 8 A.M. If you want to schedule a recurring task to start at a different time, enter that time along with the start date in the Start box of the Recurring Task Information dialog box. For example, if you want the recurring staff meeting to be scheduled for 10 A.M. starting on October 6, you would enter 10/6/08 10AM in the Start box.

- As with a summary task, the duration of a recurring task spans the earliest start to latest finish date of the individual occurrences of the recurring task.

- When you schedule a recurring task to end on a specific date, Project suggests the current project end date. If you use this date, be sure to manually change it if the project end date changes later.

- Project alerts you if you create a recurring task that would occur during nonworking time, such as a holiday. You can then choose not to create that occurrence or to schedule it for the next working day.

- You should always assign resources to recurring tasks with the Assign Resources dialog box. Entering resource names in the *Resource Name field* of the recurring task assigns the resources to the recurring task and not to the individual occurrences.

CLOSE the Short Film Project 7 file.

Key Points

- By using a combination of task relationships plus lead and lag time, you can more accurately model how work should be done.

- When entering lead time between a predecessor and successor task, entering a percentage lead time value offers more flexibility because Project recalculates the lead time value whenever the duration of the predecessor task changes.

- The constraint options in Project enable you to fully take advantage of the scheduling engine in Project or to effectively turn it off. Think through the effects of semi-flexible and inflexible constraints on your schedules, and use them sparingly.

- You can often set a deadline date for a task instead of applying a hard constraint, such as Must Finish On.

- You can record any fixed cost value you wish per task, and it is not associated with resource costs.

- The critical path indicates the series of tasks that determine the project's finish date. Project constantly recalculates the critical path, which may change as the details of your project plan change.

- You can interrupt work on a task by splitting it.

- For tasks that must be completed outside of the project's normal working time (as specified by the project calendar), you can create a new base calendar and apply it to the task.

- Project supports three different task types; fixed units is the default. A task's type determines how Project reschedules a task when you change work, duration, or assignment unit values.

- Set up a recurring task for activities, such as status meetings, that occur on a regular frequency.

Chapter at a Glance

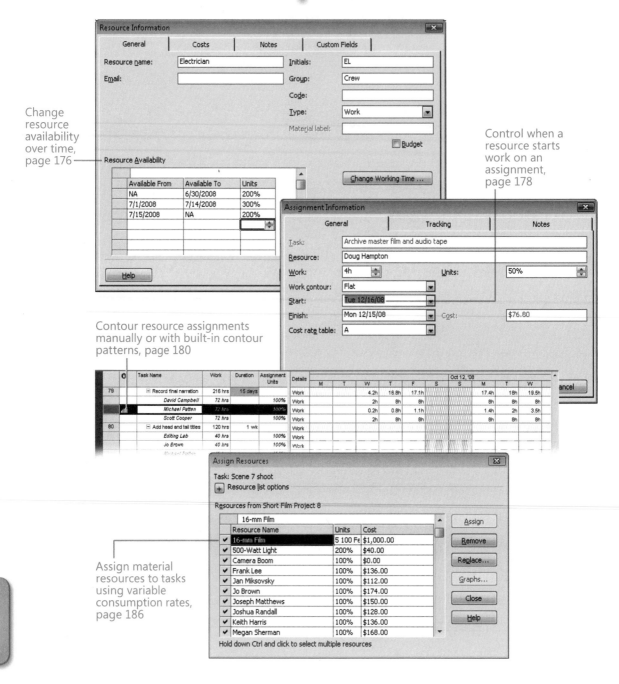

Change resource availability over time, page 176

Control when a resource starts work on an assignment, page 178

Contour resource assignments manually or with built-in contour patterns, page 180

Assign material resources to tasks using variable consumption rates, page 186

8 Fine-Tuning Resource and Assignment Details

In this chapter, you will learn how to:

- ✔ Set up different pay rates for resources.
- ✔ Set up pay rates that will change over time for a resource.
- ✔ Set resource availability to change over time.
- ✔ Delay the start of a resource assignment.
- ✔ Control how a resource's work on a task is scheduled over time by using work contours.
- ✔ Apply different cost rates for a resource assigned to different kinds of tasks.
- ✔ Enter variable consumption rates for material resources.

> **Tip** Do you need only a quick refresher on the topics in this chapter? See the Quick Reference entries on pages xxv–xlviii.

Because work resources (people and equipment) are often the most expensive part of a project, understanding how to make the best use of resources' time is an important project planning skill. In this chapter, you examine and use a variety of advanced Microsoft Office Project 2007 features relating to *resources* and their assignments to tasks.

> **Important** Before you can use the practice files provided for this chapter, you need to install them from the book's companion CD to their default locations. See "Using the Book's CD" on page xix for more information.

Entering Multiple Pay Rates for a Resource

Some *work resources* might perform different tasks with different pay rates. For example, in the short film project, the director of photography could also serve as a camera operator. Because the pay rates for director of photography and camera operator are different, you can enter two *cost rate tables* for the resource. Then, after you assign the resource to tasks, you specify which rate table should apply. Each resource can have up to five cost rate tables.

In this exercise, you create a second cost rate table for a resource.

> **BE SURE TO** start Microsoft Office Project 2007 if it's not already running.

> **Important** If you are running Project Professional, you may need to make a one-time adjustment to use the Computer account and to work offline. This ensures that the practice files you work with in this chapter do not affect your Project Server data. For more information, see "Starting Project Professional" on page 11.

> **OPEN** Short Film Project 8a from the *\Documents\Microsoft Press\Project 2007 SBS\ Chapter 8 Advanced Resources and Assignments* folder. You can also access the practice files for this book by clicking Start, All Programs, Microsoft Press, Project 2007 Step by Step, and then selecting the chapter folder of the file you want to open.

1. On the **File** menu, click **Save As**.

   The Save As dialog box appears.

2. In the **File name** box, type Short Film Project 8, and then click **Save**.

3. On the **View** menu, click **Resource Sheet**.

   The Resource Sheet view replaces the Gantt Chart view.

4. In the **Resource Sheet** view, click the name of resource 18, **Jan Miksovsky**.

Resource Information

A screenshot of Microsoft Project - Short Film Project 8 showing the Resource Sheet with the following columns and data:

	ⓘ	Resource Name	Type	Material Label	Initials	Group	Max. Units	Std. Rate	Ovt. Rate	Cost/Use	Accrue At	Base Calendar	Code
1		16-mm Camera	Work		16mm	Equipment	300%	$300.00/wk	$0.00/hr	$0.00	Start	Standard	
2		16-mm Film	Material	100 Feet	Film	Film and Lat		$25.00		$0.00	Prorated		
3		500-Watt Light	Work		5000VL	Equipment	400%	$100.00/wk	$0.00/hr	$0.00	Prorated	Standard	
4		Anne L. Paper	Work		AP	Talent	100%	$150.00/day	$0.00/hr	$0.00	Prorated	Standard	
5		Camera Boom	Work		Boom	Equipment	200%	$0.00/hr	$0.00/hr	$0.00	Prorated	Standard	
6	◈	Clair Hector	Work		CH	Production	100%	$900.00/wk	$0.00/hr	$0.00	Prorated	Standard	
7		Crane	Work		Crane	Equipment	100%	$0.00/hr	$0.00/hr	$0.00	Prorated	Standard	
8		Daniel Penn	Work		DP	Talent	100%	$150.00/day	$0.00/hr	$0.00	Prorated	Standard	
9		David Campbell	Work		DC	Talent	100%	$150.00/day	$0.00/hr	$0.00	Prorated	Standard	
10		Dolly	Work		Dolly	Equipment	200%	$0.00/hr	$0.00/hr	$0.00	Prorated	Standard	
11		Doug Hampton	Work		DH	Production	100%	$16.00/hr	$0.00/hr	$0.00	Prorated	Standard	
12		Editing Lab	Work		EL	Film and Lat	100%	$250.00/day	$0.00/hr	$25.00	Prorated	Standard	
13		Electrician	Work		EL	Crew	200%	$28.00/hr	$42.00/hr	$0.00	Prorated	Standard	
14	◈	Eric Lang	Work		EL	Production	100%	$18.50/hr	$0.00/hr	$0.00	Prorated	Standard	
15		Eric Miller	Work		EM	Talent	100%	$150.00/day	$0.00/hr	$0.00	Prorated	Standard	
16		Florian Voss	Work		FV	Production	100%	$25.00/hr	$0.00/hr	$0.00	Prorated	Standard	
17		Frank Lee	Work		FL	Crew	100%	$17.00/hr	$25.50/hr	$0.00	Prorated	Standard	
18		Jan Miksovsky	Work		JM	Production	100%	$21.75/hr	$0.00/hr	$0.00	Prorated	Standard	
19		Jim Hance	Work		JH	Talent	100%	$75.00/day	$0.00/hr	$0.00	Prorated	Standard	
20		Jo Brown	Work		JB	Production	100%	$21.75/hr	$0.00/hr	$0.00	Prorated	Standard	
21	◈	Johnathan Perrera	Work		JP	Production	100%	$25.00/hr	$0.00/hr	$0.00	Prorated	Standard	
22		Joseph Mathews	Work		JM	Talent	100%	$150.00/day	$0.00/hr	$0.00	Prorated	Standard	

5. On the **Standard** toolbar, click the **Resource Information** button.

   The Resource Information dialog box appears.

> **Tip** You can also double-click the *Resource Name* field to display the Resource Information dialog box.

6. Click the **Costs** tab.

   You see Jan's default pay rate of $21.75 per hour on rate table A. Each tab (labeled A, B, and so on) corresponds to one of the five pay rates that a resource can have.

7. Under **Cost rate tables**, click the **B** tab.

8. Select the default entry of **$0.00/h** in the field directly below the column heading **Standard Rate**, and then type 14/h.

9. In the **Overtime Rate** field in the same row, type 21/h, and then press the `Enter` key.

When you enter a pay rate, Project supplies the currency symbol if you do not.

10. Click **OK** to close the Resource Information dialog box.

    Notice that on the Resource Sheet, Jan's standard pay rate is still $21.75 per hour. (This is recorded in the Std. Rate column.) This matches the value in her rate table A, the default rate table. This rate table will be used for all of Jan's task assignments unless you specify a different rate table. You will do this in a later section.

Setting Up Pay Rates to Apply at Different Times

Resources can have both standard and overtime pay rates. By default, Project uses these rates for the duration of the project. However, you can change a resource's pay rates to be effective as of the date you choose. For example, you could initially set up a resource on January 1 with a standard rate of $16 per hour, planning to raise the resource's standard rate to $19 per hour on July 1.

Project uses these pay rates when calculating resource costs based on when the resource's work is scheduled. You can assign up to 25 pay rates to be applied at different times to each of a resource's five cost rate tables.

In this exercise, you enter different pay rates for a resource to be applied at a later date.

1. In the **Resource Name** column, select the name of resource 11, **Doug Hampton**.

2. On the **Standard** toolbar, click **Resource Information**.

    The Resource Information dialog box appears.

3. Click the **Costs** tab if it is not already selected.

Resource
Information

You'll enter a pay rate increase in cost rate table A.

4. In the **Effective Date** cell in the second row of cost rate table A, type or select 6/24/08.

5. In the **Standard Rate** cell in the second row, type 20%, and then press the [Enter] key.

Resource Information

| General | Costs | Notes | Custom Fields |

Resource Name: Doug Hampton

Cost rate tables

For rates, enter a value or a percentage increase or decrease from the previous rate. For instance, if a resource's Per Use Cost is reduced by 20%, type -20%.

A (Default) | B | C | D | E

Effective Date	Standard Rate	Overtime Rate	Per Use Cost
--	$16.00/h	$0.00/h	$0.00
Tue 6/24/08	$19.20/h	$0.00/h	$0.00

Cost accrual: Prorated

Help   Details...   OK   Cancel

If you enter a positive or negative percentage value here, Project automatically calculates the new rate value (as shown here) based on the previous rate value.

Note that Project calculates the 20% increase to produce a rate of $19.20 per hour. The previous rate of $16 per hour plus 20% equals $19.20 per hour. You can enter a specific value or a percentage increase or decrease from the previous rate. Calculating a new pay rate based on a percentage of the previous pay rate is a one-time calculation. Should you later change Doug's initial standard pay rate (currently $16.00/ hour), his next pay rate would not be affected.

> **Tip** In addition to or instead of cost rates, a resource can include a set fee that Project accrues to each task to which the resource is assigned. This is called a *cost per use*. Unlike cost rates, the cost per use does not vary with the task's duration or amount of work the resource performs on the task. In the short film project, the Editing Lab resource has a $25 cost per use that covers the cleanup costs of the lab. You specify the cost per use in the *Cost/Use* field in the Resource Sheet view or in the *Per Use Cost* field in the Resource Information dialog box.

6. Click **OK** to close the Resource Information dialog box.

Note that Doug Hampton's initial rate, $16.00 per hour, appears in his *Std. Rate* field (unless the current date is 6/24/08 or later). This field will display $16 per hour until the current date changes to 6/24/08 or later. It will then display his new standard rate of $19.20 per hour.

Setting Up Resource Availability to Apply at Different Times

One of the values that Project stores for each work resource is the resource's Max. Units value. This is the maximum capacity of a resource to accomplish tasks. A resource's working time settings (recorded in the individual resource calendars) determine when work assigned to a resource can be scheduled. However, the resource's capacity to work (measured in units and limited by the resource's Max. Units value) determines the extent to which the resource can work within those hours without becoming overallocated.

You can specify that different Max. Units values be applied at different time periods for any resource. Setting a resource's availability over time enables you to control exactly what a resource's Max. Units value is at any time. For example, you might have two electricians available for the first eight weeks, three for the next six weeks, and then two for the remainder of the project. You set resource availability over time in the Resource Availability grid on the General tab of the Resource Information dialog box. (You can open this dialog box by clicking the Resource Information command on the Project menu when in a resource view.)

> **Important** Setting the Max. Units values for different times will not prevent a resource from becoming overallocated, but Project will indicate when the resource's assignments exceed their Max. Units capacity.

In this exercise, you customize a resource's availability over time.

1. In the **Resource Name** column, click the name of resource 13, **Electrician**.

2. On the **Standard** toolbar, click **Resource Information**.

3. Click the **General** tab.

   You expect to have two electricians available to work on this project from the start of the project through June 30, 2008, three electricians from July 1 through July 14, and then only two for the remainder of the project.

4. Under **Resource Availability**, in the first row of the **Available From** column, leave **NA** (for Not Applicable).

5. In the **Available To** cell in the first row, type or select 6/30/08.

6. In the **Available From** cell in the second row, type or select 7/1/08.

7. In the **Available To** cell in the second row, type or select 7/14/08.

8. In the **Units** cell in the second row, type or select 300%.

9. In the **Available From** cell in the third row, type or select 7/15/08.

10. Leave the Available To cell in the third row blank. (Project will insert *NA* for you after you complete the next step.)

11. In the **Units** cell in the third row, type or select 200%, and then press the `Enter` key.

For the period between July 1 through July 14, you can schedule up to three electricians without overallocating them. Before and after this period, you have just two electricians to schedule.

12. Click **OK** to close the Resource Information dialog box.

Delaying the Start of Assignments

If more than one resource is assigned to a task, you might not want all of the resources to start working on the task at the same time. You can delay the start of work for one or more resources assigned to a task.

For example, assume that a task has been assigned four resources. Three of the resources initially work on the task, and the fourth later inspects the quality of the work. The inspector should start work on the task later than the other resources.

> **Tip** If you need to delay the start of all resources assigned to a task rather than adjusting each resource's assignment, you should reschedule the start date of the task.

In this exercise, you delay the start of one resource's assignment on a task.

1. On the **View** menu, click **Task Usage**.

   The Task Usage view appears. In this view, the assigned resources are listed under each task.

2. On the **Edit** menu, click **Go To**, enter 84 in the **ID** box, and then click **OK**.

> **Tip** Remember that Ctrl+G is a shortcut for displaying the Go To dialog box.

Project displays task 84, *Archive master film and audio tape.*

	❶	Task Name	Work	Duration	Assignment Units	Details	W	T	F	S	Dec 14, '06 S	M	T	W	T	F
84		⊟ Archive master film and	20 hrs	1 day		Work				5h		15h				
		Doug Hampton	4 hrs		50%	Work				1h		3h				
		Editing Lab	8 hrs		100%	Work				2h		6h				
		Michael Patten	8 hrs		100%	Work				2h		6h				
85		⊟ Hand off masters to dis	8 hrs	1 day		Work						2h	6h			
		Michael Patten	8 hrs		100%	Work						2h	6h			
						Work										

As you can see, this task currently has three resources (two people and the editing lab) assigned to it. You want to delay the start of Doug Hampton's work on this task until Tuesday, December 16.

3. Under **task 84** in the **Task Name** column, select the name of the resource, **Doug Hampton**.

4. On the **Standard** toolbar, click the **Assignment Information** button.

Assignment
Information

   The Assignment Information dialog box appears.

> **Tip** You may have noticed that the same toolbar button is used for the Resource Information and Assignment Information buttons used in this chapter, as well as the Task Information button. Which Information dialog box you see (Task, Resource, or Assignment) depends on what you have selected when you click the button.

5. Click the **General** tab if it is not already selected.

6. In the **Start** box, type or select 12/16/08

Assignment Information				[x]
General		Tracking		Notes

Task:	Archive master film and audio tape
Resource:	Doug Hampton
Work:	4h [▲▼] Units: 50% [▲▼]
Work contour:	Flat [▼]
Start:	Tue 12/16/08 [▼]
Finish:	Mon 12/15/08 [▼] Cost: $76.80
Cost rate table:	A [▼]

[OK] [Cancel]

7. Click **OK** to close the Assignment Information dialog box.

The duration of this task has increased as the work is spread over a longer period.

	❶	Task Name	Work	Duration	Assignment Units	Details					Dec 14, '06					
							W	T	F	S	S	M		W	T	F
84		⊟ Archive master film and	20 hrs	2 days		Work			4h			12h	4h			
		Doug Hampton	4 hrs		50%	Work			0h			0h	4h			
		Editing Lab	8 hrs		100%	Work			2h			6h				
		Michael Patten	8 hrs		100%	Work			2h			6h				
85		⊟ Hand off masters to dis	8 hrs	1 day		Work								8h		
		Michael Patten	8 hrs		100%	Work								8h		
						Work										
						Work										

> **Tip** If you want an assignment to start at a specific time as well as on a specific date, you can specify the time in the Start box. For example, if you want Doug Hampton's assignment to start at 1 P.M. on December 16, type 12/16/08 1:00 PM. Otherwise, Project uses the default start time as specified in the Default Start Time box on the Calendar tab of the Options dialog box.

Project adjusts Doug Hampton's assignment on this task so that he works no hours on Friday or Monday but four hours on Tuesday. The other resources assigned to the task are not affected. Note that the total work of this task did not change, but its duration did—the work was spread from two working days to three.

Applying Contours to Assignments

In the Resource Usage and Task Usage views, you can see exactly how long each re-source is scheduled to work on each task. In addition to viewing assignment details, you can change the amount of time a resource works on a task in any given time period. There are two ways to do this:

- Apply a predefined work contour to an assignment. Predefined *contours* generally describe how work is distributed over time in terms of graphical patterns. For ex-ample, the Bell predefined contour distributes less work to the beginning and end of the assignment, and distributes more work toward the middle. If you were to graph the work over time, the graph's shape would resemble a bell.

- Edit the assignment details directly. For example, in the Resource Usage or Task Usage view, you can change the assignment values directly in the timescaled grid.

How you contour or edit an assignment depends on what you need to accomplish. Predefined contours work best for assignments in which you can predict a likely pattern of effort—a task that requires considerable ramp-up time might benefit from a back-loaded contour, for example, to reflect the likelihood that the resource will be most pro-ductive toward the end of the assignment.

In this exercise, you apply a predefined contour to one task's assignments, and you man-ually edit another assignment.

1. On the **Edit** menu, click **Go To**, enter **79** in the **ID** box, and then click **OK**.

Project scrolls to task 79, *Record final narration*. This task has three resources as-signed to it.

	❶	Task Name	Work	Duration	Assignment Units	Details	M	T	W	T	F	S	Oct 12, '08 S	M	T	W	
79		⊟ Record final narration	216 hrs	9 days		Work			6h	24h	24h			24h	24h	24h	
		David Campbell	72 hrs		100%	Work			2h	8h	8h			8h	8h	8h	
		Michael Patten	72 hrs		100%	Work			2h	8h	8h			8h	8h	8h	
		Scott Cooper	72 hrs		100%	Work			2h	8h	8h			8h	8h	8h	
80		⊟ Add head and tail titles	120 hrs	1 wk		Work											
		Editing Lab	40 hrs		100%	Work											
		Jo Brown	40 hrs		100%	Work											
		Michael Patten	40 hrs		100%	Work											

As you can see in the timescaled data at the right, all three resources are scheduled to work on this task at a regular rate of eight hours per day (that is, 100 percent of their available working time)—except for the first and last days of the task. These assignments have a flat contour. This is the default work contour type that Project uses when scheduling work.

You want to change Michael Patten's assignment on this task so that, although the other assigned resources work full-time, he starts with a brief daily assignment and increases his work time as the task progresses. He should continue working on the task after the other resources have finished their assignments. To accomplish this, you will apply a back-loaded contour to the assignment.

> **Tip** The reason that each resource assigned to task 79 has just two hours of work on the task's first day and six hours on the last day is that the task is scheduled to start partway through the workday on Wednesday and finish partway through the workday on Tuesday.

2. In the **Task Name** column, select **Michael Patten**, the second resource assigned to task 79.

3. On the **Standard** toolbar, click the **Assignment Information** button.

   Assignment
   Information

   Project displays the Assignment Information dialog box.

4. Click the **General** tab if it is not already selected.

5. In the **Work Contour** box, select **Back Loaded**, and then click **OK** to close the Assignment Information dialog box.

   Project applies the contour to this resource's assignment and reschedules his work on the task.

The contour indicator matches the type of contour applied—back-loaded in this case.

The back-loaded contour causes Project to assign very little work to the resource initially and then add more work each day.

		Task Name	Work	Duration	Assignment Units	Details							Oct 12, '08			
							M	T	W	T	F	S	S	M	T	W
79		⊟ Record final narration	216 hrs	15 days		Work			4.2h	16.8h	17.1h			17.4h	18h	19.5h
		David Campbell	72 hrs		100%	Work			2h	8h	8h			8h	8h	8h
		Michael Patten	72 hrs		100%	Work			0.2h	0.8h	1.1h			1.4h	2h	3.5h
		Scott Cooper	72 hrs		100%	Work			2h	8h	8h			8h	8h	8h
80		⊟ Add head and tail titles	120 hrs	1 wk		Work										
		Editing Lab	40 hrs		100%	Work										
		Jo Brown	40 hrs		100%	Work										
		Michael Patten	40 hrs		100%	Work										

If you scroll the timescaled data to the right, you see that in each successive day of the task's duration, Michael Patten is assigned slightly more time to work on the assignment. Because Michael Patten's assignment to this task finishes later than the assignments of the other resources, Michael Patten determines the finish date of the task. One common way to phrase this is that Michael Patten is the driving resource of this task; his assignment determines, or drives, the finish date of the task.

You also see a contour indicator in the Indicators column displaying the type of contour that is applied to the assignment.

6. Point to the contour indicator.

Project displays a ScreenTip describing the type of contour applied to this assignment.

Tip Applying a contour to this assignment caused the overall duration of the task to be extended. If you do not want a contour to extend a task's duration, change the task type (on the Advanced tab of the Task Information dialog box) to Fixed Duration before applying the contour. Applying a contour to a fixed-duration task will cause Project to recalculate the resource's work value so that the resource works less in the same time period.

Next, you will directly edit another task's assignment values.

7. On the **Edit** menu, click **Go To**, enter 2 in the **ID** box, and then click **OK**.

   Project scrolls vertically to task 2, *Review script*.

Note that Clair Hector is currently assigned four hours per day for each day of the assignment's duration. Why four hours? Clair normally has eight working hours per day on these particular days (as determined by her resource calendar). She was assigned to this task at 50% assignment units, however, so the resulting scheduled work is only four hours per day.

You want to increase Clair Hector's work on the last two days of this task so that she will work full-time on it. To accomplish this, you will manually edit her assignment values.

8. In the timescaled grid in the right pane of the Project window, select Clair Hector's four-hour assignment for Wednesday, March 5.

9. Type 8h, and then press the [Tab] key.

10. In Clair's assignment for Thursday, type 8h, and then press [Enter].

Here are Clair Hector's assigned
work values for Wednesday and
Thursday, after you edited them.

O	Task Name	Work	Duration	Assignment Units	Details	Mar 2, '08							Mar 9, '08		
						S	S	M	T	W			F	S	S	M
2	⊟ Review script	40 hrs	4 days		Work			8h	8h	12h	12h					
	Clair Hector	24 hrs		100%	Work			4h	4h	8h	8h					
	Scott Cooper	16 hrs		50%	Work			4h	4h	4h	4h					
3	⊟ Develop script breakdo	80 hrs	1 wk		Work							16h				16h
	Johnathan Perrer	40 hrs		100%	Work							8h				8h
	Scott Cooper	40 hrs		100%	Work							8h				8h
4	⊟ Develop production bu	480 hrs	1 mon													

Clair is now assigned eight hours per day on these days. Project displays a contour
indicator in the Indicators column showing that a manually edited contour has
been applied to the assignment.

> **Assignment Notes**
>
> **Tip** If you want to document details about contouring an assignment or anything pertain-
> ing to an assignment, you can record the details in an assignment note. In Task Usage or
> Resource Usage view, select the assignment, and then click the Assignment Notes button on
> the Standard toolbar. Assignment notes are similar to task and resource notes.

Here are a few more capabilities that you can apply in a usage view:

- In addition to manually editing work values at the resource level as you did above,
  you can also edit work values at the task level. When you change a work value at
  the task level, Project adjusts the resulting work value per resource in accordance
  with each resource's units value on that assignment. For example, assume that on a
  specific day, two resources were assigned four hours each to a task that had a total
  work value of eight hours. If you then change the total work on the task for that
  day to 12 hours, Project will increase the work per resource from four to six hours.

- You can split a task in the Gantt Chart view to account for an interruption in the
  task, as you did in Chapter 7. You can also split a task in the Task Usage view by
  entering "0" work values in the timephased grid for the date range you want. To
  preserve the total work on the task, you should add the same amount of work
  to the end of the task as you subtracted with the split. For example, assume that
  a task starts on Monday and has eight hours total work per day for four days. Its
  work pattern (in hours per day) is 8, 8, 8 and 8. You interrupt work on the task on
  Tuesday and then add those eight hours to the end of the task (in this case, Friday).
  The new work pattern would be 8, 0, 8, 8, and 8.

- When editing values in the timephased grid, you can work with the cells somewhat
  like you might work in an Excel worksheet—you can drag and drop values and use
  the AutoFill handle to copy values to the right or downward.

Applying Different Cost Rates to Assignments

You can set as many as five pay rates per resource, which allows you to apply different pay rates to different assignments for a resource; for example, a different pay rate might depend on the skills required for each assignment. For each assignment, Project initially uses rate table A by default, but you can specify that another rate table should be used.

In the "Entering Multiple Pay Rates for a Resource" section, you set up a second rate table for Jan Miksovsky to be applied for any assignments in which she is functioning as a camera operator. Jan is currently assigned to task 27, *Scene 7 shoot*, as a camera operator, but her assignment still reflects her default pay rate as director of photography. In this exercise, you change the pay rate table to be applied to Jan for her assignment to task 27.

1. On the **Edit** menu, click **Go To**, enter 27 in the **ID** box, and then click **OK**.

   Project scrolls the Task Usage view to display task 27, *Scene 7 shoot*.

2. On the **View** menu, point to **Table: Usage**, and click **Cost**.

   Project displays the Cost table. Note the current cost of Jan's assignment to this task: $174.00.

   In the Cost table you can see the tasks and each assignment's total cost. To see other assignment cost values such as actual cost or variance, scroll the table to the right.

Task Name	Fixed Cost	Fixed Cost Accrual	Total Cost	Details	T	W	T	F	S	May 25, '08 S	M	T	W	T
27	⊟ Scene 7 shoot	$0.00	Prorated	$1,870.00	Work			68h	68h						
	16-mm Came.			$180.00	Work			12h	12h						
	500-Watt Ligt.			$40.00	Work			8h	8h						
	Camera Boon			$0.00	Work			4h	4h						
	Frank Lee			$136.00	Work			4h	4h						
	Jan Miksovsk			$174.00	Work			4h	4h						
	Jo Brown			$174.00	Work			4h	4h						
	Joseph Matth.			$150.00	Work			4h	4h						
	Joshua Rand.			$128.00	Work			4h	4h						
	Keith Harris			$136.00	Work			4h	4h						
	Megan Sherm			$168.00	Work			4h	4h						
	Scott Cooper			$176.00	Work			4h	4h						
	Sue Jackson			$120.00	Work			4h	4h						
	Ted Bremer			$144.00	Work			4h	4h						
	Tim O'Brien			$144.00	Work			4h	4h						
28	⊟ Scene 7 teardown	$0.00	Prorated	$502.00	Work			10h				10h			
	Electrician			$112.00	Work			2h				2h			
	Jo Brown			$174.00	Work			4h				4h			

Assignment
Information

3. In the **Task Name** column, select **Jan Miksovsky**, the fifth resource assigned to task 27.

4. On the **Standard** toolbar, click **Assignment Information**.

   The Assignment Information dialog box appears.

5. Click the **General** tab if it is not already selected.

6. In the **Cost Rate Table** box, type or select **B**, and then click **OK** to close the Assignment Information dialog box.

Project applies Jan's cost rate table B to the assignment. The new cost of the assignment, $112.00, appears in the Total Cost column. Because Jan's cost change also affected the total cost of the task, Project applied change highlighting to the Total Cost value, $1,808, of task 27.

	Task Name	Fixed Cost	Fixed Cost Accrual	Total Cost	Details	T	W	T	F	S	May 25, '08 S	M	T	W	T
27	⊟ Scene 7 shoot	$0.00	Prorated	$1,808.00	Work			68h	68h						
	16-mm Came.			$180.00	Work			12h	12h						
	500-Watt Ligt			$40.00	Work			8h	8h						
	Camera Boon			$0.00	Work			4h	4h						
	Frank Lee			$136.00	Work			4h	4h						
	Jan Miksovsk			$112.00	Work			4h	4h						
	Jo Brown			$174.00	Work			4h	4h						
	Joseph Matth			$150.00	Work			4h	4h						
	Joshua Rand.			$128.00	Work			4h	4h						
	Keith Harris			$136.00	Work			4h	4h						
	Mégan Sherm			$168.00	Work			4h	4h						
	Scott Cooper			$176.00	Work			4h	4h						
	Sue Jackson			$120.00	Work			4h	4h						
	Ted Bremer			$144.00	Work			4h	4h						
	Tim O'Brien			$144.00	Work			4h	4h						
28	⊟ Scene 7 teardown	$0.00	Prorated	$502.00	Work				10h			10h			
	Electrician			$112.00	Work				2h			2h			
	Jo Brown			$174.00	Work				4h			4h			

Tip If you frequently change cost rate tables for assignments, you will find it quicker to display the *Cost Rate Table* field directly in the Resource Usage or Task Usage view. Select a column heading and, on the Insert menu, click Column. In the Field Name box, select Cost Rate Table on the drop-down list, and then click OK.

Entering Material Resource Consumption Rates

The short film project includes one material resource: 16-mm film. If you completed Chapter 4, "Assigning Resources to Tasks," you assigned a material resource with a fixed amount, or *fixed consumption rate*, to a task. Another way to use material resources is to assign them with a *variable consumption rate*. The difference between the two rates is as follows:

- A fixed consumption rate means that, regardless of the duration of the task to which the material resource is assigned, an absolute quantity of the resource will be used. For example, pouring concrete for a house foundation requires a fixed amount of concrete no matter how long it takes to pour it.

- A variable consumption rate means that the quantity of the material resource consumed depends on the duration of the task. When shooting film, for example, you can shoot more film in four hours than in two, and you can determine an hourly rate at which you shoot (or consume) film. After you enter a variable consumption rate for a material resource's assignment, Project calculates the total quantity of the material resource consumed based on the task's duration. The advantage of using a variable rate of consumption is that the rate is tied to the task's duration. If the duration changes, the calculated quantity and cost of the material resource will change as well.

In either case, after you enter a standard pay rate for one unit of the material resource, Project calculates the total cost of the assignment. For example, we will assume that a 100-foot spool of 16-mm film costs $25 to purchase and process.

In this exercise, you enter an hourly variable consumption rate for a task that requires shooting (or consuming) film. You then look at the resulting quantity or number of units of film required by the duration of the task, as well as the cost of the material resource assignment.

1. On the **View** menu, click **Gantt Chart**.

   The Gantt Chart view appears.

2. Task 27 should be selected. If it not, click **Go To** on the **Edit** menu and enter 27 in the **ID** box, and then click **OK**.

   Task 27, *Scene 7 shoot*, is the first of several tasks that require film to be shot. Next, you will assign the material resource 16-mm Film to this task.

Assign Resources

3. On the **Standard** toolbar, click the **Assign Resources** button.

   The Assign Resources dialog box appears.

4. In the *Units* field for 16-mm Film in the **Assign Resources** dialog box, type 5/h and then press [Enter].

Important Be sure to select 16-mm Film and not 16-mm Camera in the Assign Resources dialog box.

Project assigns the film to the task at a consumption rate of five 100-foot spools per hour.

Because this task currently has a one-day duration, the total film assignment should be 40 spools of film (that is five spools per hour times eight hours). You can see the resulting cost—$1,000—directly in the Assign Resources dialog box. To verify the total number of spools required for this task, you will view the work values of the 16-mm Film assignment to task 27 via the Task Form.

5. On the **Window** menu, click **Split**.

   The Task Form appears.

In the Work column of the Task Form, you can see that the 16-mm Film assignment to task 27 is indeed 40 100-foot spools of film. The calculated cost of the assignment, $1,000 (which you also saw in the Assign Resources dialog box), is the 40 units of this material resource for this assignment multiplied by the $25 per-unit cost entered for this material resource. (This value is recorded in the Std. Rate field for the resource.) Should the duration of the task change, the number of units of film consumed and its total cost would change correspondingly.

6. On the **Window** menu, click **Remove Split** to close the Task Form.

7. In the Assign Resources dialog box, click **Close**.

CLOSE the Short Film Project 8 file.

Key Points

- When working with resource costs, you can specify different cost rates for different assignments and apply different cost rates at different times.

- You can account for variable resource availability over time (via a resource's Max. Units value), which allows you to more finely control when a resource will appear to be overallocated.

- In a usage view, you can edit the scheduled work values of resource assignments over time. For example, you can delay the start of one resource on an assignment without affecting the other resources assigned to the same task.

- When assigned to a task, material resources can have a fixed or variable consumption rate.

Chapter at a Glance

View work assignments per day or other time period, page 193

Edit resource assignments to manually resolve overallocations, page 199

Use resource leveling to resolve resource overallocation problems throughout a project plan, page 205

Check a project's cost and duration statistics, page 212

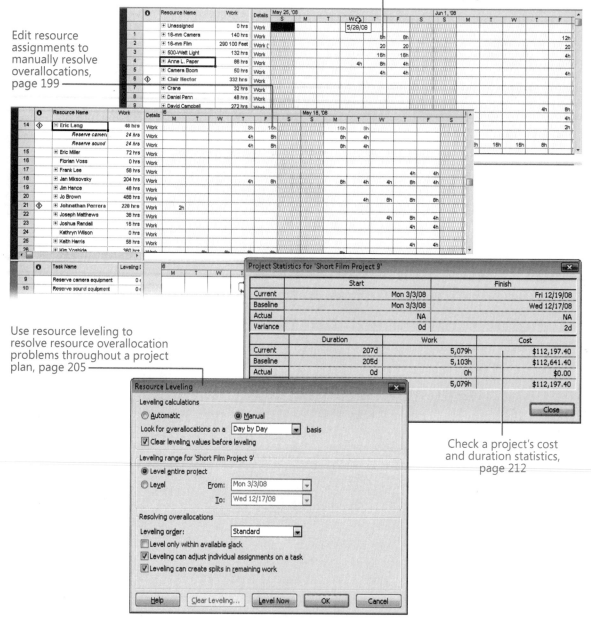

9 Fine-Tuning the Project Plan

In this chapter, you will learn how to:

✔ Look at how resources are scheduled to work over the duration of a project.

✔ Edit a resource assignment to resolve a resource overallocation.

✔ Resolve resource overallocations automatically.

✔ See detailed and overall project costs.

✔ See tasks on the critical path that determines a project's finish date.

> **Tip** Do you need only a quick refresher on the topics in this chapter? See the Quick Reference entries on pages xxv-xlviii.

In the previous two chapters, you have focused on details about tasks, resources, and assignments. Now, you will examine the results of your previous work on the schedule and dive deeper into resource assignments. You'll also observe the overall project duration and cost, as well as the sequence of tasks that determine its finish date.

> **Important** Before you can use the practice files provided for this chapter, you need to install them from the book's companion CD to their default locations. See "Using the Book's CD" on page xix for more information.

Examining Resource Allocations over Time

In this exercise, you will focus on resource allocation—how the task assignments you've made affect the workloads of the work resources (people and equipment) of a project. The relationship between a resource's capacity and his or her task assignments is called *allocation*. Each work resource is in one of three states of allocation:

● *Underallocated* The resource's assignments do not fill the resource's maximum capacity. For example, a full-time resource who has only 25 hours of work assigned in a 40-hour work week is underallocated.

- *Fully allocated* The resource's assignments fill the resource's maximum capacity. For example, a full-time resource who has 40 hours of work assigned in a 40-hour work week is fully allocated.

- *Overallocated* The resource's assignments exceed the resource's maximum capacity. For example, a full-time resource who has 65 hours of work assigned in a 40-hour work week is overallocated.

In Microsoft Office Project 2007, a resource's capacity to work is measured in units; the maximum capacity of a given resource is called *maximum units*. Units are measured either as numbers (such as three units) or as a percentage (such as 300% units).

> **Important** Concerning the scheduling engine in Project, cost and material resources do not do work; therefore, their assignments do not affect the overall duration of a project (although both cost and material resources can of course affect the overall cost of a project). When we focus on resource allocation, we mean work resources: people and equipment that do the work of a project.

Project Management Focus: Evaluating Resource Allocation

It is tempting to say that fully allocating all resources on every occasion is every project manager's goal, but that would be an oversimplification. Depending on the nature of your project and the resources working on it, some underallocations might be perfectly fine. Overallocation might not always be a problem either depending on the amount of overallocation. If one resource is overallocated for just one-half hour, Project will flag the overallocation, but such a minor overallocation might not be a problem you need to solve depending on the resource involved and the nature of the assignment. Severe overallocation—for example, a resource being assigned twice the work he or she could possibly accomplish in one day—is always a problem, however, and you should know how to identify it and maintain strategies for addressing it. This chapter helps you identify and remedy resource overallocation.

In this exercise, you look at resource allocations and focus on two resources who are overallocated.

> **BE SURE TO** start Microsoft Office Project 2007 if it's not already running.

> **Important** If you are running Project Professional, you may need to make a one-time adjustment to use the Computer account and to work offline. This ensures that the practice files you work with in this chapter do not affect your Project Server data. For more information, see "Starting Project Professional" on page 11.

> **OPEN** Short Film Project 9a from the *Documents**Microsoft Press**Project 2007 SBS*\ *Chapter 9 Advanced Plan* folder. You can also access the practice files for this book by clicking Start, All Programs, Microsoft Press, Project 2007 Step by Step, and then selecting the chapter folder of the file you want to open.

1. On the **File** menu, click **Save As**.

   The Save As dialog box appears.

2. In the **File name** box, type Short Film Project 9, and then click **Save**.

3. On the **View** menu, click **More Views**, click **Resource Allocation**, and then click the **Apply** button.

   The Resource Allocation view appears. This is a split view, with the Resource Usage view on top and the Leveling Gantt Chart view on the bottom.

On the left side of the Resource Usage view is a table (the Usage table, by default) that shows assignments grouped per resource, the total work assigned to each resource, and each assignment's work. This information is organized into an *outline* that you can expand or collapse.

The right side of the view contains assignment details (work, by default) arranged on a timescale. You can scroll the timescale horizontally to see different time periods. You can also change the tiers on the timescale to display data in units of weeks, days, hours, and so on.

The bottom pane shows the Leveling Gantt Chart view only for whatever resource or assignment (single or multiple) is selected in the upper pane.

Scroll to Task

4. On the **Standard** toolbar, click the **Scroll To Task** button.

   Project scrolls the right side of the view to show some assignment details.

   Next, you will collapse the outline in the table to see total work per resource over time.

5. Click the **Resource Name** column heading.

6. On the **Project** menu, point to **Outline** and then click **Hide Assignments**.

Hide
Assignments

> **Tip** You can also press ⌐Alt⌐+⌐Shift⌐+ ➖ or click the **Hide Assignments** button on the Formatting toolbar.

Project collapses the outline (assignments per resource) in the Resource Usage view. Resource assignments are hidden in the Usage table, and the resources' total work values over time appear in the timescaled grid on the right.

> **Tip** Notice the name of the first resource, Unassigned. This resource lists all tasks to which no specific resources are assigned.

Next, you will look at two work resources and their allocations.

7. In the **Resource Name** column, click the name of resource 4, **Anne L. Paper**.

8. On the **Standard** toolbar, click **Scroll To Task**.

Project scrolls the timescaled grid to show Anne L. Paper's earliest assignment on Wednesday.

9. Point to the **W** column heading (for Wednesday) at the top of the timescaled grid.

In any timescaled view, you can get details about dates by hovering your mouse pointer over the timescale.

A ScreenTip appears with the date of the assignment: 5/28/08. Such ScreenTips are handy in any timescaled view, such as the Resource Usage view or the Gantt Chart view.

Currently, the timescale is set to display weeks in the middle tier and days in the bottom tier. You will now change the timescale to see the work data summarized more broadly.

10. On the **Format** menu, click **Timescale**.

> **Tip** You can also double-click or right-click on the timescale and select Timescale from the shortcut menu.

The Timescale dialog box appears.

The timescale can display up to three tiers, typically in descending order of detail, such as years, months, and days. However, the top tier is disabled by default.

11. Make sure that the **Middle Tier** tab is selected, and in the **Units** box under **Middle tier formatting**, click **Months**.

12. In the **Show** box under **Timescale options**, click **One tier (Middle)**.

Timescale
Top Tier	**Middle Tier**	**Bottom Tier**	**Non-working time**

Middle tier formatting

Units: Months   Label: January   ☑ Use fiscal year

Count: 1   Align: Left   ☑ Tick lines

Timescale options

Show: One tier (Middle)   Size: 100 %   ☑ Scale separator

Preview

March	April	May	June	July	August	September	October	November

Help   OK   Cancel

13. Click **OK** to close the Timescale dialog box.

Project changes the timescaled grid to show work values per month.

	0	Resource Name	Work	Details	March	April	May	June	July	August	September	October	November	December	January	Febr
		Unassigned	0 hrs	Work												
1		16-mm Camera	140 hrs	Work			40h	56h	44h							
2		16-mm Film	290 100 Feet	Work (			80	120	90							
3		500-Watt Light	132 hrs	Work			48h	48h	36h							
4		Anne L. Paper	86 hrs	Work			16h	32h	38h							
5		Camera Boom	50 hrs	Work			16h	24h	10h							
6	⬦	Clair Hector	332 hrs	Work	32h	24h	68h				162h	46h				
7		Crane	32 hrs	Work				16h	16h							
8		Daniel Penn	48 hrs	Work				16h	32h							
9		David Campbell	272 hrs	Work			48h	56h		82h	14h	72h				
10		Dolly	56 hrs	Work			8h	24h	24h							
11		Doug Hampton	123 hrs	Work			24h	16h	31h					9h	43h	
12		Editing Lab	200 hrs	Work						72h	42h	78h			8h	
13		Electrician	104 hrs	Work			20h	84h								
14	⬦	Eric Lang	48 hrs	Work			49h									

As you can see in the timescaled grid, Anne L. Paper is underallocated in each of the three months in which she has assignments in the project: May, June, and July. Anne is one of the actors assigned to the scenes in which her character is needed, so this underallocation is really not a problem you need to address.

Notice that the names of Clair Hector and other resources appear in red. The red formatting means that these resources are overallocated: at one or more points in the schedule, their assigned tasks exceed their capacity to work. In the timescaled grid notice that Clair's 68 hours in May is formatted in red. Even though 68 hours within a month isn't an overallocation, at some point in May (perhaps even for just one day) Clair is scheduled to work more hours than she can accommodate.

You will focus in on Clair Hector first by changing the timescale settings.

14. On the **Edit** menu, click **Undo Timescale Edit**.

Undo

> **Tip** You can also press Ctrl+Z, or click the Undo button on the Standard toolbar.

Project resets the timescale back to its previous setting.

15. In the **Resource Name** column, click the name of resource 6, **Clair Hector**.

16. On the **Standard** toolbar, click **Scroll To Task**.

Project scrolls the timescaled grid to show Clair Hector's earliest assignments. It appears that Clair has no overallocations.

17. Click the **plus sign** next to Clair Hector's name in the **Resource Name** column.

Project expands the Resource Usage view to show Clair Hector's individual assignments.

18. Scroll the Resource Usage view to the right to see both of Clair's assignments on **Monday, May 5**. Use the horizontal scroll bar at the bottom of the Project window.

Clair's total work that Monday, 10 hours, is formatted red, indicating the overallocation. Clair has two assignments on May 5: the two-hour task *Staff planning meeting 9* (one instance of a *recurring task*) and the eight-hour task *Select locations*.
If necessary, drag the horizontal divider bar down to show more of the Resource
Usage view.

These two assignments make up the 10
hours of work scheduled for Monday.

These two tasks have been scheduled at times that overlap between the hours of
8 A.M. and 10 A.M. (If you want to observe this, format the timescale to display
days in the middle tier and hours in the bottom tier.) This is a real overallocation:
Clair probably cannot complete both tasks simultaneously. However, it is a relatively minor overallocation given the scope of the project, and you don't need to
be too concerned about resolving this level of overallocation. However, there are
other, more serious overallocations in the schedule that you will remedy later in this
chapter.

Here are a few other things to keep in mind when viewing resource allocation:

- By default, the Resource Usage view displays the Usage table; however, you can display different tables. On the View menu, click Table: Usage, and then click the table
  you want displayed.

- By default, the Resource Usage view displays work values in the timescaled grid.
  However, you can display additional assignment values, such as cost and remaining availability. On the Format menu, point to Details, and then click the value you
  want displayed. To add to or customize the appearance of fields displayed in the
  Resource Usage view, click Detail Styles on the Format menu.

● Instead of using the Timescale command on the Format menu to change the tiers of the timescale, you can click the Zoom In and Zoom Out buttons on the Standard toolbar. However, this method might not produce the exact level of detail you want. If it does not, use the Timescale command on the Format menu.

● To see allocations for each resource graphed against a timescale, you can display the Resource Graph view by clicking the Resource Graph command on the View menu. Use the arrow keys or horizontal scroll bar to switch between resources in this view.

● The Resource Management toolbar contains a handy collection of buttons when you're looking at allocation issues, leveling resources, or performing other common activities that relate to resources. This toolbar is hidden by default. To display it, on the View menu, point to Toolbars and then click Resource Management.

Manually Resolving Resource Overallocations

In this exercise and the next, you will continue to focus on resource allocation—how the task assignments you have made affect the workloads of the work resources (people and equipment) of the project. In this exercise, you will manually edit an assignment to resolve a resource overallocation. In the next exercise, you will automatically resolve re-source overallocations.

Manually editing an assignment is just one way to resolve a resource overallocation. Other solutions include the following:

● Replace the overallocated resource with another resource using the Replace button in the Assign Resources dialog box.

● Reduce the value in the Units field in the Assignment Information or Assign Resources dialog box.

● Assign an additional resource to the task so that both resources share the work.

If the overallocation is not too severe (such as assigning 10 hours of work in a normal eight-hour workday), you can often leave the overallocation in the schedule.

In this exercise, you will use the Resource Allocation view to examine one overallocated resource's assignments and edit the assignment to eliminate the overallocation.

1. In the Resource Usage view in the upper pane, scroll vertically through the **Resource Name** column.

Note that several names appear in red. These are overallocated resources.

2. In the **Resource Name** column, click the **plus sign** next to the name of resource 14, Eric Lang, to display his assignments.

3. On the **Standard** toolbar, click **Scroll To Task**.

Scroll to Task

Even though this resource's assignments on these days don't exceed his daily work capacity, they have been scheduled at times that overlap, resulting in an hour-by-hour overallocation.

	❶	Resource Name	Work	Details														
14	◈	– Eric Lang	48 hrs	Work					8h	16h			16h	8h				
		Reserve camera	24 hrs	Work					4h	8h			8h	4h				
		Reserve sound	24 hrs	Work					4h	8h			8h	4h				
15		+ Eric Miller	72 hrs	Work														
16		Florian Voss	0 hrs	Work														
17		+ Frank Lee	58 hrs	Work												4h	4h	
18		+ Jan Miksovsky	204 hrs	Work					4h	8h			8h	4h	4h	8h	4h	
19		+ Jim Hance	48 hrs	Work														
20		+ Jo Brown	488 hrs	Work									4h	8h	8h	8h		
21	◈	+ Johnathen Perrera	228 hrs	Work	2h													
22		+ Joseph Matthews	38 hrs	Work											4h	8h	4h	
23		+ Joshua Randall	16 hrs	Work											4h	4h		
24		Kathryn Wilson	0 hrs	Work														
25		+ Keith Harris	58 hrs	Work											4h	4h		
26		+ Kim Yoshida	360 hrs	Work		8h	8h	8h				8h						

	❶	Task Name	Leveling D									May 18, '08						
9		Reserve camera equipment	0 d										Jan Miksovsky,Eric Lang					

In the upper pane, you see that Eric is assigned full-time to two tasks that both start on Thursday, May 15. He is overallocated for the duration of both tasks. In the lower pane, you see the Gantt bars for the specific tasks that have caused Eric to be overallocated on these days. For tasks 9 and 10, Eric is assigned eight hours of work on each task Friday and Monday. This results in 16 hours of work per day, which is beyond Eric's capacity to work.

You might also notice that Eric is assigned a total of eight hours of work on Thursday and then again on the following Tuesday. These values also appear in red, indicating that Eric is overallocated on those days as well. This is because the two tasks are scheduled to start at the same time on Thursday and end at the same time on Tuesday. Thus, even though Eric has a total of eight hours of work assigned on Thursday and Tuesday, he really has two four-hour assignments in parallel. This is an overallocation.

Next, you will manually resolve this overallocation by reducing the assignment units value.

4. In the **Resource Name** column, click Eric's first assignment, **Reserve camera equipment**.

Assignment Information

5. On the **Standard** toolbar, click the **Assignment Information** button.

The Assignment Information dialog box appears.

6. Click the **General** tab if it is not already visible.

7. In the **Units** box, type or click 50%, and then click **OK** to close the Assignment Information dialog box.

Eric's daily work assignments on this task are reduced to two or four hours per day, but the task duration increased. You'd like to reduce the work but not extend the duration of the task. Note the Smart Tag indicator that appears next to the name of the assignment. You will use the Smart Tag to change the scheduling effect of the new assignment units.

Smart Tag Actions

8. Click the **Smart Tag Actions** button.

Look over the options on the list that appears.

9. On the Smart Tag Actions list, click **Change the task's total work (person-hours) to match the units and duration**.

Project reduces Eric's work assignments on the task and restores the task to its original duration.

However, Eric is still overallocated. To remedy this, you will reduce his assignment units on the second task.

10. In the **Resource Name** column, click Eric's second assignment, **Reserve sound equipment**.

11. On the **Standard** toolbar, click **Assignment Information**.

   The Assignment Information dialog box appears.

12. Click the **General** tab if it is not already visible.

13. In the **Units** box, type or click 50%, and then click **OK** to close the Assignment Information dialog box.

14. Click **Smart Tag Actions**.

15. On the Smart Tag Actions list, click **Change the task's total work (person-hours) to match the units and duration**.

Eric's total assignments on Friday and Monday are now reduced to eight hours each day. He is fully allocated on these days. By manually editing Eric's assignments to reduce his work on these days, you have resolved his overallocation. However, the manner in which you resolved Eric's overallocation was not the most direct method. You could also have edited his assignment values for Friday and Monday directly in the timescaled grid from eight to four hours each. The end result would have been the same.

Eric's overallocation on tasks 9 and 10 is a good example of the type of problem automatic leveling (described in the following section) cannot resolve. Automatic leveling can do many things to a schedule, but it cannot change resource assignment units as you did here or change assignment work. You should apply your best judgment to determine where automatic leveling can help and where you may need to manually adjust the schedule to resolve overallocations.

Next, you will look at other resource overallocations in the short film project that you can resolve automatically with resource leveling.

Leveling Overallocated Resources

In the previous section, you read about resource allocation, discovered what causes overallocation, and manually resolved an overallocation. *Resource leveling* is the process of delaying or splitting a resource's work on a task to resolve an overallocation. The options in the Level Resources dialog box enable you to set parameters concerning how you want Project to resolve resource overallocations. Project will attempt to resolve such overallocations when you choose to level resources. Depending on the options you choose, this might involve delaying the start date of an assignment or task or splitting the work on the task.

> **Important** Although the effects of resource leveling on a schedule might be significant, resource leveling never changes who is assigned to tasks nor the total work or assignment unit values of those assignments.

For example, consider the following tasks, all of which have the same full-time resource assigned.

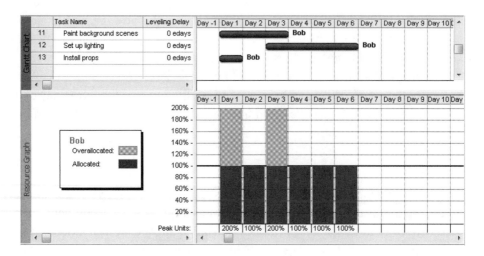

In this split view, the Resource Graph view appears below the Gantt Chart view. On day 1, the resource is overallocated at 200%. On day 2, the resource is fully allocated at 100%. On day 3, he is again overallocated at 200%. After day 3, the resource is fully allocated at 100%.

When you perform resource leveling, Project delays the start dates of the second and third tasks so that the resource is not overallocated.

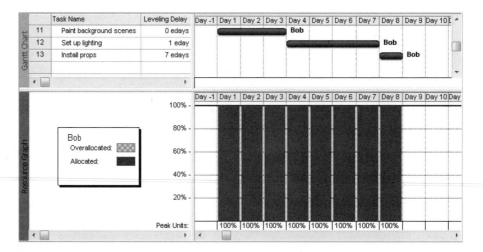

Note that the finish date of the latest task has moved from day 6 to day 8. This is common with resource leveling, which often pushes out the project finish date. There was a total of eight days of work before leveling, but two of those days overlapped, causing the resource to be overallocated on those days. After leveling, all eight days of work are still there, but the resource is no longer overallocated.

Resource leveling is a powerful tool, but it accomplishes only a few basic things: it delays tasks, splits tasks, and delays resource assignments. It does this following a fairly complex set of rules and options that you specify in the Resource Leveling dialog box. (These options are explained in the following exercise.) Resource leveling is a great fine-tuning tool, but it cannot replace your good judgment about resource availability, task durations, relationships, and constraints. Resource leveling will work with all of this information as it is entered into your project plan, but it might not be possible to fully resolve all resource overallocations within the time frame desired unless you change some of the basic task and resource values in the project plan.

> **Tip** To learn more about resource leveling, type Level resource assignments into the Search box in the upper right corner of the Project window.

In this exercise, you level resources and view the effects on assignments and the project finish date.

1. On the **Window** menu, click **Remove Split**.

2. On the **View** menu, click **Resource Sheet**.

   Overallocated

   The Resource Sheet view appears. Note that several resource names appear in red and display the Overallocated icon in the Indicators column.

> **Troubleshooting** If you do not see the Overallocated icon for any resources, try the following: On the Tools menu, click Level Resources. In the Resource Leveling dialog box, make sure that Day By Day is selected in the Look for overallocations on a ... basis box and then click OK.

3. On the **Tools** menu, click **Level Resources**.

   The Resource Leveling dialog box appears. In the next several steps, you will walk through the options in this dialog box.

4. Under **Leveling calculations**, make sure that **Manual** is selected.

   These settings determine whether Project levels resources constantly (Automatic) or only when you tell it to (Manual). Automatic leveling occurs as soon as a resource becomes overallocated.

> **Tip** All settings in the Resource Leveling dialog box apply to all project plans that you work with in Project, not only to the active project plan. Using automatic leveling might sound tempting, but it will cause frequent adjustments to project plans whether you want them or not. For that reason, we recommend you keep this setting on Manual.

5. In the **Look for overallocations on a … basis** box, make sure that **Day by Day** is selected.

   This setting determines the time frame in which Project will look for overalloca-tions. If a resource is overallocated, its name will be formatted in red. If it's over-allocated at the level you choose here, Project will also show the Overallocated indicator next to its name.

> **Tip** On most projects, leveling in finer detail than day by day can result in unrealistically precise adjustments to assignments. If you prefer not to see overallocation indicators for day-by-day overallocations, select Week by Week in the Look for overallocations on a … basis and then click OK. Doing so will not level resources, but it will determine when Project displays overallocation indicators next to resource names.

6. Make sure that the **Clear leveling values before leveling** check box is selected.

   Sometimes you will need to level resources repeatedly to obtain the results you want. For example, you might initially attempt to level week by week and then switch to day by day. If the Clear Leveling Values Before Leveling check box is se-lected, Project removes any existing leveling delays from all tasks and assignments before leveling. For example, if you previously leveled the project plan and then added more assignments, you might clear this check box before leveling again so that you wouldn't lose the previous leveling results.

7. Under **Leveling range for 'Short Film Project 9'**, make sure that **Level entire proj-ect** is selected.

   Here you choose to level either the entire project or only those assignments that fall within a date range you specify. Leveling within a date range is most useful af-ter you have started tracking actual work and you want to level only the remaining assignments in a project.

8. In the **Leveling order** box, make sure that **Standard** is selected.

   You control the priority Project uses to determine which tasks it should delay to resolve a resource conflict. The ID Only option delays tasks only according to their ID numbers: numerically higher ID numbers (for example, 10) will be delayed be-fore numerically lower ID numbers (for example, 5). You might want to use this op-tion when your project plan has no task relationships or constraints. The Standard option delays tasks according to predecessor relationships, start dates, task con-straints, *slack*, priority, and IDs. The Priority, Standard option looks at the task priority value before the other standard criteria. (*Task priority* is a numeric ranking between 0 and 1000 that indicates the task's appropriateness for leveling. Tasks with the lowest priority are delayed or split first.)

9. Make sure that the **Level only within available slack** check box is cleared.

> **Tip** Remember that to clear a check box means to remove a check from the check box and to select a check box means to put a check in it. You toggle the selection state of a check box by clicking it.

Clearing this check box allows Project to extend the project's finish date, if necessary, to resolve resource allocations.

Selecting this check box would prevent Project from extending the project's finish date to resolve resource overallocations. Instead, Project would use only the free slack within the existing schedule. Depending on the project, this might not be adequate to fully resolve resource overallocations.

10. Make sure that the **Leveling can adjust individual assignments on a task** check box is selected.

This allows Project to add leveling delay (or split work on assignments if Leveling Can Create Splits In Remaining Work is also selected) independently of any other resources assigned to the same task. This might cause resources to start and finish work on a task at different times.

11. Make sure that the **Leveling can create splits in remaining work** check box is selected.

This allows Project to split work on a task (or on an assignment if Leveling Can Adjust Individual Assignments On A Task is also selected) as a way of resolving an overallocation.

> **Tip** This tip describes enterprise project management (EPM) functionality. If you are running Project Professional, you will see an additional check box, Level Resources With The Proposed Booking Type. Leave this check box cleared. **For more information about Project Server, see Part 4, "Introducing Project Server."**

12. Click the **Level Now** button.

13. Project asks whether you want to level the entire pool or only selected resources. Leave **Entire Pool** selected, and click **OK**.

Project levels the overallocated resources.

	ⓘ	Resource Name	Type	Material Label	Initials	Group	Max. Units	Std. Rate	Ovt. Rate	Cost/Use	Accrue At	Base Calendar	Code
1		16-mm Camera	Work		16mm	Equipment	300%	$300.00/wk	$0.00/hr	$0.00	Start	Standard	
2		16-mm Film	Material	100 Feet	Film	Film and Lab		$25.00		$0.00	Prorated		
3		500-Watt Light	Work		500WL	Equipment	400%	$100.00/wk	$0.00/hr	$0.00	Prorated	Standard	
4		Anne L. Paper	Work		AP	Talent	100%	$150.00/day	$0.00/hr	$0.00	Prorated	Standard	
5		Camera Boom	Work		Boom	Equipment	200%	$0.00/hr	$0.00/hr	$0.00	Prorated	Standard	
6		Clair Hector	Work		CH	Production	100%	$900.00/wk	$0.00/hr	$0.00	Prorated	Standard	
7		Crane	Work		Crane	Equipment	100%	$0.00/hr	$0.00/hr	$0.00	Prorated	Standard	
8		Daniel Penn	Work		DP	Talent	100%	$150.00/day	$0.00/hr	$0.00	Prorated	Standard	
9		David Campbell	Work		DC	Talent	100%	$150.00/day	$0.00/hr	$0.00	Prorated	Standard	
10		Dolly	Work		Dolly	Equipment	200%	$0.00/hr	$0.00/hr	$0.00	Prorated	Standard	
11		Doug Hampton	Work		DH	Production	100%	$16.00/hr	$0.00/hr	$0.00	Prorated	Standard	
12		Editing Lab	Work		EL	Film and Lab	100%	$250.00/day	$0.00/hr	$25.00	Prorated	Standard	
13		Electrician	Work		EL	Crew	200%	$28.00/hr	$42.00/hr	$0.00	Prorated	Standard	
14		Eric Lang	Work		EL	Production	100%	$18.50/hr	$0.00/hr	$0.00	Prorated	Standard	
15		Eric Miller	Work		EM	Talent	100%	$150.00/day	$0.00/hr	$0.00	Prorated	Standard	
16		Florian Voss	Work		FV	Production	100%	$25.00/hr	$0.00/hr	$0.00	Prorated	Standard	
17		Frank Lee	Work		FL	Crew	100%	$17.00/hr	$25.50/hr	$0.00	Prorated	Standard	
18		Jan Miksovsky	Work		JM	Production	100%	$21.75/hr	$0.00/hr	$0.00	Prorated	Standard	
19		Jim Hance	Work		JH	Talent	100%	$75.00/day	$0.00/hr	$0.00	Prorated	Standard	
20		Jo Brown	Work		JB	Production	100%	$21.75/hr	$0.00/hr	$0.00	Prorated	Standard	
21		Johnathan Perrera	Work		JP	Production	100%	$25.00/hr	$0.00/hr	$0.00	Prorated	Standard	
22		Joseph Matthews	Work		JM	Talent	100%	$150.00/day	$0.00/hr	$0.00	Prorated	Standard	
23		Joshua Randall	Work		JR	Talent	100%	$16.00/hr	$24.00/hr	$0.00	Prorated	Standard	
24		Kathryn Wilson	Work		KW	Production	100%	$800.00/wk	$0.00/hr	$100.00	Prorated	Standard	
25		Keith Harris	Work		KH	Crew	100%	$17.00/hr	$25.50/hr	$0.00	Prorated	Standard	
26		Kim Yoshida	Work		KY	Production	100%	$16.40/hr	$0.00/hr	$0.00	Prorated	Standard	
27		Linda Kobara	Work		LK	Production	100%	$27.00/hr	$0.00/hr	$0.00	Prorated	Standard	
28		Lisa Garmaise	Work		LG	Production	100%	$16.00/hr	$0.00/hr	$0.00	Prorated	Standard	
29		Mark Hassall	Work		MH	Production	100%	##########	$0.00/hr	$0.00	Prorated	Standard	
30		Max Benson	Work		MB	Crew	100%	$27.00/hr	$0.00/hr	$0.00	Prorated	Standard	
31		Megan Sherman	Work		MS	Crew	100%	$21.00/hr	$0.00/hr	$0.00	Prorated	Standard	
32		Michael Patten	Work		MP	Production	100%	$820.00/wk	$0.00/hr	$0.00	Prorated	Standard	

Notice that the Overallocated indicators are gone.

> **Tip** When leveling resources with Day By Day selected, you might see the overallocation icons disappear while some resource names still appear in red. This means that some resources are still overallocated hour by hour (or minute by minute), but not day by day.

Next, you will look at the project plan before and after leveling by using the Leveling Gantt view.

14. On the **View** menu, click **More Views**, click **Leveling Gantt**, and then click **Apply**.

Project switches to the Leveling Gantt view.

15. Click the name of task 8, **Apply for filming permits**.

Scroll to Task

16. On the **Standard** toolbar, click **Scroll To Task**.

This view gives you a better look at some of the tasks that were affected by leveling.

	ⓘ	Task Name	Leveling I	May 4, '08	May 11, '08	May 18, '08	May 25, '08	Jun 1, '08	Jun 8, '08	Jun 15,
1		− Pre-Production	0 e							
2		Review script	0 (							
3		Develop script breakdo	0 (							
4		Develop production bo	0 (							
5		Scout locations	0 (	Jan Miksovsky,Max Benson,Travel[$1,000.00]						
6		Select locations	0 (	Scott Cooper,Clair Hector,Max Benson						
7		Hold auditions	0 (	Clair Hector,Scott Cooper,Doug Hampton[50%],Catering[$500.00]						
8		Apply for filming permit	0 (	Kim Yoshida						
9		Reserve camera equip	0 (	Jan Miksovsky,Eric Lang[50%]						
10		Reserve sound equipm	0 (	Eric Lang[50%]						
11		Pre-Production complet	0 (	◇ 5/22						
12	↻	+ Staff planning meeti	0 e							
23		− Production	0 e							
24		− Scene 7	0 e							
25		Scene 7 setup	0 (	Jo Brown,Max Benson,Electrician[50%]						
26		Scene 7 rehearsal	0 (	Scott Cooper,Jo Brown,Paul Borm[50%],Joseph Matthews,Sue						
27		Scene 7 shoot	0 (	Scott Cooper,Jo Brown,Joseph Matthews,Sue Jackson,Fran						
28		Scene 7 teardown	0 (	Jo Brown,Max Benson,Electrician[50%]						
29		Scene 7 prospect'd	0 (							

In the Leveling Gantt view, the bars on top represent the preleveled schedule of the task. The bar below represents the schedule after leveling.

Notice that each task now has two bars. The green bar on top represents the pre-leveled task. You can see a task's preleveled start, finish, and duration by pointing to a green bar. The blue bar on the bottom represents the leveled task.

Project was able to resolve the resource overallocations. For this particular project, leveling pushed out the project finish date by two days.

Examining Project Costs

Not all project plans include cost information, but for those that do, keeping track of project costs can be as important as or more important than keeping track of the scheduled finish date. Two factors to consider when examining project costs are the specific types of costs you want to see and how you can best see them.

The types of costs you might encounter over the life of a project include the following:

● **Baseline costs** The original planned task, resource, or assignment costs saved as part of a baseline plan.

● **Current (or scheduled) costs** The calculated costs of tasks, resources, and assignments in a project plan. As you make adjustments in a project plan, such as assigning or removing resources, Project recalculates current costs just as it recalculates task start and finish dates. After you start to incur actual costs (typically by tracking actual work), the current cost equals the actual cost plus remaining cost per task, resource, or assignment. Current costs are the values you see in fields labeled Cost or Total Cost.

- **Actual costs** The costs that have been incurred for tasks, resources, or assignments.

- **Remaining costs** The difference between the current or scheduled costs and the actual costs for tasks, resources, or assignments.

You might need to compare these costs (for example, baseline vs. actual) or examine them individually per task, resource, or assignment. Or you might need to examine cost values for summary tasks or for an entire project plan. Some common ways to view these types of costs include the following:

- You can see the entire project's current, baseline, actual, and remaining costs in the Project Statistics dialog box (on the Project menu, click Project Information, and then click Statistics).

- You can see or print formatted reports that include cash flow, budget, overbudget tasks or resources, and earned value (on the Report menu, click Reports or Visual Reports).

> **Tip** Earned value is a powerful schedule analysis tool that relies on cost information in a project plan. For more information, see Chapter 18, "Measuring Performance with Earned Value Analysis."

- You can see task-, resource-, or assignment-level cost information in usage views by displaying the Cost table (on the View menu, point to Table: Entry, and then click Cost).

> **Tip** When printing usage views, you can include cost totals. You can include row totals when printing date ranges from a usage view (on the File menu, click Page Setup, and in the Page Setup dialog box, click the View tab and select the Print Row Totals For Values Within Print Date Range check box). You can also include column totals in usage views (on the File menu, click Page Setup; in the Page Setup dialog box, click the View tab and select the Print Column Totals check box).

In this exercise, you look at the overall project costs and at individual task costs.

1. On the **View** menu, click **More Views**, click **Task Sheet**, and then click **Apply**.

   Project switches to the Task Sheet view. Next, you will display the project summary task to see the top-level or rolled-up values of the project.

2. On the **Tools** menu, click **Options**.

3. In the **Options** dialog box, click the **View** tab if it is not already visible.

4. Under the **Outline options for** label, select the **Show project summary task** check box, and then click **OK**.

   Project displays the project summary task at the top of the Task Sheet view. Next, you will switch to the Cost table.

> **Tip** Wonder where Project got this project summary task name? Project uses the title entered in the Properties dialog box (File menu) as the project summary task name. Or, if nobody has entered a distinct title property, Project uses the filename as the project summary task name. If you change the project summary task once you've displayed it, Project updates the Title property and vice versa.

5. On the **View** menu, point to **Table: Entry**, and click **Cost**.

   The Cost table appears.

6. If necessary, double-click the right edge of a column in the column heading to expand the column so that you can see the entire value.

	Task Name	Fixed Cost	Fixed Cost Accrual	Total Cost	Baseline	Variance	Actual	Remaining
0	**Short Film Project**	**$0.00**	Prorated	**$112,197.40**	**$112,641.40**	**($444.00)**	**$0.00**	**$112,197.40**
1	**Pre-Production**	**$0.00**	Prorated	**$28,528.00**	**$28,972.00**	**($444.00)**	**$0.00**	**$28,528.00**
2	Review script	$0.00	Prorated	$892.00	$892.00	$0.00	$0.00	$892.00
3	Develop script brea	$0.00	Prorated	$1,880.00	$1,880.00	$0.00	$0.00	$1,880.00
4	Develop production	$0.00	Prorated	$10,144.00	$10,144.00	$0.00	$0.00	$10,144.00
5	Scout locations	$0.00	Prorated	$6,640.00	$6,640.00	$0.00	$0.00	$6,640.00
6	Select locations	$0.00	Prorated	$2,860.00	$2,860.00	$0.00	$0.00	$2,860.00
7	Hold auditions	$0.00	Prorated	$2,600.00	$2,600.00	$0.00	$0.00	$2,600.00
8	Apply for filming pe	$500.00	Start	$1,156.00	$1,156.00	$0.00	$0.00	$1,156.00
9	Reserve camera ec	$0.00	Prorated	$744.00	$966.00	($222.00)	$0.00	$744.00
10	Reserve sound equ	$0.00	Prorated	$222.00	$444.00	($222.00)	$0.00	$222.00
11	Pre-Production com	$0.00	Prorated	$0.00	$0.00	$0.00	$0.00	$0.00
12	Staff planning me	**$0.00**	Prorated	**$1,390.00**	**$1,390.00**	**$0.00**	**$0.00**	**$1,390.00**
23	**Production**	**$0.00**	Prorated	**$47,007.00**	**$47,007.00**	**$0.00**	**$0.00**	**$47,007.00**
24	**Scene 7**	**$0.00**	Prorated	**$4,718.50**	**$4,718.50**	**$0.00**	**$0.00**	**$4,718.50**
25	Scene 7 setup	$0.00	Prorated	$502.00	$502.00	$0.00	$0.00	$502.00
26	Scene 7 rehear:	$0.00	Prorated	$906.50	$906.50	$0.00	$0.00	$906.50
27	Scene 7 shoot	$0.00	Prorated	$2,808.00	$2,808.00	$0.00	$0.00	$2,808.00
28	Scene 7 teardo	$0.00	Prorated	$502.00	$502.00	$0.00	$0.00	$502.00
29	Scene 7-proces:	$0.00	Prorated	$0.00	$0.00	$0.00	$0.00	$0.00
30	**Scene 3**	**$0.00**	Prorated	**$5,318.00**	**$5,318.00**	**$0.00**	**$0.00**	**$5,318.00**
31	Scene 3 setup	$0.00	Prorated	$614.00	$614.00	$0.00	$0.00	$614.00
32	Scene 3 rehear:	$0.00	Prorated	$1,049.00	$1,049.00	$0.00	$0.00	$1,049.00
33	Scene 3 shoot	$0.00	Prorated	$3,041.00	$3,041.00	$0.00	$0.00	$3,041.00
34	Scene 3 teardo	$0.00	Prorated	$614.00	$614.00	$0.00	$0.00	$614.00
35	Scene 3-proces:	$0.00	Prorated	$0.00	$0.00	$0.00	$0.00	$0.00
36	**Scene 1**	**$0.00**	Prorated	**$7,457.00**	**$7,457.00**	**$0.00**	**$0.00**	**$7,457.00**
37	Scene 1 setup	$0.00	Prorated	$2,514.00	$2,514.00	$0.00	$0.00	$2,514.00
38	Scene 1 rehear:	$0.00	Prorated	$1,056.50	$1,056.50	$0.00	$0.00	$1,056.50
39	Scene 1 shoot	$0.00	Prorated	$3,048.50	$3,048.50	$0.00	$0.00	$3,048.50
40	Scene 1 teardo	$0.00	Prorated	$838.00	$838.00	$0.00	$0.00	$838.00
41	Scene 1-proces:	$0.00	Prorated	$0.00	$0.00	$0.00	$0.00	$0.00

Ready

Here you can see many types of cost values for the overall project, project phases (summary tasks), and individual tasks. At this point in the project life cycle, the project plan includes a baseline; therefore, you see values in the Baseline column. Some assignment adjustments were made earlier in this chapter, so you see some values

in the Variance column; however, because it does not yet contain any actual progress, the Actual column contains only zero values.

Checking the Project's Finish Date

A project's finish date is a function of its duration and start date. Most projects have a
desired, or soft, finish date, and many projects have a "must hit," or hard, finish date.
When managing projects like these, it is essential that you know the project's current or
scheduled finish date and understand how the adjustments you make in the planning
stage affect the finish date.

In the language of project management, a project's finish date is determined by its *critical path*. The critical path is the series of tasks that will push out the project's end date
if the tasks are delayed. For this reason, when evaluating the duration of a project, you
should focus mainly on the tasks on the critical path, called critical tasks.

> **Tip** Remember that the word *critical* has nothing to do with how important these tasks are
> to the overall project. The word refers only to how their scheduling will affect the project's
> finish date.

In this exercise, you look at the project's finish date and critical path.

1. On the **Project** menu, click **Project Information**.

   The Project Information dialog box appears.

Project Information for 'Short Film Project 9'			
Start date:	Mon 3/3/08	Current date:	Mon 2/11/08
Finish date:	Fri 12/19/08	Status date:	NA
Schedule from:	Project Start Date	Calendar:	Standard
Help	Statistics...	OK	Cancel

> **Tip** This tip describes enterprise project management (EPM) functionality. If you are run-
> ning Project Professional, you will see a slightly different dialog box. The Project Information
> dialog box in Project Professional includes an Enterprise Custom Fields section. Enterprise
> custom fields are used only with Project Server. **For more information about Project
> Server, see Part 4, "Introducing Project Server."**

In the Project Information dialog box, you can see the current or scheduled finish
date for the project: December 19, 2008. Note that you can edit the start date of

the project here, but not its finish date. Project has calculated this finish date based on the start date plus the overall duration of the project. This project is scheduled from the start date, as the Schedule From box indicates. You might want to schedule a project from a finish date in some situations, in which case you enter the finish date and task information and Project calculates the start date.

> **Tip** It might sound tempting to schedule a project from a finish date, especially if it has a hard "must-hit" deadline. However, in nearly all cases, you should resist this temptation and instead schedule from a start date.

Next, you will look at the duration values for this project.

2. In the **Project Information** dialog box, click the **Statistics** button.

The Project Statistics dialog box appears.

Project Statistics for 'Short Film Project 9'

	Start	Finish
Current	Mon 3/3/08	Fri 12/19/08
Baseline	Mon 3/3/08	Wed 12/17/08
Actual	NA	NA
Variance	0d	2d

	Duration	Work	Cost
Current	207d	5,079h	$112,197.40
Baseline	205d	5,103h	$112,641.40
Actual	0d	0h	$0.00
Remaining	207d	5,079h	$112,197.40

Percent complete:

Duration: 0%   Work: 0%   Close

Here you can see the project's current, baseline, and actual start and finish dates, as well as its schedule variance.

This project currently has no actual work reported, so you see NA in the *Actual Start* and *Actual Finish* fields and zero values in the *Actual Duration* and *Actual Work* fields.

3. Click **Close** to close the Project Statistics dialog box. To conclude this exercise, you will look at the critical path.

4. On the **View** menu, click **More Views**, click **Detail Gantt,** and then click **Apply.**

The Detail Gantt view replaces the Task Sheet view.

5. On the **Edit** menu, click **Go To.**

6. In the **ID** box, type 42, and then click **OK.**

Project scrolls the view to show task 42, the *Scene 2 summary task.*

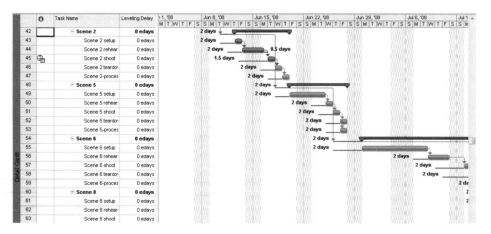

Here you can see both critical tasks (their Gantt bars are red) and noncritical tasks (blue). Any changes to the durations or timing of critical tasks will affect the project finish date. However, changes to the noncritical tasks won't necessarily affect the project finish date, depending on available slack. When you make adjustments to the project plan, and especially after you start tracking actual work, the specific tasks on the critical path are likely to change. For this reason, you should frequently check the project finish date and the critical tasks that determine it.

CLOSE the Short Film Project 9 file.

Key Points

- A work resource's maximum units (Max. Units) value determines when the resource becomes overallocated.

- The Resource Usage view enables you to view the details of assignments that cause resource overallocation.

- You can manually or automatically resolve resource overallocations.

- When editing a resource assignment value (such as assignment units), you can use a Smart Tag to change the scheduling effect of your action.

- You can view cost details from the individual assignment level all the way to the entire project level.

- The tasks on the critical path determine the project finish date.

Chapter at a Glance

Sort task or resource data, page 219

Group tasks or resources and show summary or "roll-up" values per grouping, page 226

Create custom filters to show just the data you want to see, page 227

Create your own view with the table, group and filter definitions you want, page 231

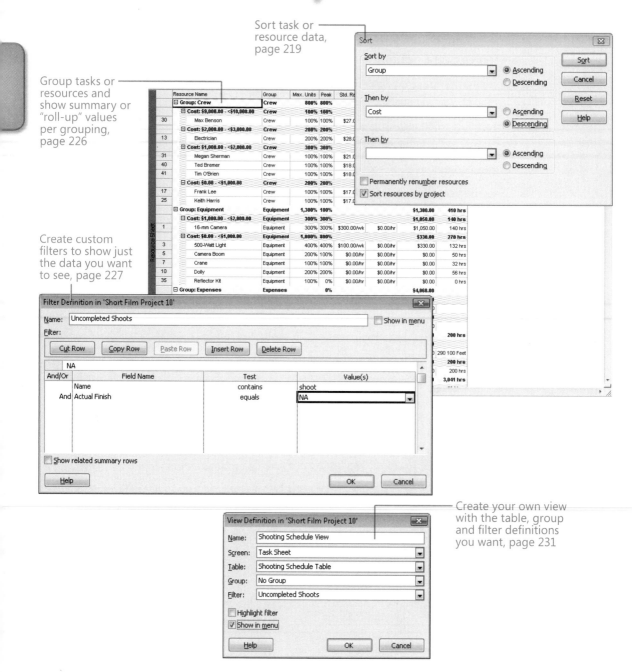

10 Organizing and Formatting Project Details

In this chapter, you will learn how to:

✔ Sort task and resource data.

✔ Display task and resource data in groups.

✔ Filter or highlight task and resource data.

✔ Create a custom table.

✔ Create a custom view.

> **Tip** Do you need only a quick refresher on the topics in this chapter? See the Quick Reference entries on pages xxv-xlviii.

After you've built a project plan, chances are you will need to examine specific aspects of the plan for your own analysis or to share with other *stakeholders*. Although the built-in views, tables, and reports in Microsoft Office Project 2007 provide many ways to examine a project plan, you might need to organize information to suit your own specific needs.

In this chapter, you use some of the formatting tools in Project to change the way your data appears. Project includes powerful features that enable you to organize and analyze data that otherwise would require separate tools, such as a spreadsheet application.

> **Important** Before you can use the practice files provided for this chapter, you need to install them from the book's companion CD to their default locations. See "Using the Book's CD" on page xix for more information.

Sorting Project Details

Sorting is the simplest way to reorganize task or resource data in Project. You can sort tasks or resources by predefined criteria, or you can create your own sort order with up to three levels of nesting. For example, you can sort resources by resource group (this is the value in the *Group field*—Crew, Equipment, and so on) and then sort by cost within each resource group.

Like grouping and filtering, which you will work with in later sections, sorting does not (with one exception) change the underlying data of your project plan; it simply reorders the data you have in the active view. The one exception is the option that Project offers to renumber task or resource IDs after sorting.

It's fine to permanently renumber tasks or resources if that's what you intend to do. For example, when building a resource list, you might enter resource names in the order in which the resources join your project. Later, when the list is complete, you might want to sort them alphabetically by name and permanently renumber them.

Each resource in the Short Film Project plan is assigned to one of several resource groups. These groups have names such as *Crew, Production, Talent,* and other names that pertain to a film production company. For your project plans, you might use resource groups to represent functional teams, departments, or whatever most logically describes collections of similar resources.

Sorting all resources by resource group enables you to see more easily the costs associated with each resource group. This can help you plan your project's budget. You can also sort resources within each group by cost from most to least expensive.

In this exercise, you sort a resource view.

BE SURE TO start Microsoft Office Project 2007 if it's not already running.

Important If you are running Project Professional, you may need to make a one-time adjustment to use the Computer account and to work offline. This ensures that the practice files you work with in this chapter do not affect your Project Server data. For more information, see "Starting Project Professional" on page 11.

> **OPEN** Short Film Project 10a from the *\Documents\Microsoft Press\Project 2007 SBS\ Chapter 10 Advanced Formatting* folder. You can also access the practice files for this book by clicking Start, All Programs, Microsoft Press, Project 2007 Step by Step, and then selecting the chapter folder of the file you want to open.

1. On the **File** menu, click **Save As**.

   The Save As dialog box appears.

2. In the **File name** box, type Short Film Project 10, and then click **Save**.

3. On the **View** menu, click **Resource Sheet**.

   The Resource Sheet view appears. By default, the Entry table appears in the Resource Sheet view; however, the Entry table does not display the cost field per resource. You will switch to the Summary table instead.

4. On the **View** menu, point to **Table: Entry**, and then click **Summary**.

   The Summary table appears.

	Resource Name	Group	Max. Units	Peak	Std. Rate	Ovt. Rate	Cost	Work
1	16-mm Camera	Equipment	300%	300%	$300.00/wk	$0.00/hr	$1,050.00	140 hrs
2	16-mm Film	Film and Lat			eet/hr	$25.00		$7,250.00 290 100 Feet
3	500-Watt Light	Equipment	400%	400%	$100.00/wk	$0.00/hr	$330.00	132 hrs
4	Anne L. Paper	Talent	100%	100%	$150.00/day	$0.00/hr	$1,812.50	86 hrs
5	Camera Boom	Equipment	200%	100%	$0.00/hr	$0.00/hr	$0.00	50 hrs
6	Clair Hector	Production	100%	100%	$900.00/wk	$0.00/hr	$7,470.00	332 hrs
7	Crane	Equipment	100%	100%	$0.00/hr	$0.00/hr	$0.00	32 hrs
8	Daniel Penn	Talent	100%	100%	$150.00/day	$0.00/hr	$900.00	48 hrs
9	David Campbell	Talent	100%	100%	$150.00/day	$0.00/hr	$5,100.00	272 hrs
10	Dolly	Equipment	200%	200%	$0.00/hr	$0.00/hr	$0.00	56 hrs
11	Doug Hampton	Production	100%	50%	$16.00/hr	$0.00/hr	$2,246.40	123 hrs
12	Editing Lab	Film and Lat	100%	100%	$250.00/day	$0.00/hr	$6,350.00	200 hrs
13	Electrician	Crew	200%	200%	$28.00/hr	$42.00/hr	$2,912.00	104 hrs
14	Eric Lang	Production	100%	100%	$18.50/hr	$0.00/hr	$444.00	24 hrs
15	Eric Miller	Talent	100%	100%	$150.00/day	$0.00/hr	$1,350.00	72 hrs
16	Florian Voss	Production	100%	0%	$25.00/hr	$0.00/hr	$0.00	0 hrs
17	Frank Lee	Crew	100%	100%	$17.00/hr	$25.50/hr	$986.00	58 hrs
18	Jan Miksovsky	Production	100%	100%	$21.75/hr	$0.00/hr	$4,375.00	204 hrs
19	Jim Hance	Talent	100%	100%	$75.00/day	$0.00/hr	$450.00	48 hrs
20	Jo Brown	Production	100%	100%	$21.75/hr	$0.00/hr	$10,614.00	488 hrs
21	Johnathan Perrera	Production	100%	100%	$25.00/hr	$0.00/hr	$5,500.00	220 hrs
22	Joseph Matthews	Talent	100%	100%	$150.00/day	$0.00/hr	$712.50	38 hrs
23	Joshua Randall	Talent	100%	100%	$16.00/hr	$24.00/hr	$256.00	16 hrs
24	Kathryn Wilson	Production	100%	0%	$800.00/wk	$0.00/hr	$0.00	0 hrs
25	Keith Harris	Crew	100%	100%	$17.00/hr	$25.50/hr	$986.00	58 hrs
26	Kim Yoshida	Production	100%	100%	$16.40/hr	$0.00/hr	$6,304.00	250 hrs

You are now ready to sort the Resource Sheet view.

5. On the **Project** menu, point to **Sort**, and click **Sort By**.

   The Sort dialog box appears.

6. Under **Sort By**, click **Cost** on the drop-down list, and next to that, click **Descending**.

7. Make sure that the **Permanently renumber resources** check box is cleared.

> **Important** The Permanently Renumber Resources (or, when in a task view, the Permanently Renumber Tasks) check box in the Sort dialog box is a Project-level (that is, application) setting; if selected, it permanently renumbers resources or tasks in any Project plan in which you sort. Because you might not want to permanently renumber resources or tasks every time you sort, it's a good idea to clear this check box.

8. Click the **Sort** button.

> **Tip** You can sort by any field, not just the fields visible in the active view. However, it's helpful to see the field by which you sort—in this case, the *Cost* field.

The Resource Sheet view is sorted by the Cost column in descending order.

The Resource Sheet view is now sorted
by cost, in descending order.

	Resource Name	Group	Max. Units	Peak	Std. Rate	Ovt. Rate	Cost	Work
38	Scott Cooper	Production	100%	100%	$880.00/wk	$0.00/hr	$11,748.00	534 hrs
20	Jo Brown	Production	100%	100%	$21.75/hr	$0.00/hr	$10,614.00	488 hrs
30	Max Benson	Crew	100%	100%	$27.00/hr	$0.00/hr	$9,720.00	360 hrs
6	Clair Hector	Production	100%	100%	$900.00/wk	$0.00/hr	$7,470.00	332 hrs
2	16-mm Film	Film and Lab		eet/hr	$25.00		$7,250.00	290 100 Feet
32	Michael Patten	Production	100%	100%	$820.00/wk	$0.00/hr	$7,216.00	352 hrs
12	Editing Lab	Film and Lab	100%	100%	$250.00/day	$0.00/hr	$6,350.00	200 hrs
26	Kim Yoshida	Production	100%	100%	$16.40/hr	$0.00/hr	$5,904.00	360 hrs
21	Johnathan Perrera	Production	100%	100%	$25.00/hr	$0.00/hr	$5,500.00	220 hrs
9	David Campbell	Talent	100%	100%	$150.00/day	$0.00/hr	$5,100.00	272 hrs
18	Jan Miksovsky	Production	100%	100%	$21.75/hr	$0.00/hr	$4,375.00	204 hrs
36	Richard Lum	Production	100%	100%	$740.00/wk	$0.00/hr	$3,700.00	200 hrs
43	Travel	Expenses		0%			$3,068.00	
13	Electrician	Crew	200%	200%	$28.00/hr	$42.00/hr	$2,912.00	104 hrs
28	Lisa Garmaise	Production	100%	100%	$16.00/hr	$0.00/hr	$2,560.00	160 hrs
11	Doug Hampton	Production	100%	50%	$16.00/hr	$0.00/hr	$2,246.40	123 hrs
4	Anne L. Paper	Talent	100%	100%	$150.00/day	$0.00/hr	$1,612.50	86 hrs
39	Sue Jackson	Talent	100%	100%	$120.00/day	$0.00/hr	$1,560.00	104 hrs
15	Eric Miller	Talent	100%	100%	$150.00/day	$0.00/hr	$1,350.00	72 hrs
34	Paul Borm	Production	50%	50%	$225.00/day	$0.00/hr	$1,125.00	40 hrs
1	16-mm Camera	Equipment	300%	300%	$300.00/wk	$0.00/hr	$1,050.00	140 hrs
31	Megan Sherman	Crew	100%	100%	$21.00/hr	$0.00/hr	$1,050.00	50 hrs
40	Ted Bremer	Crew	100%	100%	$18.00/hr	$27.00/hr	$1,044.00	58 hrs
41	Tim O'Brien	Crew	100%	100%	$18.00/hr	$27.00/hr	$1,008.00	56 hrs
42	Catering	Expenses		0%			$1,000.00	
17	Fran Lee	Crew	100%	100%	$12.20/hr	$25.50/hr	$806.00	58 hrs

This arrangement is fine for viewing resource costs in the entire project, but perhaps you'd like to see this data organized by resource group. To see this, you'll apply a two-level sort order.

> **Tip** When you sort data, the sort order applies to the active view regardless of the specific table currently displayed in the view. For example, if you sort the Gantt Chart view by start date while displaying the Entry table and then switch to the Cost table, you'll see the tasks sorted by start date in the Cost table. You can also sort in most views that do not include a table, such as the Resource Graph view.

9. On the **Project** menu, point to **Sort**, and then click **Sort By**.

The Sort dialog box appears. In it, you can apply up to three nested levels of sort criteria.

10. Under **Sort By**, click **Group** on the drop-down list, and next to that, click **Ascending**.

11. Under **Then By** (in the center of the dialog box), click **Cost** on the drop-down list, and next to that, click **Descending**.

12. Make sure that the **Permanently renumber resources** check box is cleared.

13. Click **Sort**.

Project sorts the Resource Sheet view to display resources by group (Crew, Equipment, and so on) and then by cost within each group.

Now the Resource Sheet view is sorted first by resource group and then within each group by cost.

	Resource Name	Group	Max. Units	Peak	Std. Rate	Ovt. Rate	Cost	Work
30	Max Benson	Crew	100%	100%	$27.00/hr	$0.00/hr	$9,720.00	360 hrs
13	Electrician	Crew	200%	200%	$28.00/hr	$42.00/hr	$2,912.00	104 hrs
31	Megan Sherman	Crew	100%	100%	$21.00/hr	$0.00/hr	$1,050.00	50 hrs
40	Ted Bremer	Crew	100%	100%	$18.00/hr	$27.00/hr	$1,044.00	58 hrs
41	Tim O'Brien	Crew	100%	100%	$18.00/hr	$27.00/hr	$1,008.00	56 hrs
17	Frank Lee	Crew	100%	100%	$17.00/hr	$25.50/hr	$986.00	58 hrs
25	Keith Harris	Crew	100%	100%	$17.00/hr	$25.50/hr	$986.00	58 hrs
1	16-mm Camera	Equipment	300%	300%	$300.00/wk	$0.00/hr	$1,050.00	140 hrs
3	500-Watt Light	Equipment	400%	400%	$100.00/wk	$0.00/hr	$330.00	132 hrs
5	Camera Boom	Equipment	200%	100%	$0.00/hr	$0.00/hr	$0.00	50 hrs
7	Crane	Equipment	100%	100%	$0.00/hr	$0.00/hr	$0.00	32 hrs
10	Dolly	Equipment	200%	200%	$0.00/hr	$0.00/hr	$0.00	56 hrs
35	Reflector Kit	Equipment	100%	0%	$0.00/hr	$0.00/hr	$0.00	0 hrs
43	Travel	Expenses		0%			$3,068.00	
42	Catering	Expenses		0%			$1,000.00	
2	16-mm Film	Film and Lab			eet/hr	$25.00		$7,250.00	290 100 Feet
12	Editing Lab	Film and Lab	100%	100%	$250.00/day	$0.00/hr	$6,350.00	200 hrs
38	Scott Cooper	Production	100%	100%	$880.00/wk	$0.00/hr	$11,748.00	534 hrs
20	Jo Brown	Production	100%	100%	$21.75/hr	$0.00/hr	$10,614.00	488 hrs
6	Clair Hector	Production	100%	100%	$900.00/wk	$0.00/hr	$7,470.00	332 hrs
32	Michael Patten	Production	100%	100%	$820.00/wk	$0.00/hr	$7,216.00	352 hrs
26	Kim Yoshida	Production	100%	100%	$16.40/hr	$0.00/hr	$5,904.00	360 hrs
21	Johnathan Perrera	Production	100%	100%	$25.00/hr	$0.00/hr	$5,500.00	220 hrs
18	Jan Miksovsky	Production	100%	100%	$21.75/hr	$0.00/hr	$4,375.00	204 hrs
36	Richard Lum	Production	100%	100%	$740.00/wk	$0.00/hr	$3,700.00	200 hrs

This sort offers an easy way to identify the most expensive resources in each resource group working on the short film project.

To conclude this exercise, you'll re-sort the resource information to return it to its original order.

14. On the **Project** menu, point to **Sort**, and then click **By ID**.

Project re-sorts the resource list by resource ID.

Note that there is no visual indication that a task or resource view has been sorted other than the order in which the rows of data appear. You cannot save custom sort settings that you have specified as you can with grouping and filtering. However, the sort order you most recently specified will remain in effect until you re-sort the view.

Grouping Project Details

As you develop a project plan, you can use the default views available in Project to view and analyze your data in several ways. One important way to see the data in task and resource views is by grouping. *Grouping* allows you to organize task or resource information (or, when in a usage view, assignment information) according to criteria you choose. For example, rather than viewing the resource list in the Resource Sheet view sorted by ID, you can view resources sorted by cost. Grouping goes a step beyond just sorting, however. Grouping adds summary values, or "roll-ups," at intervals that you can customize. For example, you can group resources by their cost with a $1,000 interval between groups.

> **Tip** In some respects, grouping in Project is similar to the Subtotals feature in Excel. In fact, grouping allows you to reorganize and analyze your Project data in ways that would otherwise require you to export your Project data to a spreadsheet program.

Grouping can significantly change the way you view your task or resource data, allowing for a more refined level of data analysis and presentation. Grouping doesn't change the underlying structure of your project plan; it simply reorganizes and summarizes the data. As with sorting, when you group data in a view, the grouping applies to all tables you can display in the view. You can also group the Network Diagram view, which does not contain a table.

Project includes several predefined task and resource groups, such as grouping tasks by duration or resources by standard pay rate. You can also customize any of the built-in groups or create your own.

In this exercise, you group resources by their Group name (remember, this is the value in the Group field—*Crew, Equipment,* and so on). This is similar to the sorting you did in the previous section, but this time you will see summary cost values for each resource group.

1. On the **Project** menu, point to **Group By: No Group**, and then click **Resource Group**.

Project reorganizes the resource data into resource groups, adds summary cost values per group, and presents the data in an expanded outline form.

After grouping resources by the Group field,
Project adds summary values for each group.

	Resource Name	Group	Max. Units	Peak	Std. Rate	Ovt. Rate	Cost	Work
	⊟ **Group: Crew**	**Crew**	**800%**	**800%**			**$17,706.00**	**744 hrs**
13	Electrician	Crew	200%	200%	$28.00/hr	$42.00/hr	$2,912.00	104 hrs
17	Frank Lee	Crew	100%	100%	$17.00/hr	$25.50/hr	$986.00	58 hrs
25	Keith Harris	Crew	100%	100%	$17.00/hr	$25.50/hr	$986.00	58 hrs
30	Max Benson	Crew	100%	100%	$27.00/hr	$0.00/hr	$9,720.00	360 hrs
31	Megan Sherman	Crew	100%	100%	$21.00/hr	$0.00/hr	$1,050.00	50 hrs
40	Ted Bremer	Crew	100%	100%	$18.00/hr	$27.00/hr	$1,044.00	58 hrs
41	Tim O'Brien	Crew	100%	100%	$18.00/hr	$27.00/hr	$1,008.00	56 hrs
	⊟ **Group: Equipment**	**Equipment**	**1,300%**	**100%**			**$1,380.00**	**410 hrs**
1	16-mm Camera	Equipment	300%	300%	$300.00/wk	$0.00/hr	$1,050.00	140 hrs
3	500-Watt Light	Equipment	400%	400%	$100.00/wk	$0.00/hr	$330.00	132 hrs
5	Camera Boom	Equipment	200%	100%	$0.00/hr	$0.00/hr	$0.00	50 hrs
7	Crane	Equipment	100%	100%	$0.00/hr	$0.00/hr	$0.00	32 hrs
10	Dolly	Equipment	200%	200%	$0.00/hr	$0.00/hr	$0.00	56 hrs
35	Reflector Kit	Equipment	100%	0%	$0.00/hr	$0.00/hr	$0.00	0 hrs
	⊟ **Group: Expenses**	**Expenses**		**0%**			**$4,068.00**	
42	Catering	Expenses		0%			$1,000.00	
43	Travel	Expenses		0%			$3,068.00	
	⊟ **Group: Film and Lal**	**Film and L**	**100%**	**100%**			**$13,600.00**	**200 hrs**
2	16-mm Film	Film and Lab			$25.00 /eet/hr		$7,250.00	290 100 Feet
12	Editing Lab	Film and Lab	100%	100%	$250.00/day	$0.00/hr	$6,350.00	200 hrs
	⊟ **Group: Production**	**Production**	**1,750%**	**150%**			**$63,002.40**	**3,041 hrs**
6	Clair Hector	Production	100%	100%	$900.00/wk	$0.00/hr	$7,470.00	332 hrs
11	Doug Hampton	Production	100%	50%	$16.00/hr	$0.00/hr	$2,246.40	123 hrs
14	Eric Lang	Production	100%	100%	$18.50/hr	$0.00/hr	$444.00	24 hrs
16	Florian Voss	Production	100%	0%	$25.00/hr	$0.00/hr	$0.00	0 hrs
18	Jan Miksovsky	Production	100%	100%	$21.75/hr	$0.00/hr	$4,375.00	204 hrs
20	Jo Brown	Production	100%	100%	$21.75/hr	$0.00/hr	$10,614.00	488 hrs
21	Johnathan Perrere	Production	100%	100%	$25.00/hr	$0.00/hr	$5,500.00	220 hrs
24	Kathryn Wilson	Production	100%	0%	$800.00/wk	$0.00/hr	$0.00	0 hrs
26	Kim Yoshida	Production	100%	100%	$16.40/hr	$0.00/hr	$5,904.00	360 hrs
27		Production	100%	0%		$0.00/hr	$0.00	0 hrs

Project applies colored formatting (in this case, a yellow background) to the summary data rows. Because the summary data is derived from subordinate data, you cannot edit it directly. Displaying these summary values has no effect on the cost or schedule calculations of the project plan.

This arrangement of the resource cost information is similar to the sorting you did in the previous section. To give yourself more control over how Project organizes and presents the data, you'll now create a group.

2. On the **Project** menu, point to **Group By: Resource Group**, and then click **More Groups**.

The More Groups dialog box appears.

In this dialog box, you can see all of the available predefined groups for tasks (when in a task view) and resources (when in a resource view). Your new group will be most similar to the Resource Group, so you'll start by copying it.

3. Make sure that **Resource Group** is selected, and then click the **Copy** button.

The Group Definition In dialog box appears.

> **Tip** Notice the default value in the Name field: *Copy of Resource &Group.* You will change this name shortly, but did you wonder whether the ampersand (&) is a typo? No, it's a code Project uses in the Name field, where you create what will become a new menu command. The ampersand code precedes the character that will function as the underlined keyboard shortcut for that menu command. You don't need to specify a keyboard shortcut, but they are handy if you prefer to use the keyboard to access menu commands.

4. In the **Name** box, select the displayed text, and then type Resource Groups by Cost.

5. In the **Field Name** column, click the first empty cell below **Group**.

6. Type or select Cost.

7. In the **Order** column for the Cost field, select **Descending**.

The resources will be grouped based on the values in the Group field, and then by the Cost field from highest to lowest.

Next, you'll fine-tune the cost intervals at which Project will group the resources.

8. With the Cost row still selected, click the **Define Group Intervals** button.

The Define Group Interval dialog box appears.

9. In the **Group on** box, select **Interval**.

10. In the **Group interval** box, type 1000.

11. Click **OK**.

12. Click **OK** again to close the Group Definition in dialog box.

Resource Groups By Cost appears as a new group in the More Groups dialog box.

13. Click the **Apply** button.

Project applies the new group to the Resource Sheet view. To get a better look at the groupings, you'll need to widen the Resource Name column.

14. Double-click the **Resource Name** column heading.

The Column Definition dialog box appears.

15. Click the **Best Fit** button.

Project widens the Resource Name column.

> **Tip** Using the Best Fit feature has the same effect as double-clicking the right edge of a column in the column heading to expand the column so that you can see the entire value.

After applying a two-level group, information is grouped first by resource group and then within each group by cost.

Resource Name	Group	Max. Units	Peak	Std. Rate	Ovt. Rate	Cost	Work
⊟ Group: Crew	Crew	800%	800%			$17,706.00	744 hrs
⊟ Cost: $9,000.00 - <$10,000.00	Crew	100%	100%			$9,720.00	360 hrs
30 Max Benson	Crew	100%	100%	$27.00/hr	$0.00/hr	$9,720.00	360 hrs
⊟ Cost: $2,000.00 - <$3,000.00	Crew	200%	200%			$2,912.00	104 hrs
13 Electrician	Crew	200%	200%	$28.00/hr	$42.00/hr	$2,912.00	104 hrs
⊟ Cost: $1,000.00 - <$2,000.00	Crew	300%	300%			$3,102.00	164 hrs
31 Megan Sherman	Crew	100%	100%	$21.00/hr	$0.00/hr	$1,050.00	50 hrs
40 Ted Bremer	Crew	100%	100%	$18.00/hr	$27.00/hr	$1,044.00	58 hrs
41 Tim O'Brien	Crew	100%	100%	$18.00/hr	$27.00/hr	$1,008.00	56 hrs
⊟ Cost: $0.00 - <$1,000.00	Crew	200%	200%			$1,972.00	116 hrs
17 Frank Lee	Crew	100%	100%	$17.00/hr	$25.50/hr	$986.00	58 hrs
25 Keith Harris	Crew	100%	100%	$17.00/hr	$25.50/hr	$986.00	58 hrs
⊟ Group: Equipment	Equipment	1,300%	100%			$1,380.00	410 hrs
⊟ Cost: $1,000.00 - <$2,000.00	Equipment	300%	300%			$1,050.00	140 hrs
1 16-mm Camera	Equipment	300%	300%	$300.00/wk	$0.00/hr	$1,050.00	140 hrs
⊟ Cost: $0.00 - <$1,000.00	Equipment	1,000%	800%			$330.00	270 hrs
3 500-Watt Light	Equipment	400%	400%	$100.00/wk	$0.00/hr	$330.00	132 hrs
5 Camera Boom	Equipment	200%	100%	$0.00/hr	$0.00/hr	$0.00	50 hrs
7 Crane	Equipment	100%	100%	$0.00/hr	$0.00/hr	$0.00	32 hrs
10 Dolly	Equipment	200%	200%	$0.00/hr	$0.00/hr	$0.00	56 hrs
35 Reflector Kit	Equipment	100%	0%	$0.00/hr	$0.00/hr	$0.00	0 hrs
⊟ Group: Expenses	Expenses		0%			$4,068.00	
⊟ Cost: $3,000.00 - <$4,000.00	Expenses		0%			$3,068.00	
43 Travel	Expenses		0%			$3,068.00	
⊟ Cost: $1,000.00 - <$2,000.00	Expenses		0%			$1,000.00	
42 Catering	Expenses		0%			$1,000.00	
⊟ Group: Film and Lab	Film and L	100%	100%			$13,600.00	200 hrs
⊟ Cost: $7,000.00 - <$8,000.00	Film and L					$7,250.00	
2 16-mm Film	Film and Lab			eet/hr	$25.00	$7,250.00	290 100 Feet
⊟ Cost: $6,000.00 - <$7,000.00	Film and L	100%	100%			$6,350.00	200 hrs
12 Editing Lab	Film and Lab	100%	100%	$250.00/day	$0.00/hr	$6,350.00	200 hrs
⊟ Group: Production	Production	1,750%	150%			$63,002.40	3,041 hrs

The resources are grouped by their resource group value (the yellow bands that bind together *Crew, Equipment,* and so on) and within each group by cost values at $1,000 intervals (the gray bands).

To conclude this exercise, you'll remove the grouping.

16. On the **Project** menu, point to **Group By: Resource Groups By Cost**, and click **No Group**.

Project removes the summary values and outline structure, leaving the original data. Again, displaying or removing a group has no effect on the data in the project.

Tip All predefined groups and any groups you create are available to you through the Group By button on the Standard toolbar. The name of the active group appears on this button, which resembles a box with a drop-down list. Click the arrow in the Group By button to see other group names. If no group is applied to the current table, *No Group* appears on the button.

Filtering Project Details

Another useful way to change the way you view Project task and resource information is by filtering. As the name suggests, *filtering* hides task or resource data that does not meet the criteria you specify, displaying only the data in which you're interested. Like grouping, filtering does not change the data in your Project plan; it merely changes the way that data appears.

There are two ways to use filters. You can either apply predefined filters to a view or apply an AutoFilter to a view:

- Apply a predefined or custom filter to view or highlight only the task or resource information that meets the criteria of the filter. For example, the Critical Task filter displays only the tasks on the critical path. Some predefined filters, such as the Task Range filter, prompt you to enter specific criteria—for example, a range of task IDs. If a task or resource sheet view has a filter applied, the filter name appears in the Filter button on the Formatting toolbar.

- Use *AutoFilters* for ad hoc filtering in any table in Project. When the AutoFilter feature is turned on, small arrows appear next to the names of column headings. Click the arrow to display a list of criteria by which you can filter the data. Which criteria you see depends on the type of data contained in the column—for example, AutoFilter criteria in a date column include choices such as Today and This month, as well as a Custom option, with which you can specify your own criteria. You use AutoFilter in Project in the same way you might use AutoFilter in Excel.

Both types of filters hide rows in task or resource sheet views that do not meet the criteria you specify. You might see gaps in the task or resource ID numbers. The "missing" data is only hidden and not deleted. As with sorting and grouping, when you filter data in a view, the filtering applies to all tables you can display in the view. Views that do not include tables, such as the Calendar and Network Diagram views, also support filtering (through the Filtered For command on the Project menu), but not AutoFilters.

A commonly used format for communicating schedule information on a film project is called a shooting schedule. In this exercise, you create a filter that displays only the uncompleted film shoot tasks. In later sections, you'll combine this filter with a custom table and a custom view to create a complete shooting schedule for everyone on the film project.

1. On the **View** menu, click **Gantt Chart**.

   The Gantt Chart view appears. Before you create a filter, you'll quickly see the tasks you're interested in by applying an AutoFilter.

2. On the **Project** menu point to **Filtered For: All Tasks** and then click **AutoFilter**.

Auto Filter

> **Tip** You can also click the AutoFilter button on the Formatting toolbar.

Project displays arrows to the right of the column headings.

After turning on AutoFilter, these arrows appear next to column headings. Click them to choose the AutoFilter you want.

	●	Task Name	Duration	Start	Finish
0		Short Film Project	207 days	Mon 3/3/08	Fri 12/19/08
1		Pre-Production	58.5 days	Mon 3/3/08	Thu 5/22/08
2		Review script	4 days	Mon 3/3/08	Thu 3/6/08
3		Develop script brea	1 wk	Fri 3/7/08	Fri 3/14/08
4		Develop production	1.08 mons	Fri 3/14/08	Wed 4/16/08
5		Scout locations	2 wks	Wed 4/16/08	Wed 4/30/08

3. Click the down arrow in the **Task Name** column heading, and then click **(Custom...)**.

   The Custom AutoFilter dialog box appears. You'd like to see only the tasks that contain the word *shoot*, as in "Scene 3 shoot."

4. Under **Name**, make sure **contains** appears in the first box.

5. In the adjacent box, type **shoot**.

6. Click **OK** to close the Custom AutoFilter dialog box.

   Project filters the task list to show only the tasks that contain the word *shoot* and their summary tasks.

After applying an AutoFilter, the filtered
column name is formatted in blue.

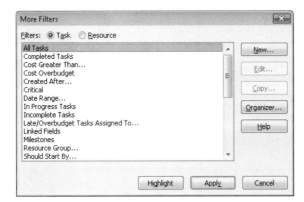

	ⓘ	Task Name	Duration	Start	Finish
0		– Short Film Project	207 days	Mon 3/3/08	Fri 12/19/08
23		– Production	53.25 days	Thu 5/22/08	Wed 8/6/08
24		– Scene 7	5 days	Thu 5/22/08	Thu 5/29/08
27		Scene 7 shoot	1 day	Mon 5/26/08	Tue 5/27/08
30		– Scene 3	4 days	Thu 5/29/08	Wed 6/4/08
33		Scene 3 shoot	1 day	Mon 6/2/08	Tue 6/3/08
36		– Scene 1	6 days	Wed 6/4/08	Thu 6/12/08
39		Scene 1 shoot	1 day	Tue 6/10/08	Wed 6/11/08
42		– Scene 2	5.5 days	Thu 6/12/08	Thu 6/19/08
45	🗐	Scene 2 shoot	1 day	Mon 6/16/08	Tue 6/17/08
48		– Scene 5	6 days	Fri 6/20/08	Fri 6/27/08
51		Scene 5 shoot	1 day	Thu 6/26/08	Thu 6/26/08
54		– Scene 6	14 days	Mon 6/30/08	Fri 7/18/08
57		Scene 6 shoot	1 day	Mon 7/14/08	Mon 7/14/08
60		– Scene 8	8 days	Mon 7/21/08	Wed 7/30/08
63		Scene 8 shoot	1 day	Mon 7/28/08	Mon 7/28/08
66		– Scene 4	4.75 days	Thu 7/31/08	Wed 8/6/08
69		Scene 4 shoot	2 hrs	Mon 8/4/08	Mon 8/4/08

Note that the Task Name column heading appears blue. This is a visual indicator
that an AutoFilter has been applied to this column.

Next, you turn off the AutoFilter and create a custom filter.

7. On the **Formatting** toolbar, click **AutoFilter**.

Project toggles the AutoFilter off, redisplaying all tasks in the project plan. Now
you are ready to create a custom filter.

8. On the **Project** menu, point to **Filtered For: All Tasks**, and then click **More Filters**.

The More Filters dialog box appears.

In this dialog box, you can see all of the predefined filters for tasks (when in a task
view) and resources (when in a resource view) that are available to you.

9. Click the **New** button.

The Filter Definition in dialog box appears.

10. In the **Name** box, type Uncompleted Shoots.

11. In the first row in the **Field Name** column, type or select Name.

12. In the first row in the **Test** column, select **contains**.

13. In the first row in the **Value(s)** column, type shoot.

   That covers the first criterion for the filter; next, you'll add the second criterion.

14. In the second row in the **And/Or** column, select **And**.

15. In the second row in the **Field Name** column, type or select Actual Finish.

16. In the second row in the **Test** column, select **equals**.

17. In the second row in the **Value(s)** column, type NA.

   NA means "not applicable" and is the way that Project marks some fields that do not yet have a value. In other words, any shooting task that does not have an actual finish date must be uncompleted.

18. Click **OK** to close the Filter Definition in dialog box.

   The new filter appears in the More Filters dialog box.

19. Click **Apply**.

   Project applies the new filter to the Gantt Chart view.

After applying a filter, Project hides information that does not meet the filter's criteria. Note the gaps in the task IDs; this is one visual clue that a filter had been applied.

	❶	Task Name	Duration	Start	Finish	
27		Scene 7 shoot	1 day	Mon 5/26/08	Tue 5/27/08	
33		Scene 3 shoot	1 day	Mon 6/2/08	Tue 6/3/08	
39		Scene 1 shoot	1 day	Tue 6/10/08	Wed 6/11/08	
45	🗐	Scene 2 shoot	1 day	Mon 6/16/08	Tue 6/17/08	
51		Scene 5 shoot	1 day	Thu 6/26/08	Thu 6/26/08	
57		Scene 6 shoot	1 day	Mon 7/14/08	Mon 7/14/08	
63		Scene 8 shoot	1 day	Mon 7/28/08	Mon 7/28/08	
69		Scene 4 shoot	2 hrs	Mon 8/4/08	Mon 8/4/08	

The tasks are now filtered to show only the uncompleted shooting tasks. Because we haven't started tracking actual work yet, all of the shooting tasks are uncompleted at this time.

> **Tip** Rather than hiding tasks that do not meet the filter criteria, you can apply blue text formatting to those that do. Click the Highlight button instead of the Apply button in the More Filters dialog box.

To conclude this exercise, you will remove the filtering.

20. On the **Project** menu, point to **Filtered For: Uncompleted Shoots**, and then click **All Tasks**.

Project removes the filter. As always, displaying or removing a filter has no effect on the original data.

> **Tip** All filters are also available to you through the Filter button on the Formatting toolbar. The name of the active filter appears in this button; click the arrow next to the filter name to see other filters. If no filter is applied to the current view, All Tasks or All Resources appears on the button, depending on the type of view currently displayed.

Customizing Tables

As you might already know, a table is a spreadsheet-like presentation of project data organized into vertical columns and horizontal rows. Each column represents one of the many fields in Project, and each row represents a single task or resource (or, in usage views, an assignment). The intersection of a column and a row can be called a cell (if you're oriented toward spreadsheets) or a field (if you think in database terms).

Project includes several tables that can be applied in views. You've already used some of these tables, such as the Entry and Summary tables. Chances are that these tables will contain the fields you want most of the time. However, you can modify any predefined table, or you can create a new table that contains only the data you want.

In this exercise, you create a table to display the information found on a shooting schedule—a common format for presenting schedule information in film projects.

1. On the **View** menu, click **More Views**.

   The More Views dialog box appears.

2. Click **Task Sheet**, and then click **Apply**.

   Project displays the Task Sheet view.

3. On the **View** menu, point to **Table: Entry**, and then click **More Tables**.

   The More Tables dialog box appears.

In this dialog box, you can see all of the available predefined tables for tasks (when in a task view) and resources (when in a resource view).

4. Make sure that **Task** is the active option, and then, in the list of tables, make sure that **Entry** is selected.

5. Click **Copy**.

   The Table Definition in dialog box appears.

6. In the **Name** box, type Shooting Schedule Table.

   Next, you will remove several fields, add others, and then put the remaining fields in the order you want.

7. In the **Field Name** column, click each of the following field names, and then click the **Delete Row** button after clicking each field name:

   Indicators
   Duration
   Finish
   Predecessors
   Resource Names

Next, you will add some fields to this table definition.

8. In the **Field Name** column, click the down arrow in the next empty cell below **Start**, and then select **Cast (Text9)** from the drop-down list.

9. In the **Align Data** column in the same row, click **Left**.

   As soon as you click in the Align Data column, Project completes row entries for the *Cast* field name by adding data to the Width and Align Title columns.

10. In the **Width** column, type or click 25.

11. In the **Field Name** column in the next empty row below **Cast**, click **Location** **(Text10)** on the drop-down list.

12. In the **Align Data** column, click **Left**.

13. In the **Width** column, type or click **15**.

The two customized text fields *Cast (Text9)* and *Location (Text10)* contain the character names and film locations for the shooting tasks. These were previously customized for you in the project plan.

The remaining work to complete this table definition is to reorder the fields to match the order commonly found on a shooting schedule.

14. In the **Field Name** column, click **Start**, and then click the **Cut Row** button.

15. In the **Field Name** column, click **Name**, and then click the **Paste Row** button.

16. In the **Date Format** box, click **1/28/02 12:33PM**.

This matches the order in which information is commonly listed on a film-shooting schedule.

17. Click **OK** to close the Table Definition in dialog box.

The new table appears in the More Tables dialog box.

18. Click **Apply**.

Project applies the new table to the Task Sheet view. If the Start column displays pound signs (###) or the values are not fully visible double-click the column headings' right edge to widen it.

In the next section, you will combine the custom filter with this custom table to create a shooting schedule view for the film project.

Customizing Views

Nearly all work you perform in Project occurs in a *view.* A view might contain elements such as tables, groups, and filters. You can combine these with other elements (such as a timescaled grid in a usage view) or with graphic elements (such as the graphic representation of tasks in the chart portion of the Gantt Chart view).

Project includes dozens of views that organize information for specific purposes. You might find that you need to see your project information in some way that is not available in the predefined views. If Project's available views do not meet your needs, you can edit an existing view or create your own view.

In this exercise, you create a film-shooting schedule view that combines the custom filter and custom table that you created in the previous sections. The view you create will more closely match a standard format used in the film industry.

1. On the **View** menu, click **More Views**.

    The More Views dialog box appears.

    In this dialog box, you can see all of the predefined views available to you.

2. Click **New**.

    The Define New View dialog box appears. Most views occupy a single pane, but a view can consist of two separate panes.

3. Make sure **Single View** is selected, and then click **OK**.

    The View Definition in dialog box appears.

> **Tip** The View Definition dialog box, like many dialog boxes in Project, includes a Help button that you can press for detailed descriptions of the settings in the dialog box.

4. In the **Name** box, type Shooting Schedule View.

5. In the **Screen** box, select **Task Sheet** from the drop-down list.

6. In the **Table** box, select **Shooting Schedule Table** from the drop-down list.

    The specific tables listed on the drop-down list depend on the type of view you selected in the Screen box in step 5.

7. In the **Group** box, select **No Group** from the drop-down list.

    The specific groups listed on the drop-down list depend on the type of view you selected in the Screen box in step 5.

8. In the **Filter** box, select **Uncompleted Shoots** from the drop-down list.

    The specific filters listed on the drop-down list depend on the type of view you selected in the Screen box in step 5.

9. Select the **Show in menu** check box.

View Definition in 'Short Film Project 10'	
Name:	Shooting Schedule View
Screen:	Task Sheet
Table:	Shooting Schedule Table
Group:	No Group
Filter:	Uncompleted Shoots

☐ Highlight filter
☑ Show in menu

Help   OK   Cancel

10. Click **OK** to close the **View Definition in** dialog box.

The new view appears and should be selected in the More Views dialog box.

11. Click **Apply**.

Project applies the new view.

This custom view is arraigned like a shooting
schedule, a standard format in the film industry.

		Start	Task Name	Cast	Location
	27	5/26/08 1:00 PM	Scene 7 shoot	Richard, Store clerk #1, Store (	Grocery store
	33	6/2/08 1:00 PM	Scene 3 shoot	Man on street, Richard	Street corner
	39	6/10/08 1:00 PM	Scene 1 shoot	Garth, Man on street, Store cle	Street corner
	45	6/16/08 5:00 PM	Scene 2 shoot	Garth, Shelly	Shelly's living room
	51	6/26/08 8:00 AM	Scene 5 shoot	Man on street, Garth, Old man,	Street corner
	57	7/14/08 8:00 AM	Scene 6 shoot	Garth, Store Clerk #1, Shelly, C	Grocery store
	63	7/28/08 8:00 AM	Scene 8 shoot	Garth, Store clerk #1, Man on s	Street corner
	69	8/4/08 1:00 PM	Scene 4 shoot	Shelly, Richard	Elevator

Only uncompleted shoots are now displayed, and the fields appear in an order consistent with a standard shooting schedule for a film project. Also, Project added the Shooting Schedule view to the View menu. This view will be saved with this Project plan, and you can use it whenever you want.

To conclude this exercise, you will adjust row height and column width to display some information that is not currently visible.

12. While holding down the ⌃ key, click the task ID numbers (not task names) for tasks **27**, **39**, **51**, **57**, and **63**.

In each of these selected rows, the names in the Cast column exceed the width of the column.

13. Drag the bottom edge of the task ID for task **27** down approximately one row.

> **Tip** While dragging the edge of the task ID, look at the status bar in the lower left corner of the Project window. The status bar indicates the new row height as you drag the edge of the task ID.

Project resizes the selected rows.

14. Double-click the right edge of the **Location** column heading.

Project resizes the column width to accommodate the widest value in the column.

To resize a row's height, drag the bottom edge of the row heading. Selected rows are also resized.

To resize a column's width, drag the right edge of the column heading.

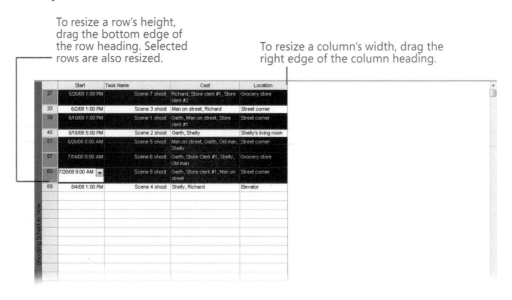

	Start	Task Name	Cast	Location
27	5/26/08 1:00 PM	Scene 7 shoot	Richard, Store clerk #1, Store clerk #2	Grocery store
33	6/2/08 1:00 PM	Scene 3 shoot	Man on street, Richard	Street corner
39	6/10/08 1:00 PM	Scene 1 shoot	Garth, Man on street, Store clerk #1	Street corner
45	6/16/08 5:00 PM	Scene 2 shoot	Garth, Shelly	Shelly's living room
51	6/26/08 8:00 AM	Scene 5 shoot	Man on street, Garth, Old man, Shelly	Street corner
57	7/14/08 8:00 AM	Scene 6 shoot	Garth, Store Clerk #1, Shelly, Old man	Grocery store
63	7/28/08 8:00 AM	Scene 8 shoot	Garth, Store clerk #1, Man on street	Street corner
69	8/4/08 1:00 PM	Scene 4 shoot	Shelly, Richard	Elevator

CLOSE the Short Film Project 10 file.

Key Points

- Common ways of organizing data in Project include sorting, grouping, and filtering. In all cases, Project never deletes the data; it simply changes how it is displayed.

- Project includes many built-in sort orders, groupings, and filters, and you can also create your own.

- Whereas sorting and filtering rearrange or selectively show only some data in a project plan, grouping adds summary values or "roll-ups" of values, such as costs, based on whatever interval you choose.

- Tables are the primary elements of most views in Project. Project includes several built-in tables, and you can also create your own.

- You work with data in Project via views. Views may contain tables, groups, filters, and in some cases graphical charts. The Gantt Chart view, for example, consists of a table on the left and a timescaled chart on the right.

- Project contains many built-in views, and you can also create your own.

Chapter at a Glance

Customize page layout and printing options for views and reports, page 242

Page Setup - Gantt Chart

Page | Margins | Header | Footer | Legend | View

Orientation

Portrait | Landscape

Scaling

Adjust to: 100 % normal size

by 1 tall

Print... | OK | Cancel

Page Setup - Gantt Chart

Page | Margins | Header | Footer | Legend | View

Preview:

Project:Short Film Project
Date: Mon 2/4/08

Start: Mon 3/3/08
Duration: 207 days

Customize the legend and other parts of views and reports, page 251

Alignment: Left | Center | Right

Start: &[Start Date]
Duration: &[Duration]

Legend on:
Every page
Legend page
None

Width: 3 in.

Legend Labels...

General: Project Start Date | Add
Project fields: Duration | Add

Print Preview... | Options... | Print... | OK | Cancel

Microsoft Project - Short Film Project 11

Page Setup... | Print... | Close | Help

See how your output will appear across pages, page 250

11 Printing Project Information

In this chapter, you will learn how to:

✔ Change page setup options for views and reports.

✔ Print a view.

✔ Print a report.

> **Tip** Do you need only a quick refresher on the topics in this chapter? See the Quick Reference entries on pages xxv–xlviii.

In this chapter, you work with some of the many views and reports in Microsoft Office Project 2007 to print your project plan. One of the most important tasks of any project manager is communicating project information to stakeholders, and that often means printing. To communicate project details in printed form, you can use the predefined views and reports as they are provided or customize them to better suit your needs.

> **Tip** This tip describes enterprise project management (EPM) functionality. Printing information from Project is a common means of communicating with stakeholders. If you are using Project Professional in conjunction with Project Server, you and your stakeholders have many additional options for communicating project information. For more information, see Part 4, "Introducing Project Server."

> **Important** Before you can use the practice files provided for this chapter, you need to install them from the book's companion CD to their default locations. See "Using the Book's CD" on page xix for more information.

Printing Your Project Plan

Printing information from a project plan to share with stakeholders is a common activity for most project managers. In Project, printing focuses on views and reports.

You've probably already seen several views and a few reports, such as the Gantt Chart view and the Project Summary report. Both views and reports organize the details of a project plan into specific formats for specific purposes. You can enter, read, edit, and print information in a view, whereas you can only print information in a report. Think of views as your general working environment in Project, and think of reports as specific formats for printing.

You can customize the way you print both views and reports; however, Project has fewer options for printing reports. When printing, many of the same options exist for both views and reports, as well as some specific options unique to views or reports. To customize printing for a view or report, you use the Page Setup and Print dialog boxes.

First, you will look at the Page Setup dialog box. To see the Page Setup dialog box for views, click Page Setup on the File menu. To see this dialog box for reports, first display a report in the Print Preview window, and then click the Page Setup button.

In the Page Setup dialog box, the Page and Margins tabs are available for both views and reports. However, the specific options you choose in the Page Setup dialog box for any view or report affect only that view or report; the settings are not shared between views or reports.

Some page setup options are unique to views or reports, and a few options are available to only specific views or reports. The following is a summary of unique page setup options:

- You can use options on the Header, Footer, and View tabs in the Page Setup dialog box for all views. The View tab in particular includes options that vary depending on which view is currently active. For views that include a legend (such as the Gantt Chart, Network Diagram, and Calendar views), the Legend tab is also available.

- You can use options on the Header and Footer tabs in most reports, but the View and Legend tabs are not available for any reports.

Project Management Focus: Communicating with Stakeholders

Besides knowing how to print, it's important to know what to print. Most project managers find that they have different *stakeholders* with different information needs. For example, what the project's financial supporters need to see at the planning stage of a project might be quite different from what the project's resources need to see after work has begun. The built-in views and reports in Project should cover nearly all stakeholder communication needs (at least when printing is the solution). The following is a summary of which views and reports best communicate project plan details to various stakeholders.

If this stakeholder	Is most interested in	Provide this printed view	Or this printed report
Project sponsor or client	Overall project duration information	Gantt Chart with project summary task displayed, filtered for summary tasks	Project Summary
	Overall project cost information	Task Sheet with project summary task displayed and Cost table applied	Budget or other reports in the Cost category
	Schedule status after work has begun	Tracking Gantt with Tracking table applied	Project Summary, Completed Tasks, or Tasks Starting Soon
Resources assigned to tasks in the project	The tasks to which they are assigned	Calendar or Resource Usage, filtered for the specific resource	To-Do List, Who Does What, or Who Does What When
Resource managers in your organization	The scope of work involving their resources in the project	Resource Sheet, Resource Graph, or Resource Usage	Resource Usage, Who Does What, or other reports in the Assignments category
Other project managers in your organization	Schedule logic, critical path, and task relationships	Network Diagram, Detail Gantt, or Tracking Gantt	Critical Tasks

> This table lists only a few of the many built-in views and reports in Project. If you have a specific information need, explore all of the views and reports before you attempt to build your own. Chances are, Project has a view or report that will meet your needs or serve as a starting point for customization.

> **Tip** To learn more about which views or reports best convey specific project information, type *Print a view* or *Create and print a basic report* into the Search box in the upper right corner of the Project window. The Search box initially contains the text *Type a question for help*.

Next, you will look at the Print dialog box. To see the Print dialog box for views, click Print on the File menu. To see this dialog box for reports, first display the report in the Print Preview window, and then click the Print button.

Depending on the active view or report, the Timescale options might not be available.

> **Tip** Depending on the printer or plotter to which you are printing, you might have additional options unique to that device. To set these options, click the Properties button for your selected printer in the Print dialog box.

In the Print dialog box, most options available for views are also available for reports. For example, some views and reports support timescale options in the Print dialog box, but others do not. The Gantt Chart view and the Who Does What When report, for example, both include a timescale. In the Print dialog boxes for both, you can print specific ranges from the timescale if you wish.

In this exercise, you compare the page setup options of views and reports.

BE SURE TO start Microsoft Office Project 2007 if it's not already running.

Important If you are running Project Professional, you may need to make a one-time adjustment to use the Computer account and to work offline. This ensures that the practice files you work with in this chapter do not affect your Project Server data. **For more information, see "Starting Project Professional" on page XXX.**

OPEN Short Film Project 11a from the *Documents\Microsoft Press\Project 2007 SBS\ Chapter 11 Printing* folder. You can also access the practice files for this book by clicking Start, All Programs, Microsoft Press, Project 2007 Step by Step, and then selecting the chapter folder of the file you want to open.

1. On the **File** menu, click **Save As**.

   The Save As dialog box appears.

2. In the **File name** box, type Short Film Project 11, and then click **Save**.

   Next, you will look at page setup options.

3. On the **File** menu, click **Page Setup**.

   The Page Setup dialog box appears. Note the title of the dialog box: Page Setup – Gantt Chart. Because the Page Setup dialog box changes depending on the active view, Project includes the view name in the dialog box title bar.

4. Click the **View** tab.

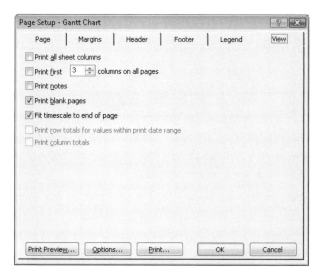

Because the Gantt Chart view includes a table, the View tab includes some options relating to columns. The Gantt Chart also includes a timescale, so you see an option relating to the timescale.

5. Click **Cancel**.

The Page Setup dialog box closes. Next, you'll switch to another view and see how the page setup options differ.

6. On the **View** menu, click **Calendar**.

The Calendar view appears. This view lacks both the table and chart elements you saw in the Gantt Chart view and instead represents tasks in a month-at-a-glance arrangement.

7. On the **File** menu, click **Page Setup**.

The Page Setup dialog box appears. Note again the title of the dialog box: Page Setup – Calendar.

8. Click the **View** tab if it is not already active.

The options available for the Calendar view are quite different from those of the Gantt Chart view. Here you have several options for controlling how details are organized in the Calendar view when printed.

The Print Notes check box, however, is available for both the Gantt Chart and Calendar views.

9. Click **Cancel**.

The Page Setup dialog box closes.

To conclude this exercise, you will see the page setup options for a report.

> **Tip** New in Project 2007 is a powerful new feature called visual reports. Visual reports can play an important role in your schedule reporting and analysis needs. Because visual reports depend on exporting Project data to other Office applications, they are described in Chapter 12, "Sharing Project Information with Other Programs."

10. On the **Report** menu, click **Reports**.

    The Reports dialog box appears.

11. Click **Custom**, and then click the **Select** button.

> **Tip** You can also double-click the Custom category.

    The Custom Reports dialog box appears.

12. In the **Custom Reports** box, click **Who Does What**, and then click the **Setup** button.

    The Page Setup dialog box appears. Note again the title of the dialog box: Page Setup – Who Does What.

    Most of the tabs you've seen for views are also available for reports, but the Legend and View tabs are not.

13. Click **Cancel** to close the Page Setup dialog box, and click **Cancel** again to close the Custom Reports dialog box.

14. Click **Close** to close the Reports dialog box.

15. On the **View** menu, click **Gantt Chart**.

> **Tip** The views available in Project are listed in the More Views dialog box. (On the View menu, click More Views.) Likewise, all available reports are listed in the Custom Reports dialog box. (On the View menu, click Reports, click Custom, and then click Select.)

Printing Views

Printing a view allows you to put on paper just about anything you see on your screen. Any customization you apply to a view, such as applying different *tables* or *groups*, will be printed as well. With a few exceptions, you can print any view you see in Project. The exceptions are as follows:

- You cannot print the Relationship Diagram or form views such as the Task Form.

- If you display two views in a combination view (one view in the top pane and the other view in the bottom pane), only the view in the active pane will be printed.

Keep in mind that the part of your project plan that you see on your screen at one time might be a relatively small portion of the full project, which could require a large number of letter-size pages to print. For example, the Gantt Chart view of a six-month project with 85 tasks can require 14 or more letter-size pages to print in its entirety. Printing Gantt Chart or Network Diagram views can use quite a bit of paper; in fact, some heavy-duty Project users make poster-size printouts of their project plans using plotters.

Whether you use a printer or a plotter, it's a good idea to preview any views you intend to print. By using the Page Setup dialog box in conjunction with the Print Preview window, you can control many aspects of the view to be printed. For example, you can control the number of pages on which the view will be printed, apply headers and footers, and determine content that appears in the legend of the Gantt Chart and some other views.

> **Tip** When printing Gantt Chart views and other views that include a timescale, adjusting the timescale before printing affects the number of pages required. To adjust the timescale so that it shows the largest time span in the smallest number of pages, on the View menu, click Zoom; then, in the Zoom dialog box, click Entire Project.
>
> To further reduce the number of pages required, you can collapse a project plan's outline to summary tasks. Click the Show button on the Formatting toolbar, and then click the outline level you want. A collapsed view showing only summary tasks might be informative enough for people who simply want an overall sense of the project plan. If you're interested in a specific time period, you can print just that portion of the timescale. You might also apply a filter to display only the information that's of greatest interest to a particular audience, such as late or overbudget tasks, for example.

In this exercise, you preview the Gantt Chart view and change options in the Page Setup dialog box.

1. On the **File** menu, click **Print Preview**.

   Project displays the Gantt Chart view in the Print Preview window.

   The Print Preview toolbar contains buttons for navigation between pages, zooming in and out, setting Page Setup options, printing, and exiting Print Preview.

   The Print Preview window has several options to explore. You will start with the page navigation buttons.

2. On the **Print Preview** toolbar, click the **Page Right** button several times to display different pages.

Page Right

3. Click the **Page Down** button once.

   To observe a broader view of the output, you'll switch to a multi-page view.

Page Down

4. Click the **Multiple Pages** button.

   The entire Gantt Chart view appears in the Print Preview window.

Multiple Pages

The multiple-page Print Preview displays the entire printed output on separate sheets (the paper size is determined by your printer settings).

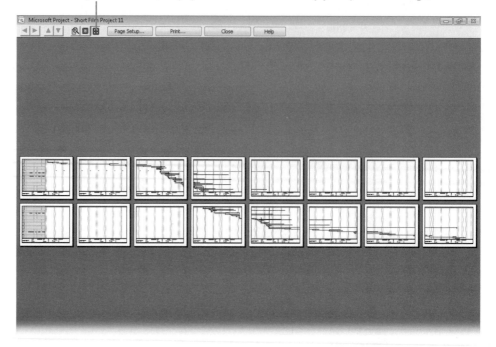

If you have a plotter selected as your default printer or you have a different page size selected for your default printer, what you see in the Print Preview window will differ from what's shown here.

The status bar text reads *2 rows by 8 columns* (the specific number of rows and columns you see may differ). We refer to rows and columns on the Gantt Chart and in other views; in the Print Preview window, however, these terms denote rows and columns of pages—in this case, two rows of pages by eight columns of pages, for a total of 16 pages. The status bar text can help you quickly determine the size (in pages) of your printed view.

Next, you'll change some options in the Page Setup dialog box.

5. On the **Print Preview** toolbar, click the **One Page** button.

One Page

Project displays the first page of the Gantt chart.

6. Click the **Page Setup** button.

The Page Setup dialog box appears. This is the same dialog box you'd see if you clicked Page Setup on the File menu. The first change you'll make to the printed Gantt Chart is to add the company name to the header that is printed on every page.

7. Click the **Header** tab.

8. On the Header tab are **Alignment** tabs. Make sure that **Center** is selected.

9. In the **General** box, click **Company Name** on the drop-down list, and then click the **Add** button.

   Project inserts the *&[Company]* code into the header and displays a preview in the Preview window of the Page Setup dialog box. The company name comes from the Properties dialog box (File menu), which has been filled out for you. Next, you'll change the content of the Gantt Chart view's legend.

10. Click the **Legend** tab.

11. On the Legend tab are **Alignment** tabs. Click the **Right** tab.

    With the current settings, Project will print the project title and the current date on the left side of the legend. You also want to print the project start date and duration on the right side of the legend.

12. Click in the text box, and type Start: followed by a space.

13. In the **General** box, click **Project Start Date** on the drop-down list, and then click **Add**.

    Project adds the label and code for the project start date to the legend.

14. Press the [Enter] key to add a second line to the legend, and then type Duration: followed by a space.

15. In the **Project fields** box, click **Duration** on the drop-down list, and then click **Add**.

    Project adds the label and code for project duration to the legend.

16. In the **Width** box, type or select 3.

    This increases the width of the box on the left side of the legend.

17. Click **OK** to close the Page Setup dialog box.

Project applies the changes you specified to the legend. To get a closer look, zoom in on the legend.

18. In the Print Preview window, click the lower left corner of the page with the magnifying-glass pointer.

Project zooms in to show the page at a legible resolution.

You can see the data you added to the legend, which will be printed on every page of the printed output.

To conclude this exercise, you will choose not to print pages that do not include any Gantt bars.

19. Click **Multiple Pages** again.

Note that several of the pages of the Gantt Chart view do not contain any Gantt bars. If you intend to print a Gantt Chart view and stitch the pages together, these pages do not add any information; therefore, you don't need to print them.

20. Click **Page Setup**.

21. In the Page Setup dialog box, click the **View** tab.

22. Clear the **Print blank pages** box, and then click **OK**.

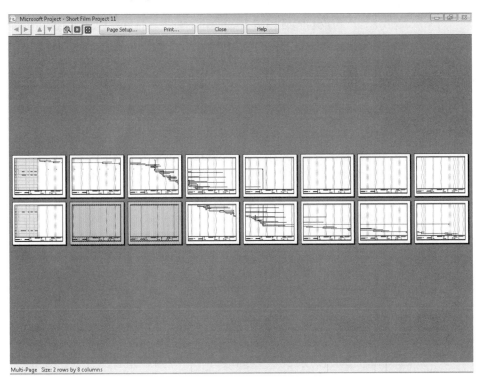

In the Print Preview window, the blank pages are formatted with a gray pattern, indicating that they will not be printed.

23. On the **Print Preview** toolbar, click **Close**.

The Print Preview window closes, and the Gantt Chart view appears. Although you did not print, your changes to the header and the legend will be saved when you save the project file.

> **Tip** You can print the project plan now if you wish; however, previewing the project plan is adequate for the purposes of the lesson. When printing in Project, you have additional options in the Print dialog box that you can open by clicking the Print command on the File menu. For example, you can choose to print a specific date range of a timescaled view, such as the Gantt Chart view, or you can print a specific page range.

Printing Reports

Reports are predefined formats intended for printing Project data. Unlike views, which you can either print or work with onscreen, reports are designed only for printing. You don't enter data directly into a report. Project includes several predefined reports that you can edit to display the information you want.

Although reports are distinct from views, some settings that you specify for a view might affect certain reports. For example:

- If subtasks are collapsed or hidden under summary tasks in a view, reports that include task lists will show only the summary tasks and not the subtasks.

- In usage views, if assignments are collapsed or hidden under tasks or resources, the usage reports (Task Usage or Resource Usage) likewise hide assignment details.

> **Tip** New in Project 2007 is a powerful new feature called visual reports. Visual reports can play an important role in your schedule reporting and analysis needs. Because visual reports depend on exporting Project data to other Office applications, we describe them in Chapter 12, "Sharing Project Information with Other Programs."

In this exercise, you see a report in the Print Preview window, and then you edit its definition (that is, the set of elements that make up the report) to include additional information.

1. On the **Report** menu, click **Reports**.

   The Reports dialog box appears, displaying the broad categories of reports available in Project.

2. Click **Custom**, and then click **Select**.

   The Custom Reports dialog box appears.

> **Tip** You can also double-click the Custom category.

This dialog box lists all predefined reports in Project as well as any custom reports that have been added.

3. In the **Reports** box, click **Task**, and then click the **Preview** button.

Project displays the Task report in the Print Preview window.

This report is a complete list of project tasks (except for summary tasks), similar to what you'd see in the Entry table of the Gantt Chart view. You'd like to see this data presented in a different way, so you'll edit this report.

4. On the **Print Preview** toolbar, click **Close**.

   The Print Preview window closes, and the Custom Reports dialog box reappears. Next, you'll create a copy of a built-in report and modify the copy.

5. In the **Reports** box, make sure that **Task** is still selected, and then click the **Copy** button.

   The Task Report dialog box appears.

> **Tip** The Task Report dialog box, like many dialog boxes in Project, includes a Help button that you can click for detailed descriptions of the settings in the dialog box.

6. In the **Name** box, select the displayed text, and then type Custom Task Report.

7. In the **Period** box, click **Months** on the drop-down list.

   Choosing Months here groups tasks by the month in which they occur. Because the report now includes a time period element, the Timescale options in the Print dialog box become available, enabling you to print data within a specific date range if you want.

8. In the **Table** box, click **Summary** on the drop-down list.

> **Tip** The tables listed in the Task Report dialog box are the same as those you can apply to any view that displays tasks in a table. In fact, if you completed Chapter 10, "Organizing and Formatting Project Details," the Shooting Schedule table you created there appears in the list here. When editing a report format, you can apply predefined or custom tables and filters, choose additional details to include in the report, and apply a sort order to the information—all in the dialog box for the report you're editing.

9. Click **OK** to close the Task Report dialog box.

10. In the Custom Reports dialog box, make sure that **Custom Task Report** is selected in the **Reports** box, and then click **Preview**.

Project applies the custom report settings you chose to the report, and the report appears in the Print Preview window. Next, you will zoom in to see the report in more detail.

11. In the Print Preview window, click the upper left corner of the page with the magnifying-glass pointer.

This custom report shows the fields displayed in the Summary Task table, but divides the tasks by month.

12. On the **Print Preview** toolbar, click **Close**.

13. In the **Custom Reports** dialog box, click **Close**.

14. Click **Close** again to close the Reports dialog box.

The Gantt Chart view reappears.

CLOSE the Short Film Project 11 file.

Key Points

- In Project, you can print views or reports. Reports are designed only for printing (or print previewing).

- When printing a view, you generally will get on paper what you see on your screen.

- With even moderately large project plans, a printed view or report might require more sheets of paper than you expect. For this reason, it's a good idea to always preview your output before printing it.

- The many reports available in Project are organized into several categories, such as Costs and Assignments. These are worth exploring (for example, by previewing) so that you know what's available.

Chapter at a Glance

Export information from Project into common formats used by data-crunching applications, page 271

Create snapshots of Project views to paste into other applications, page 262

Use the Copy Picture to Office Wizard to create new Office documents that include key Project status values and an image of the project plan, page 275

Create a visual report to represent schedule details in Excel or Visio, page 279

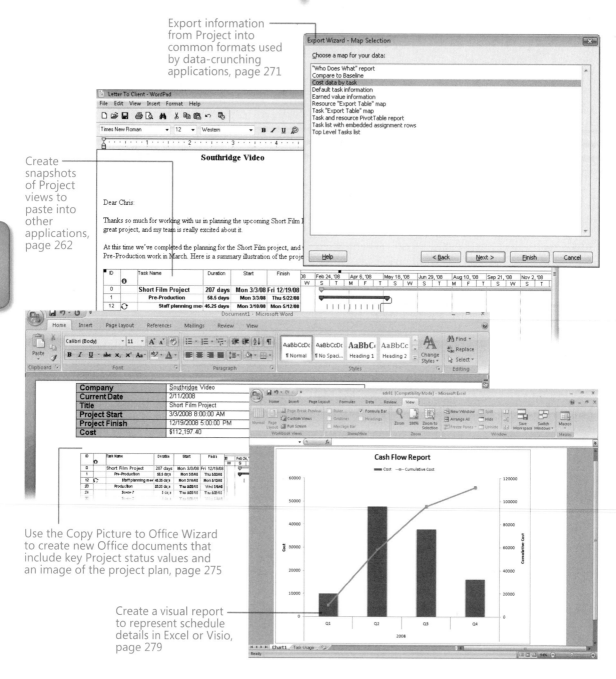

12 Sharing Project Information with Other Programs

In this chapter, you will learn how to:

✔ Copy and paste data to and from Project.

✔ Use Project to open a file produced in another program.

✔ Save Project data to other file formats using import/export maps.

✔ Generate a new Office document that contains essential project details and an illustration.

✔ Generate new Excel and Visio documents using the Visual Reports feature.

> **Tip** Do you need only a quick refresher on the topics in this chapter? See the Quick Reference entries on pages xxv-xlviii.

In this chapter, you focus on various ways of getting data into and out of Microsoft Office Project 2007. In addition to the standard Windows copy and paste features with which you might be familiar, Project offers a variety of options for importing and exporting data.

Throughout this chapter, you'll see the following terms:

● The *source program* is the program from which you copy information.

● The *destination program* is the program to which you paste information.

> **Tip** This tip describes enterprise project management (EPM) functionality. This chapter describes various ways of sharing information between Project and other applications, usually to communicate project details to stakeholders. Project Professional, when used with Project Server, offers more sophisticated ways of communicating with resources and other stakeholders online. To learn more about the enterprise collaboration tools available with Project Server, see Part 4, "Introducing Project Server."

Important Before you can use the practice files provided for this chapter, you need to install them from the book's companion CD to their default locations. See "Using the Book's CD" on page xix for more information.

Copying and Pasting with Project

You can copy and paste data to and from Project by clicking the Copy Cell, Paste, and Paste Special commands on the Edit menu and the Copy Picture command on the Report menu (or the corresponding buttons on the Standard toolbar). When copying data from Project, you can choose one of two options, depending on the results you want:

- You can copy text (such as task names and dates) from a table and paste it as text into a destination program, such as Microsoft Office Word.

- You can copy a graphic image of a view from Project and paste it as a graphic image in the destination program. With the Copy Picture command on the Report menu, you can create a graphic image of a view or a selected portion of a view. Use the Copy Picture feature to optimize the image for onscreen viewing (in PowerPoint, for example) or for printing (in Word, for example).

> **Tip** The Copy Picture feature also includes an option to save the snapshot to a GIF image file. You can then include the GIF image in a Word document or e-mail message, or post it directly to an intranet site.

There is an important distinction between using Copy Cell and Copy Picture. If you use Copy Cell, you can edit the data in the destination program. However, Copy Picture yields an image that you can edit only with a graphics editing program.

> **Tip** Many Windows programs, such as Word and Excel, have a Paste Special feature. This feature provides you with more options for pasting data from Project into the destination program. For example, you can use the Paste Special feature in Word to paste formatted or unformatted text, a picture, or a Project Document Object (an OLE object). You can also choose to paste only the data or paste it with a link to the source data in Project. For more information about using OLE with Project, type Embed an object into Project into the Search box in the upper right corner of the Project window. The Search box initially contains the text *Type a question for help.*

You also have two options when pasting data into Project from other programs:

- You can paste text (such as a list of task or resource names) into a table in Project. For example, you can paste a range of cells from Excel or a sequence of paragraphs from Word into Project. You might paste a series of task names that are organized in a vertical column from Excel or Word into the Task Name column in Project, for instance.

- You can paste a graphic image or an OLE object from another program into a graphical portion of a Gantt Chart view. You can also paste a graphic image or an OLE object into a task, resource, or assignment note; into a form view, such as the Task or Resource Form views; or into the header, footer, or legend of a view or report.

> **Important** Pasting text as multiple columns into Project requires some planning. First, make sure that the order of the information in the source program matches the order of the columns in the Project table. You can either rearrange the data in the source program to match the column order in the Project table or vice versa. Second, make sure that the columns in the source program support the same types of data—text, numbers, dates, and so on—as do the columns in Project.

For the short film project, you'd like to add a Gantt chart image to a document you've prepared for a stakeholder of the project. In this exercise, you copy a snapshot of a Gantt chart and paste it into Microsoft WordPad (or Word, if you prefer). You copy information in the same way regardless of the destination program you have in mind. For example, you could paste the snapshot into a word processor file or an e-mail message. To begin, you'll format the Gantt Chart view to show the information you want.

In this exercise, you copy an image of a Gantt Chart view to the Windows Clipboard and then paste it into another document.

> **BE SURE TO** start Microsoft Office Project 2007 if it's not already running.

> **Important** If you are running Project Professional, you may need to make a one-time adjustment to use the Computer account and to work offline. This ensures that the practice files you work with in this chapter do not affect your Project Server data. For more information, see "Starting Project Professional" on page 11.

> **OPEN** Short Film Project 12a from the \Documents\Microsoft Press\Project 2007 SBS\ Chapter 12 Sharing folder. You can also access the practice files for this book by clicking Start, All Programs, Microsoft Press, Project 2007 Step by Step, and then selecting the chapter folder of the file you want to open.

1. On the **File** menu, click **Save As**.

   The Save As dialog box appears.

2. In the **File name** box, type Short Film Project 12, and then click **Save**.

3. On the **Project** menu, point to **Filtered For: All Tasks**, and then click **Summary Tasks**.

   Project displays only the summary tasks in the project.

4. On the **View** menu, click **Zoom**.

   The Zoom dialog box appears.

5. In the **Zoom** dialog box, click **Entire project**, and then click **OK**.

   Project adjusts the timescale of the Gantt chart to show the entire project.

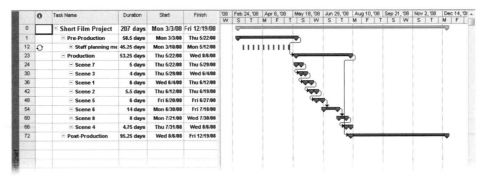

6. On the **Report** menu, click **Copy Picture**.

> **Tip** You can also click Copy Picture on the Standard toolbar.

   The Copy Picture dialog box appears.

7. Under the **Render image** label, make sure that **For screen** is selected.

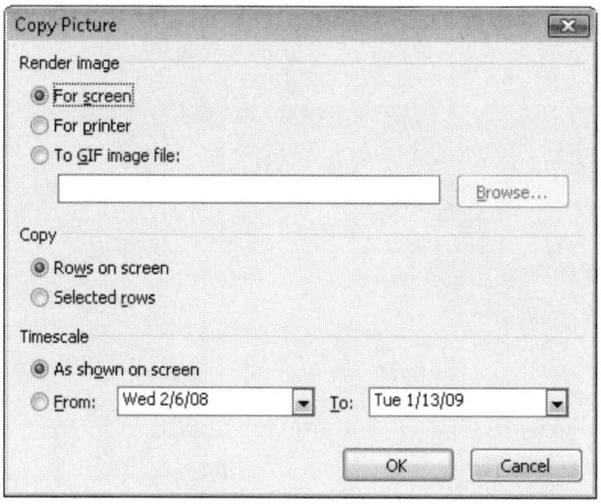

8. Click **OK.**

   Project copies a snapshot of the Gantt Chart view to the Clipboard.

   Next, you'll open a proposal document that's been created in a word processor. You can open this in WordPad (as illustrated here) or in Word if you have it.

9. Do one of the following:

   - If you do not have Word installed, click the **Windows Start** button, point to **All Programs**, click **Accessories**, and then click **WordPad.**

   - If you have Word installed, start it.

10. Do one of the following:

    - In WordPad or Word 2003 or earlier, on the **File** menu, click **Open.**

    - In Word 2007, click the **Microsoft Office** button, and then click **Open.**

11. Locate and open the document named **Letter To Client** in your Chapter 12 Sharing folder (you may have to select **All Files** in the **Files of type** box).

12. Once the document has opened, select the paragraph **(insert Gantt Chart picture here)**.

13. Press $\boxed{\text{Ctrl}}+\boxed{\text{V}}$.

    Project pastes the snapshot of the Gantt Chart view from the Clipboard to the document.

The image of the Gantt Chart view has been pasted into a WordPad document.
The Gantt chart cannot be edited in this format except as a graphic image.

Again, note that rather than pasting the image into a Word or WordPad document, you could paste this image into an e-mail message or another type of document.

14. Do one of the following:

   ● On the WordPad or Word 2003 or earlier **File** menu, click **Exit**.

   ● In Word 2007, click the **Microsoft Office** button, and then click **Exit Word**.

15. When prompted to save the document, click **No** or **Don't Save**.

Opening Other File Formats in Project

Information that you need to incorporate into a Project document can come from a variety of sources. A task list from a spreadsheet or resource costs from a database are two examples. You might want to use the unique features of Project to analyze data from another program. For example, many people keep task lists and simple project schedules in Excel, but accounting for basic scheduling issues, such as working and nonworking time, is impractical in Excel.

When saving data to or opening data from other formats, Project uses maps (also called *import/export maps* or data maps) that specify the exact data to import or export and how to structure it. You use import/export maps to specify how you want individual fields in the source program's file to correspond to individual fields in the destination program's file. After you set up an import/export map, you can use it over and over again.

> **Tip** If you have Excel installed on your computer, open the workbook named Sample Task List in the Chapter 12 Sharing folder. The important things to note about the workbook are the names and order of the columns, the presence of a header row (the labels at the top of the columns), and that the data is in a worksheet named Tasks. When you're done viewing the workbook, close it without saving changes.

In this exercise, a colleague has sent you an Excel workbook that contains her recommended tasks, durations, and sequence of activities for some work that Southridge Video will do in the future. You open the Excel workbook in Project and set up an import/export map to control how the Excel data is imported into Project.

> **Important** Project has a security setting that may prevent you from opening legacy or non-default file formats. Before you complete this section, you may need to change this setting. On the Tools menu, click **Options**. Click the Security tab, and under Legacy Formats, click **Prompt When Loading Files With Legacy Or Non Default File Format**.

1. In Project, on the **File** menu, click **Open**. The Open dialog box appears.

2. Locate the **Chapter 12 Sharing** folder in the Project 2007 Step by Step folder on your hard disk.

3. In the **Files of type** box, select **Microsoft Excel Workbooks**.

> **Tip** While scrolling through the Files Of Type box, you can see the several file formats that Project can import. If you work with programs that can save data in any of these file formats, you can import their data into Project. For more information, type File formats supported by Project into the Search box, located in the upper right corner of the Project window.

4. Select the **Sample Task List** file, and then click **Open**.

   The Import Wizard appears. This wizard helps you import structured data from a different format to Project.

5. Click the **Next** button.

   The second page of the Import Wizard appears.

The Import Wizard uses maps to organize the way that structured data from another file format is imported into Project. For this exercise, you will create a new map.

6. Make sure that **New map** is selected, and then click **Next**.

The Import Mode page of the Import Wizard appears.

7. Make sure that **As a new project** is selected, and then click **Next**.

The Map Options page of the Import Wizard appears.

8. Select the **Tasks** check box, and make sure that **Import includes headers** is selected as well.

Headers here refer to column headings.

9. Click **Next**.

The Task Mapping page of the Import Wizard appears. Here you identify the source worksheet within the Excel workbook and specify how you want to map the data from the source worksheet to Project fields.

10. On the **Source worksheet name** list, select **Tasks**.

Project analyzes the header row names from the worksheet and suggests the Project field names that are probable matches.

On this page of the Import Wizard you specify how Project should import data for other file formats; in this case an Excel workbook.

Use the Preview area to see how the data from another file format will be mapped to Project fields, based on the settings you've made above.

Import Wizard - Task Mapping

Map Tasks Data

Source worksheet name:

Tasks

Verify or edit how you want to map the data.

(Choose a source table above)

From: Excel Field	To: Microsoft Office Project Field	Data Type
Name	Name	Text
Duration	Duration	Text

Move ↑ ↓

[Add All] [Clear All] [Insert Row] [Delete Row]

Preview

Excel:	Name	Duration	
Project:	Name	Duration	
Preview:	Log footage	5 days	
	Record rough narr	4 days	
	Paper edit footage	10 days	

[Help]   [< Back] [Next >] [Finish] [Cancel]

11. Click **Next**.

The final page of the Import Wizard appears. Here you have the option of saving the settings for the new import map, which is useful when you anticipate importing similar data into Project in the future. This time, you'll skip this step.

12. Click the **Finish** button.

Project imports the Excel data into a new Project plan. (The dates you see on the timescale will differ from those shown because Project uses the current date as the project start date in the new file.)

After the task names and durations are imported, they appear as an unlinked sequence of tasks, ready for editing.

	❶	Task Name	Duration	Start	Finish
1		Log footage	5 days	Mon 2/11/08	Fri 2/15/08
2		Record rough narration	4 days	Mon 2/11/08	Thu 2/14/08
3		Paper edit footage	10 days	Mon 2/11/08	Fri 2/22/08
4		Rough cut edit	8 days	Mon 2/11/08	Wed 2/20/08
5		Fine cut edit	7 days	Mon 2/11/08	Tue 2/19/08
6		Hold formal approval show	1 day	Mon 2/11/08	Mon 2/11/08
7		Add dialog	2 days	Mon 2/11/08	Tue 2/12/08
8		Record final narration	5 days	Mon 2/11/08	Fri 2/15/08
9		Add head and tail titles	5 days	Mon 2/11/08	Fri 2/15/08
10		Add final music	3 days	Mon 2/11/08	Wed 2/13/08
11		Print internegative of film	3 days	Mon 2/11/08	Wed 2/13/08
12		Clone dubbing masters of	4 days	Mon 2/11/08	Thu 2/14/08
13		Archive master film and au	0.5 days	Mon 2/11/08	Mon 2/11/08
14		Hand off masters to distrib	0 days	Mon 2/11/08	Mon 2/11/08

This task list will become a more fully developed schedule that you'll use in a later chapter.

13. Close the new file without saving changes.

> **Tip** If you find that others need to give you task lists for creating a plan in Project and you must reorganize or clean up the lists you receive, try using the Microsoft Project Task List Import Template. Project installs this Excel template. In Excel 2003, this template appears on the Spreadsheet Solutions tab of the Templates dialog box. In Excel 2007, this template appears in the Installed Templates list of the New Workbook dialog box. The Excel template is set up with the proper field headings and column order to make importing a clean task list in Project easy.
>
> For more complex importing, see the Microsoft Project Plan Import Export Template (also an Excel template). This template contains not only task but also resource and assignment field headings and column orders for importing more complex information into Project.

> **Important** When saving an Excel file you intend to import into Project, save it in the Excel 97-2003 Workbook (xls) format. Project 2007 cannot open the Excel 2007 workbook (the XML-based xlsx) format.

Saving to Other File Formats from Project

Pasting Project data into other programs might be fine for one-time or infrequent needs, but this technique might not work as well if you must export a large volume of data from Project. Instead, you can save Project data in different file formats, which can be accomplished in various ways, including:

- You can save the entire project as Extensible Markup Language (XML) format for structured data exchange with other applications that support it. Unlike earlier versions of Project, Project 2007 does not support exporting to database formats, such as MDB or MPD, nor to the old Microsoft Project Exchange format, MPX (although Project 2007 can open these formats). The XML format is now your best option for exchanging structured data with other programs that support XML.

● You can save only the data you specify in a different format. The supported formats include Excel workbook, Excel PivotTable, and tab-delimited or comma-delimited text. When saving to these formats, you choose the format in which you want to save, pick a built-in export map (or create your own), and export the data.

Although the short film project has not yet started, the project file already contains quite a bit of planned cost data. You'd like to give this data to the financial planner of Southridge Video so she can start work on detailed budgets. However, the financial planner uses a budget program that cannot work directly with Project files. You decide to provide her with cost data as tab-delimited text, which will allow her the greatest flexibility when importing the data into her budget program.

Working with Project File Formats

Project 2000, 2002, and 2003 shared a common file format that could be opened by any version of Project from 2000 to 2003. In other words, if you were using Project 2000, 2002, or 2003, you didn't need to pay attention to the Project file format across these three versions of Project.

If you have Project 2007, you may find you need to share project plans with users of previous versions of Project. There are a few ways of doing this.

The simplest strategy is to save in Project 2000–2003 format from Project 2007 (On the File menu click Save As, and in the Save As Type box click Microsoft Project 2000-2003 (*.mpp)). However some data relating to new features in Project 2007 will be changed or discarded when saved. Cost resources, for example, will be converted to material resources.

Another strategy is to try to open a Project 2007 file in an earlier version of Project. Because the Project 2007 file format differs from that of all earlier versions of Project, you cannot open 2007 files in earlier versions of Project without first downloading a file converter from the Microsoft.com Web site. If a Project 2000, 2002, or 2003 user tries to open a 2007 file, Project will prompt them to download the converter. Even when using the converter, new features introduced in Project 2007, such as cost resources, are not supported in the earlier versions.

> **Important** At the time this book was published, the converter to open Project 2007 files in earlier versions of Project was planned but not yet available from Microsoft.

Yet another strategy familiar to users of much earlier versions of Project as well as other project management programs involves the Microsoft Project Exchange

(MPX) file format. If you must work with files from Project 95 or earlier, you can use the MPX format. Project 2007 can open files in the MPX format, which is supported by a variety of project management programs. Previous versions of Project up to 98 can save in the MPX format. If you need to migrate project plans from versions of Project 95 or earlier to Project 2007, use the MPX format. Note that Project 2007 can open, but not save in, MPX format, so it will be a one-way migration. Likewise Project 2007 can open but not save Project 98 files.

To open file formats other than Project's own or the Project 98 format, you must adjust a Project 2007 security option. On the Tools menu, click Options. Click the Security tab, and under Legacy Formats click Prompt When Loading Files With Legacy Or Non Default File Format.

In this exercise, you save project cost data to a text file using a built-in export map. At this point, you should still have Short Film Project 12 open in Project.

> **Important** Project has a security setting that may prevent you from opening legacy or non-default file formats. Before you complete this section, you may need to change this setting. On the Tools menu, click **Options**. Click the Security tab, and under Legacy Formats, click **Prompt When Loading Files With Legacy Or Non Default File Format**.

1. On the **File** menu, click **Save As**.

   The Save As dialog box appears. Project suggests saving the file in the same location from which you opened the practice file. If you see anything different in the Save As dialog box, locate the Chapter 12 Sharing folder.

2. In the **File name** box, type Short Film Project 12 Costs.

3. In the **Save as type** box, click **Text (Tab delimited)** from the list, and then click **Save**.

   The Export Wizard appears.

> **Tip** When you use import/export maps, it makes no difference what current view in Project is displayed. The current view does not affect what data can or cannot be exported.

4. Click **Next**.

   The second page of the Export Wizard appears.

5. Click **Use existing map**, and then click **Next**.

6. Under **Choose a map for your data**, select **Cost data by task**.

7. Click **Finish**.

   Project saves the text file. To view it, you will open the file in Microsoft Notepad.

8. On the **Windows Start** menu, point to **All Programs**, click **Accessories**, and click **Notepad**.

   Notepad starts.

9. In Notepad, make sure that Word Wrap is turned off. (On the **Format** menu, **Word Wrap** should not be selected.)

10. On the **File** menu, click **Open**.

11. Open the document Short Film Project 12 Costs in your Chapter 12 Sharing folder.

In this file, the fields are separated by tabs. It might not be easy for you to read, but this format is easily imported into virtually any data-crunching program.

12. On the **File** menu, click **Exit**. Notepad closes, and you return to Project.

Generating a Project Summary Report for Word, PowerPoint, or Visio

Although the Copy Picture feature is useful for moving an image of the active view to the Windows Clipboard or to a GIF file, Project makes it easy to go one step further and generate a complete document in Word, PowerPoint, or Visio. Project provides this capability with the Copy Picture To Office Wizard, which steps you through the process of specifying the exact data you want included in the new Office document and how you want it displayed. This wizard works with most views in Project, but not with the Calendar view, Relationship Diagram view, or form views.

The Copy Picture To Office Wizard generates a new Office document that contains a table of field values that apply to your entire project (such as the project finish date) as well as a GIF image of the current Project view. This wizard gives you the option of generating a new document in any of the three most common Office formats for project status reporting: PowerPoint, Word, and Visio.

In this exercise, you use the Copy Picture To Office Wizard to create a Word document with a GIF image of a Gantt chart.

> **Important** If the computer on which you are now working does not have PowerPoint, Word, or Visio 2000 or later installed, you cannot complete this procedure of using the Copy Picture To Office Wizard. If this is the case, proceed to the next section.

1. On the **View** menu, point to **Toolbars**, and click **Analysis**.

The Analysis toolbar appears.

> **Troubleshooting** If the Analysis toolbar is not listed, you may have a problem relating to COM add-ins when you installed Project 2007. To troubleshoot this problem, type **I don't see the Analysis toolbar listed in the View menu** into the Search box in the upper right corner of the Project window.

2. On the **Analysis** toolbar, click the **Copy Picture to Office Wizard** button.

The Information page of the wizard appears.

3. Click **Next**.

Step 1 of the wizard appears. Here you control the outline level of the task list.

4. Make sure that **Keep my original outline level** is selected.

5. Click **Next**.

Step 2 of the wizard appears. Here you specify exactly what you want copied and at what size.

6. Under **Copy**, make sure that **Rows on screen** is selected; under **Timescale**, make sure that **As shown on screen** is selected; under **Image Size**, make sure that **Default** is selected.

7. Click **Next**.

Step 3 of the wizard appears. Here you specify the Office application for which you want a new document created.

Before you choose an application, however, you'll preview the GIF image in your browser.

8. Click **Preview**.

Project displays the GIF image of your view in your browser.

9. Close your browser and return to step 3 of the wizard in Project.

10. Under **Application**, click **Word**.

11. Under **Orientation**, make sure that **Landscape** is selected.

12. Click **Next**.

Step 4 of the wizard appears. Here you review and, if you wish, modify the project-level fields to be included in the new document. These fields will appear in a table above the GIF image.

13. In the **Microsoft Office Project Fields** box, select **Cost**, and then click the **Add** button.

The *Cost* field name appears at the bottom of the fields list in the Fields To Export box.

14. Click **Finish**.

Project displays a confirmation message that it completed the new document creation.

15. Click **Close**.

The wizard starts Word, if it is not already running, and creates the new document.

16. If Word is minimized, click the **Word** icon on the taskbar and, if necessary, switch to the new document in Word.

The project-level fields appear in a table above the GIF image of the Gantt Chart view. For your real-world reporting needs, you could use such a document as a starting point for a recurring project status report or a one-time project write-up.

17. Close the document in Word without saving changes, and switch back to Project.

18. In Project, on the **View** menu, point to **Toolbars** and then click **Analysis**.

Project hides the Analysis toolbar.

Generating Visual Reports with Excel and Visio

Project 2007 includes a major new feature, visual reports, that focuses on sharing schedule details with other applications. Specifically, you can use the visual reports feature to export data from Project to either Excel or Visio and, once there, visually represent schedule details in compelling formats.

A visual report can include task, resource, or assignment details. When you select a visual report in Project, it generates a highly structured database, called an OLAP cube, from your project plan. Project then launches another Office application (either Excel or Visio, depending on the visual report you selected), loads and organizes the data used by that application, and generates a graphical representation of that data (an Excel chart or Visio diagram). The specific results you obtain depend on the type of visual report you choose:

- Excel visual reports utilize the PivotTable and PivotChart features in Excel. You can format the chart and modify the details in the PivotTable report from which the chart is derived. PivotTable reports are well suited to analyzing and summarizing the large volumes of data Project plans can contain. You can create Excel visual reports with Excel 2003 or later.

- Visio visual reports use a new feature introduced in Visio 2007 called PivotDiagrams. PivotDiagrams are well suited for presenting hierarchical data and can complement Project very well. Not only can you customize the visual report as a Visio diagram, but you can also filter and rearrange the data from which the diagram is derived. Visio visual reports require Visio 2007 or later.

Project includes several Excel and Visio visual report templates. You can also create your own visual reports from scratch or modify one of the supplied templates. If you are already familiar with Excel PivotTables, and/or are a Visio power user, and have the need to analyze and present Project data, you'll find visual reports of interest. However, if you're not as experienced with Excel PivotTables or Visio diagrams, you can still take a look at the visual report feature so that you have some exposure to this powerful new feature of Project 2007.

In this exercise, you generate both Excel and Visio visual reports.

> **Important** If the computer on which you are now working does not have Excel 2003 or later or Visio 2007 or later installed, you cannot complete this exercise. If this is the case, skip ahead to the "Key Points" section.

1. On the **Report** menu, click **Visual Reports**.

   The Visual Reports dialog box appears.

This dialog box groups visual reports in a number of ways: all reports; only Excel or Visio reports; and task, resource, or assignment details (divided into summary and usage reports). The dialog box includes a simplified preview of the type of graphic (chart or diagram) associated with each visual report. If desired, you can click the various tabs in the dialog box to see how the visual reports are organized.

The first visual report you'll generate is Excel based.

2. Click the **Task Usage** tab.

3. Click **Cash Flow Report** and then click **View**.

   Project generates the data required by this report, launches Excel, and creates the Cash Flow chart. You may need to adjust the zoom level to view the entire chart.

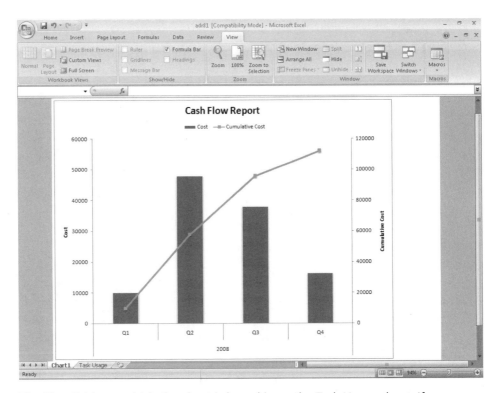

The PivotTable on which the chart is based is on the Task Usage sheet. If you are familiar with PivotTables, you can view that sheet and modify the PivotTable settings if you wish.

> **Tip** PivotTables is a powerful feature in Excel. To learn more, search for PivotTable in Excel Help.

4. When you are through working with the Excel chart, close Excel without saving changes.

To conclude this exercise, you will generate a Visio-based visual report.

> **Important** If the computer on which you are now working does not have Visio 2007 or later installed, you cannot complete this exercise. If this is the case, skip to step 11 to conclude this exercise.

In Project, the Visual Reports dialog box should still be displayed.

5. Click the **Assignment Usage** tab.

6. Click **Baseline Report (US)**, and then click **View**.

Project generates the data required by this report, launches Visio, and creates the Baseline Report diagram.

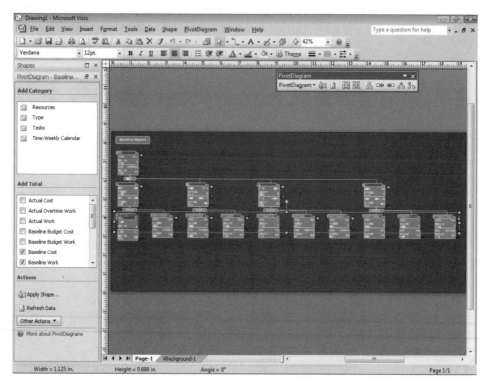

Next, you'll take a closer look at the items in this diagram.

7. In Visio, on the **View** menu, point to **Zoom**, and then **click 100%**.

8. If necessary, adjust the vertical and horizontal scroll bars until you can see the diagram details.

At this point, you could adjust the settings in the PivotDiagram pane in Visio to change the details included in the diagram.

> **Tip** PivotDiagrams is a new feature in Visio 2007. To learn more, click the More About PivotDiagrams link at the bottom of the PivotDiagram pane.

9. When you are through working with the Visio diagram, close it without saving changes.

10. In Project, click **Close** to close the Visual Reports dialog box.

> **CLOSE** the Short Film Project 12 file.

Key Points

- When sharing Project data with other Office applications, two useful techniques include copying images of the active view and generating a new Office document that includes key Project details and an image of the active view.

- You can both copy from and paste into Project just as you can with other Windows applications. However, when pasting data into a table in Project, take care to ensure that the data you want ends up in the correct fields.

- To help import Excel data into Project, Project installs two Excel templates that are properly structured for importing into Project.

- When opening other data formats in Project, Project uses import maps to help organize the imported data into the right structure for a Project table.

- Project supports saving data to common structured data formats, such as XML.

- Visual reports help you export Project data to nicely formatted Excel charts and Visio diagrams.

Chapter at a Glance

Update a baseline prior to tracking actual work, page 287

Set Baseline

- ● Set baseline
  - Baseline (last saved on Tue 10/3/06) ▼
- ○ Set interim plan
  - Copy: Start/Finish ▼
  - Into: Start1/Finish1 ▼

For:
- ● Entire project
- ○ Selected tasks

Enter actual work for tasks and assignments, page 291

	Task Name	Work	Baseline	Variance	Actual	Remaining	% W. Comp.	Details	W	T	F	S	S	M	T
1	− Pre-Production	1,452 hrs	1,452 hrs	0 hrs	82 hrs	1,370 hrs	6%	Work	12h	12h	24h			24h	
								Act. W	12h	12h	24h			18h	
2	− Review script	40 hrs	40 hrs	0 hrs	40 hrs	0 hrs	100%	Work	12h	12h					
								Act. W	12h	12h					
	Clair Hector	24 hrs	24 hrs	0 hrs	24 hrs	0 hrs	100%	Work	8h	8h					
								Act. W	8h	8h					
	Scott Cooper	16 hrs	16 hrs	0 hrs	16 hrs	0 hrs	100%	Work	4h	4h					
								Act. W	4h	4h					
3	− Develop script breakdo	144 hrs	144 hrs	0 hrs	42 hrs	102 hrs	29%	Work			24h			18h	
								Act. W			24h			18h	
	Clair Hector	48 hrs	48 hrs	0 hrs	14 hrs	34 hrs	29%	Work			8h			6h	
								Act. W			8h			6h	
	Johnathan Perrer	48 hrs	48 hrs	0 hrs	14 hrs	34 hrs	29%	Work			8h			6h	
								Act. W			8h			6h	
	Scott Cooper	48 hrs	48 hrs	0 hrs	14 hrs	34 hrs	29%	Work			8h			6h	
								Act. W			8h			6h	
4	− Develop production boi	588 hrs	588 hrs	0 hrs	0 hrs	588 hrs	0%	Work							
								Act. W							
	Johnathan Perrer	196 hrs	196 hrs	0 hrs	0 hrs	196 hrs	0%	Work							

Enter timephased actual work for tasks and assignments, page 298

	Task Name	Work	Details	F	S	S	M	T	W	T	F	S	S	M	T	W	T
1	+ Pre-Production	1,305 hrs	Work	12h													
			Act. W	12h													
24	− Production	2,495 hrs	Work				5h	26h	67h	107h	15h			24h	56h	164h	
			Act. W				5h										
25	− Scene 7	220 hrs	Work				5h	26h	67h	107h	15h						
			Act. W				5h										
26	− Scene 7 setup	20 hrs	Work				5h	15h									
			Act. W				5h										
	Electrician	4 hrs	Work				1h	3h									
			Act. W				1h										
	Jo Brown	8 hrs	Work				2h	6h									
			Act. W				2h										
	Max Benson	8 hrs	Work				2h	6h									
			Act. W				2h										
27	− Scene 7 rehearsal	44 hrs	Work					11h	33h								
			Act. W														
	Jon McKenzie	8 hrs	Work					2h	6h								

Interrupt work on the project to restart after the date you specify, page 303

Update Project

- ○ Update work as complete through: Mon 6/16/08 ▼
  - ● Set 0% - 100% complete
  - ○ Set 0% or 100% complete only
- ● Reschedule uncompleted work to start after: Wed 6/18/08 ▼

For: ● Entire project ○ Selected tasks

[Help]   [OK]   [Cancel]

13 Tracking Progress on Tasks and Assignments

In this chapter, you will learn how to:

✔ Update a previously saved baseline plan.

✔ Record actual work for tasks and assignments.

✔ Record actual work by time period.

✔ Interrupt work on a task and specify the date on which the task should start again.

> **Tip** Do you need only a quick refresher on the topics in this chapter? See the Quick Reference entries on pages xxv-xlviii.

Building, verifying, and communicating a sound project plan might take much or even most of your time as a project manager. However, *planning* is only the first phase of managing your projects. After the planning is completed, the implementation of the project starts—carrying out the plan that was previously developed. Ideally, projects are implemented exactly as planned, but this is seldom the case. In general, the more complex the project plan and the longer its planned duration, the more opportunity there is for variance to appear. *Variance* is the difference between what you thought would happen (as recorded in the project plan) and what really happened (as recorded by your tracking efforts).

Properly *tracking* actual work and comparing it against the original plan enables you to identify variance early and adjust the incomplete portion of the plan when necessary. If you completed Chapter 6, "Tracking Progress on Tasks," you were introduced to the simpler ways of tracking *actuals* in a project plan. These include recording the percentage of a task that has been completed as well as its actual start and finish dates. These methods of tracking progress are fine for many projects, but Microsoft Office Project 2007 also supports more detailed ways of tracking.

In this chapter, you track task-level and assignment-level work totals and work per time period, such as work completed per week or per day. Information distributed over time is commonly known as *timephased*, so tracking work by time period is sometimes referred to as *tracking timephased actuals*. This is the most detailed level of tracking progress available in Project.

As with simpler tracking methods, tracking timephased actuals is a way to address the most basic questions of managing a project:

- Are tasks starting and finishing as planned? If not, what will be the impact on the project's finish date?

- Are resources spending more or less time than planned to complete tasks?

- Is it taking more or less money than planned to complete tasks?

As a project manager, you must determine what level of tracking best meets the needs of your project plan and stakeholders. As you might expect, the more detailed the tracking level, the more effort required from you and the resources assigned to tasks. This chapter exposes you to the most detailed tracking methods available in Project.

In this chapter, you work with different means of tracking work and handling incomplete work. You begin, however, by updating the project baseline.

> **Tip** This tip describes enterprise project management (EPM) functionality. This chapter describes entering actual values directly in Project. Project Professional, when used with Project Server, offers more sophisticated ways of collecting information (such as actual work) from resources and other stakeholders. To learn more about the enterprise collaboration tools available with Project Server, see Part 4, "Introducing Project Server."

> **Important** Before you can use the practice files provided for this chapter, you need to install them from the book's companion CD to their default locations. See "Using the Book's CD" on page xix for more information.

Updating a Baseline

If you completed Chapter 6, you saved a baseline plan for a project plan. Recall that a *baseline* is a collection of important values in a project plan such as the planned start dates, finish dates, and costs of tasks, resources, and assignments. When you save (or set) a baseline, Project takes a "snapshot" of the existing values and saves it in the Project plan for future comparison.

Keep in mind that the purpose of the baseline is to record what you expected the project plan to look like at one point in time. As time passes, however, you might need to change your expectations. After saving an initial baseline plan, you might need to fine-tune the project plan by adding or removing tasks or assignments and so on. To keep an accurate baseline for later comparison, you have several options:

- Update the baseline for the entire project. This simply replaces the original baseline values with the currently scheduled values.

- Update the baseline for selected tasks. This does not affect the baseline values for other tasks or resource baseline values in the project plan.

- Save a second or subsequent baseline. You can save up to 11 baselines in a single plan. The first one is called Baseline, and the rest are Baseline 1 through Baseline 10.

> **Tip** To learn more about baselines in Project's online Help, type Create a baseline into the Search box in the upper right corner of the Project window. The Search box initially contains the text *Type a question for help*.

Since you completed the initial planning for the short film project and saved an initial baseline, the project plan has undergone some additional fine-tuning. This included some adjustments to assignments and task durations and a new task in the pre-production phase of the project. Because of these changes, the initial baseline does not quite match the project plan as it is currently scheduled. In this exercise, you compare the project plan as it is currently scheduled with the baseline plan and update the baseline for the project plan.

> **Important** If you are running Project Professional, you may need to make a one-time adjustment to use the My Computer account and to work offline. This ensures that the practice files you work with in this chapter do not affect your Project Server data. For more information, see "Starting Project Professional," on page 11.

> **OPEN** Short Film Project 13a from the *\Documents\Microsoft Press\Project 2007 SBS\ Chapter 13 Advanced Tracking* folder. You can also access the practice files for this book by clicking Start, All Programs, Microsoft Press, Project 2007 Step by Step, and then selecting the chapter folder of the file you want to open.

1. On the **File** menu, click **Save As**.

The Save As dialog box appears.

2. In the **File name** box, type **Short Film Project 13 Baseline**, and then click **Save**.

Next, you will switch to a different view to see baseline and scheduled values arranged for easy comparison.

3. On the **View** menu, click **Tracking Gantt**.

The Tracking Gantt view appears.

In The Tracking Gantt view, the Gantt bars for the tasks as they are currently scheduled appear in blue (or if critical, red) and their baseline schedule values appear as gray bars.

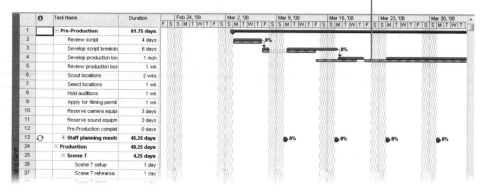

In the chart portion of this view, the tasks as they are currently scheduled appear as blue bars (if they are not critical tasks) or red bars (if they are critical). Below them, the baseline values of each task appear as gray bars.

> **Tip** In Gantt Chart views, the colors, patterns, and shapes of the bars represent specific things. To see what any item on the Gantt chart represents, just point your mouse pointer at it and a description will appear in a ScreenTip. To see a complete legend of Gantt chart items and their formatting, on the Format menu, click Bar Styles.

4. In the **Task Name** column, click the name of task 5, **Review production boards**.

5. On the **Standard** toolbar, click the **Scroll To Task** button.

Scroll to Task

The Tracking Gantt view scrolls to display the Gantt bars for task 5, *Review production boards*. This task was added to the plan after the initial baseline was saved.

This task was added to the project plan after its initial
baseline was saved, so this task has no baseline.

As you can see in the Tracking Gantt view, this task has no baseline bar, indicating that it has no baseline values.

To conclude this exercise, you will resave the baseline for the project plan. Doing so will update all baseline information for tasks, resources, and assignments prior to tracking progress.

> **Tip** This project plan includes a previously saved baseline that you will now overwrite. That's fine at this stage of the short film project, where the planning is complete and you'd like to have the most up-to-date baseline before recording any actual work. However, after work has been recorded, you should be careful about overwriting any previously saved baseline values. Once you overwrite a baseline, the original values are replaced and cannot be retrieved. Saving additional baselines is usually a better strategy after work on the project has begun.

6. On the **Tools** menu, point to **Tracking**, and then click **Set Baseline**.

   The Set Baseline dialog box appears.

7. Make sure that the **Set Baseline** option is selected. In the **For** area, make sure that the **Entire project** option is selected.

> **Tip** To update a baseline just for selected tasks, click Selected Tasks in the For area. When you do this, the options under Roll Up Baselines become available. You can control how baseline updates should affect the baseline values for summary tasks. For example, you could resave a baseline for a subtask and update its related summary task baseline values if desired. To remove a baseline, on the Tools menu, point to Tracking, and then click Clear Baseline.

8. Click **OK** to update the baseline.

Project alerts you that you are about to overwrite the previously saved baseline values.

9. Click the **Yes** button.

Project updates the baseline values for the project plan.

After resaving the baseline for the entire project, the baseline start, finish, and duration values (among others) match the scheduled values.

	❶	Task Name	Duration	Apr 6, '08	Apr 13, '08	Apr 20, '08	Apr 27, '08	May 4, '08	May 11, '08
1		⊟ Pre-Production	61.75 days						
2		Review script	4 days						
3		Develop script breakdo	6 days						
4		Develop production bo	1 mon	0%					
5		Review production bo	1 wk		0%				
6		Scout locations	2 wks			0%			
7		Select locations	1 wk				0%		
8		Hold auditions	1 wk						
		Apply for filming permit	1 wk						

Task 5 now has a baseline, and all of the other tasks' baseline values now match their scheduled values.

Save

10. On the **Standard** toolbar, click **Save**.

11. On the **File** menu, click **Close** to close the project plan.

Saving Interim Plans

After you've started tracking actual values or any time you've adjusted your schedule, you might want to take another snapshot of the current start and finish dates. You can do this with an interim plan. Like a baseline, an *interim plan* is a set of current values from the project plan that Project saves with the file. Unlike the baseline, however, an interim plan saves only the start and finish dates of tasks, not resource or assignment values. You can save up to 10 different interim plans during a project. (If you find that you need multiple snapshots of scheduled values in addition to start and finish dates, you should instead save additional baselines.)

Depending on the scope and duration of your projects, you might want to save an interim plan at any of the following junctures:

- At the conclusion of a major phase of work
- At preset time intervals, such as weekly or monthly
- Just before or after entering a large number of actual values

To save an interim plan, on the Tools menu, point to Tracking, and then click Set Baseline. In the Set Baseline dialog box, select the Set interim plan option. To learn more about interim plans, type **Create an interim plan** into the Search box in the upper right corner of the Project window.

Tracking Actual and Remaining Values for Tasks and Assignments

If you completed Chapter 6, you entered actual start, finish, and duration values for individual tasks. For tasks that have resources assigned to them, you can enter actual and remaining work values for the task as a whole or for specific assignments to that task. To help you understand how Project handles the actual values you enter, consider the following:

● If a task has a single resource assigned to it, the actual work values you enter for the task or assignment apply equally to both the task and the resource. For example, if you record that the assignment started on March 21 and has five hours of actual work, those values apply to the task as well.

● If a task has multiple resources assigned to it, the actual work values you enter for the task are distributed among or rolled down to the assignments according to their assignment units. This level of detail is appropriate if you aren't concerned about the details at the individual assignment level.

● If a task has multiple resources assigned to it, the actual work values you enter for one assignment are rolled up to the task. However, the new actual work values do not affect the other assignments' work values on the task. This level of detail is appropriate if details at the individual assignment level are important to you.

In this exercise, you record task-level and assignment-level actuals and see how the information is rolled up or down between tasks and assignments.

> **OPEN** Short Film Project 13b from the *\Documents\Microsoft Press\Project 2007 SBS\ Chapter 13 Advanced Tracking* folder. You can also access the practice files for this book by clicking Start, All Programs, Microsoft Press, Project 2007 Step by Step, and then selecting the chapter folder of the file you want to open.

1. On the **File** menu, click **Save As**.

The Save As dialog box appears.

2. In the **File name** box, type **Short Film Project 13 Actuals**, and then click **Save**.

This version of the project plan includes the updated baseline values you previously saved, as well as the first actuals reported against the first pre-production task.

3. On the **View** menu, click **Task Usage**.

The Task Usage view appears. The two sides of the usage view are split by a vertical divider bar. The Task Usage view lists resources under the tasks to which they're assigned. This information appears in the table on the left side. On the right side, you see rows organized under a timescale. The rows on the right side show you the scheduled work values for each task (for the task rows) or resource assignments (for assignment rows) on the left side. The scheduled work values for each resource are the timephased values of the assignments. The Task Usage view color-codes the rows on the right side: task rows have a yellow background, and assignment rows have a white background.

4. In the **Task Name** column, click the name of task 3, **Develop script breakdown and schedule**.

Scroll to Task

5. On the **Standard** toolbar, click the **Scroll To Task** button.

The timephased grid on the right side of the view scrolls to display the first scheduled work for the task.

Next, you'll switch the table and details shown in the view.

6. On the **View** menu, point to **Table: Usage**, and then click **Work**.

The Work table appears.

In a Task Usage view, the numbered rows are tasks. If the task has assignments, they will appear in unnumbered rows directly below the task.

In a usage view, a table appears in the left pane and a timephased grid appears in the right pane.

This timephased grid displays scheduled work per day for each assignment and task. Changing the timescale of the grid changes the level of detail it reports, though the underlying time-phased data does not change.

	Task Name	Work	Baseline	Details	T	W	T	F	S	Mar 9, '08 S	M	T	W	T	F	S
1	Pre-Production	1,452 hrs	1,452 hrs	Work	8h	8h	12h	12h	24h		24h	24h	24h	24h	24h	
2	Review script	40 hrs	40 hrs	Work	8h	12h	12h									
	Clair Hector	24 hrs	24 hrs	Work	4h	8h	8h									
	Scott Cooper	16 hrs	16 hrs	Work	4h	4h	4h									
3	Develop script breakdo	144 hrs	144 hrs	Work				24h			18h	24h	24h	24h	24h	
	Clair Hector	48 hrs	48 hrs	Work				8h			6h	8h	8h	8h	8h	
	Johnathan Perrer	48 hrs	48 hrs	Work				8h			6h	8h	8h	8h	8h	
	Scott Cooper	48 hrs	48 hrs	Work				8h			6h	8h	8h	8h	8h	
4	Develop production bor	588 hrs	588 hrs	Work												
	Johnathan Perrer	194 hrs	194 hrs	Work												
	Kim Yoshida	200 hrs	200 hrs	Work												
	Scott Cooper	194 hrs	194 hrs	Work												
5	Review production boe	80 hrs	80 hrs	Work												
	Clair Hector	40 hrs	40 hrs	Work												
	Scott Cooper	40 hrs	40 hrs	Work												
6	Scout locations	240 hrs	240 hrs	Work												
	Jan Miksovsky	80 hrs	80 hrs	Work												
	Jo Brown	80 hrs	80 hrs	Work												
	Max Benson	80 hrs	80 hrs	Work												
	Travel			Work												
7	Select locations	116 hrs	116 hrs	Work												

This table includes the Actual Work and Remaining Work columns that you will work with shortly, although they might not yet be visible. The values in the Work column are the task and assignment totals for scheduled work. Note that each task's work value is the sum of its assignment work values. For example, the work total for task 2, 40 hours, is the sum of Clair Hector's 24 hours of work on the task and Scott Cooper's 16 hours.

Next, you'll change the details shown on the timephased grid on the right side of the view.

7. On the **Format** menu, point to **Details**, and then click **Actual Work**.

For each task and assignment, Project displays the Work and Actual Work rows on the timephased grid on the right side of the view.

When you display the actual work details, the Act. Work row appears in the timephased grid for every assignment, task, and summary task.

	Task Name	Work	Baseline	Details	T	W	T	F	S	Mar 9, '08 S	M	T	W	T	F	S
1	⊟ Pre-Production	1,452 hrs	1,452 hrs	Work	8h	12h	12h	24h			24h	24h	24h	24h	24h	
				Act. W	8h	12h	12h									
2	⊟ Review script	40 hrs	40 hrs	Work	8h	12h	12h									
				Act. W	8h	12h	12h									
	Clair Hector	24 hrs	24 hrs	Work	4h	8h	8h									
				Act. W	4h	8h	8h									
	Scott Cooper	16 hrs	16 hrs	Work	4h	4h	4h									
				Act. W	4h	4h	4h									
3	⊟ Develop script breakdo	144 hrs	144 hrs	Work				24h			18h	24h	24h	24h	24h	
				Act. W												
	Clair Hector	48 hrs	48 hrs	Work				8h			6h	8h	8h	8h	8h	
				Act. W												
	Johnathan Perrer	48 hrs	48 hrs	Work				8h			6h	8h	8h	8h	8h	
				Act. W												
	Scott Cooper	48 hrs	48 hrs	Work				8h			6h	8h	8h	8h	8h	
				Act. W												
4	⊟ Develop production bor	588 hrs	588 hrs	Work												
				Act. W												
	Johnathan Perrer	196 hrs	196 hrs	Work												

Tip You can change the details (that is, fields) shown under the timescale in a usage view. You can add or remove fields and change the formatting of the fields shown. For example, you can add the Baseline Work field to the fields shown in the usage view and format it with a different colored background. To see the available fields and formatting options, on the Format menu, click Detail Styles, and then click the Usage Details tab.

In the timephased grid, you see the scheduled work values per day. If you were to add up the daily work values for a specific task or assignment, the total would equal the value in the Work column for that task or assignment. In a usage view, you see work values at two different levels of detail: the total value for a task or assignment and the more detailed timephased level. These two sets of values are directly related.

Next, you'll enter task-level and assignment-level actual work values and see how they are reflected in the timephased details.

8. Using the mouse, drag the vertical divider bar to the right until you can see all of the columns in the Work table.

Tip When the mouse pointer is in the right position to drag the vertical divider bar, it changes to a two-headed arrow that points left and right. Double-clicking the vertical divider bar will snap it to the nearest column's right edge.

To see more or less of the table on the left and the timephased grid on the right, drag this divider bar left or right. Double-clicking the divider bar will snap it to the nearest column.

	Task Name	Work	Baseline	Variance	Actual	Remaining	% W. Comp.	Details	W	T	F	S	S	M	T
1	⊟ Pre-Production	1,452 hrs	1,452 hrs	0 hrs	40 hrs	1,412 hrs	3%	Work	12h	12h	24h			24h	
								Act. W	12h	12h					
2	⊟ Review script	40 hrs	40 hrs	0 hrs	40 hrs	0 hrs	100%	Work	12h	12h					
								Act. W	12h	12h					
	Clair Hector	24 hrs	24 hrs	0 hrs	24 hrs	0 hrs	100%	Work	8h	8h					
								Act. W	8h	8h					
	Scott Cooper	16 hrs	16 hrs	0 hrs	16 hrs	0 hrs	100%	Work	4h	4h					
								Act. W	4h	4h					
3	⊟ Develop script breakdo	144 hrs	144 hrs	0 hrs	0 hrs	144 hrs	0%	Work			24h			18h	
								Act. W							
	Clair Hector	48 hrs	48 hrs	0 hrs	0 hrs	48 hrs	0%	Work			8h			6h	
								Act. W							
	Johnathan Perrer	48 hrs	48 hrs	0 hrs	0 hrs	48 hrs	0%	Work			8h			6h	
								Act. W							
	Scott Cooper	48 hrs	48 hrs	0 hrs	0 hrs	48 hrs	0%	Work			8h			6h	
								Act. W							
4	⊟ Develop production bo	588 hrs	588 hrs	0 hrs	0 hrs	588 hrs	0%	Work							
								Act. W							
	Johnathan Perre	194 hrs	194 hrs	0 hrs	0 hrs	194 hrs	0%	Work							

9. In the **Actual** column for task 3, **Develop script breakdown and schedule**, type or click 42h, and then press Enter .

Entering an actual value for the task causes Project to distribute the actual values among the assigned resources and adjust remaining work and other values.

	Task Name	Work	Baseline	Variance	Actual	Remaining	% W. Comp.	Details	W	T	F	S	S	M	T
1	⊟ Pre-Production	1,452 hrs	1,452 hrs	0 hrs	82 hrs	1,370 hrs	6%	Work	12h	12h	24h			24h	
								Act. W	12h	12h	24h			18h	
2	⊟ Review script	40 hrs	40 hrs	0 hrs	40 hrs	0 hrs	100%	Work	12h	12h					
								Act. W	12h	12h					
	Clair Hector	24 hrs	24 hrs	0 hrs	24 hrs	0 hrs	100%	Work	8h	8h					
								Act. W	8h	8h					
	Scott Cooper	16 hrs	16 hrs	0 hrs	16 hrs	0 hrs	100%	Work	4h	4h					
								Act. W	4h	4h					
3	⊟ Develop script breakdo	144 hrs	144 hrs	0 hrs	42 hrs	102 hrs	29%	Work			24h			18h	
								Act. W			24h			18h	
	Clair Hector	48 hrs	48 hrs	0 hrs	14 hrs	34 hrs	29%	Work			8h			6h	
								Act. W			8h			6h	
	Johnathan Perrer	48 hrs	48 hrs	0 hrs	14 hrs	34 hrs	29%	Work			8h			6h	
								Act. W			8h			6h	
	Scott Cooper	48 hrs	48 hrs	0 hrs	14 hrs	34 hrs	29%	Work			8h			6h	
								Act. W			8h			6h	
4	⊟ Develop production bo	588 hrs	588 hrs	0 hrs	0 hrs	588 hrs	0%	Work							
								Act. W							
	Johnathan Perre	194 hrs	194 hrs	0 hrs	0 hrs	194 hrs	0%	Work							

Project highlights the most recently changed values.

Several important things occurred when you pressed Enter:

● Project applied change highlighting to the updated values in the table.

● The amount of actual work you entered was subtracted from the Remaining column.

- The actual work was distributed to the three assignments on the task, resulting in 14 hours of actual work being recorded for each resource. Likewise, the updated remaining work value was recalculated for each assignment.

- The updated actual and remaining work values were rolled up to the pre-production summary task.

- The actual work values were also redistributed to the task and assignment timephased values.

In the timephased grid side of the view, you can observe the daily scheduled work and actual work values for the three resources on Friday and Monday, March 7 and 10. Because you entered an actual work value for the entire task, Project assumes that the work was done as scheduled (eight hours of scheduled work per resource on Friday and six hours on Monday) and records these timephased values for the resources.

To conclude this exercise, you will enter assignment work values and see the effect on the task.

10. In the **Actual** column for Clair Hector's assignment to task 3, type or click 30h, and then press [Enter].

Entering actual work on this assignment
updates remaining work and related values
on the task.

Task Name		Work	Baseline	Variance	Actual	Remaining	% W. Comp.	Details	W	T	F	S	S	M	T
1	Pre-Production	1,452 hrs	1,452 hrs	0 hrs	98 hrs	1,354 hrs	7%	Work	12h	12h	24h			24h	
								Act. W	12h	12h	24h			18h	
2	Review script	40 hrs	40 hrs	0 hrs	40 hrs	0 hrs	100%	Work	12h	12h					
								Act. W	12h	12h					
	Clair Hector	24 hrs	24 hrs	0 hrs	24 hrs	0 hrs	100%	Work	8h	8h					
								Act. W	8h	8h					
	Scott Cooper	16 hrs	16 hrs	0 hrs	16 hrs	0 hrs	100%	Work	4h	4h					
								Act. W	4h	4h					
3	Develop script breakdo	144 hrs	144 hrs	0 hrs	58 hrs	86 hrs	40%	Work			24h			18h	
								Act. W			24h			18h	
	Clair Hector	48 hrs	48 hrs	0 hrs	30 hrs	18 hrs	63%	Work			8h			6h	
								Act. W			8h			6h	
	Johnathan Perrer	48 hrs	48 hrs	0 hrs 14 hrs		34 hrs	29%	Work			8h			6h	
								Act. W			8h			6h	
	Scott Cooper	48 hrs	48 hrs	0 hrs	14 hrs	34 hrs	29%	Work			8h			6h	
								Act. W			8h			6h	
4	Develop production bo	588 hrs	588 hrs	0 hrs	0 hrs	588 hrs	0%	Work							
								Act. W							
	Johnathan Perrer	194 hrs	194 hrs	0 hrs	0 hrs	194 hrs	0%	Work							

Clair Hector's actual and remaining work values are updated, and those updates also roll up to the task and its summary task (Project highlights the changed values). However, the actual and remaining work values for the other two resources assigned to the task are not affected.

11. Drag the vertical divider bar back to the left to see the updated timephased values for the task.

The actual work value entered in the table
for the task and assignment is distributed
across the timephased grid.

Task Name	Work	Baseline	Details	T	W	T	F	S	Mar 9, '08 S	M	T	W	T	F	S	M
1	⊟ Pre-Production	1,452 hrs	1,452 hrs	Work	8h	12h	12h	24h			24h	24h	24h	24h	24h		
				Act. W	8h	12h	12h	24h			18h	8h	8h				
2	⊟ Review script	40 hrs	40 hrs	Work	8h	12h	12h										
				Act. W	8h	12h	12h										
	Clair Hector	24 hrs	24 hrs	Work	4h	8h	8h										
				Act. W	4h	8h	8h										
	Scott Cooper	16 hrs	16 hrs	Work	4h	4h	4h										
				Act. W	4h	4h	4h										
3	⊟ Develop script breakdo	144 hrs	144 hrs	Work				24h			18h	24h	24h	24h	24h		
				Act. W				24h			18h	8h	8h				
	Clair Hector	48 hrs	48 hrs	Work				8h			6h	8h	8h	8h	8h		
				Act. W				8h			6h	6h	8h				
	Johnathan Perre	48 hrs	48 hrs	Work				8h			6h	8h	8h	8h	8h		
				Act. W				8h			6h	6h					
	Scott Cooper	48 hrs	48 hrs	Work				8h			6h	8h	8h	8h	8h		
				Act. W				8h			6h	6h					
4	⊟ Develop production bo	588 hrs	588 hrs	Work													
				Act. W													
	Johnathan Perre	194 hrs	194 hrs	Work													

Again, Project assumes that the actual work value you entered for Clair was completed as scheduled; therefore, her work and actual work timephased values match
through Wednesday, March 12.

12. On the **Standard** toolbar, click **Save**.

13. On the **File** menu, click **Close** to close the project plan.

> **Tip** You are entering actual work values in this exercise, but you can also enter remaining
> work values or percentage of work complete. All of these values are related to each other—
> a change to one affects the others. You can update these values in the Work table or on the
> Tracking tab of the Assignment Information dialog box (when an assignment is selected).

Tracking a task's actual work complete value is more detailed than entering a simple
percentage complete on a task. However, neither method is as detailed as entering timephased actual work for tasks or assignments (as you will see in the next section). There's
nothing wrong with tracking actual work at the task or assignment level (or simply entering a percentage complete, for that matter) if that level of detail meets your needs. In
fact, whether you see the timephased details or not, Project always distributes any percentage complete or task-level or assignment-level actual work value that you enter into
corresponding timephased values, as you saw earlier. This is one reason why new Project
users sometimes are surprised to encounter extremely detailed values, such as 1.67 hours
of work, scheduled for a particular day. If you generally understand the math that Project
is following, however, you can figure out where such numbers come from. On the other
hand, you might not care about this level of scheduling detail—and that's OK, too.

Manually Entering Actual Costs

Whenever you've entered actual work values in this chapter, Project has calculated actual cost values for the affected task, its summary task, the resources assigned to the task, and the entire project. By default, Project calculates actual costs and does not allow you to enter them directly. In most cases, this is what we recommend and what is done with the practice files used in this book. However, if you want to enter actual cost values yourself in your own project plans, follow these steps.

> **Important** The following procedure is provided for your general information; however, do not follow this procedure now if you are completing the exercises in this book. Doing so will produce results that will not match those shown in this book.

1. On the **Tools** menu, click the **Options** command.

   The Options dialog box appears.

2. Click the **Calculation** tab.

3. Under the **Calculation options for <filename>** label, clear the **Actual costs are always calculated by Microsoft Office Project** check box.

4. Click **OK**.

After automatic cost calculation is turned off, you can enter or import task-level or assignment-level actual costs in the Actual field. This field is available in several locations, such as the Cost table. You can also enter actual cost values daily or at another interval in any timescale view, such as the Task Usage or Resource Usage view. On the Format menu, point to the Details command, and then click Actual Cost.

Tracking Timephased Actual Work for Tasks and Assignments

Entering timephased actuals requires more work on the project manager's part and might require more work from resources to inform the project manager of their daily actuals. However, doing so gives you far more detail about the project's task and resource status than the other methods used for entering actuals. Entering timephased values might be the best approach to take if you have a group of tasks or an entire project that includes the following:

- High-risk tasks

- Relatively short-duration tasks in which a variance of even one day could put the overall project at risk

- Tasks for which you'd like to develop or validate *throughput metrics*, or rates at which a given quantity of a deliverable can be completed over a given time period, such as "paint two set backdrops per day"

- Tasks in which sponsors or other stakeholders have an especially strong interest

- Tasks that require hourly billing for labor

At this point in the short film project, the pre-production work has been completed, and the production phase has just begun. Because of the large number of resources involved, the high setup and teardown costs, and the limited availability of sites at which some scenes must be filmed, these tasks are the riskiest ones of the project. In this exercise, you enter daily actuals for production tasks in the Task Usage view.

> **OPEN** Short Film Project 13c from the *\Documents\Microsoft Press\Project 2007 SBS\ Chapter 13 Advanced Tracking* folder. You can also access the practice files for this book by clicking Start, All Programs, Microsoft Press, Project 2007 Step by Step, and then selecting the chapter folder of the file you want to open.

1. On the **File** menu, click **Save As**.

   The Save As dialog box appears.

2. In the **File name** box, type **Short Film Project 13 Timephased Actuals**, and then click **Save**.

3. Click the minus sign next to task 1, **Pre-Production**, to collapse this phase of the project plan.

Scroll To Task

4. In the **Task Name** column, click the name of task 26, **Scene 7 setup**, and then, on the **Standard** toolbar, click **Scroll To Task**.

   Project scrolls the timephased grid to display the first scheduled work values of the Production phase.

	Task Name	Work	Details	F	S	S	M	T	W	T	F	S	S	M	T	W	T
						May 25, '08								Jun 1, '08			
1	⊞ Pre-Production	1,305 hrs	Work	12h													
			Act. W	12h													
24	⊟ Production	2,485 hrs	Work				20h	44h	136h	20h	24h			56h	164h	24h	
			Act. W														
25	⊟ Scene 7	220 hrs	Work				20h	44h	136h	20h							
			Act. W														
26	⊟ Scene 7 setup	20 hrs	Work				20h										
			Act. W														
	Electrician	4 hrs	Work				4h										
			Act. W														
	Jo Brown	8 hrs	Work				8h										
			Act. W														
	Max Benson	8 hrs	Work				8h										
			Act. W														
27	⊟ Scene 7 rehearsal	44 hrs	Work					44h									
			Act. W														
	Jan Miksovsk	8 hrs	Work					8h									

The first timephased actual work values you will enter are at the task level and not for specific assignments.

5. In the timephased grid, click the cell at the intersection of the **Monday, May 26** column and the task 26 actual work row. The actual work row is directly below the work row, which contains the value *20h*.

> **Tip** If you point to the name of a day on the timescale, Project will display the full date of that day in a ScreenTip.
>
> You can change the formatting of the timescale to control the time period in which you enter actual values in the timephased grid. For example, you can format the timescale to show weeks rather than days; when you enter an actual value at the weekly level, that value is distributed over the week. For more information about adjusting the timescale, type **Change the timescale to see a different level of detail** into the Search box in the upper right corner of the Project window.

6. Type **5h**, and then press the → key.

Here is the first time-
phased actual work
value you entered.

	Task Name	Work	Details	F	S	May 25, '08 S	M	T	W	T	F	S	Jun 1, '08 S	M	T	W	
1	⊞ Pre-Production	1,305 hrs	Work	12h													
			Act. W	12h													
24	⊟ Production	2,495 hrs	Work				5h	26h	67h	107h	15h			24h	56h	164h	
			Act. W				5h										
25	⊟ Scene 7	220 hrs	Work				5h	26h	67h	107h	15h						
			Act. W				5h										
26	− Scene 7 setup	20 hrs	Work				5h	15h									
			Act. W				5h										
	Electrician	4 hrs	Work				1h	3h									
			Act. W				1h										
	Jo Brown	8 hrs	Work				2h	6h									
			Act. W				2h										
	Max Benson	8 hrs	Work				2h	6h									
			Act. W				2h										
27	⊟ Scene 7 rehearsal	44 hrs	Work					11h	33h								
			Act. W														
	Jan Miksovsk	8 hrs	Work					2h	8h								

As soon as you entered the first actual value for the task, the scheduled work value changed to match it. Both work and actual work values rolled up to the task and summary task levels and were distributed among the specific assignments to the task. You can see this happen in the timephased grid on the right and the table on the left.

7. In the Tuesday, May 27 actual work cell, type **15h**, and then press Enter .

Here is the second timephased actual work value you entered. The timephased values for the task are distributed to the timephased assignment
values and affect the task and assignment totals on the table on the left.

That step concludes the actual work for this task. Next, you'll enter actual work values for the assignments on the next task.

For task 27, *Scene 7 rehearsal*, you have the actual work values for several resources
for Tuesday and Wednesday, May 27 and 28.

8. If necessary, use the scroll bars to show that all of the assignments to task 27 are
   visible.

9. In the timephased grid, click the cell at the intersection of the Tuesday, May 27 column and Jan Miksovsky's actual work row for her assignment to task 27.

10. Enter the following actual work values into the timescale grid.

> **Tip** When entering actual work, you do not need to include the "h" abbreviation (to denote
> hours). You can simply enter the number and Project will record it as hours. Hours is the de-
> fault work value for data entry. If you wish, you can change this on the Schedule tab of the
> Options dialog box (Tools menu).

Resource Name	Tuesday's Actual Work	Wednesday's Actual Work
Jan Miksovsky	3h	5h
Jo Brown	3h	5h
Joseph Matthews	2h	7h
Paul Borm	3h	1h
Scott Cooper	4h	8h
Sue Jackson	2h	6h

Task Name	Work	Details	May 25, '08								Jun 1, '08					
			F	S	S	M	T	W	T	F	S	S	M	T	W	T
27 Scene 7 rehearsal	49 hrs	Work					17h	32h								
		Act.W					17h	32h								
Jan Miksovsk	8 hrs	Work					3h	5h								
		Act.W					3h	5h								
Jo Brown	8 hrs	Work					3h	5h								
		Act.W					3h	5h								
Joseph Matth	9 hrs	Work					2h	7h								
		Act.W					2h	7h								
Paul Borm	4 hrs	Work					3h	1h								
		Act.W					3h	1h								
Scott Cooper	12 hrs	Work					4h	8h								
		Act.W					4h	8h								
Sue Jackson	8 hrs	Work					2h	6h								
		Act.W					2h	6h								
28 Scene 7 shoot	136 hrs	Work						34h	102h							
		Act.W														
16-mm Came.	24 hrs	Work						6h	18h							

Again, the individual resources' actual work values were rolled up to the tasks' actual work values. The original work values are also saved in the baseline should you ever need to refer to them later.

Save

11. On the **Standard** toolbar, click **Save**.

12. On the **File** menu, click **Close** to close the project plan.

> **Tip** In this exercise, you have seen how task and assignment values are directly related; an update to one directly affects the other. However, you can break this relationship if desired. Doing so enables you to record progress for resource assignments, for example, and manually enter actual values for the tasks to which those resources are assigned. You normally should not break this relationship unless you have special reporting needs within your organization—for example, you must follow a status reporting methodology based on something other than the actual values recorded for assignments in project plans. To break this relationship, on the Tools menu, click Options. On the Calculation tab of the Options dialog box, clear the Updating Task Status Updates Resource Status check box. This setting applies to the entire project plan that you have open at the time; you cannot apply it to only some tasks within a project plan.

When you need to track actual work at the most detailed level possible, use the timephased grid in the Task Usage or Resource Usage view. In either view, you can enter actual work values for individual assignments daily, weekly, or at whatever time period you want (by adjusting the timescale). For example, if a task has three resources assigned to it and you know that two resources worked on the task for eight hours one day and the third resource worked for six hours, you can enter these as three separate values on a timephased grid.

If your organization uses a timesheet reporting system for tracking actual work, you might be able to use this timesheet data in Project as timephased actuals. You might not need to track at this level, but if resources complete timesheets for other purposes (billing other departments within the organization, for example), you can use their data and save yourself some work.

> ## Project Management Focus: Collecting Actuals from Resources
>
> The view you used in the previous exercise is similar to a time card. In fact, to enter assignment-level actual work values, you might need some form of paper time card or its electronic equivalent. Several methods are used to collect such data from resources, assuming that you need to track actual and remaining work at this level of detail. Some collection methods include the following:
>
> - Use Project Professional in conjunction with Project Server for intranet-based team collaboration, tracking, and status reporting. To learn more about Project Server, see Part 4, "Introducing Project Server."
>
> - Collect actual values yourself. This method is feasible if you communicate with only a small group of resources on a frequent basis, such as a weekly status meeting. It's also a good opportunity to talk directly to the resources about any surprises they might have encountered (either positive or negative) while performing the work.
>
> - Collect actuals through a formal status reporting system. This technique might work through the already existing hierarchy of your organization and serve additional purposes besides project status reporting.
>
> Regardless of the data collection methods you might use, be aware that resources might have some concern about how their actual work values might reflect on their overall performance. You may need to communicate to resources that schedule actuals help in managing the schedule, but performance evaluation is a business management and not a project management focus.

Rescheduling Incomplete Work

During the course of a project, work might occasionally be interrupted for a specific task or for the entire project. Should this happen, you can have Project reschedule the remaining work to restart after the date you specify.

When you reschedule incomplete work, you specify the date after which work can resume—the rescheduled date. Here is how Project handles tasks in relation to the rescheduled date:

- If the task does not have any actual work recorded for it prior to the rescheduled date and does not have a constraint applied, the entire task is rescheduled to begin after that date.

- If the task has some actual work recorded prior to but none after the rescheduled date, the task is split so that all remaining work starts after the rescheduled date. The actual work is not affected.

- If the task has some actual work recorded for it prior to as well as after the rescheduled date, the task is not affected.

At this point in the short film project, work on the first two scenes has been completed, and the team has just started work on the next scheduled scene, Scene 1. In this exercise, you troubleshoot a delay in work caused by a problem at the studio.

> **OPEN** Short Film Project 13d from the *Documents\Microsoft Press\Project 2007 SBS\Chapter 13 Advanced Tracking* folder. You can also access the practice files for this book by clicking Start, All Programs, Microsoft Press, Project 2007 Step by Step, and then selecting the chapter folder of the file you want to open.

1. On the **File** menu, click **Save As**.

   The Save As dialog box appears.

2. In the **File name** box, type **Short Film Project 13 Reschedule**, and then click **Save**.

   The project plan is currently in the Task Usage view. Next, you'll switch to the Gantt Chart view.

3. On the **View** menu, click **Gantt Chart**.

4. In the **Task Name** column, click the name of task 38, **Scene 1 setup**.

Scroll to Task

5. On the **Standard** toolbar, click the **Scroll To Task** button.

   The Gantt Chart view scrolls to display the Gantt bar for task 38, *Scene 1 setup*. Currently, this task has one day of actual work completed and two days of scheduled work remaining.

6. Scroll the Gantt Chart view up so that the *Scene 1* summary task (task 37) appears near the top of the view.

Progress bars indicate the portion of the
task that has been completed—in this case,
one day of a three-day task.

	❶	Task Name	Duration	Start	Finish
37		⊟ Scene 1	**6 days**	**Fri 6/13/08**	**Fri 6/20/08**
38		Scene 1 setup	3 days	Fri 6/13/08	Tue 6/17/08
39		Scene 1 rehearsal	1 day	Wed 6/18/08	Wed 6/18/08
40		Scene 1 shoot	1 day	Thu 6/19/08	Thu 6/19/08
41		Scene 1 teardown	1 day	Fri 6/20/08	Fri 6/20/08
42		Scene 1-process d	1 day	Thu 6/19/08	Fri 6/20/08
43		⊟ Scene 2	**4 days**	**Mon 6/23/08**	**Fri 6/27/08**
44		Scene 2 setup	1 day	Mon 6/23/08	Mon 6/23/08
45		Scene 2 rehearsal	1 day	Tue 6/24/08	Tue 6/24/08
46		Scene 2 shoot	1 day	Tue 6/24/08	Wed 6/25/08
47		Scene 2 teardown	1 day	Thu 6/26/08	Thu 6/26/08
48		Scene 2-process d	1 day	Thu 6/26/08	Fri 6/27/08
49		⊟ Scene 5	**6 days**	**Fri 6/27/08**	**Mon 7/7/08**
50		Scene 5 setup	3 days	Fri 6/27/08	Tue 7/1/08
51		Scene 5 rehearsal	1 day	Wed 7/2/08	Wed 7/2/08
52		Scene 5 shoot	1 day	Thu 7/3/08	Thu 7/3/08
53		Scene 5 teardown	1 day	Mon 7/7/08	Mon 7/7/08

You have learned that over the weekend of June 14, a water pipe burst in the studio where Scene 1 was to be shot. None of the project's equipment was damaged,
but the cleanup will delay work through Wednesday, June 18. This effectively stops
work on the production tasks for a few days. Next, you will reschedule incomplete
work so that the project can begin again on Thursday.

7. On the **Tools** menu, point to **Tracking**, and then click **Update Project**.

The Update Project dialog box appears.

8. Select the **Reschedule uncompleted work to start after** option, and in the date
box, type or select **6/18/08**.

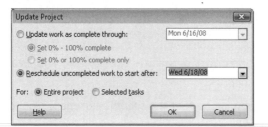

9. Click **OK** to close the Update Project dialog box.

Project splits task 38 so that the incomplete portion of the task is delayed until
Thursday.

Rescheduling work for the project causes Project to split
the task and then reschedule the remainder of it (and all
subsequent tasks) after the date you specified.

	❶	Task Name	Duration	Start	Finish
37		⊟ Scene 1	9 days	Fri 6/13/08	Wed 6/25/08
38		Scene 1 setup	3 days	Fri 6/13/08	Fri 6/20/08
39		Scene 1 rehearsal	1 day	Mon 6/23/08	Mon 6/23/08
40		Scene 1 shoot	1 day	Tue 6/24/08	Tue 6/24/08
41		Scene 1 teardown	1 day	Wed 6/25/08	Wed 6/25/08
42		Scene 1-process d	1 day	Tue 6/24/08	Wed 6/25/08
43		⊟ Scene 2	4 days	Thu 6/26/08	Wed 7/2/08
44		Scene 2 setup	1 day	Thu 6/26/08	Thu 6/26/08
45		Scene 2 rehearsal	1 day	Fri 6/27/08	Fri 6/27/08
46		Scene 2 shoot	1 day	Fri 6/27/08	Mon 6/30/08
47		Scene 2 teardown	1 day	Tue 7/1/08	Tue 7/1/08
48		Scene 2-process d	1 day	Tue 7/1/08	Wed 7/2/08
49		⊟ Scene 5	6 days	Wed 7/2/08	Thu 7/10/08
50		Scene 5 setup	3 days	Wed 7/2/08	Mon 7/7/08
51		Scene 5 rehearsal	1 day	Tue 7/8/08	Tue 7/8/08
52		Scene 5 shoot	1 day	Wed 7/9/08	Wed 7/9/08
53		Scene 5 teardown	1 day	Thu 7/10/08	Thu 7/10/08
54		Scene 5-process d	1 day	Wed 7/9/08	Thu 7/10/08

As you can see, although the duration of task 38 remains at three days, its finish date and subsequent start dates for successor tasks have been pushed out.
Although we have addressed a specific problem, in doing so, we have created other
problems in the remainder of the project. You will address this and other problems
in the project plan in later chapters.

> **Tip** You can turn off Project's ability to reschedule incomplete work on tasks for which
> any actual work has been recorded. On the Tools menu, click the Options command. In the
> Options dialog box, click the Schedule tab, and then clear the Split In-Progress Tasks check
> box.

> If you use status dates for reporting actuals, Project supports several options for
> controlling the way completed and incomplete segments of a task are scheduled
> around the status date. On the Tools menu, click the Options command. In the
> Options dialog box, click the Calculation tab. The options that control scheduling
> around the status date are Move End Of Completed Parts After Status Date Back To
> Status Date and the three other check boxes below it.
>
> > **Tip** For more information about these and other options on the tabs of the Options
> > dialog box, click the Help button that appears in the dialog box. To learn more about
> > working with status dates in Project, type Set the status date into the Search box in
> > the upper right corner of the Project window.

✕ CLOSE the Short Film Project 13 file.

Key Points

- Saving a baseline saves a large set of task, resource, and assignment values in a project plan. Saving an interim plan, however, saves only the start and finish dates of tasks.

- If you track work at the task level, work rolls down to the assignments. Conversely, if you track work at the assignment level, work rolls up to the task level.

- In usage views, you can change the time increments on the lower tier of the timescale to match the time period against which you wish to track. For example, if you wish to record actual work as full weeks, you can set the timescale to display weeks on the lower tier.

- Should work on a project be interrupted for some reason, you can reschedule the work to begin again on the date you specify.

Chapter at a Glance

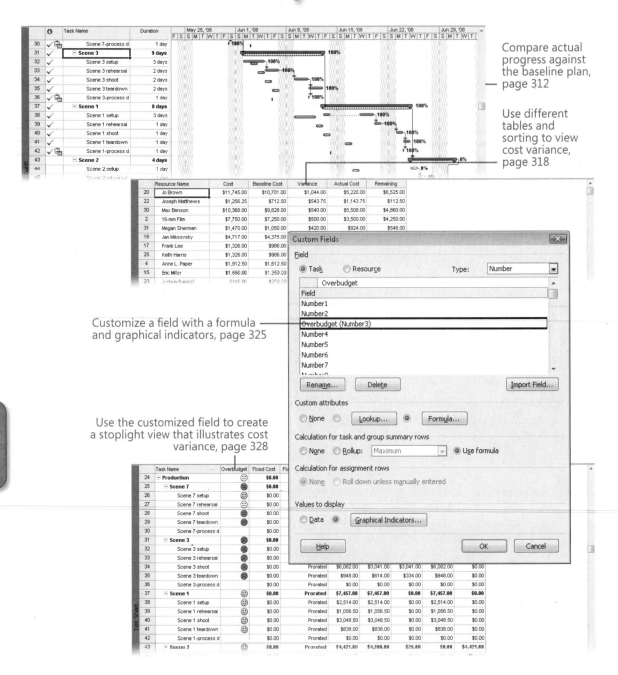

Compare actual progress against the baseline plan, page 312

Use different tables and sorting to view cost variance, page 318

Customize a field with a formula and graphical indicators, page 325

Use the customized field to create a stoplight view that illustrates cost variance, page 328

14 Viewing and Reporting Project Status

In this chapter, you will learn how to:

✔ Determine which tasks were started or completed late.

✔ View task costs at summary and detail levels.

✔ Examine resource costs and variance.

✔ Use custom fields to create a stoplight view that illustrates each task's cost variance.

> **Tip** Do you need only a quick refresher on the topics in this chapter? See the Quick Reference entries on pages xxv-xlviii.

After a project's *baseline* has been set and work has begun, the primary focus of the project manager shifts from planning to collecting, entering, and analyzing project performance details in a tool such as Microsoft Office Project 2007. For most projects, these performance details boil down to three primary questions or vital signs:

● How much work was required to complete a task?

● Did the task start and finish on time?

● What was the cost of completing the task?

Comparing the answers to these questions against the baseline provides the project manager and other *stakeholders* with a good way to measure the project's progress and to determine when corrective action might be necessary.

Communicating project status to key stakeholders, such as customers and sponsors, is arguably the most important function of a project manager and one that might occupy much of your working time. Although the perfect flow of communication cannot guarantee a project's success, a project with poor communications flow is almost guaranteed to fail.

A key to properly communicating project status is knowing the following:

● Who needs to know the project's status and for what purpose?

● What format or level of detail do these people need?

The time to answer these questions is in the initial planning phase of the project. After work on the project is under way, your main communications task will be reporting project status. This can take several forms:

● Status reports that describe where the project is in terms of cost, scope, and schedule (these are the three sides of the *project triangle*, described in Appendix A, "A Short Course in Project Management.")

● Progress reports that document the specific accomplishments of the project team

● Forecasts that predict future project performance

Where the scheduled or actual project performance differs from the baseline plan, you have variance. *Variance* is usually measured as time, such as days behind schedule, or as cost, such as dollars over budget. After initial project planning is complete, many project managers spend most of their time identifying, investigating, and, in many cases, responding to variance. However, before you can respond to variance, you must first identify, document, and report it. That is the subject of this chapter.

> **Tip** This tip describes enterprise project management (EPM) functionality. This chapter describes reporting project status to stakeholders. Project Professional, when used with Project Server, provides more sophisticated ways of not only publishing project status online, but also collecting information (such as actual work) from resources and other stakeholders. To learn more about the enterprise collaboration tools available with Project Server, see Part 4, "Introducing Project Server."

> **Important** Before you can use the practice files provided for this chapter, you need to install them from the book's companion CD to their default locations. See "Using the Book's CD" on page xix for more information.

Identifying Tasks that Have Slipped

When tasks start or finish earlier or later than planned, schedule variance is the result. One cause of schedule variance is delays in starting or finishing tasks. You'd certainly want to know about tasks that started late or future tasks that might not start as scheduled. It's also helpful to identify completed tasks that did not start on time to try to determine why this occurred.

There are different ways to view tasks with variance, depending on the type of information you want:

- Apply the Tracking Gantt view to graphically compare tasks' baseline dates with their actual or scheduled dates (on the View menu, click Tracking Gantt).

- Apply the Detail Gantt view to graphically show each task's slippage from baseline (on the View menu, click More Views, then select Detail Gantt).

- Apply the Variance table to a task view to see the number of days of variance for each task's start and finish dates (on the View menu, point to Table, and then click Variance).

- Filter for delayed or slipping tasks with the Slipped/Late Progress or Slipping Tasks filters (on the Project menu, point to Filtered For, then point to More Filters and select the filter you want to apply).

Is Variance Ever a Good Thing?

In project management, we generally look for variance that can have an adverse effect on a project, such as variance that pushes out the finish date or increases the cost of a project. However, variance includes any difference between planned and actual schedule events—even differences that have a helpful effect, such as an earlier finish date or lower cost than expected. Should you have the good fortune of managing a project that experiences such helpful variance, the techniques described here will help you identify the beneficial variance as well as any adverse variance. Your focus as a project manager is basically the same regardless of the nature of the variance—watch for it, and when it does occur, communicate it to project sponsors and other stakeholders and (if it's adverse variance) mitigate against it according to the nature of the project.

In this exercise, you apply some of these and other methods to identify variance.

BE SURE TO start Microsoft Office Project 2007 if it's not already running.

Important If you are running Project Professional, you may need to make a one-time adjustment to use the Computer account and to work offline. This ensures that the practice files you work with in this chapter do not affect your Project Server data. For more information, see "Starting Project Professional" on page 11.

> **OPEN** Short Film Project 14a from the *\Documents\Microsoft Press\Project 2007 SBS\ Chapter 14 Reporting Status* folder. You can also access the practice files for this book by clicking Start, All Programs, Microsoft Press, Project 2007 Step by Step, and then selecting the chapter folder of the file you want to open.

1. On the **File** menu, click **Save As**.

   The Save As dialog box appears.

2. In the **File name** box, type Short Film Project 14, and then click **Save**.

   To begin your analysis of tasks that have slipped, you'll start at the highest level— the project summary information.

3. On the **Project** menu, click **Project Information**.

   The Project Information dialog box appears.

4. Click the **Statistics** button.

   The Project Statistics dialog box appears.

Project Statistics for 'Short Film Project 14'				
	Start		**Finish**	
Current	Mon 3/3/08		Wed 12/31/08	
Baseline	Mon 3/3/08		Fri 12/19/08	
Actual	Mon 3/3/08		NA	
Variance	0d		6d	
	Duration	**Work**	**Cost**	
Current	212.25d	5,823h	$128,217.81	
Baseline	206.25d	5,575h	$124,536.40	
Actual	85.04d	2,512h	$53,489.31	
Remaining	127.21d	3,311h	$74,728.50	
Percent complete:				
Duration: 40%	Work: 43%			Close

Here you can see the start and finish values for the project, including the finish date's variance.

In this dialog box, you can see (among other things) that the project currently has six days of schedule variance on the finish date. In effect, the overall project finish date has slipped out by this number of days.

5. Click **Close** to close the Project Statistics dialog box.

   For the remainder of this exercise, you will use various techniques to examine the specific task variance.

6. On the **View** menu, click **Tracking Gantt**.

   Project displays the Tracking Gantt view.

7. In the **Task Name** column, click the name of task 31, the **Scene 3** summary task, and scroll the Tracking Gantt view up so that task 31 appears near the top of the view.

Scroll To Task

8. On the **Standard** toolbar, click the **Scroll To Task** button.

In the chart portion of this view, the tasks as they are currently scheduled appear as blue bars (if they are not critical tasks) or red bars (if they are critical). In the lower half of each task's row, the baseline values of each task appear as gray bars.

A gray bar represents the original (baseline) schedule in the Tracking Gantt view.

A blue or red bar represents the task as it is currently scheduled or when it was completed.

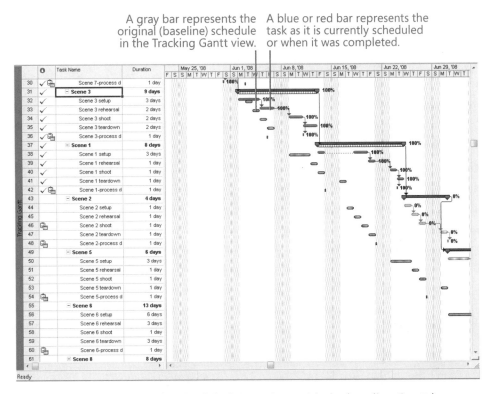

By comparing the currently scheduled Gantt bars with the baseline Gantt bars, you can see what tasks started earlier or later than planned or took longer to complete.

9. In the **Task Name** column, click the name of task 37, the **Scene 1** summary task.

10. On the **Standard** toolbar, click the **Scroll To Task** button.

Project scrolls the Tracking Gantt view to display task 37 and its adjacent tasks.

11. Scroll the Tracking Gantt view up so that task 37 appears near the top of the view.

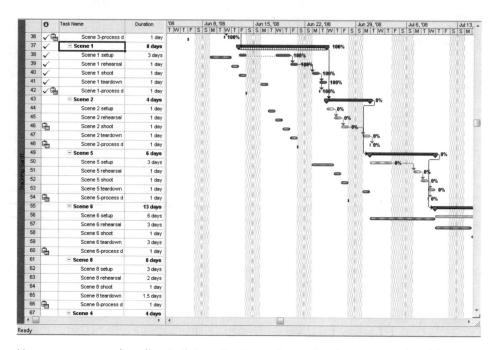

Here, you can see baseline task bars (patterned gray bars), completed task bars (solid blue bars), and bars for tasks on the *critical path* that are scheduled but not yet not started (red bars).

> **Tip** To see details about any bar or other item in a Gantt Chart view, position the mouse pointer over it. After a moment, a ScreenTip appears with details.

To focus in on only the slipping tasks, you will apply a filter.

12. On the **Project** menu, point to **Filtered For: All Tasks**, and then click **More Filters**.

The More Filters dialog box appears. In it, you can see all of the predefined filters for tasks (when in a task view) and resources (when in a resource view) available to you.

13. In the **More Filters** box, click **Slipping Tasks**, and then click the **Apply** button.

Project filters the task list to show only those tasks that, as they are now scheduled, have slipped from their baseline plan.

14. In the **Task Name** column, click the name of task 43, the **Scene 2** summary task.

15. On the **Standard** toolbar, click the **Scroll To Task** button.

Note the gaps in the task ID numbers. Tasks 1 through 23, for example, do not appear with the filter applied because they are already complete.

At this point in the schedule, the scheduled start date of tasks has slipped quite a bit. These tasks' scheduled Gantt bars are formatted red to indicate that they are critical, meaning that any delay in completing these tasks will delay the project's finish date.

16. On the **Project** menu, point to **Filtered For: Slipping Tasks**, and then click **All Tasks**.

> **Tip** You also can click the Filter button on the Formatting toolbar and then click All Tasks from the drop-down list.

Project removes the filter. As always, displaying or removing a filter has no effect on the original data.

The Tracking Gantt view graphically illustrates the difference between scheduled, actual, and baseline project performance. To see this information in a table format, you will display the Variance table in the Task Sheet view.

17. On the **View** menu, click **More Views**.

The More Views dialog box appears.

18. On the **Views** list, click **Task Sheet**, and then click **Apply**.

Project displays the Task Sheet view. Next, you'll switch to the Variance table.

19. On the **View** menu, point to **Table: Entry**, and then click **Variance**.

> **Tip** You also can right-click the Select All button in the upper left corner of the active table to switch to a different table.

Select All

The Variance table appears in the Task Sheet view.

To quickly switch to a different table, right-click here, and then click the table you want.

	Task Name	Start	Finish	Baseline Start	Baseline Finish	Start Var.	Finish Var.
1	− Pre-Production	Mon 3/3/08	Fri 5/23/08	Mon 3/3/08	Tue 5/27/08	0 days	-1.75 days
2	Review script	Mon 3/3/08	Thu 3/6/08	Mon 3/3/08	Thu 3/6/08	0 days	0 days
3	Develop script bre	Fri 3/7/08	Mon 3/17/08	Fri 3/7/08	Mon 3/17/08	0 days	0.75 days
4	Develop productio	Tue 3/18/08	Thu 4/10/08	Mon 3/17/08	Tue 4/15/08	0.75 days	-2.25 days
5	Review productio	Fri 4/11/08	Thu 4/17/08	Tue 4/15/08	Tue 4/22/08	-2.25 days	-2.25 days
6	Scout locations	Fri 4/18/08	Thu 5/1/08	Tue 4/22/08	Tue 5/6/08	-2.25 days	-2.25 days
7	Select locations	Fri 5/2/08	Thu 5/8/08	Tue 5/6/08	Tue 5/13/08	-2.25 days	-2.25 days
8	Hold auditions	Fri 5/9/08	Thu 5/15/08	Tue 5/13/08	Tue 5/20/08	-2.25 days	-2.25 days
9	Apply for filming p	Fri 5/16/08	Thu 5/22/08	Tue 5/20/08	Tue 5/27/08	-2.25 days	-2.25 days
10	Reserve camera e	Tue 5/20/08	Fri 5/23/08	Thu 5/22/08	Tue 5/27/08	-2.25 days	-2.25 days
11	Reserve sound ec	Tue 5/20/08	Fri 5/23/08	Thu 5/22/08	Tue 5/27/08	-2.25 days	-1.75 days
12	Pre-Production co	Fri 5/23/08	Fri 5/23/08	Tue 5/27/08	Tue 5/27/08	-2.25 days	-2.25 days
13	+ Staff planning m	Mon 3/10/08	Mon 5/12/08	Mon 3/10/08	Mon 5/12/08	0 days	0 days
24	− Production	Mon 5/26/08	Thu 8/14/08	Tue 5/27/08	Wed 8/6/08	-1.75 days	6 days
25	− Scene 7	Mon 5/26/08	Sat 5/31/08	Tue 5/27/08	Tue 6/3/08	-1.75 days	-1 day
26	Scene 7 setup	Mon 5/26/08	Tue 5/27/08	Tue 5/27/08	Wed 5/28/08	-1.75 days	-1 day
27	Scene 7 rehea	Tue 5/27/08	Wed 5/28/08	Wed 5/28/08	Thu 5/29/08	-1 day	-1 day
28	Scene 7 shoot	Wed 5/28/08	Thu 5/29/08	Thu 5/29/08	Fri 5/30/08	-1 day	-0.75 days
29	Scene 7 teard	Fri 5/30/08	Fri 5/30/08	Fri 5/30/08	Mon 6/2/08	-0.75 days	-0.75 days

In this table, you can view the scheduled, baseline, and variance values per task.

Here are some additional tips and suggestions for viewing slipped tasks:

- To see a legend of all Gantt bar color coding and symbols, switch to a Gantt Chart view. On the Format menu, click Bar Styles, and in the Bar Styles dialog box, look at the Name and Appearance columns.

- All filters are available to you via the Filter button on the Formatting toolbar. The name of the active filter appears in this button; click the arrow next to the filter name to see other filters. If no filter is applied to the current view, All Tasks or All Resources appears on the button, depending on the type of view currently displayed.

- You can see the criteria that most filters use to determine which tasks or resources they will display or hide. On the Project menu, point to Filter For: All Tasks, and then click More Filters. In the More Filters dialog box, click a filter and click the Edit button. In the Filter Definition dialog box, you can see the tests applied to various fields for the filter.

- The Slipping Tasks report describes tasks that are off-schedule. On the Report menu, click Reports. In the Reports dialog box, double-click Current Activities, and then double-click Slipping Tasks.

- In this exercise, you have viewed variance for a task. To see variance for assignments to a task, switch to the Task Usage view, and then apply the Variance table (to see scheduled variance) or the Work table (to see work variance).

Project Management Focus: Getting the Word Out

If you work in an organization that is highly focused on projects and project management, chances are that standard methods and formats already exist within your organization for reporting project status. If not, you might be able to introduce project status formats that are based on clear communication and project management principles.

Techniques that you can use in Project to help you report project status include the following:

- Print the Project Summary report (Reports menu).

- If you have Excel 2003 or later or Visio 2007 or later, print a status-focused visual report (Reports menu).

- Copy Project data to other applications—for example, use the Copy Picture To Office Wizard (Analysis toolbar) to copy the Gantt Chart view to Word or PowerPoint.

- Save Project data in other formats (File, Save As), such as Microsoft Excel Workbook, using the Compare To Baseline export map.

- For Project Professional users, share project status through Project Server, which enables the stakeholders you choose to view project details through their Web browsers.

All of these status-reporting tools are described elsewhere in this book.

Examining Task Costs

The schedule's status (Did tasks start and finish on time?), although critical to nearly all projects, is only one indicator of overall project health. For projects that include cost information, another critical indicator is cost variance: Are tasks running over or under budget? Task costs in Project consist of fixed costs applied directly to tasks, resource costs derived from assignments, or both. When tasks cost more or less than planned to complete, cost variance is the result. Evaluating cost variance enables you to make incremental budget adjustments for individual tasks to avoid exceeding your project's overall budget.

> **Tip** Another way of using project costs to measure past performance and predict future performance is through earned value analysis. For more information, see Chapter 18, "Measuring Performance with Earned Value Analysis."

Although tasks and resources (and their costs) are directly related, it's informative to evaluate each individually. In this exercise, you view task cost variance. Again, you'll start at the highest level—the project summary information.

1. On the **Project** menu, click **Project Information**.

   The Project Information dialog box appears.

2. Click **Statistics**.

   The Project Statistics dialog box appears.

Project Statistics for 'Short Film Project 14'			
	Start		Finish
Current		Mon 3/3/08	Wed 12/31/08
Baseline		Mon 3/3/08	Fri 12/19/08
Actual		Mon 3/3/08	NA
Variance		0d	6d

Here you can see the project's cost values.

	Duration	Work	Cost
Current	212.25d	5,823h	$128,217.81
Baseline	206.25d	5,575h	$124,536.40
Actual	85.04d	2,512h	$53,489.31
Remaining	127.21d	3,311h	$74,728.50

Percent complete:

Duration: 40%   Work: 43%   [Close]

In the Cost column, you can see the current, baseline, actual, and remaining cost values for the entire project:

- The current cost value is the sum of the actual and remaining cost values.
- The *baseline* cost value is the project's total planned cost when its baseline was set.
- The *actual* cost is the cost that's been incurred so far.
- The remaining cost is the difference between the current cost and actual cost.

Clearly, some cost variance has occurred, but you can't tell from this information when or where it occurred.

3. Click **Close** to close the Project Statistics dialog box.

Next, you will switch to views where you can examine cost variance more closely, starting with the Cost table.

4. On the **View** menu, point to **Table: Variance**, and click **Cost**.

The Cost table appears in the Task Sheet view.

	Task Name	Fixed Cost	Fixed Cost Accrual	Total Cost	Baseline	Variance	Actual	Remaining
1	− **Pre-Production**	**$0.00**	**Prorated**	**$30,672.06**	**$33,840.00**	**($3,167.94)**	**$29,172.06**	**$1,500.00**
2	Review script	$0.00	Prorated	$892.00	$892.00	$0.00	$892.00	$0.00
3	Develop script breakdo	$0.00	Prorated	$3,497.50	$3,336.00	$161.50	$3,497.50	$0.00
4	Develop production boc	$0.00	Prorated	$9,558.56	$12,398.00	($2,839.44)	$9,558.56	$0.00
5	Review production boe	$0.00	Prorated	$1,780.00	$1,780.00	$0.00	$1,780.00	$0.00
6	Scout locations	$0.00	Prorated	$6,076.00	$6,640.00	($564.00)	$5,076.00	$1,000.00
7	Select locations	$0.00	Prorated	$2,771.00	$2,771.00	$0.00	$2,771.00	$0.00
8	Hold auditions	$0.00	Prorated	$2,511.00	$2,511.00	$0.00	$2,011.00	$500.00
9	Apply for filming permit	$500.00	Start	$1,156.00	$1,156.00	$0.00	$1,156.00	$0.00
10	Reserve camera equipr	$0.00	Prorated	$744.00	$744.00	$0.00	$744.00	$0.00
11	Reserve sound equipm	$0.00	Prorated	$296.00	$222.00	$74.00	$296.00	$0.00
12	Pre-Production complet	$0.00	Prorated	$0.00	$0.00	$0.00	$0.00	$0.00
13	+ **Staff planning meeti**	**$0.00**	**Prorated**	**$1,390.00**	**$1,390.00**	**$0.00**	**$1,390.00**	**$0.00**
24	− **Production**	**$0.00**	**Prorated**	**$60,883.35**	**$54,034.00**	**$6,849.35**	**$24,317.25**	**$36,566.10**
25	− **Scene 7**	**$0.00**	**Prorated**	**$6,394.25**	**$4,718.50**	**$1,675.75**	**$6,394.25**	**$0.00**
26	Scene 7 setup	$0.00	Prorated	$502.00	$502.00	$0.00	$502.00	$0.00
27	Scene 7 rehearsal	$0.00	Prorated	$1,013.25	$906.50	$106.75	$1,013.25	$0.00
28	Scene 7 shoot	$0.00	Prorated	$4,238.00	$2,808.00	$1,430.00	$4,238.00	$0.00
29	Scene 7 teardown	$0.00	Prorated	$641.00	$502.00	$139.00	$641.00	$0.00
30	Scene 7 process d	$0.00	Prorated	$0.00	$0.00	$0.00	$0.00	$0.00

In this table, you can see each task's baseline cost, scheduled cost (in the Total Cost column), actual cost, and cost variance. The variance is the difference between the baseline cost and the scheduled cost. Of course, costs aren't scheduled in the same sense that work is scheduled; however, costs derived from work resources (that is, excluding fixed costs and costs associated with material and cost resources) are derived directly from the scheduled work.

Next, you'll focus on the top-level costs.

5. On the **Project** menu, point to **Outline**, point to **Show**, and then click **Outline Level 1**.

Show ▾
Outline

> **Tip** You can also click the Outline button on the Formatting toolbar and then Outline Level 1. The Outline button is labeled with the word "Show."

Project displays the top three summary tasks, which in this project correspond to the major phases of the short film project. Because we're currently working on tasks in the Production phase, we'll direct our attention there.

6. Click the **plus sign** next to task 24, **Production**.

Project expands the *Production* summary task to show the details for the individual scenes.

Task Name	Fixed Cost	Fixed Cost Accrual	Total Cost	Baseline	Variance	Actual	Remaining
1	+ Pre-Production	$0.00	Prorated	$30,672.06	$33,840.00	($3,167.94)	$29,172.06	$1,500.00
24	− Production	$0.00	Prorated	$60,883.35	$54,034.00	$6,849.35	$24,317.25	$36,566.10
25	− Scene 7	$0.00	Prorated	$6,394.25	$4,718.50	$1,675.75	$6,394.25	$0.00
26	Scene 7 setup	$0.00	Prorated	$502.00	$502.00	$0.00	$502.00	$0.00
27	Scene 7 rehearsal	$0.00	Prorated	$1,013.25	$906.50	$106.75	$1,013.25	$0.00
28	Scene 7 shoot	$0.00	Prorated	$4,238.00	$2,808.00	$1,430.00	$4,238.00	$0.00
29	Scene 7 teardown	$0.00	Prorated	$641.00	$502.00	$139.00	$641.00	$0.00
30	Scene 7-process d	$0.00	Prorated	$0.00	$0.00	$0.00	$0.00	$0.00
31	− Scene 3	$0.00	Prorated	$10,466.00	$5,318.00	$5,148.00	$10,466.00	$0.00
32	Scene 3 setup	$0.00	Prorated	$1,338.00	$614.00	$724.00	$1,338.00	$0.00
33	Scene 3 rehearsal	$0.00	Prorated	$2,098.00	$1,049.00	$1,049.00	$2,098.00	$0.00
34	Scene 3 shoot	$0.00	Prorated	$6,082.00	$3,041.00	$3,041.00	$6,082.00	$0.00
35	Scene 3 teardown	$0.00	Prorated	$948.00	$614.00	$334.00	$948.00	$0.00
36	Scene 3-process d	$0.00	Prorated	$0.00	$0.00	$0.00	$0.00	$0.00
37	− Scene 1	$0.00	Prorated	$7,457.00	$7,457.00	$0.00	$7,457.00	$0.00
38	Scene 1 setup	$0.00	Prorated	$2,514.00	$2,514.00	$0.00	$2,514.00	$0.00
39	Scene 1 rehearsal	$0.00	Prorated	$1,056.50	$1,056.50	$0.00	$1,056.50	$0.00
40	Scene 1 shoot	$0.00	Prorated	$3,048.50	$3,048.50	$0.00	$3,048.50	$0.00
41	Scene 1 teardown	$0.00	Prorated	$838.00	$838.00	$0.00	$838.00	$0.00
42	Scene 1-process d	$0.00	Prorated	$0.00	$0.00	$0.00	$0.00	$0.00

Looking at the Variance column, you can see that Scene 7 had some variance, and Scene 3 had significantly more. Next, you'll focus on the details for Scene 3.

Looking at the Variance column, you can see that the *Scene 3 rehearsal* and *shoot* tasks (numbers 33 and 34) account for most of the variance for the *Scene 3* summary task. As you may have noticed in the Tracking Gantt view, the actual durations of the *Scene 3* rehearsal and *shoot* tasks were longer than planned, which caused the variance on the task.

To conclude this exercise, you will use filters to help you zero in on tasks that have cost variance.

7. On the **Project** menu, point to **Outline**, point to **Show**, and then click **All Subtasks**.

Project expands the task list to show all subtasks.

8. On the **Project** menu, point to **Filtered For: All Tasks**, and then click **More Filters**.

9. In the **More Filters** dialog box, click **Cost Overbudget** and then click **Apply**.

> **Tip** You can also click the Filter box on the Formatting toolbar and then click Cost Overbudget. The Filter box initially contains the value "All Tasks."

Project filters the task list to show only those tasks that had actual and scheduled costs greater than their baseline costs.

	Task Name	Fixed Cost	Fixed Cost Accrual	Total Cost	Baseline	Variance	Actual	Remaining
1	− Pre-Production	$0.00	Prorated	$30,672.06	$33,840.00	($3,167.94)	$29,172.06	$1,500.00
3	Develop script breakdo	$0.00	Prorated	$3,497.50	$3,336.00	$161.50	$3,497.50	$0.00
11	Reserve sound equipm	$0.00	Prorated	$296.00	$222.00	$74.00	$296.00	$0.00
24	− Production	$0.00	Prorated	$60,883.35	$54,034.00	$6,849.35	$24,317.25	$36,566.10
25	− Scene 7	$0.00	Prorated	$6,394.25	$4,718.50	$1,675.75	$6,394.25	$0.00
27	Scene 7 rehearsal	$0.00	Prorated	$1,013.25	$906.50	$106.75	$1,013.25	$0.00
28	Scene 7 shoot	$0.00	Prorated	$4,238.00	$2,808.00	$1,430.00	$4,238.00	$0.00
29	Scene 7 teardown	$0.00	Prorated	$641.00	$502.00	$139.00	$641.00	$0.00
31	− Scene 3	$0.00	Prorated	$10,466.00	$5,318.00	$5,148.00	$10,466.00	$0.00
32	Scene 3 setup	$0.00	Prorated	$1,338.00	$614.00	$724.00	$1,338.00	$0.00
33	Scene 3 rehearsal	$0.00	Prorated	$2,098.00	$1,049.00	$1,049.00	$2,098.00	$0.00
34	Scene 3 shoot	$0.00	Prorated	$6,082.00	$3,041.00	$3,041.00	$6,082.00	$0.00
35	Scene 3 teardown	$0.00	Prorated	$948.00	$614.00	$334.00	$948.00	$0.00
43	− Scene 2	$0.00	Prorated	$4,421.60	$4,396.00	$25.60	$0.00	$4,421.60
45	Scene 2 rehearsal	$0.00	Prorated	$726.80	$714.00	$12.80	$0.00	$726.80
46	Scene 2 shoot	$0.00	Prorated	$2,466.80	$2,454.00	$12.80	$0.00	$2,466.80

Here again you can see that the Scene 3 tasks have accounted for nearly all cost variance in the schedule so far.

10. On the **Project** menu, point to **Filtered For: Cost Overbudget**, and then click **All Tasks**.

Project removes the filter.

What caused the task cost variance in the short film project? Because this project's costs are almost entirely derived from work performed by resources, we can conclude that more work than scheduled has been required to complete the tasks to date.

As we noted earlier, task and resource costs are closely related; in most cases, task costs are mostly or fully derived from the costs of resources assigned to tasks. Examining resource costs is the subject of the next exercise.

Here are some additional tips and suggestions for working with cost data:

● To see tasks that are over budget, you can use the Overbudget Tasks report. On the Report menu, click Reports. In the Reports dialog box, double-click Costs, and then double-click Overbudget Tasks.

● If you have Excel 2003 or later, you can use the Budget Cost Report. On the Report menu, click Visual Reports. In the Assignment Usage tab of the Visual Reports dialog box, click Budget Cost Report and then click View.

● The Cost Overbudget filter and all other filters are also available in the More Filters dialog box (on the Project menu, point to Filtered For: All Tasks, and then click More Filters) as well as the Filter button on the Formatting toolbar.

● To see work variance in the Work table, in a task view on the View menu, point to Table, and then click Work. You can also compare timephased baseline and scheduled work in a usage view. For example, in the Task Usage view, on the Format menu, point to Details, and click Baseline Work.

● In this exercise, you have viewed cost variance for a task. To see cost variance for assignments to a task, switch to the Task Usage view, and then apply the Cost table.

Examining Resource Costs

Project managers sometimes focus on resource costs as a means of measuring progress and variance within a project. However, resource cost information also serves other people and other needs. For many organizations, resource costs are the primary or even the only costs incurred while completing projects, so closely watching resource costs might directly relate to the financial health of an organization. It might not be a project manager, but instead an executive, cost accountant, or *resource manager* who is most interested in resource costs on projects as they relate to organizational costs.

Another common reason to track resource costs is for billing either within an organization (for example, billing another department for services your department has provided) or externally. In either case, the resource cost information stored in project plans can serve as the basis for billing out your department's or organization's services to others.

Because cost values in the short film project are almost entirely derived from the costs of resource assignments, you'll look at resource cost variance next.

1. On the **View** menu, click **Resource Sheet**.

   The Resource Sheet view appears.

2. On the **View** menu, point to **Table: Entry** and click **Cost**.

   The Cost table appears.

	Resource Name	Cost	Baseline Cost	Variance	Actual Cost	Remaining
1	16-mm Camera	$1,140.00	$1,050.00	$90.00	$570.00	$570.00
2	16-mm Film	$7,750.00	$7,250.00	$500.00	$3,500.00	$4,250.00
3	500-Watt Light	$420.00	$330.00	$90.00	$230.00	$190.00
4	Anne L. Paper	$1,912.50	$1,612.50	$300.00	$600.00	$1,312.50
5	Camera Boom	$0.00	$0.00	$0.00	$0.00	$0.00
6	Clair Hector	$9,427.50	$9,360.00	$67.50	$4,747.50	$4,680.00
7	Crane	$0.00	$0.00	$0.00	$0.00	$0.00
8	Daniel Penn	$900.00	$900.00	$0.00	$0.00	$900.00
9	David Campbell	$5,100.00	$5,100.00	$0.00	$300.00	$4,800.00
10	Dolly	$0.00	$0.00	$0.00	$0.00	$0.00
11	Doug Hampton	$2,336.00	$2,246.40	$89.60	$512.00	$1,824.00
12	Editing Lab	$6,350.00	$6,350.00	$0.00	$0.00	$6,350.00
13	Electrician	$9,576.00	$9,744.00	($168.00)	$2,296.00	$7,280.00
14	Eric Lang	$518.00	$444.00	$74.00	$518.00	$0.00
15	Eric Miller	$1,650.00	$1,350.00	$300.00	$900.00	$750.00
16	Florian Voss	$0.00	$0.00	$0.00	$0.00	$0.00
17	Frank Lee	$1,326.00	$986.00	$340.00	$748.00	$578.00
18	Jan Miksovsky	$4,717.00	$4,375.00	$342.00	$3,586.00	$1,131.00
19	Jim Hance	$600.00	$450.00	$150.00	$300.00	$300.00
20	Jo Brown	$11,745.00	$10,701.00	$1,044.00	$5,220.00	$6,525.00
21	Johnathan Perrera	$5,470.00	$6,550.00	($1,080.00)	$5,470.00	$0.00
22	Joseph Matthews	$1,295.25	$172.50	$945.75	$1,143.75	$112.50

In the Cost table, you can see each resource's cost, baseline cost, and related cost values. In most cases here, the cost values for work resources are derived from each resource's cost rate multiplied by the work on their assignments to tasks in the project plan.

Currently, the resource sheet is sorted by resource ID. Next, you will sort it by resource cost.

3. On the **Project** menu, point to **Sort** and click **Sort By**.

The Sort dialog box appears.

4. In the **Sort By** box, click **Cost** on the drop-down list, and click **Descending**.

5. Make sure the **Permanently renumber resources** check box is cleared, and then click the **Sort** button.

Project sorts the resources by cost from highest to lowest.

With resources sorted by cost in descending order, you can quickly identify the most expensive resources working on the project.

	Resource Name	Cost	Baseline Cost	Variance	Actual Cost	Remaining
38	Scott Cooper	$13,217.60	$13,464.00	($246.40)	$9,477.60	$3,740.00
20	Jo Brown	$11,745.00	$10,701.00	$1,044.00	$5,220.00	$6,525.00
30	Max Benson	$10,368.00	$9,828.00	$540.00	$5,508.00	$4,860.00
13	Electrician	$9,576.00	$9,744.00	($168.00)	$2,296.00	$7,280.00
6	Clair Hector	$9,427.50	$9,360.00	$67.50	$4,747.50	$4,680.00
2	16-mm Film	$7,750.00	$7,250.00	$500.00	$3,500.00	$4,250.00
32	Michael Patten	$7,216.00	$7,216.00	$0.00	$0.00	$7,216.00
12	Editing Lab	$6,350.00	$6,350.00	$0.00	$0.00	$6,350.00
26	Kim Yoshida	$5,844.96	$6,560.00	($715.04)	$3,220.96	$2,624.00
21	Johnathan Perrera	$5,470.00	$6,550.00	($1,080.00)	$5,470.00	$0.00
9	David Campbell	$5,100.00	$5,100.00	$0.00	$300.00	$4,800.00
18	Jan Miksovsky	$4,717.00	$4,375.00	$342.00	$3,586.00	$1,131.00
36	Richard Lum	$3,700.00	$3,700.00	$0.00	$0.00	$3,700.00
43	Travel	$3,068.00	$3,068.00	$0.00	$0.00	$3,068.00
28	Lisa Garmaise	$2,560.00	$2,560.00	$0.00	$0.00	$2,560.00
11	Doug Hampton	$2,336.00	$2,246.40	$89.60	$512.00	$1,824.00
4	Anne L. Paper	$1,912.50	$1,612.50	$300.00	$600.00	$1,312.50
39	Sue Jackson	$1,740.00	$1,560.00	$180.00	$660.00	$1,080.00
15	Eric Miller	$1,650.00	$1,350.00	$300.00	$900.00	$750.00
31	Megan Sherman	$1,470.00	$1,050.00	$420.00	$924.00	$546.00
17	Frank Lee	$1,326.00	$988.00	$340.00	$748.00	$578.00
25	Keith Harris	$1,326.00	$989.00	$353.00	$748.00	$578.00

This sort quickly tells you who are the most and least expensive resources (as indicated in the Cost column), but it doesn't help you see variance patterns. You will do that next.

6. On the **Project** menu, point to **Sort** and click **Sort By**.

The Sort dialog box appears.

7. In the **Sort By** box, click **Cost Variance**, and make sure **Descending** is still selected.

8. Make sure the **Permanently renumber resources** check box is cleared, and then click **Sort**.

Project re-sorts the resources by cost variance from highest to lowest.

With resources sorted by variance in descending
order, you can quickly identify those whose cost
varied the most from planned costs.

	Resource Name	Cost	Baseline Cost	Variance	Actual Cost	Remaining
20	Jo Brown	$11,745.00	$10,701.00	$1,044.00	$5,220.00	$6,525.00
22	Joseph Matthews	$1,256.25	$712.50	$543.75	$1,143.75	$112.50
30	Max Benson	$10,368.00	$9,828.00	$540.00	$5,508.00	$4,860.00
2	16-mm Film	$7,750.00	$7,250.00	$500.00	$3,500.00	$4,250.00
31	Megan Sherman	$1,470.00	$1,050.00	$420.00	$924.00	$546.00
18	Jan Miksovsky	$4,717.00	$4,375.00	$342.00	$3,586.00	$1,131.00
17	Frank Lee	$1,326.00	$986.00	$340.00	$748.00	$578.00
25	Keith Harris	$1,326.00	$986.00	$340.00	$748.00	$578.00
4	Anne L. Paper	$1,912.50	$1,612.50	$300.00	$600.00	$1,312.50
15	Eric Miller	$1,650.00	$1,350.00	$300.00	$900.00	$750.00
23	Joshua Randall	$448.00	$256.00	$192.00	$320.00	$128.00
39	Sue Jackson	$1,740.00	$1,560.00	$180.00	$660.00	$1,080.00
19	Jim Hance	$600.00	$450.00	$150.00	$300.00	$300.00
40	Ted Bremer	$1,188.00	$1,044.00	$144.00	$576.00	$612.00
41	Tim O'Brien	$1,152.00	$1,008.00	$144.00	$576.00	$576.00
1	16-mm Camera	$1,140.00	$1,050.00	$90.00	$570.00	$570.00
3	500-Watt Light	$420.00	$330.00	$90.00	$230.00	$190.00
11	Doug Hampton	$2,336.00	$2,246.40	$89.60	$512.00	$1,824.00
14	Eric Lang	$518.00	$444.00	$74.00	$518.00	$0.00
6	Clair Hector	$9,427.50	$9,360.00	$67.50	$4,747.50	$4,680.00
5	Camera Boom	$0.00	$0.00	$0.00	$0.00	$0.00
7	Crane	$0.00	$0.00	$0.00	$0.00	$0.00

With the resource list sorted by cost variance, you can quickly zero in on those resources with the greatest variance, and begin to investigate why if you so choose.

9. On the **Project** menu, point to **Sort**, and then click **By ID**.

Project re-sorts the resources by ID.

Here are some additional tips and suggestions for working with resource costs:

- You can use the Overbudget Resources report to list resources who are over budget. On the Report menu, click Reports. In the Reports dialog box, double-click Costs, and then double-click Overbudget Resources.

- You can also see timephased cost values in a usage view. For example, in the Resource Usage view, on the Format menu, click Detail Styles. In the Usage Details tab, show the Baseline Cost and Cost fields. This also works in the Task Usage view.

- If you have Excel 2003 or later, you can use the Resource Cost Summary Report. On the Report menu, click Visual Reports. In the Resource Usage tab of the Visual Reports dialog box, click Resource Cost Summary Report and then click View.

Reporting Project Cost Variance with a Stoplight View

There are many different ways to report a project's status in terms of task or budget variance or other measures. There is no shortage of features in Project that support reporting project status, but the main thing to keep in mind is that the method by which you report project status is less a technical question than a communications question. For example, what format and level of detail do your stakeholders need to see? Should project sponsors see different aspects of a project's performance than those seen by its resources? These questions are central to the project manager's job. Fortunately, as noted earlier, Project is a rich communications tool that you can use to construct the type of project status information that best meets the needs of your stakeholders.

> **Tip** Creating a stoplight view involves using formulas in custom fields. Custom fields are a very powerful and flexible feature, and the stoplight view is just one example of what you can do with them. To learn more about custom fields, type **About custom fields** into the Search box in the upper right corner of the Project window.

In this exercise, you focus on creating what is often called a stoplight report. This status report represents key indicators for tasks, such as schedule or budget status, as a simple red, yellow, or green light. Such status reports are easy for anyone to understand, and they quickly provide a general sense of the health of a project. Strictly speaking, what you'll create here is not a report in Project, so we'll call it a stoplight view instead.

1. On the **View** menu, click **More Views**.

   The More Views dialog box appears.

2. Click **Task Sheet**, and click **Apply**.

   Project displays the Task Sheet view. It currently contains the Cost table.

   To save you time, we have customized a field in this Project file containing a formula that evaluates each task's cost variance. Next, you will view the formula to understand what it does and then view the graphical indicators assigned to the field.

3. On the **Tools** menu, point to **Customize**, and then click **Fields**.

   The Custom Fields dialog box appears.

4. In the **Type** box in the upper right corner of the dialog box, click **Number** on the drop-down list.

5. In the list box, click **Overbudget (Number3)**. This is the customized field we've set up for you.

The Number3 field has been renamed "Overbudget" and customized with a formula and graphical indicators.

6. Under **Custom attributes**, click the **Formula** button.

   The Formula dialog box appears.

When writing a formula, use these buttons to insert Project fields or functions into your formula.

This formula evaluates each task's cost variance. If the task's cost is 10% or less above baseline, the formula assigns the number 10 to the task. If the cost is between 10% and 20% above baseline, it is assigned a 20. If the cost is more than 20% above baseline, it receives a 30.

7. Click **Cancel** to close the Formula dialog box.

8. In the **Custom Fields** dialog box, under **Values to display**, click the **Graphical Indicators** button.

The Graphical Indicators dialog box appears. Here, you specify a unique graphical indicator to display, depending on the value of the field for each task. Again, to save you time, the indicators are already selected.

Depending on the value returned by the formula, Project will display one of these three graphical indicators in the Overbudget column.

9. Click the first cell under the **Image** column heading (it contains a green smiley face), and then click the drop-down arrow.

   Here you can see the many graphical indicators that you can associate with the values of fields.

10. Click **Cancel** to close the Graphical Indicators dialog box, and then click **Cancel** again to close the Custom Fields dialog box.

    To conclude this exercise, you will display the Overbudget (Number3) column in the Cost table.

11. Click the **Fixed Cost** column heading.

12. On the **Insert** menu, click **Column**.

    The Column Definition dialog box appears.

13. In the **Field Name** box, click **Overbudget (Number3)** on the drop-down list, and then click **OK**.

    Project displays the Overbudget column in the Cost table.

14. Scroll the Task Sheet view down to display task 24, the Production summary task and its subtasks.

	Task Name	Overbudget	Fixed Cost	Fixed Cost Accrual	Total Cost	Baseline	Variance	Actual	Remaining
24	Production	☺	$0.00	Prorated	$60,883.35	$54,034.00	$6,849.35	$24,317.25	$36,566.10
25	Scene 7	☹	$0.00	Prorated	$6,394.25	$4,718.50	$1,675.75	$6,394.25	$0.00
26	Scene 7 setup	☺	$0.00	Prorated	$502.00	$502.00	$0.00	$502.00	$0.00
27	Scene 7 rehearsal	☺	$0.00	Prorated	$1,013.25	$906.50	$106.75	$1,013.25	$0.00
28	Scene 7 shoot	☹	$0.00	Prorated	$4,238.00	$2,808.00	$1,430.00	$4,238.00	$0.00
29	Scene 7 teardown	☹	$0.00	Prorated	$641.00	$502.00	$139.00	$641.00	$0.00
30	Scene 7-process d		$0.00	Prorated	$0.00	$0.00	$0.00	$0.00	$0.00
31	Scene 3	☹	$0.00	Prorated	$10,466.00	$5,318.00	$5,148.00	$10,466.00	$0.00
32	Scene 3 setup	☹	$0.00	Prorated	$1,338.00	$614.00	$724.00	$1,338.00	$0.00
33	Scene 3 rehearsal	☹	$0.00	Prorated	$2,098.00	$1,049.00	$1,049.00	$2,098.00	$0.00
34	Scene 3 shoot	☹	$0.00	Prorated	$6,082.00	$3,041.00	$3,041.00	$6,082.00	$0.00
35	Scene 3 teardown	☹	$0.00	Prorated	$948.00	$614.00	$334.00	$948.00	$0.00
36	Scene 3-process d		$0.00	Prorated	$0.00	$0.00	$0.00	$0.00	$0.00
37	Scene 1	☺	$0.00	Prorated	$7,457.00	$7,457.00	$0.00	$7,457.00	$0.00
38	Scene 1 setup	☺	$0.00	Prorated	$2,514.00	$2,514.00	$0.00	$2,514.00	$0.00
39	Scene 1 rehearsal	☺	$0.00	Prorated	$1,056.50	$1,056.50	$0.00	$1,056.50	$0.00
40	Scene 1 shoot	☺	$0.00	Prorated	$3,048.50	$3,048.50	$0.00	$3,048.50	$0.00
41	Scene 1 teardown	☺	$0.00	Prorated	$838.00	$838.00	$0.00	$838.00	$0.00
42	Scene 1-process d		$0.00	Prorated	$0.00	$0.00	$0.00	$0.00	$0.00
43	Scene 2	☺	$0.00	Prorated	$4,421.60	$4,396.00	$25.60	$0.00	$4,421.60
44	Scene 2 setup	☺	$0.00	Prorated	$614.00	$614.00	$0.00	$0.00	$614.00

As each task's cost variance changes, so do the graphical indicators according to the ranges specified in the formula. This is a handy format for identifying tasks whose cost variance is higher than you'd like, as indicated by the yellow or red lights.

Tip   To see a graphical indicator's numeric value in a ScreenTip, just point to the indicator.

Up to now, you've identified schedule and budget variance in a task view and budget variance in a resource view—each an important measure of project status. This is a good time to remind yourself that the final qualifier of project status is not the exact formatting of the data in Project, but the needs of your project's stakeholders. Determining what these needs are requires your good judgment and communication skills.

CLOSE the Short Film Project 14 file.

Key Points

- Schedule variance is caused by tasks that have slipped from their planned start or finish dates (as recorded in a baseline). You can use a combination of views, tables, filters, and reports to identify which tasks have slipped and caused variance.

- Schedule and cost variance are closely related—if a project plan has one, it likely has the other. As with schedule variance, you can apply a combination of views, tables, filters, and reports to locate cost variance.

- You can use formulas and graphical indicators in custom fields to create a highly customized view, such as a stoplight view, to communicate key project health indicators to your stakeholders.

Chapter at a Glance

Resolve missed deadlines by shortening task durations, page 333

Reduce resource costs by reducing their assignments on tasks, page 339

Replace resources assigned to tasks in a project plan, page 341

Compress the duration of tasks by assigning overtime work, page 344

15 Getting Your Project Back on Track

In this chapter, you will learn how to:

✔ Assign additional resources to tasks to reduce task durations.

✔ Edit work values for resource assignments and replace resources assigned to tasks.

✔ Assign overtime work to assignments and change task relationships to compress the overall project duration.

> **Tip** Do you need only a quick refresher on the topics in this chapter? See the Quick Reference entries on pages xxv-xlviii.

After work has started on a project, addressing *variance* is not a one-time event, but instead is an ongoing effort by the project manager. The specific way in which you should respond to variance depends on the type of variance and the nature of the project. In this chapter, we'll focus on some of the many variance problems that can arise during a project as work progresses. We'll frame these problems around the *project triangle* described in detail in Appendix A, "A Short Course in Project Management."

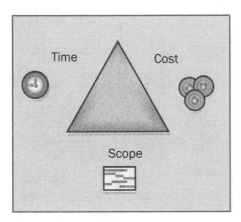

In short, the project triangle model frames a project in terms of *time* (or duration), *cost* (or budget), and *scope* (the project work required to produce a satisfactory *deliverable*).

In virtually any project of any complexity, one of these factors will be more important than the other two. The most important factor is sometimes called the driving constraint because meeting it drives your actions as a project manager. For example, for a project that must be concluded by a specific date, you might need to make cost and scope compromises to meet the deadline. Working with the project triangle provides you with a good method to analyze the trade-offs that nearly always must be made in projects. Just as importantly, it gives you a clear way of explaining the pros and cons of trade-offs to the project's *resources*, *sponsors*, and other *stakeholders*.

In the project triangle model, time, cost, and scope are interconnected; therefore, changing one element can affect the other two. For purposes of identifying, analyzing, and addressing problems in project management, it's useful to fit problems into one of these three categories.

The specific issues that we'll focus on in this chapter are not necessarily the most common problems you'll face in your own projects. Because every project is unique, there's no way to anticipate what you'll run into. However, we've attempted to highlight the most pressing issues at the midpoint of the short film project's duration and apply solutions to many common problems. Note that some of the features you'll use in this chapter are those that you might also use when planning a project. Here, however, your intent is different—getting the project plan back on track.

> **Important** Before you can use the practice files provided for this chapter, you need to install them from the book's companion CD to their default locations. See "Using the Book's CD" on page xix for more information.

Troubleshooting Time and Schedule Problems

Schedule variance will almost certainly appear in any lengthy project. Maintaining control over the schedule requires that the project manager know when variance has occurred and to what extent, and then take timely corrective action to stay on track. To help you identify when variance has occurred, the short film project plan includes the following:

- Deadline dates applied to key milestones
- A project baseline against which you can compare actual performance

The deadline dates and project baseline will help you troubleshoot time and schedule problems in Microsoft Office Project 2007. In this exercise, you address the missed deadline for the production phase of the short film project and shorten the durations of some tasks on the critical path.

> **Important** If you are running Project Professional, you may need to make a one-time adjustment to use the My Computer account and to work offline. This ensures that the practice files you work with in this chapter do not affect your Project Server data. For more information, see "Starting Project Professional" on page 11.

OPEN Short Film Project 15a from the *Documents\Microsoft Press\Project 2007 SBS\ Chapter 15 Getting Back on Track* folder. You can also access the practice files for this book by clicking Start, All Programs, Microsoft Press, Project 2007 Step by Step, and then selecting the chapter folder of the file you want to open.

1. On the **File** menu, click **Save As**.

The Save As dialog box appears.

2. In the **File name** box, type Short Film Project 15, and then click **Save**.

To begin troubleshooting the time and schedule issues, you'll get a top-level view of the degree of schedule variance in the project plan to date.

3. On the **Project** menu, click **Project Information**.

The Project Information dialog box appears.

The current date you see will probably differ.

Next, you will look at the duration values for this project.

4. In the **Project Information** dialog box, click the **Statistics** button.

The Project Statistics dialog box appears:

Based on current project performance and the remaining work as scheduled, the project will finish seven days later than planned.

In the dialog box, you can see the scheduled finish date for the project: January 2, 2009. However, you know this date must be pulled in so that the project concludes before the 2008 holiday season. You can also see that, overall, the project plan now has seven days of finish variance.

The Project Statistics dialog box also indicates some cost variance—the difference between the current and baseline cost values. You will examine this more closely in a later exercise.

5. Click **Close** to close the Project Statistics dialog box.

Before you address the overall project duration, you'll examine the missed deadline for the production phase.

6. Point to the missed deadline indicator in the **Indicators** column for task 24, the **Production** summary task.

Positioning the mouse pointer over the missed deadline indicator displays a ScreenTip in which you can see the details of the deadline and the tasks' finish date.

Enough schedule variance has occurred in the pre-production phase and the completed portion of the production phase to cause the scheduled completion of the production phase to move out beyond its deadline date of August 8.

Take a moment to look over the remaining tasks in the production phase, which consist of several more scenes to be shot. Because of the nature of this work, you cannot change task relationships (for example, from finish-to-start to start-to-start) to decrease the duration of each scene's summary task; the tasks follow a logical finish-to-start relationship. Nor can you schedule two or more scenes to be shot in parallel because many of the same resources are required for all of them. To bring the production phase back down to an acceptable duration, you'll have to shorten the duration of some of its subtasks. To do this, you'll assign additional resources to some tasks.

Looking over the remaining production tasks, you see that some of the setup and teardown tasks seem to be the longest, so you'll focus on these.

7. Click the name of task 50, **Scene 5 setup**, and then scroll the Gantt Chart view up so the task appears at the top of the view.

This three-day task currently has several resources assigned. After conferring with these resources, you all agree that they could complete the task more quickly with additional resources.

Assign Resources

8. On the **Standard** toolbar, click the **Assign Resources** button.

9. In the **Assign Resources** dialog box, under the **Resource Name** column, click **Frank Lee**, and then click the **Assign** button.

> **Troubleshooting** If Project displays a Planning Wizard message here, click Continue and then OK. It will not affect the resource assignment.

Project assigns Frank Lee to the task; because *effort-driven scheduling* is enabled for this task, Project reduces the duration of the task to 2.4 days. The total work on the task is unchanged, but it is now distributed across more resources, thereby resulting in a shorter duration.

Because effort-driven scheduling is enabled
for this task, assigning an additional resource
reduces the task's duration.

	❶	Task Name	Duration	Start	Finish
49		⊟ Scene 5	5.4 days	Wed 7/2/08	Thu 7/10/08
50		Scene 5 setup	2.4 days	Wed 7/2/08	Mon 7/7/08
51		Scene 5 rehearsal	1 day	Mon 7/7/08	Tue 7/8/08
52		Scene 5 shoot	1 day	Tue 7/8/08	Wed 7/9/08
53		Scene 5 teardown	1 day	Wed 7/9/08	Thu 7/10/08
54	📎	Scene 5-process d	1 day	Wed 7/9/08	Thu 7/10/08
55		⊟ Scene 6	13.6 days	Thu 7/10/08	Wed 7/30/08
56		Scene 6 setup	6 days	Thu 7/10/08	Fri 7/18/08
57		Scene 6 rehearsal	3 days	Fri 7/18/08	Wed 7/23/08
58		Scene 6 shoot	1 day	Wed 7/23/08	Thu 7/24/08
59		Scene 6 teardown	3 days	Thu 7/24/08	Tue 7/29/08
60	📎	Scene 6-process d	1 day	Tue 7/29/08	Wed 7/30/08
61		⊟ Scene 8	8 days	Wed 7/30/08	Sat 8/9/08
62		Scene 8 setup	3 days	Wed 7/30/08	Fri 8/1/08
63		Scene 8 rehearsal	2 days	Mon 8/4/08	Tue 8/5/08
64		Scene 8 shoot	1 day	Wed 8/6/08	Wed 8/6/08
65		Scene 8 teardown	1.5 days	Thu 8/7/08	Fri 8/8/08
66	📎	Scene 8-process d	1 day	Fri 8/8/08	Sat 8/9/08
67		⊟ Scene 4	4 days	Mon 8/11/08	Fri 8/15/08
68		Scene 4 setup	1.5 days	Mon 8/11/08	Tue 8/12/08
69		Scene 4 rehearsal	4 hrs	Tue 8/12/08	Tue 8/12/08
70		Scene 4 shoot	2 hrs	Wed 8/13/08	Wed 8/13/08
71		Scene 4 teardown	1.5 days	Wed 8/13/08	Thu 8/14/08
72	📎	Scene 4-process d	1 day	Thu 8/14/08	Fri 8/15/08
73		⊟ Post-Production	95.25 days	Fri 8/15/08	Fri 1/2/09
74		Log footage	3 days	Fri 8/15/08	Wed 8/27/08

Assign Resources dialog box:

Task: Scene 5 setup
☐ Resource list options

Resources from Short Film Project 15

	Resource Name	Units	Cost
✓	Electrician	200%	$1,075.20
✓	Frank Lee	100%	$326.40
✓	Jo Brown	100%	$417.60
✓	Max Benson	100%	$518.40
	16-mm Camera		
	16-mm Film		
	500-Watt Light		

Assign · Remove · Replace... · Graphs... · Close

To further reduce the task's duration, you'll assign another resource.

10. In the **Resource Name** column, click **Keith Harris**, and then click **Assign**.

Project further reduces the duration of the task to two days.

Next, you will reduce the durations of the setup and teardown tasks of Scene 6. This time, however, you'll make multiple assignments to multiple tasks simultaneously because it's quicker.

11. In the **Task Name** column, click the name of task 56, **Scene 6 setup**. While holding down the Ctrl key, click the name of task 59, **Scene 6 teardown**.

12. In the **Resource Name** column of the **Assign Resources** dialog box, click **Frank Lee** and then while holding down the Ctrl key click **Keith Harris**.

13. Click **Assign**.

Project assigns these two resources to tasks 56 and 59 and correspondingly reduces the durations of the two tasks.

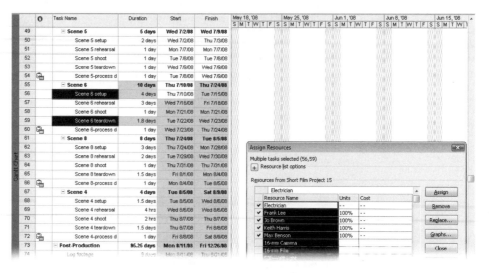

14. Scroll up to see task 24, the Production summary task.

Note that the missed deadline indicator is still visible. If you point at it with your mouse pointer, you'll see that the additional assignments you just made did indeed move in the completion date of the production phase, but not quite enough to meet its deadline date. To remedy this, you'll make some additional assignments to other tasks.

15. In the **Task Name** column, click the name of task 62, **Scene 8 setup**. While holding down the Ctrl key, click the name of task 65, **Scene 8 teardown**.

16. In the **Resource Name** column of the **Assign Resources** dialog box, click **Frank Lee** and then, while holding down the Ctrl key, click **Keith Harris**.

17. Click **Assign**.

18. Click **Close** to close the Assign Resources dialog box.

19. Scroll up to see task 24, the Production summary task.

Reducing the durations of subtasks also reduced
the duration of this summary task enough so that,
as scheduled, it no longer misses its deadline.

	①	Task Name	Duration	Start	Finish	
24		− Production	52 days	Mon 5/26/08	Thu 8/7/08	
25	✓	− Scene 7	5 days	Mon 5/26/08	Sat 5/31/08	
26	✓	Scene 7 setup	1.75 days	Mon 5/26/08	Tue 5/27/08	Jo Brown,Max Benson,Electrician[50%]
27	✓	Scene 7 rehearsal	1 day	Tue 5/27/08	Wed 5/28/08	Scott Cooper[200%],Jo Brown[150%],Paul Borm[150%],Joseph N
28	✓	Scene 7 shoot	1.25 days	Wed 5/28/08	Thu 5/29/08	Scott Cooper[600%],Jo Brown[600%],Joseph Matthews[600
29	✓	Scene 7 teardown	1 day	Fri 5/30/08	Fri 5/30/08	Jo Brown[150%],Max Benson[150%],Electrician[25%]

The missed deadline indicator is gone. Next, you'll see how the production phase is
now scheduled. Recall that the deadline date of the Production summary task was
August 8.

20. On the **Edit** menu, click **Go To**.

21. In the **Date** box (not the ID box), type or click 8/8/08, and then click **OK**.

Project scrolls the Gantt Chart to show the end of the *Production* summary task.

You can visually verify that the summary
task concludes prior to its deadline in the
chart portion of the Gantt Chart view.

	①	Task Name	Duration	Start	Finish	
24		− Production	52 days	Mon 5/26/08	Thu 8/7/08	
25	✓	− Scene 7	5 days	Mon 5/26/08	Sat 5/31/08	
26	✓	Scene 7 setup	1.75 days	Mon 5/26/08	Tue 5/27/08	
27	✓	Scene 7 rehearsal	1 day	Tue 5/27/08	Wed 5/28/08	
28	✓	Scene 7 shoot	1.25 days	Wed 5/28/08	Thu 5/29/08	

With the updated setup and teardown durations, the overall duration of the production phase now ends on August 7, just prior to its deadline. However, given the
amount of variance that occurred in the production phase already, you should keep
a close watch on this phase as work progresses.

Troubleshooting Cost and Resource Problems

In projects where you've entered cost information for resources, you might find that
you must fine-tune resource and assignment details to address many cost problems.
Although this might not be your intention, changing resource assignment details not
only affects costs, but can affect task durations as well.

As you saw in the previous exercise, the short film project plan has some cost variance.
As it is currently scheduled, the project plan will end up costing about $5,000 more than
planned, or about 4% over budget. This cost variance has resulted from some longer-
than-expected assignment durations and the resulting increased costs of the assigned
resources.

After researching the high cost of the electricians on the setup and teardown assignments, you discover that, in most cases, they're really needed for only a portion of the tasks' durations. After discussing the issue with the production manager, you agree that the electricians' assignments on the remaining setup and teardown tasks should be halved. While you're updating the project, you'll also handle the upcoming departure of another resource.

In this exercise, you adjust work values for resource assignments and replace one resource with another on upcoming assignments. You begin, however, by checking the total cost of the electricians' assignments.

1. On the **View** menu, click **Resource Sheet**.

2. On the **View** menu, point to **Table: Entry** and then click **Cost**.

   The Cost table appears in the Resource Sheet view. Note the current total cost of resource 13, Electrician: $7,784. This figure is a combination of the electricians' actual cost to date and their anticipated cost for scheduled assignments yet to be completed. You would like to reduce this cost by reducing the electricians' work on upcoming tasks.

3. On the **View** menu, click **Resource Usage**.

   The Resource Usage view appears.

4. In the **Resource Name** column, click the **plus sign** next to the name of resource 13, **Electrician**.

   The Electricians' assignments are displayed.

   Because Scenes 7, 3, and 1 have already been completed, you'll focus on the electricians' assignments to the remaining scenes.

Scroll To Task

5. On the **Standard** toolbar, click the **Scroll To Task** button.

   Project scrolls the timephased grid portion of the Resource Usage view so that some of the electricians' assignments are visible. As you edit assignment work values in the steps below, you can scroll the timephased grid to see the effect on the scheduled work per day.

6. In the **Work** column in the table in the left pane for **Scene 2 setup**, type 8h, and then press the [Enter] key.

   Project adjusts the work of the electricians on this task to four hours.

7. In the **Work** column, enter the new work values in the following list for the electricians' remaining assignments:

For this assignment	Enter this work value
Scene 2 teardown	4h
Scene 5 setup	16h
Scene 5 teardown	8h
Scene 6 setup	32h
Scene 6 teardown	7h
Scene 8 setup	8h
Scene 8 teardown	4h
Scene 4 setup	6h
Scene 4 teardown	6h

After reducing the work on the electricians' assignments, their total work (and resulting cost) is correspondingly reduced.

Note that because the electricians were not the only resource assigned to these tasks, reducing the electricians' scheduled work in this way will reduce the cost of their assignments, but not necessarily the durations of these tasks. The other resources assigned to these tasks may have assignments of longer durations.

To verify the reduction in the electricians' costs, you'll switch back to the Resource Sheet view.

8. On the **View** menu, click **Resource Sheet**.

The Resource Sheet view appears.

The electricians' updated cost
includes their actual cost plus
remaining cost.

	Resource Name	Cost	Baseline Cost	Variance	Actual Cost	Remaining
1	16-mm Camera	$1,140.00	$1,050.00	$90.00	$570.00	$570.00
2	16-mm Film	$7,750.00	$7,250.00	$500.00	$3,500.00	$4,250.00
3	500-Watt Light	$420.00	$330.00	$90.00	$230.00	$190.00
4	Anne L. Paper	$1,912.50	$1,612.50	$300.00	$600.00	$1,312.50
5	Camera Boom	$0.00	$0.00	$0.00	$0.00	$0.00
6	Clair Hector	$9,427.50	$9,360.00	$67.50	$4,747.50	$4,680.00
7	Crane	$0.00	$0.00	$0.00	$0.00	$0.00
8	Daniel Penn	$900.00	$900.00	$0.00	$0.00	$900.00
9	David Campbell	$5,100.00	$5,100.00	$0.00	$300.00	$4,800.00
10	Dolly	$0.00	$0.00	$0.00	$0.00	$0.00
11	Doug Hampton	$2,336.00	$2,246.40	$89.60	$512.00	$1,824.00
12	Editing Lab	$6,350.00	$6,350.00	$0.00	$0.00	$6,350.00
13	Electrician	$5,068.00	$9,744.00	($4,676.00)	$2,520.00	$2,548.00
14	Eric Lang	$518.00	$444.00	$74.00	$518.00	$0.00
15	Eric Miller	$1,650.00	$1,350.00	$300.00	$900.00	$750.00
16	Florian Voss	$2,400.00	$0.00	$2,400.00	$0.00	$2,400.00
17	Frank Lee	$2,754.00	$986.00	$1,768.00	$748.00	$2,006.00
18	Jan Miksovsky	$4,717.00	$4,375.00	$342.00	$3,586.00	$1,131.00
19	Jim Hance	$600.00	$450.00	$150.00	$300.00	$300.00

Note the updated total cost of resource 13, Electrician: $5,068. Only the Cost and
Remaining Cost values changed; the costs relating to work already performed (that
is, actual work) are not affected, nor is the baseline cost.

To conclude this exercise, you will update the project plan to reflect that a resource
will be leaving the project early and his assignments will be taken over by another resource. Max Benson will be leaving the project just after the start of work
on Scene 2. You will reassign Max Benson's work on subsequent tasks to Megan
Sherman. Megan happens to be a slightly less expensive resource, so the replacement will help slightly with the cost variance as well.

9. On the **View** menu, click **Task Usage**.

   The Task Usage view appears.

10. On the **View** menu, point to **Table: Usage** and then click **Work**.

    The Work table appears in the Task Usage view.

11. Drag the vertical divider bar to the right to show the Percent Work Complete col-
    umn (labeled % W. Comp).

    Next, you'll filter the Task Usage view to show only those tasks to which Max
    Benson is assigned. In that way, when you replace Max Benson with Megan
    Sherman, the replacement will affect only the tasks to which Max Benson is
    assigned.

12. On the **Project** menu, point to **Filtered For: All Tasks**, and then click **Using
    Resource**.

    The Using Resource dialog box appears.

13. In the **Show Tasks Using** box, click **Max Benson**, and then click **OK**.

    Project filters the Task Usage view to show only those tasks to which Max Benson is assigned.

Here is the first incomplete assignment for Max Benson.

ID	Task Name	Work	Baseline	Variance	Actual	Remaining	% W. Comp.	Details	M	T	W	T	F	S	Jun 29 S
1	Pre-Production	1,305 hrs	1,452 hrs	-147 hrs	1,305 hrs	0 hrs	100%	Work							
6	Scout locations	216 hrs	240 hrs	-24 hrs	216 hrs	0 hrs	100%	Work							
	Max Benson	72 hrs	80 hrs	-8 hrs	72 hrs	0 hrs	100%	Work							
7	Select locations	116 hrs	116 hrs	0 hrs	116 hrs	0 hrs	100%	Work							
	Max Benson	40 hrs	40 hrs	0 hrs	40 hrs	0 hrs	100%	Work							
24	Production	2,813 hrs	2,495 hrs	318 hrs	1,231 hrs	1,582 hrs	44%	Work	144h	32h	24h	16h	135h		
25	Scene 7	351 hrs	220 hrs	131 hrs	351 hrs	0 hrs	100%	Work							
26	Scene 7 setup	20 hrs	20 hrs	0 hrs	20 hrs	0 hrs	100%	Work							
	Max Benson	8 hrs	8 hrs	0 hrs	8 hrs	0 hrs	100%	Work							
29	Scene 7 teardown	26 hrs	20 hrs	6 hrs	26 hrs	0 hrs	100%	Work							
	Max Benson	12 hrs	8 hrs	4 hrs	12 hrs	0 hrs	100%	Work							
31	Scene 3	532 hrs	268 hrs	264 hrs	532 hrs	0 hrs	100%	Work							
32	Scene 3 setup	54 hrs	24 hrs	30 hrs	54 hrs	0 hrs	100%	Work							
	Max Benson	24 hrs	8 hrs	16 hrs	24 hrs	0 hrs	100%	Work							
35	Scene 3 teardown	38 hrs	24 hrs	14 hrs	38 hrs	0 hrs	100%	Work							
	Max Benson	16 hrs	8 hrs	8 hrs	16 hrs	0 hrs	100%	Work							
37	Scene 1	324 hrs	324 hrs	0 hrs	324 hrs	0 hrs	100%	Work	144h	32h					
38	Scene 1 setup	96 hrs	96 hrs	0 hrs	96 hrs	0 hrs	100%	Work							
	Max Benson	24 hrs	24 hrs	0 hrs	24 hrs	0 hrs	100%	Work							
41	Scene 1 teardown	32 hrs	32 hrs	0 hrs	32 hrs	0 hrs	100%	Work			32h				
	Max Benson	8 hrs	8 hrs	0 hrs	8 hrs	0 hrs	100%	Work			8h				
43	Scene 2	228 hrs	216 hrs	12 hrs	24 hrs	204 hrs	11%	Work			24h	16h	135h		
44	Scene 2 setup	40 hrs	24 hrs	16 hrs	24 hrs	16 hrs	60%	Work			24h	16h			
	Max Benson	16 hrs	8 hrs	8 hrs	8 hrs	8 hrs	50%	Work			8h	8h			
47	Scene 2 teardown	20 hrs	24 hrs	-4 hrs	0 hrs	20 hrs	0%	Work							
	Max Benson	8 hrs	8 hrs	0 hrs	0 hrs	8 hrs	0%	Work							
49	Scene 5	328 hrs	352 hrs	-24 hrs	0 hrs	328 hrs	0%	Work							
50	Scene 5 setup	80 hrs	96 hrs	-16 hrs	0 hrs	80 hrs	0%	Work							
	Max Benson	16 hrs	24 hrs	-8 hrs	0 hrs	16 hrs	0%	Work							
53	Scene 5 teardown	24 hrs	32 hrs	-8 hrs	0 hrs	24 hrs	0%	Work							
	Max Benson	8 hrs	8 hrs	0 hrs	0 hrs	8 hrs	0%	Work							
55	Scene 6	604.6 hrs	644 hrs	-39.4 hrs	0 hrs	604.6 hrs	0%	Work							

Ready

Looking at the *Percent Work Complete* field, you can see that Max has uncompleted work starting with task 44 and concluding with task 71. You can see in the Percent Work Complete column that Max Benson's assignment to task 44, *Scene 2 setup*, is 50% complete.

14. In the **Task Name** column, select the task names and assignments for tasks 44 through 71.

    Next, you will make the resource replacement. Keep an eye on Max Benson's partial work on task 44.

Assign Resources

15. On the **Standard** toolbar, click **Assign Resources**.

    The Assign Resources dialog box appears.

16. In the **Resource Name** column, click **Max Benson**, and then click the **Replace** button.

    The Replace Resource dialog box appears.

17. In the **Resource Name** column, click **Megan Sherman**, and then click **OK**.

Project replaces Max Benson's future assignments with Megan Sherman.

18. Click **Close** to close the Assign Resources dialog box.

After replacing Max Benson with Megan Sherman, Max's actual work on the partially completed task is preserved... ...and his remaining work on the task is assigned to Megan.

	Task Name	Work	Baseline	Variance	Actual	Remaining	% W. Comp.	Details	M	T	W	T	F	S	S
43	⊟ Scene 2	228 hrs	216 hrs	12 hrs	24 hrs	204 hrs	11%	Work			24h	16h	135h		
44	⊟ Scene 2 setup	40 hrs	24 hrs	16 hrs	24 hrs	16 hrs	60%	Work			24h	16h			
	Max Benson	8 hrs	8 hrs	0 hrs	8 hrs	0 hrs	100%	Work			8h				
	Megan Sherm	8 hrs	0 hrs	8 hrs	0 hrs	8 hrs	0%	Work			0h	8h			
47	⊟ Scene 2 teardown	20 hrs	24 hrs	–4 hrs	0 hrs	20 hrs	0%	Work							
	Megan Sherm	8 hrs	8 hrs	0 hrs	0 hrs	8 hrs	0%	Work							
49	⊟ Scene 5	328 hrs	352 hrs	–24 hrs	0 hrs	328 hrs	0%	Work							
50	⊟ Scene 5 setup	80 hrs	96 hrs	–16 hrs	0 hrs	80 hrs	0%	Work							
	Megan Sherm	16 hrs	24 hrs	–8 hrs	0 hrs	16 hrs	0%	Work							
53	⊟ Scene 5 teardown	24 hrs	32 hrs	–8 hrs	0 hrs	24 hrs	0%	Work							

Note that for task 44, Project preserved Max Benson's eight hours of actual work on the task and assigned the remaining work on the task (also eight hours) to Megan. For the subsequent tasks to which Max was assigned, he has been replaced by Megan.

19. On the **Project** menu, point to **Filtered For: Using Resource**, and then click **All Tasks**.

Project unfilters the Task Usage view.

Troubleshooting Scope-of-Work Problems

A project's scope should include all of the work required—and only the work required—to successfully deliver the product of the project to its intended customer. After project work has started, managing its scope usually requires making trade-offs: trading time for money, quality for time, and so on. You might have the goal of never making such trade-offs, but a more realistic goal might be to make the best-informed trade-offs possible.

Recall from the previous exercises that the project finish date extended into 2009. With the actions taken in the previous exercise, the finish date has been pulled into late December 2008, but you want it to end around mid-December 2008 at the latest. In this exercise, you focus on the project's finish date and make several trade-offs to ensure that the project will deliver its product within the time frame that you want.

1. On the **Project** menu, click **Project Information**.

The Project Information dialog box appears. As the project is now scheduled, it will be completed on December 22, 2008—that is, if all of the remaining work is completed as scheduled. However, realistically, you expect the holiday season to interfere with concluding the project, so you'll need to take steps to pull in the finish date.

2. Click **Cancel** to close the Project Information dialog box.

   Because the project finish date is controlled by tasks on the *critical path*, you'll begin by viewing only those tasks.

3. On the **View** menu, click **More Views**.

4. In the **More Views** dialog box, click **Detail Gantt**, and then click the **Apply** button.

   The Detail Gantt view appears.

5. On the **Project** menu, point to **Filtered For: All Tasks**, and then click **Critical**.

   Project displays only the critical tasks. The remaining production tasks are already as compressed as they can be, so you'll focus on compressing the post-production tasks. To begin, you'll allow overtime work for several tasks to shorten their durations.

6. On the **Edit** menu, click **Go To**.

7. In the **ID** box, type 75, and then click **OK**.

   Project displays task 75, *Record rough narration*.

8. To see the effect of the following steps on the duration of task 75 and successor tasks, scroll the Detail Gantt view in the upper pane until task 75 appears near the top of the screen.

9. On the **Window** menu, click **Split**.

   The Task Form appears below the Detail Gantt view.

10. Click anywhere in the **Task Form**. Then, on the **Format** menu, point to **Details**, and click **Resource Work**.

    The Resource Work details appear in the Task Form.

11. In the **Task Form**, in the **Ovt. Work** column for the resource named **David Campbell**, type or click **30h**, and press Enter.

12. In the **Ovt. Work** column for **Michael Patten**, type or click **30h**, and click **OK** in the upper right corner of the Task Form.

    The overtime work values cause Project to adjust the daily work assignments for these resources and shorten the overall duration of the task.

Assigning overtime work reduces the duration of the task but not the total amount of work required to complete the task.

Note that each resource's total work on this task remains at 96 hours. Now, however, 30 of those 96 hours per resource will be scheduled as overtime. The same amount of work will be performed, but in a shorter time span. Project will apply overtime cost rates, if they have been set up, to the overtime portion of the assignment.

13. In the Gantt Chart view, click the name of task 76, **Paper edit footage**.

14. In the **Task Form**, enter 25 hours (**25h**) of overtime work for each of the four assigned resources, and then click **OK**.

Project schedules the overtime work and recalculates the task's duration.

15. On the **Window** menu, click **Remove Split**.

16. On the **Project** menu, click **Project Information**.

The Project Information dialog box appears. The adjustments you've made to the schedule have pulled in the project's finish date to 12/11/08. Although that meets the target you had in mind, you can expect some additional variance given the overall performance to date. In anticipation of this, you'll make further adjustments to the post-production tasks.

17. Click **Cancel** to close the Project Information dialog box.

18. In the **Task Name** column, click the name of task 83, **Print internegative of film**.

Task 83, *Print internegative of film*, isn't really dependent on its predecessor being completed before it can start and does not use the same resources as its predecessor. After talking with the resources assigned to it and its predecessor task, you all agree that, given the schedule crunch, work on task 83 can begin at the same time as its predecessor, task 82.

Task Information

19. On the **Standard** toolbar, click the **Task Information** button.

The Task Information dialog box appears.

20. Click the **Predecessors** tab.

21. In the **Type** field for the task's predecessor, click **Start-to-Start (SS)** on the drop-down list.

22. Click **OK** to close the Task Information dialog box.

Scroll To Task

23. On the **Standard** toolbar, click **Scroll To Task**.

	❶	Task Name	Leveling Delay	Oct 12, '08	Oct 19, '08	Oct 26, '08	Nov 2, '08	Nov 9, '08	Nov 16, '08	N
73		⊟ **Post-Production**	**0 edays**							
74		Log footage	0 edays							
75		Record rough narration	0 edays							
76		Paper edit footage	0 edays							
77		Rough cut edit	0 edays							
78		Fine cut edit	0 edays							
79		Hold formal approval sl	0 edays							
80		Record final narration	0 edays							
81		Add head and tail titles	0 edays							
82		Add final music	0 edays							
83		Print internegative of fil	0 edays							
84		Clone dubbing masters	0 edays							
85		Archive master film and	0 edays							
86		Hand off masters to dis	0 edays							

Changing the predecessor relationship between these tasks to start-to-start decreases the overall duration of the project because these tasks are on the critical path.

Project reschedules task 83 to start when task 82 starts and reschedules all subsequent linked tasks as well. Note that task 84 will now start and end before task 82 is completed.

24. On the **Project** menu, click **Project Information**.

The Project Information dialog box appears. The project's finish date is now pulled back to mid November—a workable date at this time.

To conclude this exercise, you'll see what effects these final adjustments have had on the project's final cost values as well.

25. Click **Statistics**.

The Project Statistics dialog box appears.

Project Statistics for 'Short Film Project 15'				
	Start		**Finish**	
Current	Mon 3/3/08		Mon 11/17/08	
Baseline	Mon 3/3/08		Fri 12/19/08	
Actual	Mon 3/3/08		NA	
Variance	0d		-21.88d	
	Duration	**Work**	**Cost**	
Current	184.38d	5,846h	$122,779.31	
Baseline	206.25d	5,575h	$124,536.40	
Actual	78.88d	2,536h	$53,671.31	
Remaining	105.5d	3,310h	$69,108.00	
Percent complete:				
Duration: 43% Work: 43%			Close	

The project's current cost calculation is now slightly below the baseline cost, although you know it's likely to go up as the remainder of the project experiences more variance.

26. Click **Close** to close the Project Statistics dialog box.

You confer with the project sponsors, who are pleased that you can wrap up the short film project before the holiday season. Although producing the project deliverable within these constraints will be a challenge, you're both realistic and optimistic about the project's future performance and comfortable with your project management skills and knowledge of Project. Good luck!

CLOSE the Short Film Project 15 file.

Key Points

- When addressing variance in a project plan, it is useful to evaluate your plan (and variance) in terms of time, cost, and scope: the three sides of the project triangle.

- When addressing schedule problems, focus your remedies on tasks on the critical path; these drive the finish date of the project.

- When addressing cost or scope problems, focus on expensive resources and especially on their longer assignments.

Part 3

Special Projects

Chapter at a Glance

Change the formatting of different types of bars in the Gantt Chart view, page 355

Use gridlines to make your Gantt Chart views easier to read, page 357

Create new box styles in the Network Diagram view, page 360

Change the formatting of other types of views, such as the Calendar view, page 362

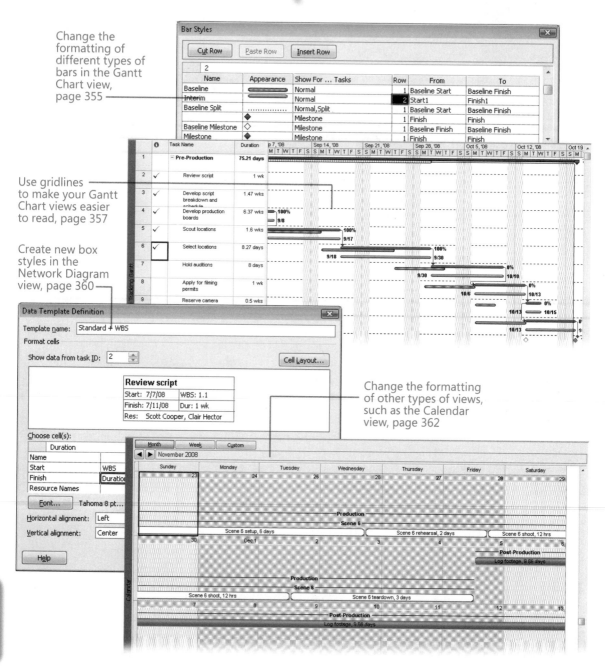

16 Applying Advanced Formatting

In this chapter, you will learn how to:

✔ Format the Gantt Chart view.

✔ Format the Network Diagram view.

✔ Format the Calendar view.

> **Tip** Do you need only a quick refresher on the topics in this chapter? See the Quick Reference entries on pages xxv-xlviii.

This chapter introduces you to some of the more advanced formatting features in Microsoft Office Project 2007. A well-formatted project plan is essential for communicating details to resources, customers, and other stakeholders. Some of the formatting capabilities in Project are similar to those of a style-based word processor, such as Word, in which defining a style once affects all content in the document to which that style has been applied. In Project, you can use styles to change the appearance of a specific type of Gantt bar, such as a summary bar, throughout a project plan. Other formatting options introduced in this chapter focus on the different ways of identifying tasks and formatting some of the more commonly used views.

> **Important** Before you can use the practice files provided for this chapter, you need to install them from the book's companion CD to their default locations. See "Using the Book's CD" on page xix for more information.

Formatting a Gantt Chart View

You can directly format specific items (a milestone, for example) in a Gantt chart view or use the Gantt Chart Wizard (on the Format menu) to change the look of a Gantt Chart view in limited ways. If you completed Chapter 5, "Formatting and Printing Your Plan," you worked with the Gantt Chart Wizard. In this section, you will customize specific items, such as Gantt bars and gridlines, in ways that the Gantt Chart Wizard cannot.

> **Tip** Remember that several views are Gantt chart views, even though only one view is specifically called the Gantt Chart view. Other Gantt chart views include the Detail Gantt, Leveling Gantt, Multiple Baselines Gantt, and Tracking Gantt. Gantt chart view generally refers to a type of presentation that shows Gantt bars organized along a timescale.

In addition to changing the formatting of objects that appear by default in a Gantt chart view (such as a task's Gantt bar), you can add or remove objects. For example, it may be useful to compare baseline, interim, and *actual* plans in a single view. Doing so helps you evaluate the schedule adjustments you have made.

In this exercise, you display the current schedule along with the baseline and the interim plan. (The baseline and the interim plan were previously set in the project plan.) You begin by customizing a copy of the Tracking Gantt chart view.

> **BE SURE TO** start Microsoft Office Project 2007 if it's not already running.

> **Important** If you are running Project Professional, you may need to make a one-time adjustment to use the Computer account and to work offline. This ensures that the practice files you work with in this chapter do not affect your Project Server data. For more information, see "Starting Project Professional" on page 11.

> **OPEN** Parnell Film 16a from the \Documents\Microsoft Press\Project 2007 SBS\Chapter 16 Advanced Formatting folder. You can also access the practice files for this book by clicking Start, All Programs, Microsoft Press, Project 2007 Step by Step and then selecting the chapter folder of the file you want to open.

1. On the **File** menu, click **Save As**.

   The Save As dialog box appears.

2. In the **File name** box, type Parnell Film 16, and then click **Save**.

3. On the **View** menu, click **More Views**.

   The More Views dialog box appears.

4. On the **Views** list, click **Tracking Gantt**, and click the **Copy** button.

   The View Definition dialog box appears.

5. In the **Name** box, type Interim Tracking Gantt, and click **OK**.

   The new view is listed in the More Views dialog box.

6. Click the **Apply** button.

   Project displays the new view, which at this point is identical to the Tracking Gantt view. Next, you will customize this new view so that your original Tracking Gantt view will not be altered. You will add the interim plan bars to the view.

7. On the **Format** menu, click **Bar Styles**.

   The Bar Styles dialog box appears.

> **Tip** You can also display this dialog box by double-clicking the background of the chart portion of a Gantt chart view or by right-clicking in the background and selecting Bar Styles in the shortcut menu.

8. Scroll down the list of the bar styles, and in the **Name** column, click **Baseline Split**.

9. Click the **Insert Row** button.

   Project inserts a row for a new bar style in the table. Project draws Gantt bars in the order in which they are listed in the Bar Styles dialog box. Inserting a new bar style above the Baseline Split will help ensure that it won't be obscured by another type of Gantt bar.

10. In the new cell in the **Name** column, type Interim.

    Interim is the name you'll give to the new task bar that will appear on the chart portion of the view.

> **Tip** The names of most task bars will appear in the legend of printed Gantt chart views. If you do not want a task bar name to appear in the legend, type an asterisk (*) at the beginning of the task bar name. For example, if you wanted to prevent *Interim* from appearing in the legend, you would enter its name here as **Interim*. In the Bar Styles dialog box, you can see that the Rolled Up task bar name (among others) is prefaced with an asterisk, so it does not appear in the legend of a printed Gantt chart view.

11. In the same row, click the cell under the **Show For...Tasks** column heading, and then click **Normal** on the drop-down list.

The Show For ... Tasks value indicates the type of task the bar will represent (such as a normal task, a summary task, or a milestone) or the status of the task (such as critical or in progress).

> **Tip** This is a fairly complex dialog box in Project, but it is extensively documented in online Help. To see Help for this dialog box, click the Help button.

12. Click the cell under the **From** column heading, and click **Start1** on the drop-down list.

13. Click the cell under the **To** column heading, and then click **Finish1** on the drop-down list.

The From and To values represent the start and end points for the bar.

Here is the new bar style you are creating.

The options on these tabs apply to the active bar style above; in this case, "Interim."

The *Start1* and *Finish1* items are the fields in which the first interim plan values were previously set for you in the project plan. The current start date and finish date of each task in the project were saved to these fields when the interim plan was set. If you completed Chapter 13, "Tracking Progress on Tasks and Assignments," you have already been introduced to interim plans.

You have now instructed Project to display the first interim plan's start and finish dates as bars. Next, you will specify what these bars should look like.

14. Click the cell under the **Row** column heading, and click **2** on the drop-down list.

This causes Project to display multiple rows of Gantt bars for each task in the view. Next, focus your attention on the lower half of the Bar Styles dialog box.

15. In the **Shape** box under the **Middle** label, click the half-height bar, the third option from the top of the list.

> **Troubleshooting** The Bar Styles dialog box is one of several dialog boxes in Project that contains tabs (and is referred to as a tabbed dialog box). If you don't see the Shape box mentioned in the previous step, verify that the Bars tab is active and not the Text tab.

16. In the **Pattern** box under the **Middle** label, click the solid bar, the second option from the top of the list.

17. In the **Color** box, click **Green**.

Because this custom view focuses on the interim plan, next you'll format the interim bars to include their start and finish dates.

18. In the **Bar Styles** dialog box, click the **Text** tab.

19. In the **Left** box, click **Start1** on the drop-down list.

> **Tip** You can type a letter in a field name list to go directly to fields that begin with that letter. For example, you can type S to go to the items that begin with S.

20. In the **Right** box, click **Finish1** on the drop-down list.

Selecting these values will cause the Start1 and Finish1 dates to appear on either side of the bar.

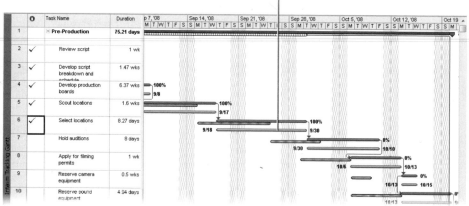

21. Click **OK** to close the Bar Styles dialog box.

Project displays the interim bars on the Interim Tracking Gantt view. Next, you will get a better look at the Gantt bars.

22. In the **Task Name** column, click the name of task 6, **Select locations**.

Scroll To Task

23. On the **Standard** toolbar, click the **Scroll To Task** button.

Project scrolls the view to display the Gantt bars for task 6 and its adjacent tasks.

In this custom view, the interim plan appears
as green bars and the interim start and finish
dates appear at either end of the interim bars.

Here you can see that the completed task 6 (shown as a solid blue bar at the top of the task row) corresponds exactly to its interim plan bar (the green bar at the bottom of the task row) and that both were scheduled later than the baseline (the patterned gray bar in the middle of the task row). This occurred because, after the baseline was set, changes to the schedule were made that pushed out the scheduled start date of the task. Then the interim plan was saved.

To conclude this exercise, you'll display horizontal gridlines on the chart portion of the Interim Tracking Gantt view to better distinguish the rows of Gantt bars per task.

24. On the **Format** menu, click **Gridlines**.

The Gridlines dialog box appears.

25. In the **Line to change** box, make sure that **Gantt Rows** is selected. Then, in the **Type** box, click the long dashed line, the last option on the list.

26. Click **OK** to close the Gridlines dialog box.

Project draws gridlines between task rows in the chart.

Horizontal gridlines help separate the sets of Gantt bars for each task from those of the other tasks.

Displaying gridlines like this is a great idea when you print multiple Gantt bars for each task.

Project supports several additional Gantt Chart formatting features than those we've worked with in this section. If you wish to explore other formatting options, look at these commands on the Format menu:

- Timescale—for setting time increments, such as weeks and days, and how non-working time is displayed.

- Text Styles—for formatting text associated with a specific task type, such as summary task text.

- Layout—for formatting link lines and Gantt bar visual effects.

Formatting the Network Diagram View

In traditional project management, the Network Diagram is a standard way of representing project activities and their relationships. Tasks are represented as boxes, or nodes, and the relationships between tasks are drawn as lines connecting the nodes. Unlike a Gantt chart, which is a timescaled view, a Network Diagram enables you to view project activities in a manner more closely resembling a flowchart format. This is useful if you'd like to place more focus on the relationships between activities rather than on their durations.

Project provides substantial formatting options for the Network Diagram. In this section, you will use only a few of these formatting options. If you're a heavy-duty Network Diagram user, you'll want to explore the formatting options in greater detail on your own.

In this exercise, you format items in the Network Diagram view.

1. On the **View** menu, click **Network Diagram**.

   The Network Diagram view appears. In this view, each task is represented by a box or node, and each node contains several pieces of information (or fields) about the task.

The Network Diagram view focuses more on task relationships than on durations or sequence. Each task is represented as a box or node, and the relationships between tasks are represented as arrows.

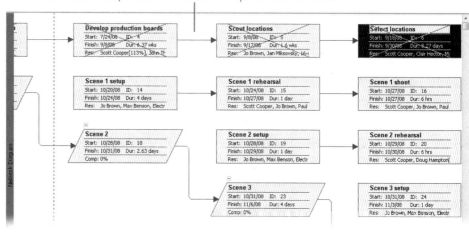

Tip Nodes with an X drawn through them represent completed tasks.

Next, you'll replace the task ID values with the *Work Breakdown Structure (WBS)* codes.

2. On the **Format** menu, click **Box Styles**.

Note that commands on the Format menu may change depending on the type of active view.

The Box Styles dialog box appears.

On the Style Settings For list, you can see all of the node box styles available in Project. The Preview box shows you the specific labels and fields displayed in each box style.

3. Click **More Templates**.

The Data Templates dialog box appears. Templates determine what fields appear in boxes (nodes) as well as their layout.

4. On the **Templates in "Network Diagram"** list, make sure that **Standard** is selected, and then click **Copy**.

The Data Template Definition dialog box appears. You want to add the WBS code value to the upper right corner of the node.

5. In the **Template name** box, type Standard + WBS.

6. Below **Choose cell(s)**, click **ID**. This is the field you will replace.

7. Click **WBS** on the drop-down list of fields, and then press the ⌈Enter⌉ key.

Pressing the ⌈Enter⌉ key causes Project to update the preview in the dialog box.

8. Click **OK** to close the Data Template Definition dialog box.

9. Click **Close** to close the Data Templates dialog box.

10. In the **Box Styles** dialog box, under **Style settings for**, select **Critical**, and while holding the ⌈Shift⌉ key, click **Noncritical Milestone**.

The four types of subtasks are selected.

11. In the **Data template** box, select **Standard + WBS** from the drop-down list.

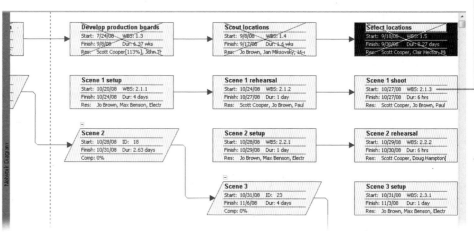

12. Click **OK** to close the Box Styles dialog box.

Project applies the revised box style to nodes in the Network Diagram.

After you reformat the box style in the Network Diagram view, the WBS code replaces the task ID for select box styles.

Now for these box styles, the WBS value appears in the upper right corner of each box rather than the Task ID.

Here are some additional things to consider when working in the Network Diagram view:

- In the Network Diagram view, you can format all boxes with the Box Styles command on the Format menu, or you can format just the active box with the Box command. This is similar to the Bar Styles and Bar commands available on the Format menu when you have a Gantt Chart view displayed.

- If you have Visio 2007 or later, you can generate a Visio visual report that is similar to a network diagram view. Visio visual reports are PivotDiagrams that you can customize. For more information about visual reports, see Chapter 12, "Sharing Project Information with Other Programs."

Formatting the Calendar View

The Calendar view is probably the simplest view available in Project; however, even the Calendar view offers several formatting options. This view is especially useful for sharing schedule information with resources or other stakeholders who prefer a traditional "month-at-a-glance" format rather than a more detailed view, such as the Gantt Chart view.

In this exercise, you reformat summary and critical tasks in the Calendar view.

1. On the **View** menu, click **Calendar**.

   The Calendar view appears. It displays four weeks at a time, and it draws task bars on the days on which tasks are scheduled. Depending on your screen resolution, you might see additional task bars in the Calendar view.

The Calendar view resembles a traditional "month-at-
a-glance" calendar and displays tasks as bars spanning
the days on which they are scheduled to occur.

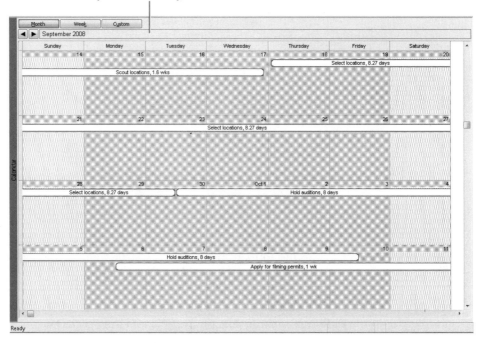

2. On the **Format** menu, click **Bar Styles**.

   The Bar Styles dialog box appears. The additional item type you would like to show
   on the Calendar view is a summary bar.

3. In the **Task type** box, click **Summary**.

4. In the **Bar type** box, click **Line** on the drop-down list.

   The next item type to reformat is critical tasks.

5. In the **Task type** box, click **Critical**.

6. In the **Pattern** box, select the second option on the drop-down list: the solid bar.

7. In the **Color** box, select **Red** from the drop-down list.

8. Click **OK** to close the Bar Styles dialog box.

   Project applies the format options to the Calendar view. To conclude this exercise, you'll display a month that includes some critical tasks.

9. On the **Edit** menu, click **Go To**.

10. In the **Date** box, type or select 11/23/08, and then click **OK**.

    Project displays parts of November and December 2008, which includes the newly formatted critical tasks. Next, you will change how the bars are laid out.

11. On the **Format** menu, click **Layout**.

12. In the **Layout** dialog box, click **Attempt to fit as many tasks as possible**, and then click **OK**.

As with the other views you've customized in this chapter, the Calendar view has additional formatting options available on the Format menu.

After you reformat the Calendar view, critical tasks appear in red and summary tasks appear as lines.

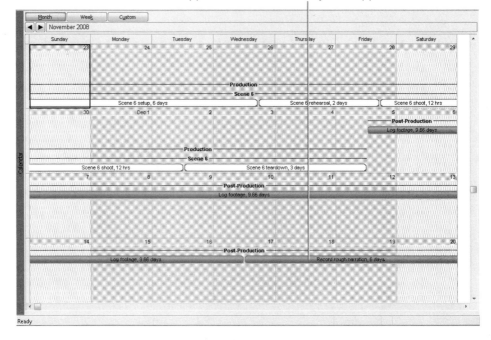

CLOSE the Parnell Film 16 file.

Key Points

- Many different types of bars can appear in the chart portion of a Gantt chart view. Each type of bar can represent a type of task (such as a summary task) or a condition of a task (such as completed).

- The Gantt Chart Wizard offers limited Gantt bar formatting, but the Format Bar Styles command (Format menu) gives you complete control over Gantt bar formatting.

- Although the Gantt Chart view is often synonymous with project plans, the Network Diagram view (sometimes incorrectly referred to as a PERT chart) is useful for focusing on the relationships between activities.

- The Calendar view is especially helpful for those who prefer a traditional "month-at-a-glance" format.

- The specific commands available on the Format menu vary with the view displayed, but most views in Project support some degree of customization.

Chapter at a Glance

Work with the global template and Organizer to share customized elements between project plans, page 370

Record a VBA macro to perform an often-repeated sequence of actions, page 374

Edit VBA macro code in the Visual Basic Editor, page 377

Create a custom toolbar, page 382

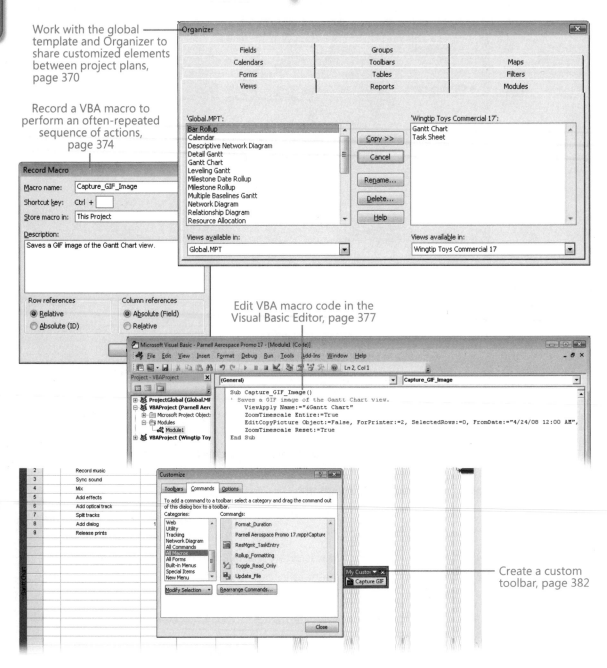

17 Customizing Project

In this chapter, you will learn how to:

✔ Copy a customized element, such as a table, from one project plan to another by using the Organizer.

✔ Record and play back a macro.

✔ Edit a macro in the Visual Basic Editor.

✔ Create a custom toolbar.

> **Tip** Do you need only a quick refresher on the topics in this chapter? See the Quick Reference entries on pages xxv-xlviii.

This chapter describes some of the ways that you can customize Microsoft Office Project 2007 to fit your own preferences. Project has some customization features, such as the Organizer and global template, that are unique to Project. In addition, Project has customization features, such as recording Visual Basic for Applications (VBA) macros, that are similar to what you might be familiar with from other Microsoft Office applications.

> **Important** Some of the actions you perform in this chapter can affect your overall settings in Project regardless of the specific project plan you are using. To keep your Project environment unaffected or at the "factory settings" throughout this chapter, we include steps to undo some actions.

> **Important** Before you can use the practice files provided for this chapter, you need to install them from the book's companion CD to their default locations. See "Using the Book's CD" on page xix for more information.

Sharing Custom Views and Other Elements Between Project Plans

The *Organizer* is the feature you use to share customized elements, such as views, among project plans. The complete list of elements that you can copy between project plans with the Organizer is indicated by the names of the tabs in the Organizer dialog box, which you will see shortly.

One Project feature that you can work with through the Organizer is the *global template*, named Global.mpt. The global template is installed as part of Project and provides the default views, tables, and other elements in Project. The list of elements provided by the global template includes the following:

- Calendars
- Filters
- Forms
- Groups
- Maps (import/export)

- Reports
- Tables
- Menus and toolbars
- Modules (VBA macros)
- Views

> **Tip** This tip describes enterprise project management (EPM) functionality. Project Standard always uses the global template. Project Professional, when used with Project Server, has a different configuration. When Project Professional is connected to Project Server, it uses the global template but is supplemented with details from the enterprise global template as well. For more information about Project Server, see Part 4, "Introducing Project Server."

Initially, the specific definitions of all views, tables, and similar elements are contained in the global template. For example, the fact that the default usage table contains one set of fields and not others is determined by the global template. The very first time you display a view, table, or similar element in a project plan, it is automatically copied from the global template to that project plan. Thereafter, the element resides in the project plan. Any subsequent customization of that element in the project plan (for example, changing the fields displayed in a table) applies to only that one project plan and does not affect the global template. The exception to this is macros, toolbars, and import/export maps. By default, Project stores these elements in the global template rather than in the active project plan.

You could use Project extensively and never need to touch the global template. However, when you do work with the global template, you do so through the Organizer. Some results that you can accomplish relating to the global template include:

● Create a customized element, such as a custom view, and make it available in all project plans you work with by copying the custom view into the global template.

● Replace a customized element, such as a view or table, in a project plan by copying the original, unmodified element from the global template to the project plan in which you've customized the same element.

● Copy one customized element, such as a custom view, from one project plan to another.

The settings in the global template apply to all project plans you work with in Project. Because we don't want to alter the global template you use, in this exercise we'll focus on copying customized elements between two project plans. Keep in mind, though, that the general process of using the Organizer shown here is the same whether you are working with the global template and a project plan or two project plans. In fact, any custom element that you copy into the global template becomes available in all of the project plans you use.

> **Important** In the Organizer, when you attempt to copy a view, table, or other element from a project plan to the global template, Project alerts you as to whether you will overwrite that same element in the global template. If you choose to overwrite it, that customized element (such as a customized view) will be available in all new project plans and any other project plans that do not already contain that element. If you choose to rename the customized element, it becomes available in all project plans but does not affect the existing elements already stored in the global template. It's generally a good idea to give your customized elements unique names, such as *Custom Gantt Chart*, so that you can keep the original element intact.

In this exercise, you will copy a custom table from one project plan to another.

> **Important** If you are running Project Professional, you may need to make a one-time adjustment to use the My Computer account and to work offline. This ensures that the practice files you work with in this chapter do not affect your Project Server data. For more information, see "Starting Project Professional" on page XX.

> **OPEN** Parnell Aerospace Promo 17a and Wingtip Toys Commercial 17b from the *Documents\Microsoft Press\Project 2007 SBS\Chapter 17 Customizing* folder. You can also access the practice files for this book by clicking Start, All Programs, Microsoft Press, Project 2007 Step by Step and then selecting the chapter folder of the file you want to open.

1. On the **File** menu, click **Save As**.

   The Save As dialog box appears.

2. In the **File name** box, type Wingtip Toys Commercial 17, and then click **Save**.

3. Repeat steps 1 and 2 to save Parnell Aerospace Promo 17a as Parnell Aerospace Promo 17.

4. On the **Window** menu, click **Wingtip Toys Commercial 17**.

   The Wingtip Toys Commercial 17 project plan contains a custom table named Custom Entry Table, which is currently displayed in the Task Sheet view. The Custom Entry Table was previously added to this project plan for you.

Pointing to the Select All button will give you a ScreenTip that identifies the current view and table.

The table in this view has been customized by inserting and removing columns.

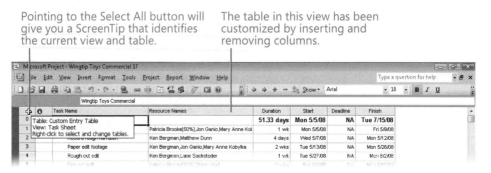

You'd like to copy this custom table to the Parnell Aerospace Promo 17 project plan.

5. On the **Tools** menu, click **Organizer**.

   The Organizer dialog box appears.

Every tab in the Organizer dialog box has a similar structure—the elements in the global template are on the left, and those in the active project plan are on the right.

6. Click several of the tabs in the dialog box to get an overview of the available options, and then click the **Tables** tab.

   As you can see, every tab of the Organizer dialog box has a similar structure: elements from the global template appear on the left side of the dialog box, and the same types of elements from the active project plan appear on the right.

   You might notice that the list of tables in the Wingtip plan is not the complete list of tables that you can display. The list you see for the Wingtip plan in the Organizer includes only the tables that have actually been displayed already in the Wingtip plan. If you were to display another table, such as the Schedule table, Project would copy that table definition from the global template into the Wingtip plan.

   Selecting an element on the left side of the dialog box and then clicking the Copy button will copy that element to the project plan listed on the right. Conversely, selecting an element on the right side of the dialog box and then clicking the Copy button will copy that element to the file listed on the left.

7. On the **Tables available in** drop-down list on the left side of the **Organizer** dialog box, select **Parnell Aerospace Promo 17**.

   This project plan appears in the list because it is open in Project.

   The side of the dialog box in which you've selected an element determines the direction in which you copy the element.

   As you can see, the Parnell plan (on the left) does not have the Custom Entry Table and the Wingtip plan (on the right) does.

8. In the list of tables on the right side of the dialog box, click **Custom Entry Table**.

> **Tip** Notice that the two arrow symbols (>>) in the Copy button switch direction (<<) when you select an element on the right side of the dialog box.

9. Click **Copy**.

   Project copies the Custom Entry Table from the Wingtip plan to the Parnell plan.

   After clicking the Copy button, the Custom Entry Table is copied from the Wingtip plan to the Parnell plan.

10. Click **Close** to close the Organizer dialog box.

    To conclude this exercise, you will display the newly copied custom table.

11. On the **Window** menu, click **Parnell Aerospace Promo 17**.

    Project switches to the Parnell plan, which is the plan to which you just copied the custom table.

12. On the **View** menu, click **More Views**.

    The More Views dialog box appears.

13. On the **Views** list, click **Task Sheet**, and then click **Apply**.

14. On the **View** menu, point to **Table: Entry**, and then click **Custom Entry Table**.

    Project displays the custom table in the Parnell plan.

15. On the **View** menu, click **Gantt Chart**.

> **Important** In this exercise, you copied a table between project plans. When copying an entire view, however, keep in mind that most views are comprised of tables, filters, and groups. When copying custom views between plans, you might also need to copy a custom table, filter, or group that is part of the custom view. For a refresher about the elements of a view, see Chapter 1, "Getting Started with Project."

Recording Macros

Many activities you perform in Project can be repetitive. To save time, you can record a *macro* that captures keystrokes and mouse actions for later playback. The macro is recorded in Microsoft Visual Basic for Applications (VBA), the built-in macro programming language of the Microsoft Office System. You can do sophisticated things with VBA, but you can record and play back simple macros without ever directly seeing or working with VBA code.

The macros you create are stored in the global template by default, so they are available to you whenever Project is running. (In fact, macros, toolbars, and import/export maps are unique in that, when you create or customize them, Project will store them in the global template rather than the active project plan by default.) The project plan for which you originally created the macro need not be open to run the macro in other project plans. If you want, you can use the Organizer to copy the macro from the global template to another project plan to give it to a friend, for example.

Creating a graphic image snapshot of a view is a great way to share project details with others. However, it's likely the details you initially capture will become obsolete quickly as the project plan is updated. Capturing updated snapshots is a repetitive task that is ideal for automation through a macro. In this exercise, you record and run a macro in the Parnell Aerospace Promo 17 project plan that creates a GIF image snapshot and saves it locally. From there, you could attach the GIF image to an e-mail message, publish it to a Web site, insert it into a document, or share it in other ways.

1. On the **Tools** menu, point to **Macro**, and then click **Record New Macro**.

   The Record Macro dialog box appears.

2. In the **Macro name** box, type Capture_GIF_Image

> **Tip** Macro names must begin with a letter and cannot contain spaces. To improve the readability of your macro names, you can use an underscore (_) in place of a space. For example, rather than naming a macro CaptureGIFImage, you can name it Capture_GIF_Image.

   For this macro, we will not use a shortcut key. When recording other macros, note that you cannot use a `Ctrl`+ combination already reserved by Project, so combinations like `Ctrl`+`Enter` (the keyboard shortcut for Find) and `Ctrl`+`G` (Go To) are unavailable. When you click OK to close the dialog box, Project alerts you whether you need to choose a different key combination.

3. In the **Store macro in** box, click **This Project** to store the macro in the active project plan.

   When a macro is stored in a project plan, the macro can be used by any project plan when the project plan that contains the macro is open. The default option, Global File, refers to the global template. When a macro is stored in the global template, the macro can be used by any project at any time because the global template is open whenever Project is running. In this exercise, since we don't want to customize your global template, you'll store the macro in the active project plan.

4. In the **Description** box, select the current text, and replace it by typing Saves a GIF image of the Gantt Chart view.

   The description is useful to help identify the actions the macro will perform.

5. Click **OK**.

Project begins recording the new macro. Project does not literally record and play back every mouse movement and passing second, but records only the results of the keystrokes and mouse actions you make. Do not feel rushed to complete the recording of the macro.

6. On the **View** menu, click **Gantt Chart**.

Even though the project plan is already showing the Gantt Chart view, including this step in the macro thereby records the action so that, if the project plan were initially in a different view, the macro would switch to the Gantt Chart view.

7. On the **View** menu, click **Zoom**.

8. In the **Zoom** dialog box, select **Entire Project**, and then click **OK**.

Project adjusts the timescale to display the entire project.

9. On the **Report** menu, click **Copy Picture**.

The Copy Picture dialog box appears.

10. Under **Render image**, click **To GIF image file**, and then click **Browse**.

11. In the **Browse** dialog box, navigate to the **Chapter 17 Customizing** folder, and then click **OK**.

12. Click **OK** to close the Copy Picture dialog box.

Project saves the GIF image.

13. On the **View** menu, click **Zoom**, click **Reset**, and then click **OK**.

Now you are ready to stop recording.

14. On the **Tools** menu, point to **Macro**, and then click **Stop Recorder**.

Next, you will run the macro to see it play back.

15. On the **Tools** menu, point to **Macro**, and then click **Macros**.

The Macros dialog box appears.

16. In the **Macro name** box, click **Parnell Aerospace Promo 17.mpp!Capture_GIF_ Image**, and then click the **Run** button.

The macro begins running, but pauses as soon as Project generates a confirmation message to replace the existing GIF image file (the one you just created while recording the macro).

> **Important** Your security level setting in Project affects Project's ability to run macros that you record or receive from others. You may not have set the security level directly, but it may have been set when you installed Project or by a system policy within your organization.

17. Click **Overwrite** to overwrite the previously created GIF image file.

The macro resaves the GIF image. Next, you'll see the results of the macro's actions.

18. In Windows Explorer, navigate to the Chapter 17 Customizing folder, and double-click the **Parnell Aerospace Promo 17 GIF** image file to open it in your image editor or viewer application.

The GIF image appears in your image application. In the following figure, we are displaying the GIF image in Internet Explorer.

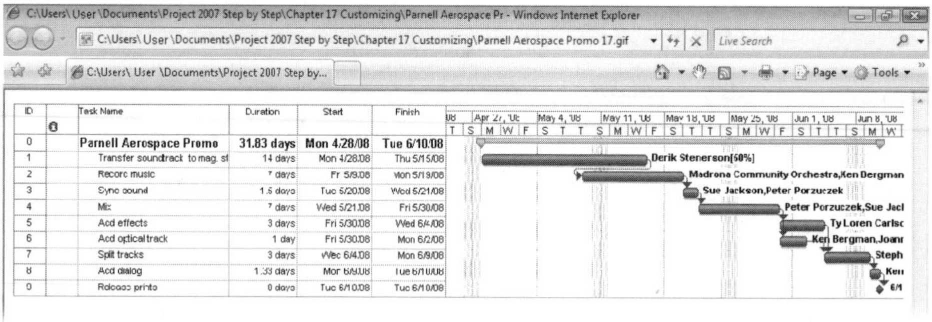

19. Close your image viewing application, and then switch back to the **Parnell Aerospace Promo 17** project plan in Project.

This macro would be very useful if the Parnell project manager needed to recapture the project plan snapshot frequently. For example, the project manager could recapture it at regular intervals during the planning stage—when the details are being developed—and then again during the execution stage—when the effects of actual progress change the remaining scheduled work.

Editing Macros

As handy as the Capture_GIF_Image macro is to use, it can be improved. Remember that when you ran it in the previous exercise, you had to confirm that Project should overwrite the existing GIF image. Because the intent of the macro is to capture the most current information, you would always want to overwrite the older information. You can change the macro code directly to accomplish this. The macro code resides in a VBA module, and you work with the code in the Visual Basic Environment.

> **Tip** The VBA language and Visual Basic Environment are standard in many of the programs in the Microsoft Office System (including Project). Although the specific details of each program differ, the general way in which you use VBA in each is the same. VBA automation is a powerful tool you can master, and that knowledge can be used in many Microsoft programs.

In this exercise, you work in the Visual Basic Editor to fine-tune and enhance the macro you recorded in the previous exercise and then run it.

1. On the **Tools** menu, point to **Macro**, and then click **Macros**.

2. Under **Macro name**, click **Parnell Aerospace Promo 17.mpp! Capture_GIF_Image**, and then click the **Edit** button.

   Project loads the module that contains the macro in the Visual Basic Editor.

   This VBA code was generated when
   Project recorded your macro.

A full explanation of the VBA language is beyond the scope of this book, but we can walk you through some steps to change the behavior of the previously recorded macro. You might also recognize some of the actions that you recorded earlier by the names used in the VBA code.

3. Click at the beginning of the line, **ViewApply Name:="&Gantt Chart"**, and press Enter .

4. Click in the new line you just created, press Tab , and type
Application.Alerts False

This line of code will suppress the prompt you received when running the macro and accept the default option of replacing the existing GIF image file with the same name.

Here is the text you typed.

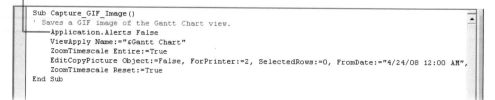

```
Sub Capture_GIF_Image()
' Saves a GIF image of the Gantt Chart view.
    Application.Alerts False
    ViewApply Name:="&Gantt Chart"
    ZoomTimescale Entire:=True
    EditCopyPicture Object:=False, ForPrinter:=2, SelectedRows:=0, FromDate:="4/24/08 12:00 AM",
    ZoomTimescale Reset:=True
End Sub
```

Tip Note that as you were typing, selection boxes and ScreenTips might have appeared. The Visual Basic Editor uses such tools and feedback to help you enter text in a module correctly.

5. In the line that begins with **EditCopyPicture**, select the date and time "**4/24/08 12:00 AM**" (including the quotation marks) that follows **FromDate:=**, and type
ActiveProject.ProjectStart

Note that the specific date you see might not be 4/24/08.

This VBA code describes the project start date of the active project.

Here is the text string you typed to return the project start date.

```
he Gantt Chart view.
alse
ntt Chart"
:=True
ct:=False, ForPrinter:=2, SelectedRows:=0, FromDate:=ActiveProject.ProjectStart, ToDate:="6/13/0
=True
```

This causes the macro to get the current start date of the active project for the GIF image that the macro creates.

6. In the same line, select the date and time "**6/15/08 12:00 AM**" (including the quotation marks) that follows **ToDate:=**, and type ActiveProject.ProjectFinish

Again, note that the specific date you see might not be 6/15/08.

Here is the text string you typed to
return the project finish date.

```
, SelectedRows:=0, FromDate:=ActiveProject.ProjectStart, ToDate:=ActiveProject.ProjectFinish, Fi
```

This causes the macro to get the current finish date of the active project for the GIF image that the macro creates. Now, if the project plan's start or finish date changes, the date range for the GIF image will change as well.

Next, you'll add new macro capabilities while in the VBA Editor.

7. Click at the beginning of the line **EditCopyPicture**, and press ⎆Enter.

8. Click in the new line you just created, press ⇥Tab, and type
   FilterApply Name:="Incomplete Tasks"

   This line of code will apply the Incomplete Tasks filter to the current view.

9. Click at the beginning of the line **ZoomTimescale Reset:=True**, and press ⎆Enter.

10. Click in the new line you just created, press ⇥Tab, and type
    FilterApply Name:="All Tasks"

    This line of code will remove the Incomplete Tasks filter to the current view.

Here are the two new lines of text you added to this macro.

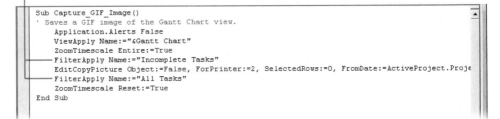

```
Sub Capture_GIF_Image()
' Saves a GIF image of the Gantt Chart view.
    Application.Alerts False
    ViewApply Name:="&Gantt Chart"
    ZoomTimescale Entire:=True
    FilterApply Name:="Incomplete Tasks"
    EditCopyPicture Object:=False, ForPrinter:=2, SelectedRows:=0, FromDate:=ActiveProject.Proje
    FilterApply Name:="All Tasks"
    ZoomTimescale Reset:=True
End Sub
```

11. On the **File** menu in the **Visual Basic Editor**, click **Close and Return to Microsoft Project**.

    The Visual Basic Editor closes, and you return to the Parnell plan.

    You could run the updated macro now, but first you'll make some changes to the project plan.

12. On the **Project** menu, click **Project Information**.

    The Project Information dialog box appears.

Note the current start and finish dates: *4/28/08* and *6/10/08*.

13. In the **Start date** box, type or select 5/5/08, and then click **OK** to close the Project Information dialog box.

Project reschedules the start (and all subsequent dates) of the project plan. Before you rerun the macro, however, you'll make one more change to the plan. You'll record some progress on tasks.

14. Click the name of task 1, **Transfer soundtrack to mag. stock**.

15. On the **Tools** menu, point to **Tracking**, and then click **Update Tasks**.

The Update Tasks dialog box appears.

16. In the **Actual dur** field, type 20d, and then click **OK**.

Next, you'll record partial progress on task 2.

17. Click the name of task 2, **Record music**.

18. On the **Tools** menu, point to **Tracking**, and then click **Update Tasks**.

The Update Tasks dialog box appears.

19. In the **Actual dur** field, type 5d, and then click **OK**.

Now you are ready to rerun the macro.

20. On the **Tools** menu, point to **Macro**, and then select **Macros**.

The Macros dialog box appears.

21. In the **Macro name** box, click **Parnell Aerospace Promo 17.mpp! Capture_GIF_ Image**, and then click **Run**.

The macro runs, and this time you are not prompted to overwrite the previously saved files. To verify that the macro ran correctly, you'll view the updated GIF image in your image application.

22. In Windows Explorer, navigate to the Chapter 17 Customizing folder, and double-click the **Parnell Aerospace Promo 17** GIF image file to open it in your image application.

The GIF image appears in your image application.

Here The macro detected the updated project start and finish dates, and filtered out the completed task 1 before saving the GIF image. is the text string you typed to return the project finish date.

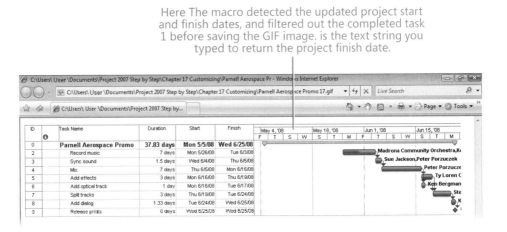

The updated screenshot includes the updated project start and finish dates, and displays only incomplete tasks (note that task 1, which is now completed, does not appear). Now you can run the macro as frequently as needed to capture the most up-to-date information.

23. Close your image viewing application, and then switch back to the **Parnell Aerospace Promo 17** project plan in Project.

Here are some additional tips for working with VBA macros in Project.

- VBA is a rich and well-documented programming language. If you would like to take a closer look at VBA in Project, on the Tools menu, click Macro, and then click Visual Basic Editor. In the Microsoft Visual Basic window, on the Help menu, click Microsoft Visual Basic Help.

- While working in a module, you can get help on specific items such as objects, properties, and methods. Click a word, and then press the F1 key.

- To close the Microsoft Visual Basic window and return to Project, on the File menu, click Close and Return to Microsoft Project.

Customizing a Toolbar

As with other Office applications, you have several choices concerning how to work with Project. Some of the many customization settings include the following:

- Setting up Project to save the active file or all open files automatically at the time interval you specify. (On the Tools menu, click Options, and on the Save tab of the Options dialog box, select Save Every and enter the time interval you want.)

- Creating customized toolbars that include buttons for any commands you want. (You will do this in the following exercise.)

In this exercise, you create a custom toolbar and assign the macro you recorded earlier to a button on the custom toolbar.

1. On the **Tools** menu, point to **Customize**, and then click **Toolbars**.

   The Customize dialog box appears.

2. Click the **Toolbars** tab.

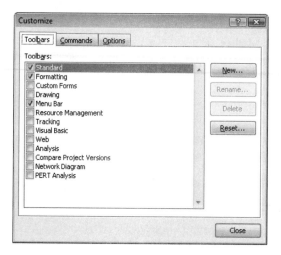

A check mark indicates the toolbars that are currently displayed; what you see on your screen might differ.

> **Tip** Toolbars are either docked or floating. When docked, a toolbar appears at one edge of the Project window. This is typically the top edge, but you can dock a toolbar at any edge of the window. When a toolbar is floating, it contains a title bar displaying the toolbar's name. To move a docked toolbar, point to the far left edge and drag the toolbar either into the Project window to make it float or to another edge of the window to redock it.

3. Click **New**.

The New Toolbar dialog box appears.

4. In the **Toolbar Name** box, type My Custom Toolbar, and then click **OK**.

The new toolbar appears in the list of toolbars and is displayed by default. (Initially, it's a floating, empty toolbar.)

Initially the new toolbar floats in the
Project window; it might not appear in
this exact spot on your screen.

Next, you'll add a command to the toolbar that runs the previously recorded macro.

5. Click the **Commands** tab.

On the Categories list, you can see several categories of commands. Many of these, such as File and Edit, correspond to menu names.

6. On the **Categories** list, click **All Macros**.

The commands in the All Macros category appear in the Commands list on the right.

Most of the commands listed for the All Macros category relate to macros included with Project; what you see on your screen might differ. However, you should see the Parnell Aerospace Promo 17.mpp!Capture_GIF_Image macro listed because it is stored in the active project plan.

7. Drag the **Parnell Aerospace Promo 17.mpp!Capture_GIF_Image** macro from the Customize dialog box onto the My Custom Toolbar.

The My Custom Toolbar widens to show the full title of the macro. If necessary, drag the toolbar so you can see all of the title.

Next, you'll change the text that appears on the button and add a graphic image.

8. In the **Customize** dialog box, click **Modify Selection**, and then click **Image and Text**.

This setting makes room on the button for an image as well as a text label.

9. Click **Modify Selection**, and then point to **Change Button Image**.

A submenu of button images appears.

10. Click the first item on the last row, which is the clapperboard figure.

    Project adds the button image to the button. Next, you will change the text label of the button.

11. Click **Modify Selection**, and then position your mouse pointer in the **Name** box and select the full name of the macro.

12. With the name of the macro selected, type Capture GIF, and then press [Enter].

    Project changes the text label on the button.

13. Click **Close** to close the Customize dialog box.

    The custom toolbar remains floating in your Project window. Next, you'll try it out.

14. On **My Custom Toolbar**, click the **Capture GIF** button.

    The Capture_GIF_Image macro runs. If you want, view the updated results in your image application, and then switch back to Project.

Custom toolbars and any other customizations made to built-in toolbars apply to all project plans you view in Project. This is because toolbar settings must reside in the global template. To conclude this exercise, you'll delete My Custom Toolbar from your global template so it doesn't affect your overall Project environment.

15. On the **Tools** menu, click **Organizer**.

The Organizer dialog box appears.

16. Click the **Toolbars** tab.

17. In the **Global.MPT** box, click **My Custom Toolbar**, and then click **Delete**.

18. Project prompts you to confirm that you want to delete the toolbar; click **Yes**.

19. Click **Close** to close the Organizer dialog box.

> **Tip** You can also delete a toolbar on the Toolbars tab of the Customize dialog box (Tools menu).

CLOSE the Parnell Aerospace Promo 17 and Wingtip Toys Commercial 17 files.

Key Points

- In Project, you share elements that you customize, such as tables or filters, between project plans and the global template via the Organizer.

- Project, like many other programs in the Microsoft Office System, uses the Visual Basic for Applications (VBA) macro programming language. Among other things, macros enable you to automate repetitive tasks.

- If you want to work directly with VBA code, you do so in the Visual Basic Editor, which is included in Project as well as other Office applications.

- You can substantially customize the toolbars in Project to include the commands and features that interest you the most.

Chapter at a Glance

Set the status date and view earned value schedule indicators to evaluate past schedule performance and forecast future performance, page 392

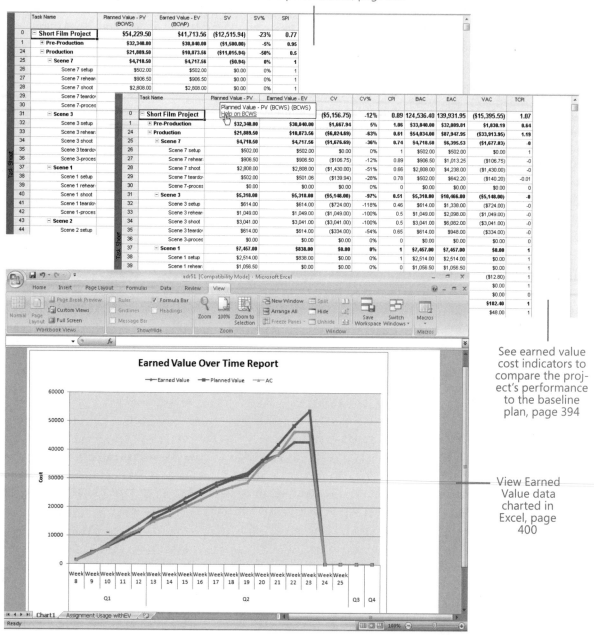

See earned value cost indicators to compare the project's performance to the baseline plan, page 394

View Earned Value data charted in Excel, page 400

18 Measuring Performance with Earned Value Analysis

In this chapter, you will learn how to:

✔ Set a status date and see earned value indicators for schedule performance.

✔ See earned value cost performance indicators.

✔ Generate the earned value visual report.

> **Tip** Do you need only a quick refresher on the topics in this chapter? See the Quick Reference entries on pages xxv-xlviii.

Looking at task and resource *variance* throughout a project's duration is an essential project management activity, but it does not give you a complete picture of the project's long-term health. For example, a task might be over budget and ahead of schedule (possibly not good) or over budget and behind schedule (definitely not good). Viewing schedule or cost variance alone does not tell you much about performance trends that might continue for the duration of the project.

To get a more complete picture of overall project performance in terms of both time and cost, you can use *earned value analysis* (also called earned value management, or EVM). The purpose of earned value analysis is to measure the project's progress and help predict its outcome. Earned value analysis involves comparing the project's progress to what you expected to achieve (as reflected in a baseline plan) at a specific point in the schedule or budget of a project plan and then forecasting future project performance.

The main differences between earned value analysis and simpler schedule and cost variance analysis can be summed up as follows:

● Simple variance analysis answers the question, "What current performance results are we obtaining?"

- Earned value analysis addresses the question, "For the current performance results we are obtaining, are we getting our money's worth?"

The difference is subtle but important. Here is an example. Assume that a project has a baseline duration of 160 days and a budget of $82,000. After approximately one-half of the baseline duration has elapsed, the actual costs incurred are about $40,000. But what is the project's status? You cannot tell based on this information alone. A simple distribution of cost over time would suggest that $40,000 spent by the midpoint of an $82,000 project is just about right. But perhaps the project is running ahead of schedule—more work has been completed by midpoint than planned. That would be good news; the project might finish ahead of schedule. On the other hand, the project might be running behind schedule—less work has been accomplished than was planned. This would be bad news; the project will likely miss its planned finish date, exceed its budget, or both.

Earned value analysis enables you to look at project performance in a more sophisticated way. It helps you to determine two important variables: the true cost of project results to date and the performance trend that is likely to continue for the remainder of the project.

Earned value analysis has its origins in large projects carried out for the U.S. Department of Defense, and it remains an essential project status reporting tool for major government projects. However, because of the usefulness of earned value analysis in predicting future project performance, it is gaining popularity in the private sector and on smaller projects as well.

> **Important** Before you can use the practice files provided for this chapter, you need to install them from the book's companion CD to their default locations. See "Using the Book's CD" on page xix for more information.

Viewing Earned Value Schedule Indicators

For Microsoft Office Project 2007 to calculate earned value amounts for a project plan, you must first do the following:

- Set a baseline plan so Project can calculate the budgeted cost of the work scheduled before you start tracking actual work. (On the Tools menu, point to Tracking, and then click Set Baseline.)
- Record actual work on tasks or assignments.

- Set the status date so Project can calculate actual project performance up to a certain point in time. (On the Project menu, click Project Information, and then select a status date.) If you do not specify a status date, Project uses the current date.

Earned value analysis uses the following three key values to generate all schedule indicator and cost indicator values:

- The budgeted cost of work scheduled, called *BCWS*. This is the value of the work scheduled to be completed as of the status date. Project calculates this value by adding up all of the timephased baseline values for tasks up to the status date. BCWS is also more generally called *planned value* (PV).

- The actual cost of work performed, called *ACWP*. This is the actual cost incurred to complete each task's actual work up to the status date.

- The budgeted cost of work performed, called *BCWP* or earned value. This is the portion of the budgeted cost that should have been spent to complete each task's actual work performed up to the status date. This value is also more generally called *earned value* (EV) because it is literally the value earned by the work performed.

The earned value analysis schedule and the cost variance are directly related, but it's simpler to examine each independently. To accommodate this, Project groups the earned value schedule and cost indicator fields into different *tables*, along with a third table that combines the key fields of both schedule and cost indicators:

- Earned Value Schedule Indicators, which focuses on schedule values through the status date, including the schedule performance index (SPI) value.

- Earned Value Cost Indicators, which focuses on cost values through the status date, including the cost performance index (CPI) value.

- Earned Value, which shows combined schedule and cost values through the status date.

In this exercise, you set the status date and view earned value schedule indicators for the project plan.

> **BE SURE TO** start Microsoft Office Project 2007 if it's not already running.

> **Important** If you are running Project Professional, you may need to make a one-time adjustment to use the Computer account and to work offline. This ensures that the practice files you work with in this chapter do not affect your Project Server data. For more information, see "Starting Project Professional" on page 11.

> **OPEN** Short Film Project 18a from the *Documents\Microsoft Press\Project 2007 SBS \Chapter 18 Earned Value* folder. You can also access the practice files for this book by click-ing Start, All Programs, Microsoft Press, Project 2007 Step by Step, and then selecting the chapter folder of the file you want to open.

1. On the **File** menu, click **Save As**.

   The Save As dialog box appears.

2. In the **File name** box, type **Short Film Project 18**, and then click **Save**.

3. On the **View** menu, point to **Table: Entry**, and click **More Tables**.

   The More Tables dialog box appears. In it, you see the three earned value tables.

4. On the **Tables** list, select **Earned Value Schedule Indicators**, and click the **Apply** button.

   Project displays the Earned Value Schedule Indicators table in the Task Sheet view. Next, you will set the project status date. Unless you specify a status date, Project uses the current date when performing earned value calculations.

5. On the **Project** menu, click **Project Information**.

   The Project Information dialog box appears.

6. In the **Status Date** box, type or select **6/20/2008**, and click **OK**.

   June 20 is the date that includes recent work completed on this project.

   Here you can see the earned value schedule indicators for the project plan, sum-mary tasks, and subtasks.

> **Tip** If any column displays pound signs (###) or the values are not fully visible, double-click the column heading's right edge to widen it.

Project-level earned value indicators.

Summary task-level earned value indica-tors.

Task-level earned value indicators.

	Task Name	Planned Value - PV (BCWS)	Earned Value - EV (BCWP)	SV	SV%	SPI
0	Short Film Project	$54,229.50	$41,713.56	($12,515.94)	-23%	0.77
1	+ Pre-Production	$32,340.00	$30,840.00	($1,500.00)	-5%	0.95
24	Production	$21,889.50	$10,873.56	($11,015.94)	-50%	0.5
25	Scene 7	$4,718.50	$4,717.56	($0.94)	0%	1
26	Scene 7 setup	$502.00	$502.00	$0.00	0%	1
27	Scene 7 rehear	$906.50	$906.50	$0.00	0%	1
28	Scene 7 shoot	$2,808.00	$2,808.00	$0.00	0%	1
29	Scene 7 teardo	$502.00	$501.06	($0.94)	0%	1
30	Scene 7-proces	$0.00	$0.00	$0.00	0%	0
31	Scene 3	$5,318.00	$5,318.00	$0.00	0%	1
32	Scene 3 setup	$614.00	$614.00	$0.00	0%	1
33	Scene 3 rehear	$1,049.00	$1,049.00	$0.00	0%	1
34	Scene 3 shoot	$3,041.00	$3,041.00	$0.00	0%	1
35	Scene 3 teardo	$614.00	$614.00	$0.00	0%	1
36	Scene 3-proces	$0.00	$0.00	$0.00	0%	0
37	Scene 1	$7,457.00	$838.00	($6,619.00)	-89%	0.11

All earned value numbers are reported either as dollars or as index ratios for easy comparison; negative cost values appear in parentheses. Note the information in the following columns:

- *Planned Value - PV or BCWS* The budgeted cost of work scheduled, as described earlier. As of the status date, a total of $54,229.50 was scheduled to be spent on tasks. In the baseline plan, the short film project would have incurred this amount by the status date. Project uses this value for comparison with the earned value and to derive other values.

- *Earned Value - EV or BCWP* The budgeted cost of work performed. The value of the work performed as of the status date in the short film project is only $41,713.56—quite a bit less than the planned value.

- *SV* The schedule variance, which is simply the difference between the earned value and planned value. The short film project has a negative schedule variance of $12,515.94.

- *SV%* The ratio of the schedule variance to the planned value, expressed as a percentage. This value tells you whether the current level of completion on tasks is ahead of or behind the performance predicted in the baseline. The short film project is 23% behind or under baseline performance.

- *SPI* The schedule performance index. This is the earned value divided by the planned value, and it is the most common way to compare earned value schedule performance between tasks, summary tasks, or projects. Because it's an index value, SPI alone tells you nothing about the specific earned or planned values on which it is based, but it does tell you how they relate to each other. You can also compare how this index value relates to the comparable index value for other tasks, summary tasks, or projects. For example, you can see that the pre-production phase of the short film project has an SPI of 0.95; the planned value was very close to the earned value. However, the second phase, Production, has a considerably lower SPI value: 0.5. The project summary task has a 0.77 SPI value. One way you can interpret this information (and this is where an index value is especially useful) is that for every dollar's worth of work you had planned to accomplish by the status date, only 77 cents' worth was actually accomplished.

Tip Here's a quick way to get help about an earned value field or any field in a table in Project. Point to the column heading, and in the ScreenTip that appears, click the Help On <Field Name> link. Information about that field appears in the Help window.

You can use these schedule indicator values to address the question, "At the rate you're making progress, is there enough time left to complete the project?" In the case of the short film project, one area to investigate is the low SPI for the production work completed thus far and whether the cause of that problem is likely to affect the remaining production work.

The values in the Earned Value Schedule Indicators table inform us about schedule performance, but they do not directly inform us about cost performance. You examine cost performance in the next section.

Viewing Earned Value Cost Indicators

The flip side of the question, "Is there enough time left to complete the project?" relates to cost: "Is there enough money available to complete the project?" Focusing on earned value cost indicators can help you answer this question. To calculate cost indicators, Project uses the actual cost of work performed, or ACWP, as derived from the actual work values recorded in a project plan.

In this exercise, you display earned value cost indicators for the project plan.

1. On the **View** menu, point to **Table: Earned Value Schedule Indicators**, and click **More Tables**.

    The More Tables dialog box appears.

2. On the **Tables** list, select **Earned Value Cost Indicators**, and click **Apply**.

    Project displays the Earned Value Cost Indicators table in the Task Sheet view.

> **Tip** If any column displays pound signs (###) or the values are not fully visible, double-click the column heading's right edge to widen it.

To get help about any field in a table, point to
the column heading, and in the ScreenTip that
appears, click the Help link.

	Task Name	Planned Value - PV	Earned Value - EV	CV	CV%	CPI	BAC	EAC	VAC	TCPI
		Planned Value - PV (BCWS) (BCWS)								
0	⊟ **Short Film Project**	Help on BCWS		($5,156.75)	-12%	0.89	124,536.40	139,931.95	($15,395.55)	1.07
1	⊞ Pre-Production	$32,340.00	$30,840.00	$1,667.94	5%	1.06	$33,840.00	$32,009.81	$1,830.19	0.64
24	⊟ Production	$21,889.50	$10,873.56	($6,824.69)	-63%	0.61	$54,034.00	$87,947.95	($33,913.95)	1.19
25	⊟ Scene 7	$4,718.50	$4,717.56	($1,676.69)	-36%	0.74	$4,718.50	$6,395.53	($1,677.03)	-0
26	Scene 7 setup	$502.00	$502.00	$0.00	0%	1	$502.00	$502.00	$0.00	1
27	Scene 7 rehear	$906.50	$906.50	($106.75)	-12%	0.89	$906.50	$1,013.25	($106.75)	-0
28	Scene 7 shoot	$2,808.00	$2,808.00	($1,430.00)	-51%	0.66	$2,808.00	$4,238.00	($1,430.00)	-0
29	Scene 7 teardov	$502.00	$501.06	($139.94)	-28%	0.78	$502.00	$642.20	($140.20)	-0.01
30	Scene 7-proces	$0.00	$0.00	$0.00	0%	0	$0.00	$0.00	$0.00	0
31	⊟ Scene 3	$5,318.00	$5,318.00	($5,148.00)	-97%	0.51	$5,318.00	$10,466.00	($5,148.00)	-0
32	Scene 3 setup	$614.00	$614.00	($724.00)	-118%	0.46	$614.00	$1,338.00	($724.00)	-0
33	Scene 3 rehear	$1,049.00	$1,049.00	($1,049.00)	-100%	0.5	$1,049.00	$2,098.00	($1,049.00)	-0
34	Scene 3 shoot	$3,041.00	$3,041.00	($3,041.00)	-100%	0.5	$3,041.00	$6,082.00	($3,041.00)	-0
35	Scene 3 teardov	$614.00	$614.00	($334.00)	-54%	0.65	$614.00	$948.00	($334.00)	-0
36	Scene 3-proces	$0.00	$0.00	$0.00	0%	0	$0.00	$0.00	$0.00	0
37	⊟ Scene 1	$7,457.00	$838.00	$0.00	0%	1	$7,457.00	$7,457.00	$0.00	1
38	Scene 1 setup	$2,514.00	$838.00	$0.00	0%	1	$2,514.00	$2,514.00	$0.00	1
39	Scene 1 rehear	$1,056.50	$0.00	$0.00	0%	0	$1,056.50	$1,056.50	$0.00	1
40	Scene 1 shoot	$3,048.50	$0.00	$0.00	0%	0	$3,048.50	$3,061.30	($12.80)	1
41	Scene 1 teardov	$838.00	$0.00	$0.00	0%	0	$838.00	$838.00	$0.00	1
42	Scene 1-proces	$0.00	$0.00	$0.00	0%	0	$0.00	$0.00	$0.00	0
43	⊟ Scene 2	$4,396.00	$0.00	$0.00	0%	0	$4,396.00	$4,213.60	$182.40	1
44	Scene 2 setup	$614.00	$0.00	$0.00	0%	0	$614.00	$595.00	$19.00	1

Here you can see the earned value cost indicators for the project plan, summary
tasks, and subtasks. Because planned value and earned value are key values for
both schedule and cost indicators, they appear in both tables and were described
in the previous section. Note that the *ACWP* field (Actual Cost of Work Performed)
does not appear on either the schedule indicators or cost indicators tables; it does
appear on the Earned Value table, however. Note the project summary task (task 0)
values in the following columns:

- *CV* The cost variance, or the difference between earned value and ACWP. The
  short film project has relatively low cost variance.

- *CV%* The ratio of cost variance to planned value, expressed as a percentage.
  This value tells you how close you are (under or over) to the budget plan per
  task. The short film project is below baseline cost performance.

- *CPI* The cost performance index. The short film project's CPI (as of the status
  date) is 0.89. One way you can interpret this is that for every dollar's worth of
  work you have paid for, 89 cents worth of work was actually accomplished.

- *BAC* The budget at completion. This is simply the total baseline cost of a task,
  summary task, or project. You evaluate this figure against the EAC to derive
  the VAC.

- *EAC* The estimate at completion. This value represents the forecasted cost to
  complete a task, summary task, or project based on performance so far (up to
  the status date).

- *VAC* The variance at completion, or the difference between the BAC and the
  EAC. The VAC represents the forecasted cost variance to complete a task,

summary task, or project based on performance so far (up to the status date). The short film project has some variance at completion value.

- *TCPI* The to complete performance index. This index value demonstrates the ratio of remaining work to remaining budget as of the status date. The short film project's TCPI value is 1.07, meaning remaining work and remaining budget are almost equal. Depending on your screen resolution, you might need to scroll right to see this column.

> **Important** Although it might seem odd and even confusing to consider being ahead of or behind schedule in terms of dollars, remember that dollars buy work and work drives the completion of tasks.

From a pure cost variance analysis standpoint, the short film project appears to be in relatively good shape. Yet the schedule variance analysis suggests otherwise. The heart of the issue is that, as of the status date, quite a bit of work has started later than planned but has not cost more than planned. The true health of the project is often not obvious and requires a comparison of both cost and schedule variance based on past performance, as well as forecasts of future performance.

Now let's all take a deep breath. Earned value analysis is one of the more complicated procedures you can do in Project, but the information it provides on project status is invaluable. Earned value analysis is also a great example of the benefits of entering task and resource cost information in a project plan.

> **Tip** To quickly see the selected task's earned value numbers in any task view, click the Task Earned Value button on the Custom Forms toolbar. To display this toolbar, on the View menu, point to Toolbars, and then click Custom Forms.

Changing How Project Calculates Earned Value Numbers

All of the earned value calculations shown in the previous exercises use the default calculation options in Project. However, you can change settings to give yourself more flexibility in how earned value is calculated. Some important settings you can change include the following:

- Rather than using the percent complete of tasks that is based on actuals recorded in a project plan, you can tell Project to use a percent complete value that you enter—regardless of a task's calculated percent complete. The manual or override value is called physical percent complete.

- Rather than using the initial baseline values stored in the default Baseline fields for earned value comparisons, you can tell Project to use any baseline set you want—Baseline or Baseline 1 through Baseline 10.

You can set these options for an entire project plan or change only the calculation method for a specific task:

- To change these options for an entire project plan, on the Tools menu, click Options, and then in the Options dialog box, click the Calculation tab. Next, click the Earned Value button. In the Earned Value dialog box, choose the calculation method and baseline options you want.

- To change the earned value calculation method for a selected task, on the Project menu, click Task Information, and then in the Task Information dialog box, click the Advanced tab. In the Earned Value Method box, click the method you want.

If you choose to use the physical percent complete method for either an entire project plan or a specific task, you must enter a percent complete value manually. This field is displayed in the Tracking table, and you can insert it into any other task table.

Generating an Earned Value Visual Report

Visual reports are a major new feature of Project 2007. If you completed the section "Generating Visual Reports with Excel and Visio" in Chapter 12, you've worked with some visual reports. One of the Excel visual reports available in Project, the Earned Value Over Time Report, generates the classic "S-curve" line chart that graphs cumulative values over time for the three key indicators associated with earned value analysis. They are:

- Actual Cost of Work Performed (ACWP), labeled in the visual report's legend as *AC*.
- Budgeted Cost of Work Scheduled (BCWS), labeled as *Planned Value*.
- Budgeted Cost of Work Performed (BCWP), labeled as *Earned Value*.

In previous versions of Project, to generate a similar chart in Excel, you used an add-in named Analyze Timescaled Data in Excel. In Project 2007, this functionality is provided by the visual report. As with all Excel visual reports in Project, you end up with the chart as well as the Excel PivotTable on which the chart is based that you can modify as you wish.

> **Important** If the computer on which you are now working does not have Excel 2003 or later installed, you cannot complete this exercise. If this is the case, skip ahead to the "Key Points" section.

In this exercise, you generate an Earned Value Over Time Report.

1. On the **Report** menu, click **Visual Reports**.

   The Visual Reports dialog box appears:

   This dialog box groups visual reports in a number of ways: all reports, only Excel or Visio reports, and task, resource, or assignment details (divided into summary and usage reports). The dialog box includes a simplified preview of the type of graphic (chart or diagram) associated with each visual report. You can click the various tabs in the dialog box to see how the visual reports are organized if you wish.

2. Click the **Assignment Usage** tab.

3. Click **Earned Value Over Time Report.**

4. In the **Select level of usage data to include in the report** box, make sure that **Weeks** is selected.

   This setting determines the time increment that will be included in the Excel PivotTable and charted in the line graph.

5. Click **View**.

Project generates the data required by this report, launches Excel, and creates the report. Next, you'll adjust the PivotTable outline to change the level of detail shown in the line chart.

6. In Excel, click the tab name of the **Assignment Usage withEV** sheet.

This is the PivotTable on which the earned value chart is based.

On the PivotTable Field List, you can see all of the fields for which timephased data was exported from Project. You can add any of these fields to the PivotTable by clicking them.

To show more detail in the earned value chart, you'll expand the PivotTable outline.

7. Click the **plus signs** next to the **Q1** and **Q2** values.

The PivotTable expands to show the weekly values you exported from Project.

8. Click the tab name of the **Chart1** sheet.

9. In Excel, adjust the zoom setting such that the entire chart is visible.

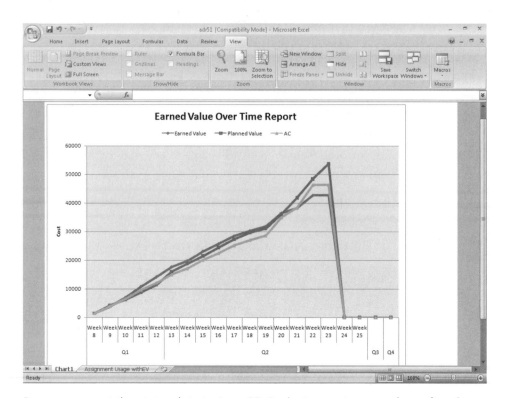

Because you set the status date to June 20, Project reports zero values after that date, causing the lines in the chart to return to zero after week 23 of the project's overall duration.

Now the earned value chart shows the level of detail we want. The key to reading this type of chart is to locate earned value and actual cost as they relate to planned cost. Recall that the planned costs represent the cumulative amount of money you planned to spend at any given time. Where the earned value line falls below the planned value line around week 20, you see the project effectively fell behind schedule. The actual cost (AC) line, when it is below the planned value line, tells you the project was running below budget. Around week 21, however, actual cost shot well above budget. As the earned value indicators you saw in Project suggested, the project has been underperforming in terms of both schedule and cost indicators. The earned value chart helps you visualize the specific trends that are driving project performance and hopefully allows you time to address these issues through the remainder of the project.

10. Close Excel without saving the workbook.

11. In Project, click **Close** to close the Visual Reports dialog box.

CLOSE the Parnell Film 18 file.

Key Points

- Earned value analysis is a complex and robust means of evaluating project performance and predicting its outcome.

- When performing earned value analysis, remember that it is essential to set the project status date.

- Project organizes key earned value indicators into schedule indicators and cost indicators tables, as well as an overall earned value table.

- The earned value visual report allows you to graph key earned value indicators in Excel.

Chapter at a Glance

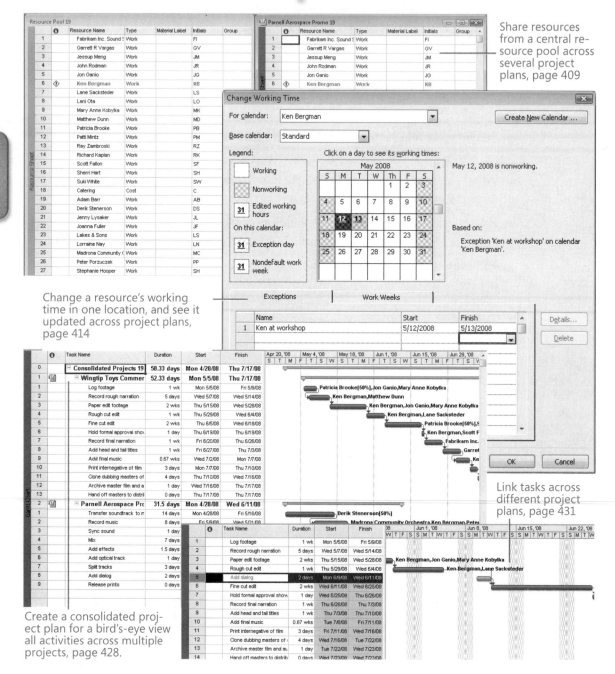

Share resources from a central resource pool across several project plans, page 409

Change a resource's working time in one location, and see it updated across project plans, page 414

Link tasks across different project plans, page 431

Create a consolidated project plan for a bird's-eye view all activities across multiple projects, page 428.

19 Consolidating Projects and Resources

In this chapter, you will learn how to:

✔ Create a resource pool to share resources across multiple projects.

✔ Look at resource allocation across multiple projects.

✔ Change resource assignments in a sharer plan, and see the effects in the resource pool.

✔ Change a resource's working time in the resource pool, and see the effects in the sharer plan.

✔ Make a specific date nonworking time in the resource pool, and see the effects in the sharer plan.

✔ Create a project plan, and make it a sharer plan for the resource pool.

✔ Manually update the resource pool from a sharer plan.

✔ Insert project plans to create a consolidated project.

✔ Link tasks between two project plans.

Tip Do you need only a quick refresher on the topics in this chapter? See the Quick Reference entries on pages xxv-xlviii.

Important This chapter describes various ways of sharing resources and managing multiple projects. This process is more generally called portfolio management or enterprise project management. Project Professional, when used with Project Server, offers much more sophisticated ways of managing a portfolio of projects and resources across an enterprise. To learn more about the portfolio management tools available with Project Server, see Part 4, "Introducing Project Server."

Most project managers must juggle more than one project at a time. These projects often share resources and are worked on simultaneously. Microsoft Office Project 2007 has several features to make it easier to work with multiple projects. In this chapter, you share resource information between multiple project plans and pull together separate project plans as a single consolidated plan.

> **Important** Before you can use the practice files provided for this chapter, you need to install them from the book's companion CD to their default locations. See "Using the Book's CD" on page xix for more information.

Creating a Resource Pool

When managing multiple projects, it is common for *work resources* (people and equipment) to be assigned to more than one project at a time. It might become difficult to coordinate the work resources' time among the multiple projects, especially if those projects are managed by different people. For example, a sound engineer in a film studio might have task assignments for a TV commercial, a promotional program, and a documentary film—three projects proceeding simultaneously. In each project, the engineer might be *fully allocated* or even *underallocated*. However, if you add together all of her tasks from these projects, you might discover that she has been overallocated, or assigned to work on more tasks than she can handle at one time. When working with cost resources in multiple projects, you might want to see not only the cost per project associated with a cost resource, but the cumulative costs across projects as well. Likewise, when working with material resources in multiple projects, you'd see cumulative consumed material resources in whatever unit of consumption you've used.

A *resource pool* can help you see how resources are utilized across multiple projects. The resource pool is a project plan from which other project plans draw their resource information. It contains information about all resources' task assignments from all project plans linked to the resource pool. You can change resource information—such as maximum units, cost rates, and nonworking time—in the resource pool, and all linked project plans will use the updated information.

The project plans that are linked to the resource pool are called *sharer plans*. The following is one way of visualizing a resource pool and sharer plans.

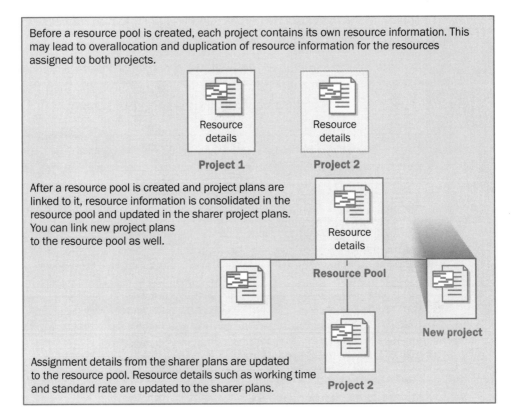

Before a resource pool is created, each project contains its own resource information. This may lead to overallocation and duplication of resource information for the resources assigned to both projects.

Resource details

Resource details

Project 1

Project 2

After a resource pool is created and project plans are linked to it, resource information is consolidated in the resource pool and updated in the sharer project plans. You can link new project plans to the resource pool as well.

Resource details

Resource Pool

New project

Assignment details from the sharer plans are updated to the resource pool. Resource details such as working time and standard rate are updated to the sharer plans.

Project 2

If you manage just one project with resources that are not used in other projects, a resource pool provides you no benefit. However, if your organization plans to manage multiple projects, setting up a resource pool enables you to do the following:

- Enter resource information once, but use it in multiple project plans.
- View resources' assignment details from multiple projects in a single location.
- View assignment costs per resource across multiple projects.
- View cost resources cumulative costs across multiple projects.
- View material resources cumulative consumption values across multiple projects.
- Find resources who are overallocated across multiple projects, even if those resources are underallocated in individual projects.
- Enter resource information, such as nonworking time, in any of the sharer plans or in the resource pool so that it is available in other sharer plans.

A resource pool is especially beneficial when working with other Project users across a network. In those cases, the resource pool is stored in a central location, such as a network server, and the individual owners of the sharer plans (which might be stored locally or on a network server) share the common resource pool.

In this exercise, you arrange the windows of two project plans that will become sharer plans; this helps you see the effects of creating a resource pool. You then create a project plan that will become a resource pool and link the two sharer plans to it.

> **BE SURE TO** start Microsoft Office Project 2007 if it's not already running.

> **Important** If you are running Project Professional, you may need to make a one-time adjustment to use the Computer account and to work offline. This ensures that the practice files you work with in this chapter do not affect your Project Server data. For more information, see "Starting Project Professional" on page 11.

> **OPEN** Wingtip Toys Commercial 19a from the *Documents\Microsoft Press\Project 2007 SBS\Chapter 19 Consolidating* folder. You can also access the practice files for this book by clicking Start, All Programs, Microsoft Press, Project 2007 Step by Step and then selecting the chapter folder of the file you want to open.

1. On the **File** menu, click **Save As**.

   The Save As dialog box appears.

2. In the **File name** box, type Wingtip Toys Commercial 19, and then click **Save**.

Open

3. On the **Standard** toolbar, click the **Open** button.

   The Open dialog box appears.

4. Double-click the **Parnell Aerospace Promo 19b** file.

5. On the **File** menu, click **Save As**.

   The Save As dialog box appears.

6. In the **File name** box, type Parnell Aerospace Promo 19, and then click **Save**.

   These two project plans were previously created, and both contain resource information. Next, you will create a new project plan that will become a resource pool.

New

7. On the **Standard** toolbar, click the **New** button.

   Project creates a new project plan, with the Gantt Chart view displayed.

8. On the **View** menu, click **Resource Sheet**.

   The Resource Sheet view replaces the Gantt Chart view.

9. On the **File** menu, click **Save As**.

10. Navigate to the *Documents\Microsoft Press\Project 2007 SBS\ Chapter 19 Consolidating* folder.

11. In the **File name** box, type Resource Pool 19, and then click **Save**.

> **Tip** You can name a resource pool with any name you want, but it is a good idea to indicate that it is a resource pool in the file name.

12. On the **Window** menu, click **Arrange All**.

Project arranges the three project plan windows within the Project window.

Title bar

Prior to being linked to a resource pool, some resource names and other details are duplicated in these project plans.

> **Tip** You do not need to arrange the project windows in this way to create a resource pool, but it is helpful to see the results as they occur in this chapter.

Looking at the resource names in the two project plans (Parnell Aerospace Promo 19 and Wingtip Toys Commercial 19), you can see that several of the same resources appear in both project plans. These include Fabrikam Inc. Sound Studio, Jon Ganio, Ken Bergman, Catering (a cost resource), and others. None of these resources are overallocated in either project.

13. Click the title bar of the Wingtip Toys Commercial 19 window.

14. On the **Tools** menu, point to **Resource Sharing**, and click **Share Resources**.

The Share Resources dialog box appears.

15. Under **Resources for 'Wingtip Toys Commercial 19'**, select the **Use resources** option.

The Use Resources From list contains the open project plans that can be used as a resource pool.

16. On the **From** list, make sure that **Resource Pool 19** is selected in the drop-down list.

```
Share Resources                                    ⊠

Resources for 'Wingtip Toys Commercial 19'
   ○ Use own resources
   ◉ Use resources
      From:  | Resource Pool 19            | ▼ |

On conflict with calendar or resource information
   ◉ Pool takes precedence
   ○ Sharer takes precedence

   [ Help ]           [    OK    ]    [ Cancel ]
```

17. Click **OK** to close the Share Resources dialog box.

You see the resource information from the Wingtip Toys Commercial 19 project plan appear in the Resource Pool 19 plan. Next, you will set up the Parnell Aerospace Promo 19 project plan as a sharer plan with the same resource pool.

18. Click the title bar of the Parnell Aerospace Promo 19 window.

19. On the **Tools** menu, point to **Resource Sharing**, and then click **Share Resources**.

20. Under **Resources for 'Parnell Aerospace Promo 19'**, click the **Use resources** option.

21. On the **From** list, make sure that **Resource Pool 19** is selected.

Resource Pool 19 is selected by default. The Wingtip Toys Commercial 19 project plan is already a sharer plan, and Project won't allow a sharer plan to be a resource pool for another project plan.

22. Under **On conflict with calendar or resource information**, make sure that the **Pool takes precedence** option is selected.

Selecting this option causes Project to use resource information (such as cost rates) in the resource pool rather than in the sharer plan should it find any differences between the two project plans.

23. Click **OK** to close the Share Resources dialog box.

You see the resource information from the Wingtip Toys Commercial 19 project plan appear in the resource pool.

After these two sharer plans have been linked to the resource pool, the combined resource information appears in all their files.

The resource pool contains the resource information from both sharer plans. Project will consolidate resource information from the sharer plans based on the name of the resource. Jon Ganio, for example, is listed only once in the resource pool, no matter how many sharer plans list him as a resource.

> **Important** Project cannot match variations of a resource's name—for example, Jon Ganio from one sharer plan and J. Ganio from another. For this reason, it is a good idea to develop a convention for naming resources in your organization, and then stick with it.

Again, you do not have to arrange the project windows as you did in this exercise to link the sharer plans to the resource pool. However, it is helpful in this chapter to see the results as they occur.

Tip If you decide that you do not want to use a resource pool with a project plan, you can break the link. On the Tools menu, point to Resource Sharing, and click Share Resources. Under Resources For <Current Project Name>, select the Use Own Resources option.

Creating a Dedicated Resource Pool

Any project plan, with or without tasks, can serve as a resource pool. However, it is a good idea to designate a project plan that does not contain tasks as the resource pool. This is done because any project with tasks will almost certainly conclude at some point, and you might not want assignments for those tasks (with their associated costs and other details) to be included indefinitely in the resource pool.

Moreover, a dedicated resource pool without tasks can enable people, such as *line managers* or resource managers, to maintain some information about their resources, such as nonworking time, in the resource pool. These people might not have a role in project management, and they will not need to deal with task-specific details in the resource pool.

Viewing Assignment Details in a Resource Pool

One of the most important benefits of using a resource pool is that it allows you to see how resources are allocated across projects. For example, you can identify resources that are overallocated across the multiple projects to which they are assigned.

Let's look at a specific example. As you might have noticed in the previous section, the resource Ken Bergman, who was not overallocated in either of the individual project plans, did appear overallocated after Project accounted for all of his assignments across the two project plans. When Ken's assignments from the two sharer plans were combined, they exceeded his capacity to work on at least one day. Although Ken most likely was aware of this problem, the project manager may not have known about it without setting up a resource pool (or hearing about the problem directly from Ken).

In this exercise, you look at the information in the resource pool.

1. Double-click the title bar of the Resource Pool 19 window.

   The resource pool window is maximized to fill the Project window. In the resource pool, you can see all of the resources from the two sharer plans. To get a better view of resource usage, you will change views.

2. On the **View** menu, click **Resource Usage**.

The Resource Usage view appears.

3. In the **Resource Name** column, click the name of resource 6, **Ken Bergman**, and then scroll the Resource Usage view to display all of Ken's assignments below his name.

Scroll to Task

4. On the **Standard** toolbar, click the **Scroll To Task** button.

The timescale details on the right side of the Project window scroll horizontally to show Ken Bergman's earliest task assignments. The red numbers (for example, 16 hours on Friday through Monday, May 9 through 19) indicate days on which Ken is overallocated. Next, you will display the Resource Form to get more detail about Ken's assignments.

5. On the **Window** menu, click **Split**.

In this combination view, you can see both the resource's assigned tasks and details about each assignment.

The Resources Form shows assignments across multiple projects when using a resource pool.

In this combination view, you can see all resources in the resource pool and their assignments (in the upper pane), as well as the selected resource's details (in the lower pane) from all sharer plans. You can see, for example, that the *Record rough narration* task to which Ken is assigned is from the Wingtip Toys Commercial 19 project, and the *Record music* task is from the Parnell Aerospace Promo 19 project. Ken was not overallocated in either project, but he is overallocated when you see his assignments across projects in this way.

If you want, click different resource names in the Resource Usage view to see their assignment details in the Resource Form.

6. On the **Window** menu, click **Remove Split**.

> **Tip** In a resource pool, the Resource Form is just one way to see the details of specific assignments from sharer plans. Other ways include inserting the Project or Task Summary Name columns into the table portion of the Resource Usage view. (On the Insert menu, click Column.)

Updating Assignments in a Sharer Plan

You might recall that an assignment is the matching of a resource to a task. Because a resource's assignment details originate in sharer plans, Project updates the resource pool with assignment details as you make them in the sharer plan.

In this exercise, you change resource assignments in a sharer plan, and you see the changes posted to the resource pool.

1. On the **Edit** menu, click **Go To.**

2. In the **ID** field, enter 21, and then click **OK.**

   Project displays the information for Jenny Lysaker. You can see that Jenny has no task assignments in either sharer plan. (The value of her *Work* field is zero.) Next, you will assign Jenny to a task in one of the sharer plans, and you will see the result in the resource pool as well as in the project.

3. On the **Window** menu, click **Parnell Aerospace Promo 19**.

4. On the **View** menu, click **Gantt Chart**.

Assign Resources

5. On the **Standard** toolbar, click the **Assign Resources** button.

6. In the **Task Name** column, click the name of task 5, **Add effects**.

7. In the **Resource Name** column in the **Assign Resources** dialog box, click **Jenny Lysaker**, and click the **Assign** button.

8. Click **Close** to close the Assign Resources dialog box.

9. On the **Window** menu, click **Resource Pool 19** to switch back to the resource pool.

Scroll to Task

10. Make sure that resource 21, Jenny Lysaker, is selected, and then on the **Standard** toolbar, click **Scroll to Task**.

	ⓘ	Resource Name	Work	Details	Jun 1, '08													Jun 8, '08	
					T	W	T	F	S	S	M	T	W	T	F	S	S	S	
21		− Jenny Lysaker	12 hrs	Work				4h			8h								
		Add effects	12 hrs	Work				4h			8h								
22		− Joanna Fuller	8 hrs	Work				4h			4h								
		Add optical trac	8 hrs	Work				4h			4h								

As expected, Jenny Lysaker's new task assignment appears in the resource pool.

When the resource pool is open in Project, any changes you make to resource assignments or other resource information in any sharer plans immediately show up in all other open sharer plans and the resource pool. You don't need to switch between sharer plans and the resource pool, as you did in this chapter, to verify the updated resource assignments.

Updating a Resource's Information in a Resource Pool

Another important benefit of using a resource pool is that it gives you a central location in which to enter resource details, such as cost rates and working time. When a resource's information is updated in the resource pool, the new information is available in all of the sharer plans. This can be especially useful in organizations with a large number of resources working on multiple projects. In larger organizations, people such as line managers, resource managers, or staff in a *program office* are often responsible for keeping general resource information up to date.

Ken Bergman has told you that he will be unavailable to work on May 12 and 13. In this exercise, you update a resource's working time in the resource pool, and you see changes in the sharer plans.

1. On the **Edit** menu, click **Go To**.

2. In the **ID** field, enter 6, and in the **Date** field, type or select 5/12/2008 and then click **OK**.

   Project displays Ken's assignments during the week of May 11 and later.

	ⓘ	Resource Name	Work	Details	May 11, '08										May 18, '08			
					F	S	S	M	T	W	T	F	S	S	M	T	W	
6	◇	− Ken Bergman	261.33 hrs	Work	16h			16h	16h	16h	16h	16h			16h	8h	8h	
		Record rough m	32 hrs	Work	8h			8h										
		Paper edit footა	80 hrs	Work					8h	8h	8h	8h			8h	8h	8h	
		Rough cut edit	40 hrs	Work														
		Hold formal app	8 hrs	Work														
		Add final music	26.67 hrs	Work														
		Record music	56 hrs	Work	8h			8h	8h	8h	8h	8h			8h			
		Add optical trac	8 hrs	Work														
		Add dialog	10.67 hrs	Work														
7		− Lane Sacksteder	90.67 hrs	Work														
		Rough cut edit	40 hrs	Work														
		Add final music	25.57 hrs	Work														

3. On the **Tools** menu, click **Change Working Time**.

The Change Working Time dialog box appears.

4. In the **For calendar** box, make sure that **Ken Bergman** is selected.

Ken Bergman's resource calendar appears in the Change Working Time dialog box. Ken has told you that he will not be available to work on Monday and Tuesday, May 12 and 13, because he plans to attend a workshop.

5. On the **Exceptions** tab in the Change Working Time dialog box, click in the first row under **Name** and type Ken at workshop.

The description for the calendar exception is a handy reminder for you and others who may view the project plan later.

6. Click in the **Start** field and type or select 5/12/2008.

7. Click in the **Finish** field and type or select 5/13/ 2008, and then press Enter .

8. Click **OK** to close the Change Working Time dialog box.

> **Tip** When making such changes in the resource pool, you should have it open as read-write (as you do now). Whenever you open a resource pool, Project asks whether you want to open it as read-only (the default) or read-write.

Now Ken has no work scheduled (as he did previously).

Because May 12 and 13 have been set as nonworking days for this resource, no work is scheduled on these days.

To verify that Ken's nonworking time setting was updated in the sharer plans, you will look at his working time in one of those project plans.

9. On the **Window** menu, click **Parnell Aerospace Promo 19**.

10. On the **Tools** menu, click **Change Working Time**.

The Change Working Time dialog box appears.

11. In the **For calendar** box, click **Ken Bergman**. His name appears toward the top of the list.

On the Exceptions tab, you can see that May 12 and 13 are flagged as nonworking days for Ken; the change to this resource's working time in the resource pool has been updated in the sharer plans.

> **Tip** To quickly scroll the calendar to May 2008 in the Change Working Time dialog box, just select either the Start or Finish date for Ken's exception.

12. Click **Cancel** to close the Change Working Time dialog box.

Updating All Plans' Working Times in a Resource Pool

In the previous exercise, you changed an individual resource's working time in the re-source pool, and you saw the change posted to the sharer plans. Another powerful ca-pability of a resource pool enables you to change working times for a base calendar and see the changes updated to all sharer plans that use that calendar. For example, if you specify that certain days (such as holidays) are to be nonworking days in the resource pool, that change is posted to all sharer plans.

> **Important** By default, all sharer plans share the same base calendars, and any changes you make to a base calendar in one sharer plan are reflected in all other sharer plans through the resource pool. If you have a specific sharer plan for which you want to use dif-ferent base calendar working times, change the base calendar that sharer plan uses.

In this exercise, you set nonworking time in a base calendar in the resource pool, and you see this change in all sharer plans.

1. On the **Window** menu, click **Resource Pool 19**.

   The entire company will be attending a local film festival on May 12, and you want this to be a nonworking day for all sharer plans.

2. On the **Tools** menu, click **Change Working Time**.

   The Change Working Time dialog box appears.

3. In the **For calendar** box, select **Standard (Project Calendar)** on the drop-down list.

   Changes in working time to the Standard base calendar in the resource pool affect all project plans that are sharer plans of the resource pool.

4. On the **Exceptions** tab in the **Change Working Time** dialog box, click in the first row under **Name** and type Local Film Festival.

5. Click in the **Start** field and type or select 5/12/2008, and then click the **Finish** field.

   Project fills in the same value in the *Finish Date* field.

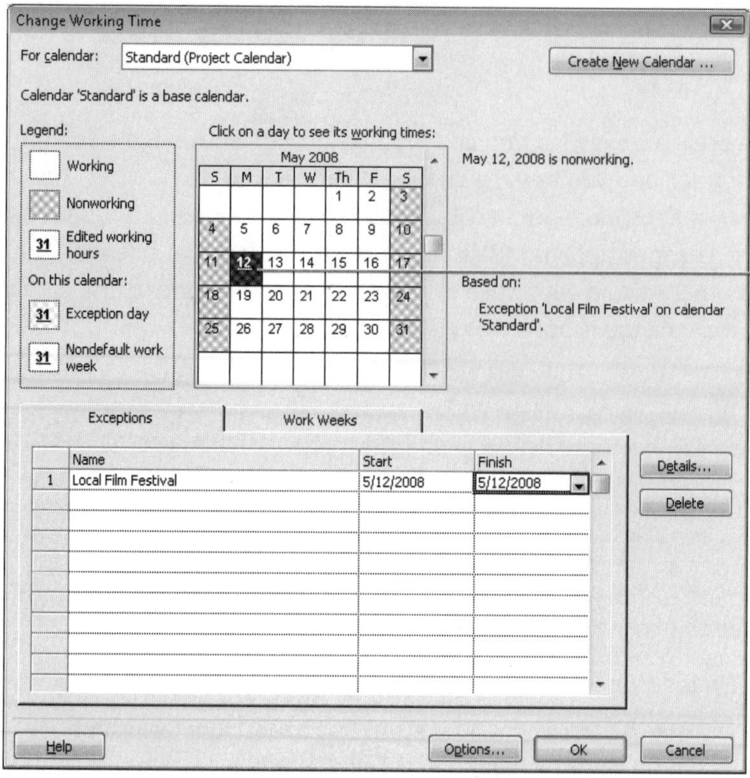

Change Working Time dialog box, with the callout:

May 12 is set as a nonworking day in the resource pool.

6. Click **OK** to close the Change Working Time dialog box.

To verify that this change to the Standard base calendar in the resource pool was updated in the sharer plans, you will look at working time in one of the sharer plans.

7. On the **Window** menu, click **Wingtip Toys Commercial 19**.

8. On the **Tools** menu, click **Change Working Time**.

The Change Working Time dialog box appears.

9. In the **For calendar** box, **click Standard (Project Calendar)** on the drop-down list.

> **Tip** Base calendars, such as 24 Hours, Night Shift, and Standard, appear at the top of the list in the For Calendar box. Resource names appear below the base calendars.

Note the *Local Film Festival* exception on May 12. All project plans that are sharer plans of the same resource pool will see this change in this base calendar.

In the sharer plans linked to the resource pool, May 12 is set as a nonworking day in the Standard base calendar.

10. Click **Cancel** to close the Change Working Time dialog box.

If you want, you can switch to the Parnell Aerospace Promo 19 project plan and verify that May 12 is also a nonworking day for that project.

11. Close and save changes to all open project plans, including the resource pool.

> **Important** When working with sharer plans and a resource pool, it is important to understand that when you open a sharer plan, you must also open the resource pool if you want the sharer plan to be updated with the most recent changes to the resource pool. For example, assume that you change the project calendar's working time in the resource pool, save it, and close it, If you later open a sharer plan but do not also open the resource pool, that sharer plan will not reflect the updated project calendar's working time.

Linking New Project Plans to a Resource Pool

You can make a project plan a sharer plan for a resource pool at any time: when initially entering the project plan's tasks, after you have assigned resources to tasks, or even after work has begun. After you have set up a resource pool, you might find it helpful to make sharer plans of all new projects along with the sharer plans of projects already created. In that way, you get used to relying on the resource pool for resource information.

> **Tip** A definite timesaving advantage of creating new project plans as sharer plans of a resource pool is that your resource information is instantly available. You do not have to reenter any resource data.

In this exercise, you create a project plan and make it a sharer plan for the resource pool.

Open

1. On the **Standard** toolbar, click **Open**.

   The Open dialog box appears.

2. Navigate to the Chapter 19 Consolidating folder, and double-click **Resource Pool 19**.

   Project prompts you to select how you want to open the resource pool.

   Open Resource Pool

   This file is the resource pool for many projects. What do you want to do?

   You can:

   ○ Open resource pool read-only allowing others to work on projects connected to the pool.

   ○ Open resource pool read-write so that you can make changes to resource information (like pay rates, etc.), although this will lock others out of updating the pool with new information.

   ○ Open resource pool read-write and all other sharer files into a new master project file. You can access this new master project file from the Window menu command.

   [OK]   [Cancel]   [Help]

> **Important** The default option is to open the resource pool as read-only. You might want to choose this option if you and other Project users are sharing a resource pool across a network. If you store the resource pool locally, however, you should open it as read-write. To read more about how to open a resource pool, click the Help button in the Open Resource Pool dialog box.

3. Click the second option to open the project plan as read-write, and then click **OK**.

4. On the **View** menu, click **Resource Sheet**.

   The Resource Sheet view appears.

New

5. On the **Standard** toolbar, click **New**.

6. On the **File** menu, click **Save As**.

   The Save As dialog box appears.

7. Navigate to the *Documents\Microsoft Press\Project 2007 SBS\Chapter 19 Consolidating* folder.

8. In the **File name** box, type Hanson Brothers Project 19, and then click **Save**.

Assign Resources

9. On the **Standard** toolbar, click **Assign Resources**.

   The Assign Resources dialog box is initially empty because you have not yet entered any resource information in this project plan.

10. On the **Tools** menu, point to **Resource Sharing**, and then click **Share Resources**.

    The Share Resources dialog box appears.

11. Under **Resources for 'Hanson Brothers Project 19'**, select the **Use resources** option.

12. On the **From** list, make sure that **Resource Pool 19** is selected on the drop-down list, and then click **OK** to close the Share Resources dialog box.

    In the Assign Resources dialog box, you see all of the resources from the resource pool appear.

Assign Resources			
No task selected			
[+] Resource list options			
Resources from Hanson Brothers Project 19			

Resource Name	Units	Cost	
Adam Barr			Assign
Catering			Remove
Derik Stenerson			Replace...
Fabrikam Inc. Sound Studio			
Garrett R Vargas			Graphs...
Jenny Lysaker			Close
Jessup Meng			
Joanna Fuller			Help
John Rodman			
Jon Ganio			

Hold down Ctrl and click to select multiple resources

Now these resources are ready for assignments to tasks in this project.

13. Click **Close** to close the Assign Resources dialog box.

14. On the **File** menu, click **Close**. When prompted, click the **Yes** button to save your changes.

   The Hanson Brothers Project 19 project plan closes, and the Resource Pool 19 plan remains open.

15. On the **File** menu, click **Close**. When prompted, click **Yes** to save your changes to Resource Pool 19.

> **Important** You save changes to the resource pool because it records the names and locations of its sharer plans.

> **Troubleshooting** If a sharer plan is deleted, assignment information from that sharer plan is still stored in the resource pool. To clear this assignment information from the resource pool, you must break the link to the sharer plan. Open the resource pool as read-write. On the Tools menu, click Resource Sharing, and then click Share Resources. In the Share Resources dialog box, click the name of the now-deleted sharer plan, and click the Break Link button.

Opening a Sharer Plan and Updating a Resource Pool

If you are sharing a resource pool with other Project users across a network, whoever has the resource pool open as read-write prevents others from updating resource information, such as standard cost rates, or making other project plans sharers of that resource pool. For this reason, it is a good idea to open the resource pool as read-only and use the Update Resource Pool command only when you need to update the resource pool with assignment information. You can click the Update Resource Pool command from the Resource Sharing submenu of the Tools menu. This command updates the resource pool with new assignment information; once that is done, anyone else who opens the resource pool will see the latest assignment information.

In this chapter, you are working with the resource pool and sharer plans locally. If you are going to use a resource pool over a network, it is a good idea to understand the updating process. This exercise introduces you to that process.

In this exercise, you change assignments in a sharer plan and then manually send updated assignment information to the resource pool.

Open

1. On the **Standard** toolbar, click **Open**.

2. Navigate to the Chapter 19 Consolidating folder, and double-click the **Parnell Aerospace Promo 19** file.

Because this project plan is a sharer plan linked to a resource pool, Project gives you the following options.

> **Open Resource Pool Information**
>
> This file shares resources from a resource pool. What do you want to do?
>
> You can:
>
> ○ Open resource pool to see assignments across all sharer files.
>
> ○ Do not open other files.
>
> [OK]   [Cancel]   [Help]

3. Click the **Open resource pool to see assignments across all sharer plans** option, and then click **OK**.

Choosing the second option, Do Not Open Other Files, allows you to see assignments only in the single sharer project plan.

The resource pool opens as read-only in the background. (If you want to verify this, look at the items on the Window menu.) Next, you will change some assignments in the sharer plan.

Assign Resources

4. On the **Standard** toolbar, click **Assign Resources**.

The Assign Resources dialog box appears. First, you will assign a resource to a task.

5. In the **Task Name** column, click the name of task 6, **Add optical track**.

6. In the **Resource Name** column in the **Assign Resources** dialog box, click **Stephanie Hooper**, and click **Assign**.

Next, you will remove a resource from a task.

7. In the **Task Name** column, click the name of task 8, **Add dialog**.

8. In the **Resource Name** column in the **Assign Resources** dialog box, click **Sue Jackson** (located at the top of the Resource Name column), and then click the **Remove** button.

You have made two assignment changes in the sharer plan. Because the resource pool is open as read-only, those changes have not been permanently saved in the resource pool. Next, you will update the resource pool.

9. On the **Tools** menu, point to **Resource Sharing**, and then click **Update Resource Pool**.

Project updates the assignment information in the resource pool with the new details from the sharer plan. Anyone else who opens or refreshes the resource pool now will see the updated assignment information.

> **Important** Only assignment information is saved to the resource pool from the sharer plan. Any changes you make to resource details, such as maximum units, in the sharer plan are not saved in the resource pool when you update. When you want to change the resource details, open the resource pool as read-write. After it is open as read-write, you can change resource details in either the resource pool or the sharer plan, and the other project plans will be updated.

Next, you will change an assignment in the sharer plan, close the project plan, and then update the resource pool.

10. In the **Task Name** column, click the name of task 3, **Sync sound**.

11. In the **Resource Name** column in the **Assign Resources** dialog box, click **Lane Sacksteder**, and then click **Assign**.

12. Click **Close** to close the Assign Resources dialog box.

13. On the **File** menu, click **Close**.

14. When prompted to save changes, click **Yes**.

Project determines that, because the resource pool was open as read-only, the latest assignment changes from the sharer plans have not been updated in the resource pool. You are offered the choices shown in the following illustration.

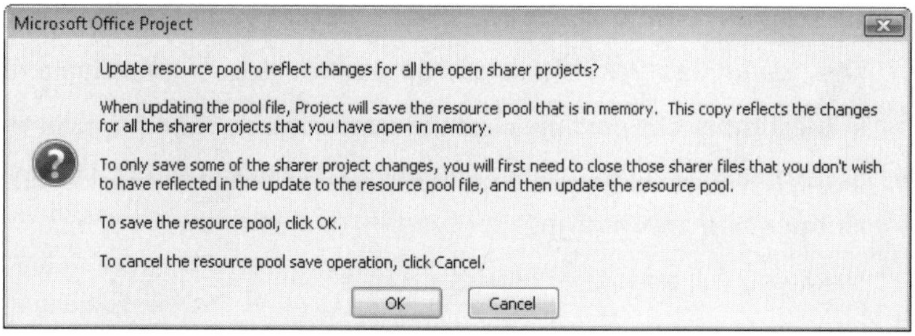

15. Click **OK**.

Project updates the assignment information with the new details from the sharer plan. The resource pool remains open as read-only.

16. On the **File** menu, click **Close**.

Because the resource pool was opened as read-only, Project closes it without prompting you to save changes.

Consolidating Project Plans

Most projects often involve several people working on tasks at different times, sometimes in different locations, and frequently for different supervisors. Although a resource pool can help you manage resource details across projects, it might not give you the level of control that you want over tasks and relationships between projects.

A good way to pull together far-flung project information is to use a *consolidated project*. This is a project plan that contains other project plans, called *inserted projects*. The inserted projects do not reside within the consolidated project plan, but are linked to it in such a way that they can be viewed and edited from it. If a project plan is edited outside of the consolidated project, the updated information appears in the consolidated project plan the next time it is opened.

> **Tip** Consolidated project plans are also known as master projects, and inserted project plans are also known as subprojects; however, this chapter uses the terms consolidated and inserted. To learn more about consolidated project plans, type Insert a project into a master project into the Search box in the upper right corner of the Project window. The Search box initially contains the text *Type a question for help*.

Using consolidated project plans enables you to do the following:

- See all tasks from your organization's project plans in a single view.
- "Roll up" project information to higher levels of management. For example, you might insert a team's project plan into the larger department's consolidated project plan and then insert that plan into the larger organization's consolidated project plan.
- Divide your project data into different project plans to match the nature of your project such as by phase, component, or location. Then you can pull the information back together in a consolidated project plan for a comprehensive look at the whole.
- See all of your projects' information in one location so that you can filter, sort, and group the data.

Consolidated project plans use Project's outlining features. An inserted project plan appears as a summary task in the consolidated project plan, except that its summary Gantt bar is gray and an inserted project icon appears in the Indicators column. When you save a consolidated project plan, you are also prompted to save any changes you have made to inserted project plans as well.

> **Tip** If you normally work on a set of project plans, but you don't want to combine them into one consolidated project plan, consider saving them as part of a workspace instead. A workspace simply records the names and window sizes of the open project plans into one file that you can later open. On the File menu, click Save Workspace.

In this exercise, you create a new consolidated project plan and insert two project plans.

New

1. On the **Standard** toolbar, click **New**.

   Project creates a new project plan.

2. On the **Insert** menu, click **Project**.

3. Navigate to the Chapter 19 Consolidating folder, and while holding down the Ctrl key, select **Wingtip Toys Commercial 19** and **Parnell Aerospace Promo 19**.

4. Click **Insert**.

   Project inserts the two projects into the consolidated project as collapsed summary tasks.

5. On the **File** menu, click **Save As**.

6. Navigate to the *Documents\Microsoft Press\Project 2007 SBS\Chapter 19 Consolidating* folder.

7. In the **File name** box, type Consolidated Projects 19, and then click **Save**.

   Next, you will display the details of the two inserted projects.

8. Select the names of the summary tasks 1 and 2, the Wingtip and Parnell projects.

9. On the **Project** menu, point to **Outline**, and then click **Show Subtasks**.

   Project asks whether you want to open the resource pool. Project hasn't actually loaded the content of the inserted project plans yet, and showing the subtasks in the consolidated project is akin to opening them.

10. Make sure that **Open resource pool to see assignment across all sharer files** is selected, and then click **OK**.

    Project expands the Wingtip and Parnell project details. If any duration or date values are not fully visible, double-click the right edge of the column heading.

11. On the **Standard** toolbar, click the **Scroll To Task** button.

Scroll to Task

Note the Inserted Project icon in the Indicators
column and the gray summary tasks bars.

	❶	Task Name	Duration	Start	Finish
1	🗐	⊟ **Wingtip Toys Comm**	**52.33 days**	**Mon 5/5/08**	**Thu 7/17/08**
1		Log footage	1 wk	Mon 5/5/08	Fri 5/9/08
2		Record rough narration	5 days	Wed 5/7/08	Wed 5/14/08
3		Paper edit footage	2 wks	Thu 5/15/08	Wed 5/28/08
4		Rough cut edit	1 wk	Thu 5/29/08	Wed 6/4/08
5		Fine cut edit	2 wks	Thu 6/5/08	Wed 6/18/08
6		Hold formal approval sh	1 day	Thu 6/19/08	Thu 6/19/08
7		Record final narration	1 wk	Fri 6/20/08	Thu 6/26/08
8		Add head and tail titles	1 wk	Fri 6/27/08	Thu 7/3/08
9		Add final music	0.67 wks	Wed 7/2/08	Mon 7/7/08
10		Print internegative of fil	3 days	Mon 7/7/08	Thu 7/10/08
11		Clone dubbing masters	4 days	Thu 7/10/08	Wed 7/16/08
12		Archive master film and	1 day	Wed 7/16/08	Thu 7/17/08
13		Hand off masters to dis	0 days	Thu 7/17/08	Thu 7/17/08
2	🗐	⊟ **Parnell Aerospace F**	**31.5 days**	**Mon 4/28/08**	**Wed 6/11/08**
1		Transfer soundtrack to	14 days	Mon 4/28/08	Fri 5/16/08
2		Record music	8 days	Fri 5/9/08	Wed 5/21/08
3		Sync sound	1 day	Thu 5/22/08	Thu 5/22/08
4		Mix	7 days	Fri 5/23/08	Mon 6/2/08
5		Add effects	1.5 days	Tue 6/3/08	Wed 6/4/08
6		Add optical track	1 day	Tue 6/3/08	Tue 6/3/08
7		Split tracks	3 days	Wed 6/4/08	Mon 6/9/08
8		Add dialog	2 days	Mon 6/9/08	Wed 6/11/08
9		Release prints	0 days	Wed 6/11/08	Wed 6/11/08

Note that the task IDs within both inserted projects start at 1, and the summary
tasks representing the inserted projects are numbered 1 and 2. Next, you'll take a
look at the details of the inserted projects.

12. On the **View** menu, click **Zoom**.

13. In the **Zoom** dialog box, click the **Entire Project** option, and then click **OK**.

Project adjusts the timescale in the Gantt chart so that the full duration of the two
inserted projects is visible.

	❶	Task Name	Duration	Start	Finish
1	🗐	⊟ **Wingtip Toys Comm**	**52.33 days**	**Mon 5/5/08**	**Thu 7/17/08**
1		Log footage	1 wk	Mon 5/5/08	Fri 5/9/08
2		Record rough narration	5 days	Wed 5/7/08	Wed 5/14/08
3		Paper edit footage	2 wks	Thu 5/15/08	Wed 5/28/08
4		Rough cut edit	1 wk	Thu 5/29/08	Wed 6/4/08
5		Fine cut edit	2 wks	Thu 6/5/08	Wed 6/18/08
6		Hold formal approval sh	1 day	Thu 6/19/08	Thu 6/19/08
7		Record final narration	1 wk	Fri 6/20/08	Thu 6/26/08
8		Add head and tail titles	1 wk	Fri 6/27/08	Thu 7/3/08
9		Add final music	0.67 wks	Wed 7/2/08	Mon 7/7/08
10		Print internegative of fil	3 days	Mon 7/7/08	Thu 7/10/08
11		Clone dubbing masters	4 days	Thu 7/10/08	Wed 7/16/08
12		Archive master film and	1 day	Wed 7/16/08	Thu 7/17/08
13		Hand off masters to dis	0 days	Thu 7/17/08	Thu 7/17/08
2	🗐	⊟ **Parnell Aerospace F**	**31.5 days**	**Mon 4/28/08**	**Wed 6/11/08**
1		Transfer soundtrack to	14 days	Mon 4/28/08	Fri 5/16/08
2		Record music	8 days	Fri 5/9/08	Wed 5/21/08
3		Sync sound	1 day	Thu 5/22/08	Thu 5/22/08
4		Mix	7 days	Fri 5/23/08	Mon 6/2/08
5		Add effects	1.5 days	Tue 6/3/08	Wed 6/4/08
6		Add optical track	1 day	Tue 6/3/08	Tue 6/3/08
7		Split tracks	3 days	Wed 6/4/08	Mon 6/9/08
8		Add dialog	2 days	Mon 6/9/08	Wed 6/11/08
9		Release prints	0 days	Wed 6/11/08	Wed 6/11/08

To conclude this exercise, you will display the project summary task of the consolidated project plan.

14. On the **Tools** menu, click **Options**.

15. In the **Options** dialog box, click the **View** tab.

16. Under **Outline options for 'Consolidated Projects 19'**, select the **Show project summary task** box, and then click **OK**.

Project displays the Consolidated Projects 19 summary task.

The values of this summary task, such as duration and work, represent the rolled-up values of both inserted projects. As Southridge Video takes on more projects, inserting them into the consolidated project plan in this way gives you a single location in which to view all activities of the organization.

17. Close and save changes to all open files.

> **Tip** To quickly create a consolidated project plan and insert projects that are open in Project, on the Window menu, click New Window. Under Projects, select the open projects you want inserted, and then click OK.

Creating Dependencies Between Projects

Most projects do not exist in a vacuum. Tasks or phases in one project might depend on tasks in other projects. You can show such dependencies by linking tasks between projects.

Reasons that you might need to create dependencies between projects include the following:

● The completion of one task in a project might enable the start of a task in another project. For example, another project manager might need to complete an environmental impact statement before you can start to construct a building. Even if these two tasks are managed in separate project plans (perhaps because separate departments of a development company are completing them), one project has a logical dependency on the other.

● A person or a piece of equipment might be assigned to a task in one project, and you need to delay the start of a task in another project until that resource completes the first task. The two tasks might have nothing in common other than needing that resource.

Task relationships between project plans look similar to links between tasks within a project plan, except that external predecessor and successor tasks have gray task names and Gantt bars. Such tasks are sometimes referred to as *ghost tasks* because they are not linked to tasks within the project plan, only to tasks in other project plans.

In this exercise, you link tasks in two project plans, and you see the results in the two project plans as well as in a consolidated project plan.

Open

1. On the **Standard** toolbar, click **Open**.

   The Open dialog box appears.

2. Navigate to the Chapter 19 Consolidating folder, and double-click the **Wingtip Toys Commercial 19** file.

3. Click **Open resource pool to see assignment across all sharer files**, and then click **OK**.

4. On the **Standard** toolbar, click **Open**.

5. Navigate to the Chapter 19 Consolidating folder, and double-click the **Parnell Aerospace Promo 19** file.

6. In the **Task Name** column, click the name of task 8, **Add dialog**.

7. On the **Standard** toolbar, click **Scroll to Task**.

Scroll to Task

To the right of the task's Gantt bar, one of the resources assigned to this task is named Fabrikam Inc. Sound Studio. You want to use this studio for work on the Wingtip Toys project after this task is completed. Next, you will link task 8 to a task in the Wingtip Toys Commercial 19 project plan.

8. On the **Window** menu, click **Wingtip Toys Commercial 19**.

9. On the **View** menu, click **Gantt Chart**.

10. Click the name of task 5, **Fine cut edit**.

Scroll to Task

11. On the **Standard** toolbar, click **Scroll to Task**.

   Project scrolls the Gantt Chart view to display task 5.

Task Information

12. On the **Standard** toolbar, click the **Task Information** button.

   The Task Information dialog box appears. In the next two steps, you will enter the file name and task ID of the predecessor task in this format: File Name\Task ID.

13. Click the **Predecessors** tab.

14. In the **ID** column, click the next empty cell below task 4 and type **Parnell Aerospace Promo 19**.

Task Information						
General	Predecessors	Resources	Advanced	Notes		Custom Fields

Name: Fine cut edit   Duration: 2w   ☐ Estimated

Predecessors:

Parnell Aerospace Promo 19\8

ID	Task Name	Type	Lag
4	Rough cut edit	Finish-to-Start (FS)	0d
Parnell Aerospace Promo 19\8			

Help   OK   Cancel

15. Press the ⎆ Enter key, and then click **OK** to close the Task Information dialog box.

   Project inserts the ghost task named *Add dialog* in the project. The ghost task represents task 8 from the Parnell project.

The ghost task appears in the project to
which it is linked with its task name in gray.   The ghost tasks' Gantt bar is gray.

		Task Name	Duration	Start	Finish
1		Log footage	1 wk	Mon 5/5/08	Fri 5/9/08
2		Record rough narration	5 days	Wed 5/7/08	Wed 5/14/08
3		Paper edit footage	2 wks	Thu 5/15/08	Wed 5/28/08
4		Rough cut edit	1 wk	Thu 5/29/08	Wed 6/4/08
5		Add dialog	2 days	Mon 6/9/08	Wed 6/11/08
6		Fine cut edit	2 wks	Wed 6/11/08	Wed 6/25/08
7		Hold formal approval show	1 day	Wed 6/25/08	Thu 6/26/08
8		Record final narration	1 wk	Thu 6/26/08	Thu 7/3/08
9		Add head and tail titles	1 wk	Thu 7/3/08	Thu 7/10/08
10		Add final music	0.67 wks	Tue 7/8/08	Fri 7/11/08
11		Print internegative of film	3 days	Fri 7/11/08	Wed 7/16/08
12		Clone dubbing masters of	4 days	Wed 7/16/08	Tue 7/22/08
13		Archive master film and au	1 day	Tue 7/22/08	Wed 7/23/08
14		Hand off masters to distrib	0 days	Wed 7/23/08	Wed 7/23/08

Tip If you point to the ghost task's Gantt bar, Project displays a ScreenTip that contains details about the ghost task, including the full path to the external project plan where the external predecessor task (the ghost task) resides.

Next, you'll look at the ghost task in the Parnell project.

16. On the **Window** menu, click **Parnell Aerospace Promo 19**.

Here you can see that ghost task 9, *Fine cut edit*, is a successor for task 8, *Add dialog*. Because task 9 is a successor task with no other links to this project, it has no effect on other tasks here.

The link between these two project plans will remain until you break it. Deleting a task in the source plan or the ghost task in the destination plan deletes the corresponding task or ghost task in the other plan.

17. Close and save changes to all open files.

To conclude this exercise, you will display the link between these two projects in the consolidated project plan.

18. On the **Standard** toolbar, click **Open**.

19. Navigate to the Chapter 19 Consolidating folder, and double-click the **Consolidated Projects 19** file.

20. Click **Open resource pool to see assignment across all sharer files**, and then click **OK**.

21. In the Parnell project, click the name of task 8, *Add dialog*.

22. On the **Standard** toolbar, click **Scroll to Task**.

You can see the link line between the task *Add dialog* in one inserted project and the task *Fine cut edit* in the other inserted project.

In the consolidated project plan, the cross-project
link appears as a normal task link.

Because you are looking at a consolidated project plan that shows the tasks from
both project plans, the cross-project link does not appear as a ghost task.

The following are a few additional tips and suggestions for working with consolidated
projects and cross-project links:

- If you do not want to see cross-project links, on the Tools menu, click Options. On
  the View tab, clear the Show External Successors or Show External Predecessors
  check box.

- When viewing a consolidated project, you can quickly create cross-project links by
  clicking the Link Tasks button on the Standard toolbar. Dragging the mouse between two task bars will do the same thing.

- Each time you open a project plan with cross-project links, Project will prompt you
  to update the cross-project links. You can suppress this prompt if you would rather
  not be reminded, or you can tell Project to automatically accept updated data from
  the linked project plan. On the Tools menu, click Options, and then click the View
  tab. Under Cross Project Linking Options For <File Name>, select the options you
  want.

CLOSE all open files.

Key Points

- If you have resource information duplicated in more than one project plan, a re-source pool is an excellent way to collect resource information across project plans and spot problems, such as resource overallocation.

- Besides indicating individual resources' nonworking time in a resource pool, you can edit the project calendar in a resource pool (for example, marking holidays as nonworking time) and that information will be propagated to all sharer plans of the resource pool file.

- Resource assignment details from all sharer plans are available for viewing (but not editing) in the resource pool file.

- Consolidating project plans into a single plan is useful when you want to see all of the aggregate details in one place (the consolidated project plan), yet continue to work with the individual project plans.

- When a task in one project plan has a logical dependency on a task in another project plan, you can link the two with a cross-project link. This produces what is sometimes called a ghost task (the predecessor or successor task) in both project plans.

Part 4

Introducing Project Server

Chapter at a Glance

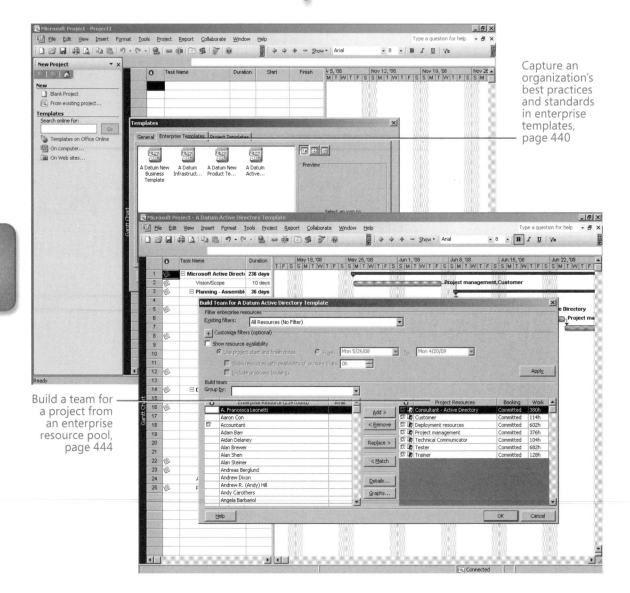

Capture an organization's best practices and standards in enterprise templates, page 440

Build a team for a project from an enterprise resource pool, page 444

20 Planning Work with Project Server

In this chapter, you will learn how to:

✔ Understand the components of a Project Server–based enterprise project management solution.

✔ Create a new project plan based on an enterprise template.

✔ Assign work resources from an enterprise resource pool.

✔ Publish a plan to Project Server after developing it in Project Professional.

This chapter introduces some of the key differences between desktop project management (as you've practiced it in this book) and Project Server–based *enterprise project management*. Project Server is the cornerstone of the *Microsoft Office Enterprise Project Management (EPM) Solution* (we'll refer to this as Project Server–based EPM). EPM is one of the more complex but potentially rewarding practices that a large organization can adopt.

Some organizational benefits of Project Server-based EPM include:

● Capture your organization's best practices with regard to workflow models and resource skills in enterprise templates.

● Gain insight into resource workload and availability across all projects and other activities in your organization.

● Develop consistent ways of describing and tracking project activities across your organization.

Although you might be the sole user of Project in your organization, the real "user" of EPM is the entire organization; thus, the software toolset is correspondingly more complex than Project simply running on a single computer. For this reason, fully addressing the details of EPM is far beyond the scope of this book. However, we want to illustrate the key features and processes of Project Server–based EPM so that you can start to determine whether it can serve a useful role in your organization. For most organizations, we think the answer will be "Yes," but getting from initial interest in Project Server–

based EPM to full implementation is a series of complex steps. We hope that this and the following chapters can help you formulate some ideas of how Project Server–based EPM can improve your organization's performance.

Chances are that you currently don't have access to Project Server in your organization. In fact, it takes quite a bit of software planning and deployment to reach the point where you can see the Project Server interface. For this reason, we do not require you to purchase and install Project Server to complete the exercises in this chapter. Instead, we'll play tour guide and walk you through the planning (this chapter), tracking (Chapter 21), and information management (Chapter 22) aspects of Project Server–based EPM.

> **Important** This chapter does not use practice files and is not written for hands-on practice. We do not assume that you have access to Project Professional and Project Server or to the Project Server sample database that we illustrate here. Instead, this and the other chapters in Part 4 describe and illustrate important features of a Project Server–based EPM system.

Understanding the Key Pieces of Enterprise Project Management

If you've completed the previous chapters in this book, you have a good introduction to project management on the scale of a single project manager with projects that have dozens of resources working on hundreds of tasks. You may be practicing project management at this scale now. Indeed, with a resource pool and multi-project features, such as consolidated projects, a single project manager should be able to stay on top of several different projects in various stages of completion with Project Standard running on a single computer.

Now, imagine dozens of project managers planning and tracking hundreds of projects, each with hundreds or even thousands of resources and tasks—all within a single organization. Project management at this scale requires a high degree of planning, coordination, and standardization. This is the realm of EPM: a large organization planning, coordinating, and executing a large number of projects simultaneously.

Think about any past or current experiences you've had working on projects in a large organization, and try answering these questions:

- Were potential projects evaluated against the goals and objectives of the organization such that the projects selected for execution aligned well with the strategic goals of the organization?

- Were the projects defined and scoped in a consistent way that would enable apples-to-apples comparisons?

- Were resource assignments made with full knowledge of each resource's skills, location, and availability?

- Did the executive leadership of the organization have a clear picture of the status of each project?

If your answer to these questions is "No," the organization was probably not practicing EPM. There is no question that many large organizations can gain great benefits by adopting EPM; however, this is no easy task, or they would have implemented EPM already. Succeeding with EPM requires a strong willingness from the leadership of the organization (executive sponsorship), a well-trained group of administrators, project and resource managers, and a software infrastructure capable of enabling it.

The Project Server–based EPM toolset includes the following:

- Project Professional 2007

- Project Web Access, the browser-based interface to Project Server

- Project Server 2007, running on Windows Server 2003 SP1 or later

- SQL Server 2000 or later, the database for enterprise project and resource data

- Windows SharePoint Services 3.0

- Microsoft .NET Framework 3.0

Deploying a complete Project Server–based EPM system requires considerable research, planning, and coordination within an organization that is well beyond the scope of this book. However, we want to give you a chance to see what Project Server–based EPM looks like and determine whether it could play a beneficial role in your organization. To illustrate the capabilities of Project Server, we'll use a sample database from a fictitious company, the A. Datum Corporation. The following are some resources to help with your evaluation, planning, and deployment of a Project Server–based EPM solution:

- Review all of the relevant material on the Project Server area of the Office Online Web site at microsoft.com. Find it on the Web at *http://office.microsoft.com*, and then navigate to the Project Server page.

- Consider attending classroom training on EPM deployment from Microsoft Learning. Here is the link to the Project Server 2003 course; check the Microsoft Learning Web site for Project Server 2007 information: *http://www.microsoft.com /learning/syllabi/en-us/2732Afinal.mspx*. You can also investigate the new Project Server certification, described in Appendix B.

- If you are in an organization that is relatively new to the project management discipline or lacks an experienced internal Information Technology (IT) group, consider working through the Project Server deployment process with a recognized Project Partner. You can begin your search for a qualified partner firm with the Microsoft Resource Directory listed here: *http://directory.microsoft.com/mprd/*

- **See also the learning and community resources described in Appendix B, "What's Next?"** Many of these resources scale from the Project desktop to EPM.

> **Tip** Portfolio management is an even higher degree of enterprise focus. In the Microsoft Office Enterprise Project Management Solution, portfolio management is supported by Microsoft Office Project Portfolio Server 2007. Portfolio management focuses on aligning the strategic goals of an organization with project selection. Project Portfolio Server is a new offering. Find more information about it on the Web at *http://office.microsoft.com*, and then navigate to the Project Portfolio Server page.

Building a New Plan from an Enterprise Template

One of the principal goals of practicing EPM is to maintain standard ways of describing work in projects across the organization. Previously in this book, you've been introduced to templates for Project on the desktop. Templates are an excellent way to help ensure consistent project structures and schedule logic, task names, and even initial resource assignments. Such consistency is essential for multi-project or portfolio management within an organization.

In a Project Server–based EPM setting, an organization can implement enterprise templates that reside in Project Server and are available to Project Professional users. *Enterprise templates* can help enforce organizational standards and give project managers a quicker start when developing new project plans. In this section, you'll view an enterprise template used at the fictitious A. Datum Corporation.

As noted above, we do not require that you have access to Project Server. Instead, we will guide you through some common Project Server–based EPM scenarios by playing the roles of various users in the A. Datum Corporation.

1. Steve Masters, a project manager at A. Datum Corporation, starts Project Professional.

2. On the File menu, Steve clicks New. In the New Project task pane, he then clicks On Computer to view the enterprise templates for Project Professional.

In a Project Server-based EPM system, enterprise templates are stored in Project Server and are available to Project Professional users in the organization.

Like all enterprise templates, these are stored in Project Server and are available to Project Professional users at A. Datum Corporation. The people who set up Project Server–based EPM at A. Datum Corporation created the enterprise templates for the most common types of projects the organization performs and populated each enterprise template with task lists, schedule logic, and other information that reflects the best practices of the organization.

3. Steve creates a new project plan based on the A. Datum New Product Template.

An enterprise template can include not only
task lists and dependencies, but generic
resource assigned to tasks.

This project plan contains a task list and links between tasks as well as *generic resources* assigned to tasks.

Similar to regular work resources in a resource pool, generic resources reside in the *enterprise resource pool* that all Project Server–based EPM users share. Generic resources, as the name suggests, are placeholder resources usually identified by a specific role or job title, such as *Manufacturing engineer* or *Safety*. Just like a regular enterprise resource, a generic resource can include cost and skills details. One way to think of a generic resource is as a resource starting point; a certain type of task should be performed by a certain type of resource. The generic resource describes that type of resource but doesn't represent a specific person or group of people. As a project manager develops a project plan, he or she can initially work with generic resources to make sure the right types of roles are assigned to the right tasks and then replace the generic resources with real resources before the tracking stage of the project begins. This replacement can be manual or automated and is shown later in this chapter.

4. To wrap up his initial work, in the Project Information dialog box, Steve adjusts the start date for the new project he is planning to May 26, 2008.

Staffing an Enterprise Project with Resources

As with a single project plan on the desktop (in Project Standard, for example), one key result of the planning stage in Project Server–based EPM is identifying the correct resources to perform work in the project and assigning them to the correct tasks. The combination of the enterprise resource pool (stored in Project Server) and the features in Project Professional makes the task of resource identification and assignment a sophisticated and powerful step in planning an enterprise project.

The Project Professional feature that we'll investigate in this section is *Build Team from Enterprise*. A related feature that we won't look at here, the Resource Substitution Wizard, enables you to replace generic resources with enterprise resources based on matching skills or other attributes (such as location or availability) of your choice. Both of these features rely on the enterprise resource pool and certain information recorded within it.

1. Steve Masters, a project manager at A. Datum Corporation, is developing a new project plan in Project Professional based on the A. Datum Active Directory enterprise template.

So far, Steve has adjusted the project start date. Next, he's ready to replace the generic resources assigned to tasks in this project with real work resources (that is, specific people and teams) from the enterprise resource pool. To do this, Steve will use the *Build Team from Enterprise* feature, which makes enterprise resources available for assignments in a specific project plan.

2. Steve clicks Build Team from Enterprise on the Tools menu.

Enterprise resources must be added to a
project plan before they become available
for assignments to tasks in the project.

In this dialog box, Steve sees the full enterprise resource pool on the left and the
local generic resources already associated with the project plan on the right. If
Steve wished, he could filter the enterprise resource list based on resource fields or
show only resources who have working time available in a specific date range.

3. Because Steve is familiar with the enterprise resources he wants for this project, he
just adds them to the project plan.

After adding enterprise resources to a project plan, they are still available to other projects.

Steve is now ready to replace the generic resources with the enterprise resources. Part of the value of this template is that it included the generic resource assignments to specific tasks based on skill or role. Steve can take advantage of that organizational knowledge by replacing each generic resource assignment with an enterprise resource, which he does through the Assign Resources dialog box.

4. Steve displays the Assign Resources dialog box, which now contains a mix of generic and enterprise resources.

5. Steve clicks the Select All button (the upper left corner of the table in the Gantt Chart view) to select all tasks.

    Now he's ready to make the resource replacements. He'll start with the Project Management generic resource, which he'll replace with himself.

6. In the Assign Resource dialog box, Steve clicks Project Management, and then clicks Replace.

7. In the Replace Resource dialog box, Steve locates his own name.

With all tasks selected, replacing
one resource with another replaces all
assignments of the initial resource.

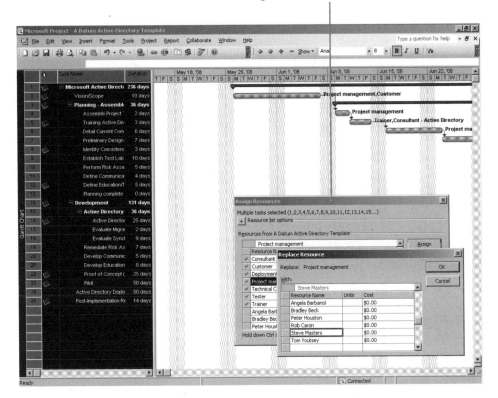

8. Steve clicks OK, and Project replaces all task assignments of the Project Manager generic resource with Steve Masters the enterprise resource.

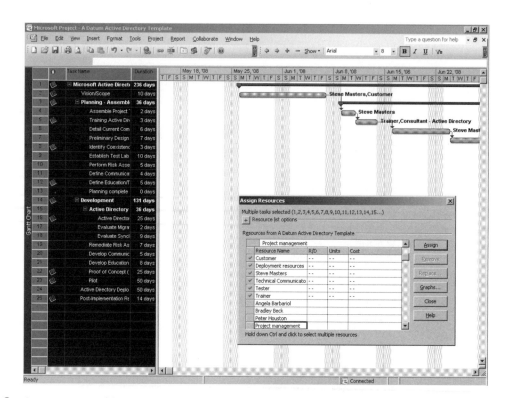

9. Steve repeats this process to replace most of the other generic resources with enterprise resources. He then adjusts the zoom level to see the resulting project plan.

Steve's next steps would be to review the enterprise resources that now have assignments in this project plan and, if desired, to fine-tune the assignments before publishing the plan to Project Server.

Publishing a Plan to Project Server

To make a project plan viewable by other *stakeholders* (such as resources with assignments in the project plan), the project manager must publish the project plan to Project Server. After initially publishing a project plan to Project Server, the project manager should republish updated information to keep fresh the data that stakeholders and others will see. In the following example, a project manager publishes a project plan to Project Server.

Steve Masters, a project manager at A. Datum Corporation, has previously saved his new project plan while he continued to fine-tune it. The new plan, Active Directory Northwest, is based on the A. Datum Active Directory enterprise template. Now, Steve is ready to publish the project plan to Project Server.

1. In Project Professional, Steve clicks Publish on the File menu.

   After Steve clicks Publish, Project publishes the plan to Project Server. The resources assigned to tasks in this project will now see their assignments. Likewise, executives at A. Datum Corporation will be able to view this project plan.

Key Points

- Project Server–based enterprise project management (EPM) enables an organization to practice project management in a consistent, efficient way.

- Enterprise templates are available to Project Professional users in a ProjectServer–based EPM system and help ensure consistent schedules within an organization.

- The Resource Substitution Wizard and Build Team From Enterprise are both features enabled by Project Server that help identify optimal work resources for task assignments.

Chapter at a Glance

Record progress on assignments in the Tasks Center in Project Web Access, page 452

Use the Outlook Integration add-in to record progress on assignments from within Outlook, page 455

Use a "stoplight" view to convey the status of all projects under way in the organization, page 459

21 Tracking Work with Project Server

In this chapter, you will learn how to:

✔ See how resources report their progress on assignments through the timesheet in Project Web Access (PWA).

✔ See how resources report their progress from the Outlook calendar to Project Server via the Outlook integration add-in.

✔ See how project managers approve task changes (such as actual work) from resources in PWA and update project plans in Project Professional.

✔ See how executives and other stakeholders can see project status at a glance and drill into the details that most interest them in PWA.

This chapter focuses on the role of a Project Server–based *enterprise project management (EPM)* system in tracking *actual* work and other schedule-related details in projects that are under way. The specific tools involved can vary with the role of the user—Project Web Access (PWA) serves the needs of resources, project managers, and executive *stakeholders*. Resources can also use Microsoft Office Outlook for submission to Project Server, and project managers also use Project Professional to manage the schedule changes processed through Project Server.

> **Important** This chapter does not use practice files and is not written for hands-on practice. We do not assume that you have access to Project Professional and Project Server or to the Project Server sample database that we illustrate here. Instead, this and the other chapters in Part 4 describe and illustrate important features of a Project Server–based EPM system.

Reporting Actual Work Through Project Web Access

After the project manager has published a project plan to Project Server, resources can review their assignments in Project Web Access (PWA), the browser-based interface for Project Server. Resources can report progress on their assigned tasks. Project Server can maintain a full audit log of progress reported and can lock tasks and projects from future time tracking. Resources can also report various activities that they want their project manager to know about; these activities need not be associated with tasks. The project manager associated with a project reviews progress submissions from resources before the submissions affect the schedules.

In this example, a resource records actual work in PWA and then submits that information to a project manager.

1. Brad Sutton, a resource at A. Datum Corporation, logs on to PWA.

   After logging on, Brad sees a personalized Home page that summarizes all Project Server details that relate to Brad.

   Every Project Server-based EPM user who logs on to Project Web Access sees a customized Home page. The options available vary per user, depending on the roles to which they are assigned.

The links under the Reminders heading lead to the major areas of PWA, called *centers*. The Tasks link displays the Tasks Center, for example.

2. Brad clicks Tasks to view his Tasks Center. Here, Brad can see his assignments across multiple projects.

In the Tasks Center, resources see all their current assignments and can record progress on those assignments.

3. Brad switches to the Timesheet view, then reports his progress on some tasks to which he is assigned.

Resources can see the scheduled work on their assignments (that is, the amount of work for which they were scheduled), and enter actual work values.

Brad can report overall progress in terms of percent complete, actual and remaining work, or detailed daily actual progress. He can recalculate the actual and remaining work so that he always sees the most current values.

4. Brad submits the progress he has recorded to his project manager, Steve Masters.

Reporting Actual Work Through Outlook

Project Server includes a COM add-in for Outlook that enables Outlook users to see their task assignments and report their status. This information is submitted to Project Server for project manager approval and is eventually incorporated into the project plan as actual work. The Outlook integration add-in allows team members who would rather work in Outlook than in the Tasks Center in PWA to see their assignments and keep the project manager up to date on their status.

In this section, we'll illustrate how a team member works with his Project Server–based EPM task assignments in Outlook. Brad Sutton, a team member at A. Datum Corporation, has task assignments in several active and upcoming project plans. Brad has previously used PWA to record progress on his assignments, but now he'd like to work in Outlook. Brad has previously installed the Outlook integration add-in from Project Server.

1. Brad checks his Outlook To-Do List and sees his task assignments from Project Server.

Imported assignments appear as tasks in Outlook.

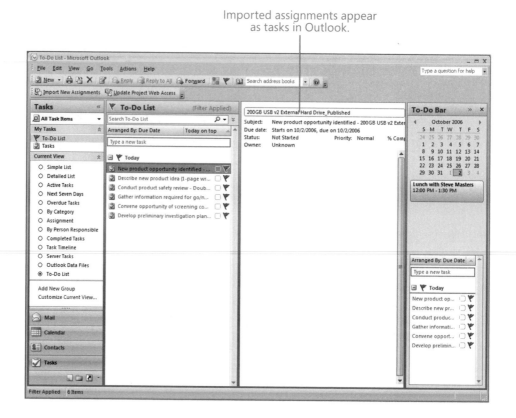

2. Brad double-clicks one of the tasks. The task details appear in a new window.

The interface of the Outlook
Integration add-in is similar to
what a resource would see in
Project Web Access.

Here, Brad sees the key information for this assignment—the task and project from which his assignment originated as well as his timesheet view.

Brad can choose to display this and his other tasks in PWA by clicking the Go To Web Timesheet button. However, the timesheet for the task that's visible here is sufficient for his reporting needs.

3. Brad reports on the task health and updates his remaining work estimate.

The resource can record progress on their assignments and submit the information to the project manger—without ever leaving Outlook.

At this point, his status is entered in the form but has not been submitted to the project manager. Brad takes care of this detail next.

4. Brad clicks the Save to Project Web Access button in the Project Web Access Appointment dialog box. The add-in submits Brad's task status to Steve Masters, the project manager of the Active Directory West project. This update will remain in Project Server until the project manager approves it. It then will be recorded in the Active Directory West project plan.

As far as the project manager is concerned, the actual work submitted through Outlook is essentially the same as actuals submitted through PWA. For reporting status on assignments, the Outlook integration add-in makes Outlook a reasonable substitute for PWA for resources who prefer to work in Outlook.

Handling Actuals from Resources

When the project manager logs on to PWA, he or she sees immediately whether resources have submitted new actual work, or other information. The project manager can then review the submissions and have them posted to the project plan. After they are included in the project plan, Project Professional responds to actuals by recalculating task durations and rescheduling remaining work, as needed.

In this section, we'll illustrate how a project manager reviews and processes information submitted by resources.

1. Steve Masters, a project manager at A. Datum Corporation, logs on to PWA. Steve immediately sees that he has pending task changes from resources.

Project managers, like all Project Web Access users, see a custom Home page when they log on. In this case, the project manager sees that he has new task changes from resources to evaluate.

2. Steve clicks the three task updates from resources under the Approvals label, and PWA switches to the Task Updates Center, where Steve can view the details of the task changes from resources.

In the Task Updates Center, project managers can see the details of task changes submitted by resources, and approve, reject, or hold on to all or some of them.

3. Today, Steve is focused primarily on Brad Sutton's most recent work on the 200GB USB v2 External Hard Drive project.

4. Steve selects the tasks for which Brad has submitted actuals, and clicks Accept.

   Project Server records the progress in the 200GB USB v2 External Hard Drive project and reports that Steve has no additional updates.

Next, Steve can evaluate the actual work submitted by Brad Sutton and other resources in Project and make schedule adjustments as needed.

With PWA and the Outlook integration add-in, all of the actual work recorded in the project plan can come directly from the resources; the project manager does not need to reenter this information into the project plan. However, the project manager always maintains control over what information is and is not incorporated into the project plan.

Keeping Stakeholders Informed

One of the primary purposes of a Project Server–based EPM system is to keep the status of active projects accurate, timely, and visible. Executive stakeholders and sponsors are often especially interested in the high-level status of a collection of related projects, often called a *portfolio* or *program*, and want to drill into the details of a specific project only when they see some indication of a problem. The Project Center in PWA is where executives and other stakeholders can most easily see multi-project status at a glance. The Project Center can be substantially customized with display options and custom views, as we'll see here.

Jo Brown is an executive at A. Datum Corporation and oversees several of the projects under way there (she manages the project managers). Jo relies on the project managers within her organization to keep their project status accurate and uses the Project Center as the primary way to view project status. When she sees something in the Project Center that concerns her, she digs deeper into the project details and then consults with the project manager.

1. Jo Brown logs on to PWA and sees her custom Home page.

2. Jo navigates to the Project Center and, in the View box, selects A. Datum Executive Summary.

In this customized stoplight view, red, yellow, and green icons indicate key schedule status values (in this case, budget and schedule variance) for each project.

The Executive Summary view displays each project as an item on a Gantt chart, as well as status indicators for the overall budget and schedule. This is one of several custom views that the Project Server administrators at A. Datum Corporation have created to better meet the needs of their stakeholders. As with other views in PWA, Jo can alter this view to focus on the data in which she is most interested or switch to another view.

The Executive Summary view is sometimes called a *stoplight view* because it represents key project status measures (in this case, budget and schedule) with green (good), yellow (moderate problem), or red (major problem) indicators. Jo likes this view because she can scan for the "red light" projects and focus her limited time on those projects to determine what is causing the budget or schedule variance.

3. Jo can see that work is under way on the 100X DVD Drive project. Jo clicks the project's name to view the schedule directly in PWA.

In this custom stoplight view, The Budget and Schedule indicator values are determined by predefined thresholds.

Like other stakeholders at A. Datum Corporation, Jo Brown can get a wide range of details about projects, depending on her interest.

Key Points

- Both the Tasks Center in PWA and calendar appointments in Outlook (with the support of the Outlook integration add-in) serve as timesheets for resources to report progress on their assignments.

- The Updates Center in PWA allows project managers to evaluate, approve, or reject task change submissions from resources. Approved task changes cause Project Server to update the affected project plans in Project Professional.

- The Project Center in PWA enables executives and other stakeholders to view project status across the organization and drill into the project plans that most interest them.

Chapter at a Glance

Create a new risk and associate it with a project plan, page 464

Create an issue for a project plan and assign it to someone for resolution, page 467

Set up alerts to notify you via e-mail when a document, risk and issue you are interested in changes for any reason, page 470

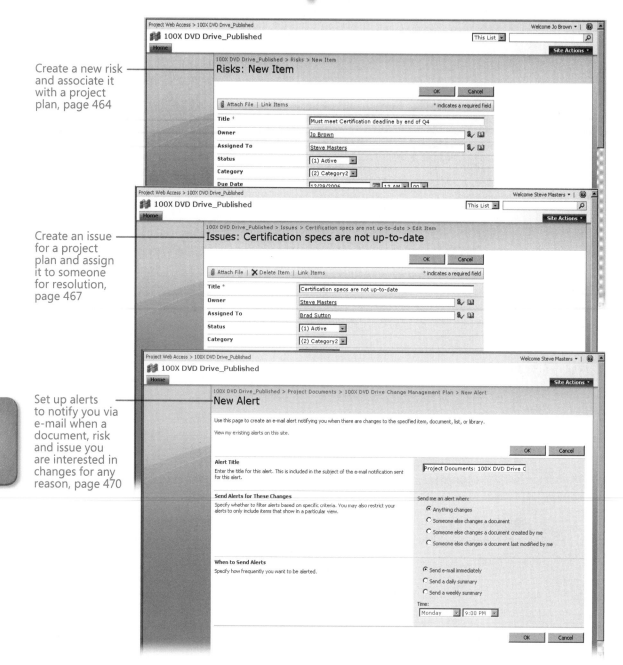

22 Managing Risks, Issues, and Documents with Project Server

In this chapter, you will learn how to:

✔ Create a risk in Project Web Access and associate it with a project.

✔ Create an issue, associate it with a project, and assign it to someone for resolution.

✔ Create a document library for a project and upload a document.

Project Server integrates with Windows SharePoint Services (WSS). In fact, the Project Web Access (PWA) interface is built from WSS Web parts. This integration adds the risk, issue, and document management capabilities of WSS to a Project Server–based *enterprise project management (EPM) system*.

With WSS integrated with Project Server, some features of WSS are applied in ways that make them more applicable to EPM. Document lists in WSS, for example, can now be associated with specific projects in the Project Server database or with tasks within those projects.

Each project published to Project Server receives a WSS subweb provisioned for it. PWA users then interact with the WSS Risks, Issues, and Documents pages directly in PWA. Risks, issues, and documents can all play essential roles in supporting Project Server–based EPM, and we'll walk through each of these on the following pages.

> **Important** This chapter does not use practice files and is not written for hands-on practice. We do not assume that you have access to Project Professional and Project Server or to the sample database in Project Server that we illustrate here. Instead, this and the other chapters in Part 4 describe and illustrate important features of a Project Server–based enterprise project management (EPM) system.

Managing Risks

WSS integration with Project Server affords an excellent tool for identifying, tracking, and mitigating threats to project success, that is, for risk management. As the term is used in Project Server, a *risk* is a record of a potential threat (or less likely, an opportunity) that could affect the completion of a task or project. The Risks functionality in Project Server allows an organization to identify, rank, and track the risks they are most interested in. You can also associate risks with issues, documents, or other risks.

Risks and issues (another feature enabled in Project Server by WSS and described in the next section) have some similarities. However, one distinguishing aspect of a risk is the *trigger*. A trigger is the criteria or threshold that needs to be met before a risk's contingency plan goes into effect. In a large organization, different people may be involved in defining or quantifying risks, developing contingency plans, and specifying a risk's trigger. Should a risk materialize into an actionable item, it may become an issue for ongoing tracking and mitigation. You can enable e-mail notification and alerts to keep track of risk status and thereby see the status of all risks associated with a project or all risks within an organization.

In this section, we'll see how to create a new risk (that is, formally identify something as a risk) for a project.

1. Jo Brown, an executive at A. Datum Corporation, logs in to Project Server and navigates to the Project Center.

2. There, she selects the 100X DVD Drive project and goes to the Risk Center for that project.

Jo wants to create a new risk for the 100X DVD Drive project. Currently, this project has no risks associated with it.

Risks, which are potential problems or opportunities, can be associated with projects published to Project Server; with tasks within those projects; or with other risks, issues, or documents.

3. Jo clicks New Item on the New menu and displays the Risks: New Item page.

The values contained within a risk help identify the nature of the risk (threat or opportunity), trigger points, mitigation plans, and owner.

4. Jo enters the risk information and assigns the risk to the project manager of the 100X DVD Drive project, Steve Masters.

5. Jo clicks OK to record the risk and returns to the Risks page for this project. The new risk appears there.

After a risk is created, its status and owner are visible on the Risks page for the project with which the risk is associated.

Steve can now review the details of the risk item, change its Status value and other details, or assign the risk to someone else. Jo can keep track of any changes to the risk item by pointing to the risk title and clicking Alert Me in the menu that appears.

Managing Issues

Issues, as the term is used in Project Server, are action items with a structured discussion about a specific topic. At all times, an issue has an owner (such as a project manager or team member) and a status (such as active or resolved). Using issues is an excellent way to keep track of the action items of those projects in which the action items should not appear in the projects themselves. You can also think of issues as risks that evolved into actionable items that now require tracking and mitigation.

As with risks and documents (described in the next section), you can associate issues with specific projects or tasks. You can also enable e-mail notification and alerts to keep track of issue status and thereby see the status of all issues associated with a project.

In this section, we'll see how to create a new issue and assign it to someone for resolution.

1. Steve Masters, a project manager at A. Datum Corporation, logs in to Project Server and navigates to the Project Center.

2. There, he selects the 100X DVD Drive project and goes to the Issue Center for that project. This project currently has no issues.

3. Steve wants to create a new issue for a task in the 100X DVD Drive project, so he clicks New.

A new, blank issue for the 100X DVD Drive project appears.

Unlike a risk, an issue is an actual, action-able item. The issue properties specify the nature of the issue, owner, and importance.

4. Steve enters the information he wants for the issue and then assigns the issue to Brad Sutton, a resource who has assignments in the 100X DVD Drive project.

5. When he's finished, Steve clicks OK.

The new issue appears on the project's Issues page, ready for Brad Sutton to resolve.

As with risk items, Steve can monitor progress on this issue by pointing to the issue title and clicking Alert Me in the menu that appears. Brad will see the issue assigned to him the next time he logs in to PWA. He can review the details of the issue, change its Status value and other details, or assign the issue to someone else.

Managing Documents

Associating documents with projects or tasks is an extremely useful capability afforded by the Project Server–WSS integration. Common types of documents you might want to link to projects or tasks include specifications, budgets, and various project management documents, such as risk management plans.

There are two types of document libraries: project and public. In project document libraries, project managers set up the properties of the document libraries associated with their projects. Project managers can specify options, such as the default templates to use for Office documents and access permissions to the documents. In public document libraries, all Project Server users have access unless the server administrator specifies otherwise. Both types of libraries support e-mail notification when a document has been changed. You'll see visual indicators and links to documents in a project document library in the Project Center and Tasks Center.

In this section, we'll see how to create a document library for a project and upload a document to the library.

1. Steve Masters, a project manager at A. Datum Corporation, logs in to Project Server and navigates to the Project Center.

2. There, he selects the 100X DVD Drive project and goes to the Document Center for that project. This project currently has no documents.

3. Steve already has the document he wants to add to this project's document library, so he clicks Upload Document from the Upload menu.

4. Steve browses to the document he wants and clicks OK.

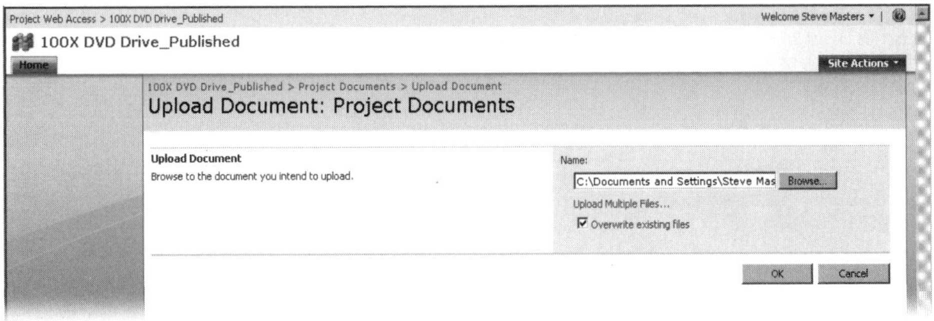

5. Steve clicks OK.

The uploaded document appears in the project's document library.

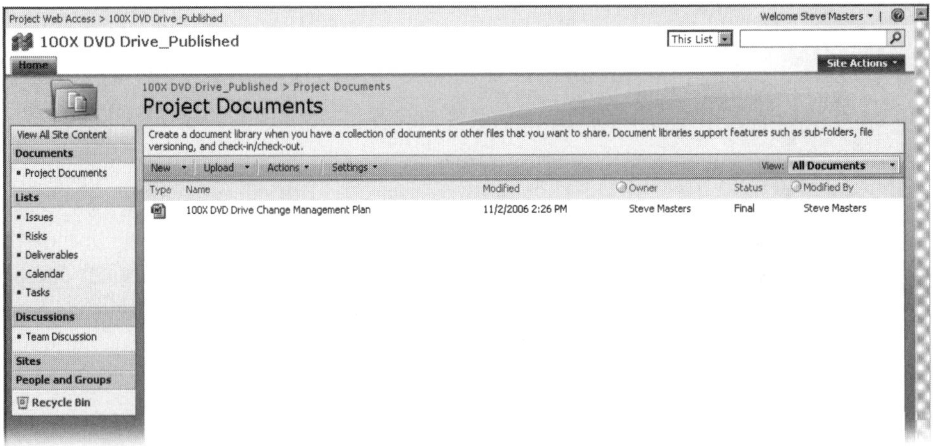

Steve wants to keep close track of any changes made to this document by anyone on the project team. He'll set up PWA to alert him via e-mail when the document is modified.

6. Steve points to the document name, clicks the Down Arrow that appears next to the document name, and clicks Alert Me.

The New Alert screen appears.

7. Steve sets the alert options he wants.

Documents, risks, and issues can have alerts set up for
them that notify you by e-mail when the document,
risk, or issue changes for any reason.

Steve can set up similar alerts for the entire document library associated with the
project, as well as risks and issues.

Key Points

- Project Server integrates with Windows SharePoint Services (WSS) for document, issue, and risk management with an enterprise project management focus.

- Risks and issues are similar; however, risks are potential problems or opportunities, whereas issues are actionable items.

- Documents, issues, and risks can be associated with projects, tasks within projects, or with other documents, issues, or risks.

- Project Server users can set up e-mail notification to alert them when any changes are made to documents, issues, or risks.

Part 5

Appendices

A A Short Course in Project Management

Throughout this book, we've included advice on how best to use Microsoft Office Project 2007 while following sound project management practices. This appendix focuses on the basics of project management, regardless of any software tools you may use to help you manage projects. While project management is a broad, complex subject, in this appendix we focus on the "project triangle" model. In this model, you consider projects in terms of time, cost, and scope.

Understanding What Defines a Project

Succeeding as a project manager requires that you complete your projects on time, finish within budget, and make sure your customers are happy with what you deliver. That sounds simple enough, but how many projects have you heard of (or worked on) that were completed late, cost too much, or didn't meet the needs of their customers?

A Guide to the Project Management Body of Knowledge (3rd edition, published by the Project Management Institute, 2004)—referred to as the PMBOK and pronounced "pim-bok"—defines a project as "a temporary endeavor undertaken to create a unique product or service." Let's walk through this definition to clarify what a project is and is not.

> **Tip** For more information about the Project Management Institute and the PMBOK, see Appendix B, "What's Next?"

First, a project is *temporary*. A project's duration might be just one week or it might go on for years, but every project has an end date. You might not know that end date when the project begins, but it's out there somewhere in the future. Projects are not the same as ongoing operations, although the two have a great deal in common. *Ongoing operations*, as the name suggests, go on indefinitely; you don't establish an end date. Examples include most activities of accounting and human resources departments. People who run ongoing operations might also manage projects; for example, a manager of a human resources department for a large organization might plan a college recruiting fair. Yet, projects are distinguished from ongoing operations by an expected end date, such as the date of the recruiting fair.

Next, a project is an *endeavor*. *Resources*, such as people and equipment, need to do work. The endeavor is undertaken by a team or an organization, and therefore projects have a sense of being intentional, planned events. Successful projects do not happen spontaneously; some amount of preparation and planning happens first.

Finally, every project creates a *unique product* or *service*. This is the *deliverable* for the project and the reason that the project was undertaken. A refinery that produces gasoline does not produce a unique product. The whole idea, in this case, is to produce a standardized commodity; you typically don't want to buy gas from one station that is significantly different from gas at another station. On the other hand, commercial airplanes are unique products. Although all Boeing 777 airplanes might look the same to most of us, each is, in fact, highly customized for the needs of its purchaser.

By now, you may realize that much of the work that goes on in the world is project work. If you schedule, track, or manage any of this work, then congratulations are in order: you are already doing some project management work!

Project management has been a recognized profession since about the 1950s, but project management work in some form has been occurring for as long as people have been doing complex work. When the Great Pyramids at Giza in Egypt were built, somebody somewhere was tracking resources, schedules, and specifications in some fashion.

> **Tip**   Project management is now a well-recognized profession in most industries. To learn more about organizations that train project managers and advance project management as a profession, see Appendix B, "What's Next?"

The Project Triangle: Viewing Projects in Terms of Time, Cost, and Scope

You can visualize project work in many ways, but our favorite method is what is sometimes called the *project triangle* or triangle of triple constraints.

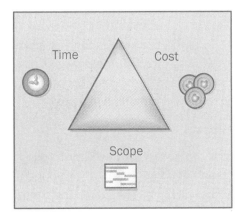

This theme has many variations, but the basic concept is that every project has some element of a time constraint, has some type of budget, and requires some amount of work to complete. (In other words, it has a defined scope.) The term *constraint* has a specific meaning in Project, but here we're using the more general meaning of a limiting factor. Let's consider these constraints one at a time.

Time

Have you ever worked on a project that had a deadline? (Maybe we should ask whether you've ever worked on a project that did not have a deadline.) Limited time is the one constraint of any project with which we are all probably most familiar. If you're working on a project right now, ask your team members to name the date of the project deadline. They might not know the project budget or the scope of work in great detail, but chances are they all know the project deadline.

The following are examples of time constraints:

- You are building a house and must finish the roof before the rainy season arrives.
- You are assembling a large display booth for a trade show that starts in two months.
- You are developing a new inventory-tracking system that must be tested and running by the start of the next fiscal year.

Since we were children, we have been trained to understand time. We carry wristwatches, paper and electronic organizers, and other tools to help us manage time. For many projects that create a product or event, time is the most important constraint to manage.

Cost

You might think of cost simply in monetary terms, but project *cost* has a broader meaning: costs include all of the resources required to carry out the project. Costs include the people and equipment who do the work, the materials they use, and all of the other events and issues that require money or someone's attention in a project.

The following are examples of cost constraints:

- You have signed a fixed-price contract to deliver an inventory-tracking software system to a client. If your costs exceed the agreed-upon price, your customer might be sympathetic but probably won't be willing to renegotiate the contract.

- The president of your organization has directed you to carry out a customer research project using only the staff and equipment in your department.

- You have received a $5,000 grant to create a public art installation. You have no other funds.

For virtually all projects, cost is ultimately a limiting constraint; few projects could go over budget without eventually requiring corrective action.

Scope

You should consider two aspects of *scope*: product scope and project scope. Every successful project produces a unique product: a tangible item or service. Customers usually have some expectations about the features and functions of products they consider purchasing. *Product scope* describes the intended quality, features, and functions of the product—often in minute detail. Documents that outline this information are sometimes called product specifications. A service or event usually has some expected features as well. We all have expectations about what we'll do or see at a party, concert, or sporting event.

Project scope, on the other hand, describes the work required to deliver a product or service with the intended product scope. Project scope is usually measured in tasks and phases.

The following are examples of scope constraints:

- Your organization won a contract to develop an automotive product that has exact requirements—for example, physical dimensions measured to 0.01 mm. This is a product scope constraint that will influence project scope plans.

- You are constructing a building on a lot that has a height restriction of 50 feet.

- You can use only internal services to develop part of your product, and those services follow a product development methodology that is different from what you had planned.

Product scope and project scope are closely related. The project manager who manages project scope well must also understand product scope or must know how to communicate with those who do.

Time, Cost, and Scope: Managing Project Constraints

Project management gets most interesting when you must balance the time, cost, and scope constraints of your projects. The project triangle illustrates the process of balancing constraints because the three sides of the triangle are connected, and changing one side of a triangle affects at least one other side.

The following are examples of constraint balance:

- If the duration (time) of your project schedule decreases, you might need to increase budget (cost) because you must hire more resources to do the same work in less time. If you cannot increase the budget, you might need to reduce the scope because the resources you have cannot complete all of the planned work in less time.

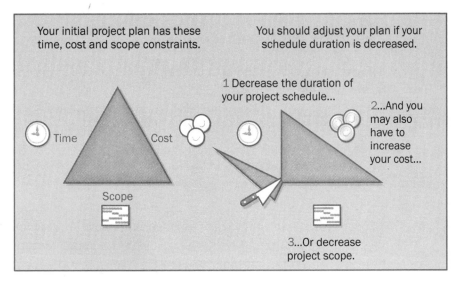

Your initial project plan has these time, cost and scope constraints.

You should adjust your plan if your schedule duration is decreased.

Time   Cost

Scope

1 Decrease the duration of your project schedule...

2...And you may also have to increase your cost...

3...Or decrease project scope.

If you must decrease a project's duration, make sure that overall project quality is not unintentionally lowered. For example, testing and quality control often occur last in a software development project; if project duration is decreased late in the project, those tasks might be the ones to suffer with cutbacks. You must weigh the benefits of decreasing the project duration against the potential downside of a deliverable with poorer quality.

● If the budget (cost) of your project decreases, you might need more time because you cannot pay for as many resources or for resources of the same efficiency. If you cannot increase the time, you might need to reduce project scope because fewer resources cannot complete all of the planned work in the time remaining.

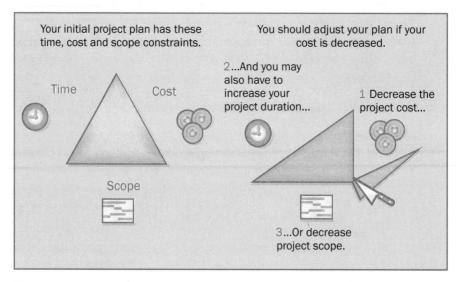

If you must decrease a project's budget, you could look at the *grades* of material resources for which you had budgeted. For example, did you plan to shoot a film in 35 mm when cheaper digital video would do? A lower-grade material is not necessarily a lower-quality material. As long as the grade of material is appropriate for its intended use, it might still be of high quality. As another example, fast food and gourmet are two grades of restaurant food, but you may find high-quality and low-quality examples of each.

You should also look at the costs of the human and equipment resources you have planned to use. Can you hire less experienced people for less money to carry out simpler tasks? Reducing project costs can lead to a poorer-quality deliverable, however. As a project manager, you must consider (or, more likely, communicate to the decision makers) the benefits versus the risks of reducing costs.

● If your project scope increases, you might need more time or resources (cost) to complete the additional work. When project scope increases after the project has started, it's called *scope creep*. Changing project scope midway through a project is not necessarily a bad thing; for example, the environment in which your project deliverable will operate may have changed or become clearer since beginning the project. Changing project scope is a bad thing only if the project manager doesn't recognize and plan for the new requirements—that is, when other constraints (cost, time) are not correspondingly examined and, if necessary, adjusted.

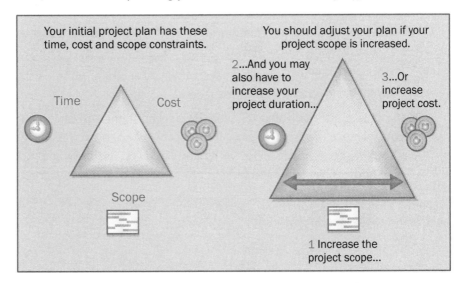

Time, cost, and scope are the three essential elements of any project. To succeed as a project manager, you should know quite a bit about how all three of these constraints apply to your projects.

Here is our final word about the project triangle model. Like all simple models of complex subjects, this model is a useful learning tool but not always a reflection of the real world. If real projects always performed as the project triangle suggests they should, you might see projects delivered late but at planned cost or with expected scope. Or, projects might be completed on time and with expected scope but at higher cost. In other words, you'd expect to see at least one element of the project triangle come in as planned. But the sad truth is that many projects, even with rigorous project management oversight, are delivered late, over budget, *and* with far less than expected scope of functionality. You've probably participated in a few such projects yourself. As you well know, project management is just plain difficult. Success in project management requires a rare mix of skills and knowledge about schedule practices and tools, as well as skill in the domain or industry in which a project is executed.

Managing Your Projects with Project

The best project management tool in the world can never replace your good judgment. However, the right tool can and should help you accomplish the following:

- Track all of the information you gather about the work, duration, and resource requirements for your project.

- Visualize your project plan in standard, well-defined formats.

- Schedule tasks and resources consistently and effectively.

- Exchange project information with *stakeholders* over networks and the Internet using standard file formats.

- Communicate with resources and other stakeholders while leaving ultimate control in the hands of the project manager.

In the chapters of this book, you were introduced to the rich functionality of Project in a realistic context: managing a project from conception to completion. Not everything in this book might have applied to your needs, and you probably have needs that this book did not address. Yet, after completing this tutorial, you're off to a great start with Project.

B What's Next?

If you've completed most or all of the chapters in this book, you're well on your way to mastering Microsoft Office Project 2007. However, one book can only get you so far. To help further your Project and project management knowledge, a few sources are available to you.

Joining a Project Learning Community

If there's one thing we can say about Project users, it's that they love to talk about the program and their work with it and to share ideas with others. Whether you work in a large organization or independently, you're likely to find a community of Project users nearby.

If you're in a large organization, especially one with a strong project management focus, you might find an internal Project user group or support group there. Such groups often meet informally to provide peer training and support, critique project plans, and share best practices. If such a group does not exist in your organization, you might well start one.

In the public realm, there are many Project user groups around the world. These groups typically meet on a regular basis to share tips and tricks about Project. For example, in the Puget Sound area in the northwest United States—where the authors live—there's an active Microsoft Project Association chapter that meets most months for informal idea sharing and formal presentations by industry experts. Joining a user group is a great way to broaden your exposure to Project usage; it also can be a great source for informal product support, training, and career networking.

The following are a few places where you can investigate Project user groups and related resources:

- The Microsoft Project Association (MPA) is the official industry association for Project. MPA offers both free and membership-based information about a variety of Project and project management resources, as well as a directory of Project user groups around the world. Find it on the Web at *www.mympa.org.*

- The Project area of the Office Online Web site at microsoft.com includes a variety of tools and information from Microsoft and other Project users to help you manage your projects. Find it on the Web at *http://office.microsoft.com,* and then navigate to the Project page.

- The official Project newsgroup offers help and discussions with other Project users, including Microsoft Most Valuable Professionals (MVPs). You can use any newsreader software to access this newsgroup. To view or subscribe to this newsgroup, point your newsreader to *news://msnews.microsoft.com/microsoft.public.project.*

- The Microsoft Project MVPs are independent Project experts (not Microsoft employees) officially given MVP status by Microsoft in recognition of their product expertise and work in helping the larger user community utilize Project successfully. MVPs frequently respond to questions in the newsgroups. Find the MVP Web site at *http://project.mvps.org.*

- To discuss Visual Basic for Applications (VBA) in Project, point your newsreader to *news://msnews.microsoft.com/microsoft.public.project.vba.*

- The Project Server area of the Office Online Web site at microsoft.com includes evaluation, deployment, and IT administration information for the Microsoft Office Enterprise Project Management (EPM) Solution. Find it on the Web at *http://office.microsoft.com,* and then navigate to the Project Server page.

- To discuss Project Server, point your newsreader to *news://msnews.microsoft.com/microsoft.public.project.server.*

- The Project Portfolio Server area of the Office Online Web site at microsoft.com describes the new portfolio management solution. Find it on the Web at *http://office.microsoft.com,* and then navigate to the Project Portfolio Server page.

> **Tip** To view the full list of available Microsoft newsgroups or to use a newsgroup through your browser rather than a newsreader, go to *www.microsoft.com/communities/newsgroups/default.mspx.*

To formally showcase your Project or EPM expertise, you can become certified. Microsoft has worked with the Project Management Institute (PMI, described in the next section) and others to develop a new set of certifications for Project and the EPM solution—the Microsoft Office Project 2007 Certification Program. These new certifications are aligned with the *Project Management Body of Knowledge* (PMBOK, described in Appendix A). The certifications include:

- Desktop Technology Specialist, focusing on competency with the features found in Project Standard or those in Project Professional when used as a stand-alone.

- EPM Technology Specialist, focusing on competency with Project Professional and Project Server.

- EPM Professional, focusing on Project Professional and Project Server competency with large projects and programs.

To learn about training opportunities and certification requirements for Project 2007 certification, look on the Web at *www.microsoft.com/learning*.

> **Important** The new Project 2007 Certification Program was announced as this book went to press. Therefore, by the time you read this, some details may have changed.

Joining a Project Management Learning Community

Perhaps more than other desktop programs, Project requires you to be involved in a specific formal activity: project management. Project management can be an exciting mix of technical, organizational, and social challenges. The Project Management Institute (PMI) is the leading organization of professional project management. PMI focuses on setting project management standards, developing and offering educational programs, and certifying project managers. The most widely recognized PMI certification is the Project Management Professionals (PMP) certification.

The PMI's PMBOK describes generally accepted project management practices, knowledge areas, and terminology. In addition, the PMI publishes the journals *Project Management Journal* and *PM Network*. You can learn more about the PMI on the Web at *www.pmi.org*. If you are professionally invested in the practice of project management, you should be in the PMI.

Final Words

There are, of course, many worthwhile commercial and nonprofit organizations dedicated to Project and project management besides those we have described here. Project enjoys a leading position in the diverse, sometimes contentious, but always interesting world of project management. Wherever you are in your own Project and project management knowledge and career development, you can find a great variety of supporting organizations and peers today. Good luck!

Glossary

8/80 rule   A general guideline regarding the estimation of task duration. Task durations between eight hours (or one day) and 80 hours (10 working days, or two weeks) are generally sized to a manageable duration.

Accrual   The method by which a project incurs the cost of a task or a resource. The three types of accrual are start, prorated, and end.

Actual   A detail about task completion recorded in a Project plan. Prior to recording actuals, the project plan contains scheduled or planned information. Comparing planned project information to actuals helps the project manager better control project execution.

ACWP   An earned value indicator; the acronym stands for Actual Cost of Work Performed. In earned value analysis, this is the actual cost of tasks that have been completed (or the portion completed of each) by the status date.

allocation   The portion of the capacity of a resource devoted to work on a specific task.

assignment   The matching of a work resource (a person or a piece of equipment) to a task. You can also assign a material resource to a task, but those resources have no effect on work or duration.

AutoFilter   In a table, a quick way to view only the task or resource information that meets the criteria you choose. To turn on AutoFilter, on the Project menu, point to Filtered For <filter name>, and then click AutoFilter. To filter a table with AutoFilter, click the arrow next to a column heading, and choose the criteria you want.

BAC   An earned value indicator; the acronym stands for Budget At Completion. This is the same as baseline cost.

base calendar   A calendar that can serve as the project calendar or a task calendar. A base calendar defines the default working times for resources. Project includes three base calendars named Standard, 24 Hours, and Night Shift. You can customize these, or you can use them as a basis for your own base calendar.

baseline   The original project plan, saved for later comparison. The baseline includes the planned start and finish dates of tasks and assignments, as well as their planned costs. Project plans can have up to 11 baselines.

BCWP   An earned value indicator; the acronym stands for Budgeted Cost of Work Performed. In earned value analysis, this is the budgeted cost of tasks that have been completed (or the portion completed of each) by the status date. BCWP is also called Earned Value (EV) because it represents the value earned in the project by the status date.

BCWS   An earned value indicator; the acronym stands for Budgeted Cost of Work Scheduled. In earned value analysis, this is the portion of the project's budget that is scheduled to be spent by the status date. BCWS is also called Planned Value (PV).

bottom-up planning   A method of developing a project plan that starts with the lowest-level tasks and organizes them into broad phases.

burdened labor rate   A resource cost rate that reflects not only the resource's direct payroll cost, but also some portion of the organization's costs that are not directly related to the resource's assignments on a project. Note that Project doesn't support a burdened labor rate directly; if you want to use one, simply enter it as a resource's standard or overtime cost rate.

calendar   The settings that define the working days and time for a project, resources, and tasks.

consolidated project   A Project plan that contains one or more inserted project plans. The inserted projects are linked to the consolidated project so that any changes to the inserted projects are reflected in the consolidated plan, and vice versa. A consolidated project plan is also known as a master project plan.

constraint   A restriction, such as Must Start On (MSO) or Finish No Later Than (FNLT), that you can place on the start or finish date of a task.

contour   The manner in which a resource's work on a task is scheduled over time. Project includes several predefined work contours that you can apply to an assignment. For example, a back-loaded contour schedules a small amount of work at the beginning of an assignment and then schedules increasing amounts of work as time progresses. You can also manually contour an assignment by editing work values in a usage view, such as the Resource Usage. Applying a predefined contour or manually contouring an assignment causes Project to display a work contour icon in the Indicators column.

Copy Picture   The feature that enables you to copy images and create snapshots of a view.

cost   The resources required to carry out a project, including the people who do the work, the equipment used, and the materials consumed as the work is completed. Cost is one side of the project triangle model.

cost rate table   The resource pay rates that are stored on the Costs tab of the Resource Information dialog box. You can have up to five separate cost rate tables per resource.

cost resource   A type of resource used to represent financial costs associated with tasks in a project. Use cost resources to account for standard categories of costs you want to track in a project, such as costs for travel or catering. A cost resource does no work and has no effect on the scheduling of a task to which it is assigned.

CPI   An earned value indicator; the acronym stands for Cost Performance Index. In earned value analysis, this is the ratio of budgeted to actual cost (CPI = BCWP / ACWP).

critical path   A series of tasks that, if delayed, will push out the end date of a project.

CV   An earned value indicator; the acronym stands for Cost Variance. In earned value analysis, this is the difference between budgeted and actual cost (CV = BCWP − ACWP).

CV%   The ratio of cost variance to BCWS, expressed as a percentage (CV% = [(BCWP − ACWP) / BCWP] × 100). This is an earned value indicator.

deadline   A date value you can enter for a task that indicates the latest date by which you want the task to be completed. If the scheduled completion date of a task is later than its deadline, you are notified. The benefit of entering deadline dates is that they do not constrain tasks.

deliverable   The final product, service, or event a project is intended to create.

dependency   A link between a predecessor task and a successor task. A dependency controls the start or finish of one task relative to the start or finish of the other task. The most common dependency is finish-to-start, in which the finish date of the predecessor task determines the start date of the successor task.

destination program   The program into which you place the data when exchanging data between Project and another program.

duration   The span of working time you expect it will take to complete a task.

EAC   An earned value indicator; the acronym stands for Estimate At Completion. In earned value analysis, this is the forecasted cost to complete a task based on performance up to the status date (EAC = ACWP + [BAC − BCWP] / CPI).

earned value analysis   A sophisticated form of project performance analysis that focuses on schedule and budget performance compared with baseline plans. Earned value uses your original baseline estimates and progress to date to show whether you're ahead, behind, or on schedule compared with the actual costs incurred.

effort-driven scheduling   A scheduling method in which the work of a task remains constant regardless of the number of resources assigned to it. As resources are added to a task, the duration decreases, but the work remains the same and is distributed among the assigned resources. Effort-driven scheduling is the default scheduling method in Project, but it can be turned off for any task.

elapsed duration   The amount of time it will take to finish a task, based on a 24-hour day and a 7-day week.

enterprise project management   Project management practiced in a formal, consistent way throughout an organization.

enterprise resource pool   When using a Project Server–based enterprise project management system, a central repository of generic and work resources that can be shared by all projects published to Project Server.

enterprise template   When using a Project Server–based enterprise project management system, templates that are stored in Project Server and available to Project Professional users. Enterprise templates help ensure consistent use of best practices and metrics within an organization.

Entry table   The grid on the left side of the default Gantt Chart view.

export map   The specifications for exporting fields from Project to other file formats, such as HTML. Project includes several export maps, which you can use as they are or modify.

field   The lowest-level information about a task, resource, or assignment.

filtering   In a view, a way to see or highlight only the task or resource information that meets the criteria you choose.

fixed consumption rate   A fixed quantity of a material resource to be consumed in the completion of an assignment.

fixed cost   A set amount of money budgeted for a task. This amount is independent of resource costs and task duration.

fixed duration   A task type in which the duration value is fixed. If you change the amount of work you expect a task to require, Project recalculates units for each resource. If you change duration or units, Project recalculates work.

fixed units   A task type in which the units value is fixed. If you change the duration of a task, Project recalculates the amount of work scheduled for the task. If you change units or work, Project recalculates duration.

fixed work   A task type in which the work value is fixed. If you change the duration of the task, Project recalculates units for each resource. If you change units or work, Project recalculates duration.

flexible constraint   A constraint type that gives Project the flexibility to change the start and finish dates (but not the duration) of a task. As Soon As Possible (ASAP) and As Late As Possible (ALAP) are both flexible constraints.

free slack   The amount of time that a task can be delayed without delaying the start date of another task.

fully allocated   The condition of a resource when the total work of his or her task assignments is exactly equal to his or her work capacity.

Gantt Chart view   A predefined view in Project consisting of a table (the Entry table by default) on the left and a graphical bar chart on the right that shows the project plan over time.

generic resource   When using a Project Server–based enterprise project management system, a special type of resource that can describe the expected skills of a specific type of work resource. Project managers can plan with generic resources and then replace them with work resources based on matching skills (and other factors).

ghost task   A task that represents a link from one Project plan to another. Ghost tasks appear as gray bars.

Global template   A Project template named Global.mpt that contains the default views, tables, filters, and other items that Project uses.

group   A way to reorder task or resource information in a table and display summary values for each group. You can specify several levels of groups. (The term group is also used to refer to the Resource Group field, which is unrelated.)

Group field   A field in which you can specify a group name (such as a department) with which you want to associate a resource. If you organize resources into groups, you can sort, filter, or group resources by group.

HTML template   A set of HTML tags and codes applied to Project data as it's exported through a map. Project includes several HTML templates, which you can use as they are or modify.

hyperlink   A link to another file, a specific location in a file, a page on the World Wide Web, or a page on an intranet.

import/export map   A set of specifications for importing specific data to or from Project fields. Project includes several built-in maps, which you can use as they are or modify. Import and export maps are sometimes referred to as data maps.

inflexible constraint   A constraint type that forces a task to begin or end on a certain date. Must Start On (MSO) and Must Finish On (MFO) are both inflexible constraints.

inserted project   A Project plan that is inserted into another Project plan, called a consolidated plan. An inserted project is also known as a subproject.

interim plan   A task's start and finish values, saved for later comparison. Each Project plan can have, at most, 10 interim plans.

lag time   A delay between tasks that have a task relationship. For example, lag time causes the successor task in a finish-to-start relationship to begin some time after its predecessor task concludes.

lead time   An overlap between tasks that have a task relationship. For example, lead time causes the successor task in a finish-to-start relationship to begin before its predecessor task concludes. In the Project interface, you enter lead time as negative lag time.

line manager   A manager of a group of resources; also called a functional manager. A line manager might also have project management skills and responsibilities, depending on the organization's structure.

link   A logical relationship between tasks that controls sequence and dependency. In the Gantt Chart and Network Diagram views, links appear as lines between tasks.

macro   A recorded or programmed set of instructions that carry out a specific action when initiated. Macros in Project use Visual Basic for Applications.

material resources   The consumables that are used up as a project progresses. As with work resources, you assign material resources to tasks. Unlike work resources, material resources have no effect on the total amount of work scheduled on a task.

maximum units   The maximum capacity (as entered in the Max. Units field) of a resource to accomplish tasks. If you allocate the resource beyond capacity, Project alerts you that the resource is overallocated.

Microsoft Office System Enterprise Project Management Solution The set of tools and practices built upon Project Server and (optionally) Windows SharePoint Services.

milestone A significant event that is reached within the project or imposed upon the project. In Project, milestones are normally represented as tasks with zero duration.

negative slack The amount of time that tasks overlap due to a conflict between task relationships and constraints.

night shift A base calendar included with Project designed to accommodate an 11:00 P.M.–8:00 A.M. "graveyard" work shift.

noncritical tasks The tasks that have slack. Noncritical tasks can finish within their slack time without affecting the project completion date.

note The information (including linked or embedded files) that you want to associate with a task, resource, or assignment.

OLE A protocol that enables you to transfer information, such as a chart or text (called an object), to documents in different programs.

ongoing operation An activity that has no planned end date and is repetitive in nature. Examples include accounting, managing human resources, and some manufacturing.

Organizer A dialog box with which you can copy views, tables, filters, and other items between the Global.mpt template and other Project plans or between two different Project plans.

outline A hierarchy of summary tasks and subtasks within Project, usually corresponding to major phases of work.

outline number Numbers that indicate the position of a task in the project's hierarchy. For example, a task with an outline number of 4.2 indicates that it's the second subtask under the fourth top-level task.

overallocated The condition of resources when they are assigned to do more work than is their normal work capacity.

phase A sequence of tasks that represent a major portion of the project's work. In Project, phases are represented by summary tasks.

planning The first major phase of project management work. Planning includes all of the work in developing a project schedule up to the point where the tracking of actual work begins.

predecessor A task whose start or end date determines the start or finish of another task or tasks, called successor tasks.

product scope The quality, features, and functions (often called specifications) of the deliverable of the project.

program office A department within an organization that oversees a collection of projects (such as producing wings and producing engines), each of which contributes to a complete deliverable (such as an airplane) and the organization's strategic objectives.

progress bar A graphical representation on a bar in the Gantt Chart view that shows how much of a task has been completed.

project A temporary endeavor undertaken to create a unique product or service.

project calendar The base calendar that is used by the entire project. The project calendar defines normal working and nonworking days and times.

project scope The work required to produce a deliverable with agreed-upon quality, features, and functions.

project summary task A summary task that contains top-level information such as duration, work, and costs for the entire project. The project summary task has a task ID of 0 and is displayed through the View tab of the Options dialog box, which is available by clicking the Options command on the Tools menu.

project triangle A popular model of project management in which time, cost, and scope are represented as the three sides of a triangle. A change to one side will affect at least one of the other two sides. There are many variations on this model.

recurring task A task that repeats at established intervals. You can create a recurring task that repeats for a fixed number of times or that ends by a specific date.

relationship The type of dependency between two tasks, visually indicated by a link line. The types of relationships include finish-to-start, start-to-start, finish-to-finish, and start-to-finish. Also known as a link, a logical relationship, a task dependency, or a precedence relationship.

report A format designed for printing. Project includes several predefined reports, each focusing on specific aspects of your project data. You can also define your own reports.

resource calendar The working and nonworking days and times of an individual work resource.

resource leveling A method of resolving resource overallocation by delaying the start date of an assignment or an entire task or splitting up the work on a task. Project can level resources automatically, or you can do it manually.

resource manager A person who oversees resource usage in project activities specifically to manage the time and costs of resources. A resource manager might also have project management skills and responsibilities, depending on the organization's structure.

resource pool A Project plan that other projects use for their resource information. Resource pools contain information about resources' task assignments from all project plans (called sharer plans) linked to the resource pool.

resources People, equipment, and material (and the associated costs of each) needed to complete the work on a project.

risk An event that decreases the likelihood of completing the project on time, within budget, and to specification (or, less likely, an opportunity to improve project performance).

scheduling formula A representation of how Project calculates work, based on the duration and resource units of an assignment. The scheduling formula is Duration × Units = Work.

scope The products or services to be provided by a project, and the work required to deliver it. For project planning, it's useful to distinguish between product scope and project scope. Scope is one side of the project triangle model.

ScreenTip A short description of an item on the screen, such as a toolbar, button, or bar. To see a ScreenTip, point to an item until the ScreenTip appears.

semi-flexible constraint A constraint type that gives Project the flexibility to change the start and finish dates of a task within one date boundary. Start No Earlier Than (SNET), Start No Later Than (SNLT), Finish No Earlier Than (FNET), and Finish No Later Than (FNLT) are all semi-flexible constraints.

sequence The chronological order in which tasks occur. A sequence is ordered from left to right in most views that include a timescale, such as the Gantt Chart view.

sharer plan A project plan that is linked to a resource pool. Sharer plans use resources from a resource pool.

shortcut menu A menu you display by pointing to an item on the screen and then right-clicking. Shortcut menus contain only the commands that apply to the item to which you are pointing.

slack The amount of time that a task can be delayed without delaying a successor task (free slack) or the project end date (total slack). Slack is also known as float.

sorting   A way of ordering task or resource information in a view by the criteria you choose.

source program   When exchanging data between Project and another program, the program in which the data resided originally.

SPI   An earned value indicator; the acronym stands for Schedule Performance Index. In earned value analysis, this is the ratio of performed to scheduled work (SPI = BCWP / BCWS).

split   An interruption in a task, represented in the Gantt bar as a dotted line between segments of a task. You can split a task multiple times.

sponsor   An individual or organization that both provides financial support and champions the project team within the larger organization.

stakeholders   The people or organizations that might be affected by project activities (those who "have a stake" in its success). These also include the resources working on the project as well as others (such as customers) external to the project work.

Standard base calendar   A base calendar included with Project designed to accommodate an 8:00 A.M.–5:00 P.M. Monday through Friday work shift.

status date   The date you specify (not necessarily the current date) that determines how Project calculates earned value indicators.

successor   A task whose start or finish is driven by another task or tasks, called predecessor tasks.

summary task   A task that is made up of and summarizes the subtasks below it. In Project, phases of project work are represented by summary tasks.

SV   An earned value indicator; the acronym stands for Schedule Variance. In earned value analysis, this is the difference between current progress and the baseline plan (SV = BCWP − BCWS).

SV%   The ratio of schedule variance to BCWS, expressed as a percentage (SV% = [SV / BCWS] × 100). This is an earned value indicator.

table   A spreadsheet-like presentation of project data, organized in vertical columns and horizontal rows. Each column represents one of the many fields in Project, and each row represents a single task or resource. In a usage view, additional rows represent assignments.

task   A project activity that has a starting and finishing point. A task is the basic building block of a project.

task calendar   The base calendar that is used by a single task. A task calendar defines working and nonworking times for a task, regardless of settings in the project calendar.

task ID   A unique number that Project assigns to each task in a project. In the Entry table, the task ID appears in the far left column.

task priority   A numeric ranking between 0 and 1000 of a task's importance and appropriateness for leveling. Tasks with the lowest priority are delayed or split first. The default value is 500.

task type   A setting applied to a task that determines how Project schedules the task, based on which of the three scheduling formula values is fixed. The three task types are fixed units, fixed duration, and fixed work.

TCPI   An earned value indicator; the acronym stands for To Complete Performance Index. In earned value analysis, this is the ratio of remaining work to remaining budget, as of the status date (TCPI = [BAC − BCWP] / [BAC − ACWP]).

template   A Project file format that enables you to reuse existing project plans as the basis for new project plans. Project includes several templates that relate to a variety of industries, and you can create your own templates.

time   The scheduled durations of individual tasks and the overall project. Time is one side of the project triangle model.

Throughput metric   A measurement of the quantity of a deliverable that can be completed over a given time period, usually expressed as a ratio. For example, "paint one wall per day" describes a quantity of a deliverable (a painted wall) that can be produced in a given time period (a day). Note that the time period used in a metric is work, not elapsed duration.

timephased field   The task, resource, or assignment values that are distributed over time. The values of timephased fields appear in the timescale grid on the right side of views, such as the Task Usage or Resource Usage view.

timescale   The timescale appears in views, such as the Gantt Chart and Resource Usage views, as a band across the top of the grid and denotes units of time. You can customize the timescale in the Timescale dialog box, which you can open from the Format menu.

top-down planning   A method of developing a project plan by identifying the highest-level phases or summary tasks before breaking them into lower-level components or subtasks.

total slack   The amount of time that a task can be delayed without delaying the project's end date.

tracking   The second major phase of project management work. Tracking includes all of the collecting, entering, and analyzing of actual project performance values, such as work on tasks and actual durations.

underallocated   The condition of resources when they are assigned to do less work than is their normal work capacity. For example, a full-time resource who has only 25 hours of work assigned in a 40-hour work week is underallocated.

units   A standard way of measuring the capacity of a resource to work when you assign the resource to a task in Project. Units are one variable in the scheduling formula: Duration × Units = Work.

VAC   An earned value indicator; the acronym stands for Variance At Completion. In earned value analysis, this is the forecasted cost variance to complete a task based on performance up to the status date (VAC = BAC − EAC).

variable consumption rate   A quantity of a material resource to be consumed that will change if the duration of the task to which it is assigned changes.

variance   A deviation from the schedule or budget established by the baseline plan.

view   A visual representation of the tasks or resources in your project. The three categories of views are charts, sheets, and forms. Views enable you to enter, organize, and examine information in a variety of formats.

WBS   (work breakdown structure) The identification of every task in a project that reflects that task's location in the hierarchy of the project.

work   The total scheduled effort for a task, resource, resource assignment, or entire project. Work is measured in person-hours and might not match the duration of the task. Work is one variable in the scheduling formula: Duration × Units = Work.

work resources   The people and equipment that do the work of the project.

workspace   A set of project plans and settings that you can save and reopen by opening a single workspace file. Workspace files have the .mpw extension.

Index

D

E

F

G

See also Change Working Time dialog
    box
Working time settings, 176
Work resource costs, 91
Work resources
    assigning, to tasks, 78–83
    defined, 60
    examples of, 60
    See also Resource(s)
Work table, 321–322
WSS. *See* Windows SharePoint Services
    (WSS)
WSS subweb, 463

Z

Zoom dialog box, 248
Zoom In, 199
Zoom Out, 199

About the Authors

Carl S. Chatfield

Carl is a content project manager and trainer in Engineering Excellence, an organization within Microsoft that develops and promotes best practices among software engineering teams at Microsoft. Previously, Carl has worked on Office applications as a technical writer and documentation manager since 1991. Carl is a graduate of the Masters program in Technical Communication at the University of Washington and is certified as a Project Management Professional (PMP) by the Project Management Institute. He lives in Redmond, Washington.

Timothy D. Johnson

Tim was a technical/developmental editor in the Microsoft Project User Assistance team for several years. Prior to joining the Project User Assistance team in 2000, he was a Project support professional for six years (going all the way back to Project 3.0—if you called Microsoft Product Support Services with a Project question, there's a good chance you talked to Tim). Tim is still involved in the computer industry and continues to look for ways to help customers better understand and use their computer applications. Tim makes his home in Issaquah, Washington.

Acknowledgments

From Carl: I'd like to thank the members and officers of the Puget Sound chapter of the Microsoft Project Association, our local Project user group. From Tim: thank you Ratsamy (Mimi), Brian, and Brenda. The authors also wish to acknowledge our technical reviewer Brian Kennemer, and Adrian Jenkins of the Project Business Unit at Microsoft, who provided valuable and timely answers to our technical questions.

What do you think of this book?

We want to hear from you!

Do you have a few minutes to participate in a brief online survey?

Microsoft is interested in hearing your feedback so we can continually improve our books and learning resources for you.

To participate in our survey, please visit:

www.microsoft.com/learning/booksurvey/

...and enter this book's ISBN-10 number (appears above barcode on back cover*). As a thank-you to survey participants in the United States and Canada, each month we'll randomly select five respondents to win one of five $100 gift certificates from a leading online merchant. At the conclusion of the survey, you can enter the drawing by providing your e-mail address, which will be used for prize notification only.

Thanks in advance for your input. Your opinion counts!

* Where to find the ISBN-10 on back cover

ISBN-13: 000-0-0000-00000
ISBN-10: 0-0000-00000

00000

0 000000 000000

Example only. Each book has unique ISBN.

Microsoft *Press*

No purchase necessary. Void where prohibited. Open only to residents of the 50 United States (includes District of Columbia) and Canada (void in Quebec). For official rules and entry dates see:

www.microsoft.com/learning/booksurvey/

welcome to the ribbon

Your quick reference to the new user interface in Microsoft® Office

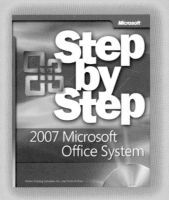

See more learning resources at
microsoft.com/mspress

Part No. X13-27587
Copyright © 2007 Microsoft Corporation. All rights reserved.

Customizing Your Workspace

Add frequently used commands to the Quick Access Toolbar

1. Click the **Microsoft® Office Button** and then click **Options**.

2. In the list at the left, click **Customize** then choose your commands.

    or

1. Right-click a command or command group on the Ribbon.

2. Click **Add to Quick Access Toolbar**.

Collapse the Ribbon

To reduce the Ribbon to a single line of tabs, press **CTRL +F1** or click **Customize Quick Access Toolbar** and then click **Minimize the Ribbon**.

Clicking on a tab while the Ribbon is minimized will temporarily restore the Ribbon. After you have made your selection, it will collapse again.

Use keyboard shortcuts to access commands

1. Press and release the **ALT** key.

    KeyTips are displayed for each Tab on the Ribbon, as well as the **Microsoft Office Button** and the **Quick Access Toolbar**.

2. Type the letter(s) shown in the KeyTip for the feature you want to use. Typing the letter associated with a Tab will display KeyTips for every command on that Tab.